THE EVOLUTION OF MIND

The Evolution of Mind

Fundamental Questions and Controversies

Edited by
STEVEN W. GANGESTAD
JEFFRY A. SIMPSON

THE GUILFORD PRESS
New York   London

© 2007 The Guilford Press
A Division of Guilford Publications, Inc.
72 Spring Street, New York, NY 10012
www.guilford.com

Printed in the United States of America

This book is printed on acid-free paper.

Last digit is print number: 9 8 7 6 5 4 3 2 1

Library of Congress Cataloging-in-Publication Data

The evolution of mind : fundamental questions and controversies / edited by Steven W.
Gangestad, Jeffry A. Simpson.
　　p. cm.
　Includes bibliographical references and index.
　ISBN-10: 1-59385-408-0　　ISBN-13: 978-1-59385-408-9 (hardcover)
　1. Evolutionary psychology.　2. Human evolution.　I. Gangestad, Steven W.
II. Simpson, Jeffry A.
　BF698.95.E955 2007
　155.7—dc22
　　　　　　　　　　　　　　　　　　　　　　　　　　　　　　　2006026955

About the Editors

Steven W. Gangestad, PhD, is Distinguished Professor of Psychology at the University of New Mexico. His research has covered a variety of topics in evolutionary behavioral science, including the determinants of sexual attraction, changes in women's sexual psychology across the ovarian cycle, the effects of genetic compatibility between mates on relationship qualities, individual variation in developmental precision and its manifestations in neuropsychology, and influences of men's testosterone levels.

Jeffry A. Simpson, PhD, is Professor of Psychology and Director of the Doctoral Minor in Interpersonal Relationships at the University of Minnesota. His research interests include adult attachment processes, human mating, idealization in relationships, empathic accuracy in relationships, and dyadic social influence. Dr. Simpson is a fellow of the American Psychological Association and the Association for Psychological Science. He serves as Associate Editor for the *Journal of Personality and Social Psychology: Interpersonal Relations and Group Processes.*

Contributors

C. Athena Aktipis, MA, Department of Psychology, University of Pennsylvania, Philadelphia, Pennsylvania

Richard Alexander, PhD, Museum of Zoology, University of Michigan, Ann Arbor, Michigan

Paul W. Andrews, JD, PhD, Department of Psychology, Virginia Commonwealth University, Richmond, Virginia

H. Clark Barrett, PhD, Department of Anthropology, University of California, Los Angeles, California

Monique Borgerhoff Mulder, PhD, Department of Anthropology, University of California, Davis, California

Robert Boyd, PhD, Department of Anthropology, University of California, Los Angeles, California

Pascal Boyer, PhD, Department of Anthropology, Washington University, St. Louis, Missouri

David M. Buss, PhD, Department of Psychology, University of Texas at Austin, Austin, Texas

Kathryn Coe, PhD, College of Public Health, University of Arizona, Tucson, Arizona

Leda Cosmides, PhD, Department of Psychology and Center for Evolutionary Psychology, University of California, Santa Barbara, California

Charles B. Crawford, PhD, Department of Psychology, Simon Fraser University, Burnaby, British Columbia, Canada

Peter DeScioli, MA, Department of Psychology, University of Pennsylvania, Philadelphia, Pennsylvania

Robin Dunbar, PhD, School of Biological Sciences, University of Liverpool, Liverpool, United Kingdom

Alice H. Eagly, PhD, Department of Psychology, Northwestern University, Evanston, Illinois

Elsa Ermer, MA, Department of Psychology and Institute for Policy Research, University of California, Santa Barbara, California

Barbara L. Finlay, PhD, Department of Psychology, Cornell University, Ithaca, New York

Mark Flinn, PhD, Department of Anthropology, University of Missouri, Columbia, Missouri

Steven W. Gangestad, PhD, Department of Psychology, University of New Mexico, Albuquerque, New Mexico

David C. Geary, PhD, Department of Psychological Sciences, University of Missouri, Columbia, Missouri

Michael Gurven, PhD, Department of Anthropology, University of California, Santa Barbara, California

Edward H. Hagen, PhD, Institute for Theoretical Biology, Humboldt University, Berlin, Germany

Kim Hill, PhD, Department of Anthropology, University of New Mexico, Albuquerque, New Mexico

Hunter Honeycutt, PhD, Department of Psychology, Bridgewater College, Bridgewater, Virginia

Satoshi Kanazawa, PhD, Interdisciplinary Institute of Management, London School of Economics and Political Science, London, United Kingdom

Hillard S. Kaplan, PhD, Department of Anthropology, University of New Mexico, Albuquerque, New Mexico

Douglas T. Kenrick, PhD, Department of Psychology, Arizona State University, Tempe, Arizona

Robert Kurzban, PhD, Department of Psychology, University of Pennsylvania, Philadelphia, Pennsylvania

Jane B. Lancaster, PhD, Department of Anthropology, University of New Mexico, Albuquerque, New Mexico

Robert Lickliter, PhD, Department of Psychology, Florida International University, Miami, Florida

Debra Lieberman, PhD, Department of Psychology, University of Hawaii at Manoa, Honolulu, Hawaii

Geoffrey Miller, PhD, Department of Psychology, University of New Mexico, Albuquerque, New Mexico

Steven Mithen, PhD, Department of Archaeology, University of Reading, Reading, United Kingdom

H. Kern Reeve, PhD, Department of Neurobiology and Behavior, Cornell University, Ithaca, New York

Peter J. Richerson, PhD, Department of Environmental Science and Policy, University of California, Davis, California

Mark Schaller, PhD, Department of Psychology, University of British Columbia, Vancouver, British Columbia, Canada

Paul W. Sherman, PhD, Department of Neurobiology and Behavior, Cornell University, Ithaca, New York

Joan B. Silk, PhD, Department of Anthropology, University of California, Los Angeles, California

Jeffry A. Simpson, PhD, Department of Psychology, University of Minnesota, Minneapolis, Minnesota

Eric Alden Smith, PhD, Department of Anthropology, University of Washington, Seattle, Washington

Craig B. Stanford, PhD, Department of Anthropology, University of Southern California, Los Angeles, California

Kim Sterelny, PhD, Department of Philosophy, Victoria University of Wellington, Wellington, New Zealand

Jill M. Sundie, PhD, Bauer College of Business, University of Houston, Houston, Texas

Donald Symons, PhD, Department of Anthropology, University of California, Santa Barbara, California

Randy Thornhill, PhD, Department of Biology, University of New Mexico, Albuquerque, New Mexico

John Tooby, PhD, Department of Anthropology and Center for Evolutionary Psychology, University of California, Santa Barbara, California

David Sloan Wilson, PhD, Department of Biological Sciences, Binghamton University, Binghamton, New York

Wendy Wood, PhD, Department of Psychology, Duke University, Durham, North Carolina

Contents

Contents

An Introduction to *The Evolution of Mind*

Why We Developed This Book

Steven W. Gangestad
Jeffry A. Simpson

In the history of ideas, Darwin's theory of evolution through natural selection stands as one of most awe inspiring. His ideas profoundly changed the way scientists understand and appreciate the biological world. As Theodosius Dobzhansky (1973) once quipped, ever since Darwin, "nothing in biology makes sense except in the light of evolution" (p. 125). Just as influential, however, have been the theory's implications for how we, as human beings, understand ourselves. According to modern evolutionary biology, modern-day *Homo sapiens* represent merely a pixel of a present-day snapshot of the recurrent stream of replication, variation, and selection that began over 3 billion years ago. This stream, which all humans are a part of, operates according to certain principles. And these principles can divulge a great deal about who we are.

Despite being a formative influence on the emerging science of psychology in the late 1800s, evolutionary biology did little to shape the social and behavioral sciences for nearly a century after Darwin's death. The ethologists Tinbergen, Lorenz, and von Frisch, of course, reminded psychologists that animals, including humans, were shaped by selection pressures to adapt to their natural environments and that, accordingly, much can be learned via careful observation of behavior in natural habitats. But ethological theory itself was not deeply informed by evolutionary biology at that point in time.

This fact was largely a reflection of the state of affairs within biology, not within psychology. For the first half of the 20th century, the major theoretical task in evolutionary biology was to complete the grand synthesis of Darwinism and Mendelism. Evolutionary genetics, in fact, enjoyed great progress during this period. With a few notable exceptions (e.g., Cole, 1954; Lack, 1966), however, evolutionary biologists had not turned their attention to developing broad theories of how selection might have shaped the phenotypes of organisms, including how organisms evolved to interact with both their physical environments and with one another.

When theorists eventually turned their attention to this task in the 1960s and 1970s, they discovered that many of the phenotypes of interest happened to be behavioral in nature. Examples included how organisms are shaped to relate to kin, how they are shaped to reproduce; the general nature of their lifecourses, how the sexes relate to one another, and how cooperation can evolve and be sustained. The optimality and game theoretic approaches developed during these decades quickly generated a multitude of new theories that remain foundational in evolutionary biology today, such as life history theory, parental investment theory, parent–offspring conflict theory, sperm competition theory, the concept of reciprocal altruism, optimal foraging theory, and sex allocation theory. In 1975, Edward O. Wilson's *Sociobiology* promised a "new synthesis" of the life and social sciences based on some of these new principles. Debates over precisely how these principles could be applied to understand human behavior quickly ensued. Within a decade, several promising alternative approaches were founded, including human behavioral ecology (e.g., Chagnon & Irons, 1979), gene–culture coevolutionary approaches (e.g., Boyd & Richerson, 1985), and evolutionary psychology (Tooby & Cosmides, 1989).

During the last two decades, the study of the evolutionary foundations of human nature has grown at an exponential rate. In fact, it is now a booming interdisciplinary scientific enterprise, one that sits at the cutting edge of the social and behavioral sciences.

Textbooks and handbooks often chronicle the emergence of new fields. Although not one textbook on evolutionary psychology was on the market a decade ago, today textbooks on human evolution abound. Within the past 10 years, a dozen new textbooks touting different evolutionary perspectives have appeared, including Buss's *Evolutionary Psychology: The New Science of the Mind* (1999), Gaulin and McBurney's *Psychology: An Evolutionary Approach* (2001), Cartwright's *Evolution and Human Behavior* (2000), Barrett, Dunbar, and Lycett's *Human Evolutionary Psychology* (2002), and Palmer and Palmer's *Evolutionary Psychology: The Ultimate Origins of Human Behavior* (2002), to name a few. These textbooks provide excellent introductions to the field and the major topics within it. In addition, several major handbooks have been or will soon be published, including edited volumes by Buss (2005), Crawford and Krebs (1998), and Dunbar and Barrett (2007).

Precisely because of the profound implications that evolutionary biology holds for understanding human nature, the new evolutionary behavioral sciences have also inspired popular press books. Authors such as Steven Pinker (*The Language Instinct*, 1994; *How the Mind Works*, 1997; *The Blank Slate*, 2003), Robert Wright (*The Moral Animal*, 1994), Frank Sulloway (*Born to Rebel*, 1996), Sarah Hrdy (*Mother Nature*, 1999), Geoffrey Miller (*The Mating Mind*, 2000), and Matt Ridley (*The Red Queen*, 1993; *The Origins of Virtue*, 1996; *Nature via Nurture*, 2003) have all written influential works. Moreover, Dawkin's *The Selfish Gene* (1976) and Dennett's *Darwin's Dangerous Idea* (1995) remain among the most widely read treatises on the foundations of evolutionary biology.

Needless to say, evolutionary approaches to understanding human behavior have also been criticized. Wilson's *Sociobiology* (1975), for example, was castigated by some evolutionary biologists, most notably Stephen Jay Gould and Richard Lewontin (1979). Evolutionary psychology has also been criticized for similar reasons. Some criticism expresses fear that evolutionary approaches serve right-wing agendas. Other criticism has been directed at the adaptationist approach in evolutionary biology (see Gould & Lewontin, 1979). The former criticisms hold little water; many evolutionary theorists, such as John Maynard Smith and Robert Trivers, publicly endorse liberal social and political views. Many of the latter criticisms regarding the adaptationist approach have been addressed (see Alcock, 2001, for a review). Thus, although human evolutionary behavioral science has hardly won over all critics, many behavioral scientists are open to hearing and learning more about the insights into human nature that evolutionary biology has to offer. As a result, the most important debates today do not center on *whether* evolutionary approaches can offer deeper insights into human nature and behavior, but on *which* approaches might offer the most significant insights. One purpose of this book is to foster effective clarification and resolution of the most important debates and controversies.

THEORETICAL APPROACHES IN HUMAN
EVOLUTIONARY BEHAVIORAL SCIENCE

Four main perspectives can be identified in human evolutionary behavioral science (Laland & Brown, 2002). They include human sociobiology and three counterreactions to sociobiology that address genetic evolution— human evolutionary ecology, evolutionary psychology, and gene–culture coevolution. We briefly describe, compare, and contrast the major tenets of each approach below.

Human Sociobiology

Wilson's *Sociobiology* (1975) brought together many breakthroughs in evolutionary theory that occurred in the 1960s and 1970s, especially Hamilton's (1964) notion of inclusive fitness, the gene's-eye view championed by Hamilton (1964) and Williams (1966), life-history theory, four major theories introduced by Trivers (1971, 1972, 1974; Trivers & Willard, 1973), and the evolutionary economic strategy of modeling selection pressures on phenotypes through analysis of their fitness benefits and costs. The first six chapters of *Sociobiology* laid out these ideas. The remainder of the book applied them to the behavior of organisms within various taxa—with the final chapter focusing on humans. Shortly thereafter, Wilson (1978) published *On Human Nature*, which expanded the ideas sketched out in that final chapter on humans.

Perhaps the most lasting influence of *Sociobiology* was Wilson's (1975) declaration that a new evolutionary perspective on the behavior of animals had emerged, one that was based on the new "gene's-eye view" and rigorous modeling of selection pressures on behavioral phenotypes. The ideas presented in his first six chapters, followed by additional theoretical developments rooted in kindred evolutionary economic modeling (e.g., optimal foraging theory, sex allocation theory, evolutionary game theory) soon transformed the way biologists thought about and studied animal behavior. The focus of ethologists on naturalistic observation and the identification of behavioral "fixed action patterns" was replaced by the focus of behavioral ecologists on behavioral function in response to selection pressures, the approach that currently defines the study of animal behavior (see Krebs & Davies, 1997). With an intellectual heritage indebted to the ideas and perspective captured in Wilson's 1975 book, some current animal behavioral ecologists still refer to themselves as sociobiologists (e.g., Alcock, 2001), and a leading journal in the field is entitled *Behavioral Ecology and Sociobiology*.

Wilson's (1978) writings on human behavior, however, spawned few direct intellectual descendants of his approach. Most of his ideas were highly speculative and not well documented, especially with respect to humans. Much of his evidence was anecdotal, and he neglected to review and incorporate relevant theory and data from various fields in the social and behavioral sciences. To complicate matters, Wilson adopted a hereditarian stance; that is, he wrote of genes "for" particular behaviors, implying that behavior itself is inherited and relatively insensitive to environmental influences. For these reasons, most major approaches in human evolutionary behavioral science today fashion themselves as reactions largely *against* sociobiology.

Human Behavioral Ecology

By the 1970s, several anthropologists had become attracted to new adaptationist ideas in evolutionary biology. In addition to primatologists such as Irven DeVore (who worked at Harvard with Wilson and Trivers) and Jane Lancaster, the individuals included Napoleon Chagnon, William Irons, and Kristen Hawkes. Anthropologists were struck by the variability of behavior across cultures. People in different groups eat different foods, spend differing amounts of time hunting or fishing, have different customs involving sexual relations and marriage, divide tasks between men and women differently, and raise children differently. Wilson's hereditarian sociobiological approach failed to offer sufficient explanations for this variability. The emerging animal behavioral ecology approach did, however. Behavioral ecologists wanted to understand differences in behavior across species as different adaptive solutions to problems posed by the varying ecologies in which different species reside. They did so by modeling and measuring selection on phenotypes imposed by particular local ecologies. Human behavioral ecologists (also known as evolutionary or Darwinian anthropologists) began to apply this approach to account for variation within and between human populations. In different ecological settings, different behavioral strategies for tasks such as foraging, mating, parental investment, and childrearing were found to optimize reproductive success (e.g., Smith & Winterhalder, 1992). Accordingly, behavioral ecologists wanted to know whether actual variations in these domains both within and between different cultures reflected variations in optimal strategies.

To address these questions, human behavioral ecologists developed theoretical tools and research strategies similar to those used by animal behavioral ecologists. Specifically, they developed quantitative models to identify which kinds of behavior tend to be optimal in promoting reproductive fitness within a given ecology. For instance, what allocation of time to hunting in a particular group tends to maximize net calorie gain? To derive optima when testing these models, researchers must estimate parameters within the model with actual data, such as the rate of return per unit time as a function of hunting, gathering roots, picking fruits, and so on. In some instances, this might include estimating the rate of actual reproduction as a function of a particular behavior. Human behavioral ecologists then measure actual performance (e.g., the actual amount of time spent hunting) and compare it to the estimated optimum. If a discrepancy exists, they usually refine the model by taking into account benefits or costs not specified in the initial optimality model, such as considering the benefits of obtaining mates through hunting success in addition to the benefits of energy capture.

Human behavioral ecologists seldom focus on the proximate mechanisms through which people make optima decisions. In this regard, they are similar to animal behavioral ecologists. Empirical success reflects understanding the *function* of a behavior in terms of a rigorous selection model. Precisely how an animal achieves optimal behavior through a psychological process tends to be of little concern to most behavioral ecologists. Instead, human behavioral ecologists assume that individuals in different groups behave differently because they facultatively, flexibly, and adaptively adjust their behavior in response to the particular contingencies imposed by certain environments. In that sense, they differ from most animal behavioral ecologists. Although animal behavioral ecologists recognize that individuals in species may have evolved to enact different strategies in different circumstances (e.g., to adjust clutch size in response to changes in resource abundance), cross-species differences are typically presumed to reflect differences in gene pools. Evolutionary psychologists, on the other hand, seek to specify the precise proximate psychological mechanisms through which individuals facultatively adjust their behavior.

Evolutionary Psychology

In the late 1980s, two synergistic events led to the emergence of what is now known as evolutionary psychology. First, anthropologist Donald Symons (1987, 1990) and the team of anthropologist John Tooby and psychologist Leda Cosmides critiqued the "adaptivist" orientation in human behavioral ecology and claimed that a truly adaptationist approach was needed. Second, Tooby and Cosmides (1989, 1990, 1992) developed a metatheory for an adaptationist approach.

Darwinism, Symons (1987) argued, offers a *historical* explanation for the evolution of phenotypic traits. Some of these traits, namely, specific adaptations, were favored by natural selection for their reproductive benefits. Other traits, called "by-products," were not directly selected, but were incidental effects of selection for other adaptive features. A Darwinian approach applied to understanding human behavior, therefore, must shed light on the nature of adaptations that were recurrently favored in ancestral environments, as evidenced by their phenotypic design. Human behavioral ecologists, Symons charged, do not study adaptations. Rather, they study *adaptiveness*; their approach asks whether behaviors themselves (e.g., polyandry, bridewealth, matrilineal inheritance) are adaptive. But behaviors themselves, Symons argued, are not aspects of phenotypic design; they are merely *outputs* of design that interact with specific environmental inputs. Some behaviors may be adaptive but are not the product of actual adaptations. Behaviors that are not adaptive but *are* the product of adaptations may be fairly common (Tooby & Cosmides, 1990).

Symons (1987) illustrated the difference between adaptiveness and adaptation with a familiar example, taste preferences. People prefer foods high in sugar and fat. These preferences most likely reflect adaptations to a hunter-gatherer existence in which calories were limited and humans had to be motivated to find and consume energy-rich foods. In modern societies, of course, calories are not restricted and, hence, these preferences contribute to unhealthy, maladaptive dietary habits. An adaptationist approach asks whether the preferences themselves were selected historically and, if so, for what benefits? An adaptivist approach, by comparison, focuses only on whether the behavior itself is *currently* adaptive. The former approach is truly Darwinian, according to Symons; the latter approach is not.

Tooby and Cosmides (1990, 1992) then proposed a specific version of psychological adaptationism, which has become the primary approach identified with evolutionary psychology. Psychological adaptations can be described at multiple levels of analysis. One can, for instance, ask what brain features could have been selected to give rise to particular forms of adaptive behavior. Cosmides and Tooby suggested that the most useful level of description from a functional perspective is the *cognitive* one. This level addresses questions about *which* cues in ancestral environments (i.e., which recurrent cues in the environments in which the adaptation was selected) are processed to generate *which* specific cognitive, emotional, or behavioral responses. Precise description should specify the particular computational procedures (or "Darwinian algorithms") that mediate information available in the environment as it leads to the response. Cosmides's

(1989) "cheater detection algorithm" is one paradigmatic example of how theories about psychological adaptations can be derived, developed, and tested.

Evolutionary psychologists also focus on "adaptive problems," circumstances in ancestral environments in which an adaptation arose and for which the adaptation offers a solution. Taste preferences for sugar and fat, for example, solved the adaptive problem to obtain and consume energy-rich food sources. Adaptive problems, therefore, are a common way in which evolutionary psychologists discuss ancestral (rather than current) selection pressures. Adaptive problems in past environments should have been numerous (problems associated with foraging, mating, kin recognition, alliance formation, etc.). Different problems should have demanded different solutions. According to Tooby and Cosmides (1992), a "general problem solver" cannot proficiently solve different kinds of problems. Accordingly, most evolutionary psychologists believe that psychological adaptations are functionally specialized in nature and diverse in number, each one having been designed to solve a particular ancestral adaptive problem. In the parlance of Tooby and Cosmides, an adaptationist approach anticipates that psychological architecture should be characterized by "massive modularity." In other words, the mind should have evolved to have many specialized information-processing procedures (algorithms), each one dedicated to detecting and solving a particular adaptive problem.

In the early 1990s, debates between human behavioral ecologists and evolutionary psychologists began. More recently, the evolutionary psychology approach has also been criticized by developmental scientists. Before discussing these debates, we turn to the third major response to sociobiology, the gene–culture coevolutionary approach.

The Gene–Culture Coevolutionary Approach

In his widely-acclaimed book *The Selfish Gene*, Richard Dawkins (1976) proposed that just as genes evolve via differential replication, ideas also undergo a Darwinian-like selection process. Ideas are passed from individual to individual, from one mind to another. Some ideas, however, more effectively "replicate" themselves in new minds (i.e., they are more effectively transmitted across individuals), spreading rapidly and becoming popular. Dawkins coined the term "meme" (shortened from *mimeme*, the Greek root of "imitation") to refer to the unit of replication in the evolution of ideas. These notions gave rise to the science of memetics, which examines the processes through which memes spread and are maintained. The differential spread of ideas, practices, and norms, according to this viewpoint, explains cultural evolution.

According to this perspective, selection operates on two systems of "inherited" information: one system based on the replication of genes (genetic evolution), and the other based on the replication of ideas (cultural evolution). In classic work, Boyd and Richerson (1985) have shown that population genetic mathematical models developed for genetic evolution also model parallel processes of cultural evolution. This perspective is called *dual inheritance theory*.

The two systems of inheritance, however, do not evolve independently. Lumsden and Wilson (1981) and Cavilli-Svorza and Feldman (1981) recognized that the way in which cultural information is transmitted and evolves depends on human development and learning, with genes playing a role in each. Genetic evolution, therefore, affects cultural evolution. But cultural evolution can also affect genetic evolution, in that cultural innovation changes the selective environments of genes, stimulating genetic evolution. Cavilli-Svorza and Feldman labeled this approach *gene–culture coevolutionary theory*, a term now applied to other major theories within this approach (e.g., Boyd & Richerson, 1985; see also Laland & Brown, 2002).

Gene–culture evolutionary models have several interesting implications. First, they predict that some behaviors or beliefs selected against at the genetic level can be strongly culturally selected and, hence, spread. Because of this process, "maladaptive" behavior or beliefs can and do culturally evolve. One example is the common belief that effective birth control should be used to regulate and suppress fertility. At a superficial level, this observation appears to be similar to the claim of evolutionary psychologists that, in the modern world, some behaviors may be maladaptive. At a deeper level, however, it is very different. Evolutionary psychologists contend that maladaptive behavior often is a result of modern environments not matching ancestral ones; in ancestral environments, currently maladaptive behaviors (e.g., eating energy-rich foods) would have been adaptive. Gene–culture coevolutionary theorists, in contrast, contend that some behaviors or beliefs that *are not and would never have been adaptive* (e.g., using effective birth control) may nonetheless evolve via cultural selection.

Second, transmission processes may cause group practices that have evolved through cultural selection to persist even when substantial changes in the environment are operating on *genetic* variants. This possibility is inconsistent with most human behavioral ecology approaches. Strong forms of behavior ecology, for instance, claim that changes in behaviors that are adaptive in certain ecologies should *produce* behavioral change.

Third, cultural evolution can operate via group selection. Williams (1966) argued that only under highly restrictive conditions should genetically based adaptations evolve if they are good for the group but detrimental to individual fitness (e.g., the tendency to warn others about a predator, calling perhaps lethal attention to oneself). The rate at which groups become extinct would have to be substantial to cause group selection on genetic variation between groups to counteract selection on individuals to act in their best self-interest within groups (cf. Sober & Wilson, 1998). Boyd and Richerson (1985) suggest that group selection may, however, operate to cause *cultural* evolution. Accordingly, cultural selection may create and maintain substantial variation across groups relative to within-group variation due to enforcement of and conformity to norms or tendencies to copy others. The differential success of groups, then, may cause substantial "spread" of cultural practices that foster group success if successful groups produce descendant splinter groups that adopt similar practices.

MAJOR DEBATES IN HUMAN EVOLUTIONARY BEHAVIORAL SCIENCE

The Adaptationist versus Adaptivist Debates

Following major critiques by Symons (1987, 1990) and Tooby and Cosmides (1990, 1992), the behavioral ecologists responded. A vigorous debate—known as the evolutionary anthropology versus evolutionary psychology debate—ensued. Indeed, one entire issue of the journal *Ethology and Sociobiology* (1990) was dedicated to it.

This debate centered on several questions and issues. First, what is the appropriate level of analysis for studying the outcomes of evolutionary processes? Evolutionary psychologists argued it should be psychological adaptations. Evolutionary anthropologists, on the other hand, defended their focus on behavior. Behaviors do, of course, qualify as "phenotypes" of organisms, and they are subjected to selection pressures. Although psychological adaptations could mediate how selection operates on genes, evolutionary anthropologists argued that there are advantages to keeping description at the level of direct observation rather than risking incorrect inferences about unseen, underlying psychological adaptations.

Second, what is the nature of psychological outcomes produced by selection? Evolutionary psychologists argued that selection should have produced many specialized psychological adaptations, each designed to solve an important and specific ancestral problem. In addition, these adaptations should be virtually universal. Behavioral ecologists, in contrast, accentuated the flexibility of human behavior. However, they typically did not try to specify or study the psychological mechanisms responsible for generating different behaviors, which is central to the mission of evolutionary psychology. Behavioral ecologists emphasized the ability of humans to generate novel solutions to adaptive problems, which they believe casts doubt on evolutionary psychologists' assumptions that adaptations are modular and specialized.

Third, is there any utility to examining *current* fitness outcomes or adaptiveness to test evolutionary theories? Evolutionary psychologists have argued that there is not, stating that selection relevant to understanding current adaptations and behavior has already occurred in our ancestral past. Current adaptiveness (or selection) is irrelevant (Thornhill, 1997). Organisms ought to be viewed as "adaptation executers," not "fitness maximizers." Historically shaped adaptations that guide current behavior, whether adaptive or not, can be inferred by examining the design of organisms today. Behavioral ecologists have countered this point by contending that evolutionary psychologists assume that modern environments have changed in crucial ways from ancestral environments. However, current environments may not have changed as much as some evolutionary psychologists believe, particularly in the more traditional cultures that behavioral ecologists often study.

Fourth, what should explanations of the evolution of human behavior look like? Evolutionary psychologists have argued that these explanations should focus on the specific kinds of adaptive problems in ancestral environments that current adaptations were designed to solve. Human behavioral ecologists have countered that evolutionary psychologists' treatment of selection pressures tends to be oversimplified. Organisms undoubtedly face trade-offs when solving adaptive problems. The effort put into solving one problem may detract from effort that could be put into solving other problems. As a result, according to behavioral ecologists, organisms *are* selected to maximize fitness, at least within the constraints of specific trade-offs. In so doing, organisms must compromise solutions to any one adaptive problem. Human behavioral ecologists also have claimed that only through explicit optimality modeling can one appreciate how organisms are shaped by selection. Evolutionary psychologists, they have noted, rarely use mathematical optimality modeling to test their speculations.

During these debates, each side has occasionally caricatured the other in an overly critical light, or has presented an oversimplified, monolithic view of the other's positions. Many human behavioral ecologists, for instance, recognize that modern environments are different in significant ways from ancestral ones, meaning that some adaptations that are "mismatched" to current environments could be the source of certain maladaptive behaviors (e.g., Smith, Borgerhoff Mulder, & Hill, 2001). Some behavioral ecologists also acknowledge specialized design in certain domains (e.g., Kaplan, Hill, Lancaster, & Hurtado, 2000). By the same token, some evolutionary psychologists not only recognize but have also written about human capacities to innovate, although most have claimed that these capacities are adaptations specialized for innovation per se (e.g., Tooby & Cosmides, 2000). Other evolutionary psychologists have also written on how humans should respond "flexibly" to different ecologies, resulting in the sort of ecology-dependent variation that behavioral ecologists emphasize (e.g., Gangestad & Simpson, 2000). Still other evolutionary psychologists have started to employ optimality and game theoretical models, though most note that the selection pressures being modeled are relevant to explaining current adaptations shaped by similar ancestral selection pressures (see DeScioli & Kurzban, Chapter 13, this volume; Kaplan & Gangestad, Chapter 12, this volume). Attempts to resolve these debates are likely to proceed more quickly and in more fruitful directions if participants appreciate both the subtleties and the variations that exist within different theoretical vantage points.

Tensions with Gene–Culture Coevolutionary Theory

Whereas debates between behavioral ecologists and evolutionary psychologists have at times been vociferous, gene–culture coevolutionary theorists have more quietly criticized other approaches. These theorists contend that practices, beliefs, and norms can and do persist via cultural selection despite significant changes in local ecologies. Contrary to the expectations of behavioral ecologists, these components of culture may not track ecology (see Richerson & Boyd, 2005). Moreover, although evolutionary psychologists acknowledge that transmission of information and cultural practices are important evolved outcomes in humans, gene–culture coevolutionary theorists complain that most evolutionary psychologists do not sufficiently recognize either the extent to which cultural transmission and selection can generate maladaptive behaviors or the extent to which culture itself affects genetic selection.

Proponents of other perspectives have critiqued gene–culture coevolutionary approaches as well. Cultural inheritance does not proceed along distinct lineages, as genetic evolution does; that is, ideas are not replicated in the same way that genes are; rather, they are repeatedly reconstructed in the mind of each individual (Sperber, 1996). The units of cultural inheritance, therefore, are not easy to define. Variants of new ideas do not arise through a random process, such as mutation; rather, they may emerge through systematic processes (e.g., creative innovation); therefore, cultural evolution does not obey the same principles that genetic evolution does. To their credit, Boyd and Richerson (1985) have emphasized many differences between genetic and cultural evolution in their coevolutionary model. The critical issue is not whether differences between cultural and genetic evolution exist; they do (see Laland & Brown, 2002). The critical issue is what implications these differences have for understanding how each "evolutionary process" impacts human perceptions and behavior.

Critiques of Evolutionary Psychology within Psychology

As evolutionary psychology has gained prominence within psychology, some psychologists and psychologically minded philosophers have questioned some of its foundations and core assumptions. One set of criticisms has come from neurobiologists, developmental neuropsychologists, and philosophers, who argue that the assumption of "massive modularity" is untenable. According to this critique, evolutionary psychologists should expect brain maturation to be precisely programmed by genetic information needed to yield the many postulated Darwinian modules. In addition, many "modules" should be established early in life. Advances in developmental neurobiology, however, indicate that precise genetic programming does not characterize brain development. Instead, interactions with the physical and social world shape development of neural areas, and these effects persist for prolonged periods of time, often through adolescence. Higher cortical areas—those that integrate and organize information to create complex representations of the world and then dictate basic information processing—are characterized by prolonged, environmentally contingent development. The general picture emerging from developmental neurobiology, therefore, is one in which how humans process information is constructed through prolonged interactions with the physical and social world, not precise "prewired" programming (see Quartz & Sejnowski, 2002). In fact, Buller (2005) recently concluded that the basic neural adaptation of higher cortical regions is "plasticity"—the ability to adapt to the specific world in which one develops.

A related set of criticisms has come from developmental systems theorists (e.g., Oyama, Griffiths, & Gray, 2001), who claim that evolutionary psychology is grounded on naive and misleading views of how development actually occurs. Development transpires through interactions between elements that comprise a "developmental system," some of which emerge as development proceeds (maternal environments, intracellular entities, environmental interactions with the world that influence gene expression, etc.). The outcomes of a system depend on all of its elements, whose effects are not only additive but may also be interactive. Importantly, no single set of developmental elements is privileged. Thus, according to this view, it is incorrect to conceive of genes as "blueprints" that act as master plans for development and then orchestrate it. It is also incorrect to believe that orchestration of development by genetic "blueprints" leads to specific developmental outcomes that are "prespecified" by genes. Developmental processes are much more dynamic and highly epigenetic; the introduction of new environmental influences can sometimes generate unexpected outcomes that cannot be anticipated from the selective history of an organism.

Selective history, therefore, cannot serve as a complete explanation of evolved outcomes. Selection does not generate variants; it selects between existing variants. Variation is introduced through alterations in developmental processes. As a result, a complete understanding of how a given outcome evolved requires more sophisticated developmental science, which many evolutionary psychologists seem to ignore (see Lickliter & Honeycutt, 2003).

Evolutionary psychologists have, of course, addressed these criticisms. They have argued that an adaptation does not imply that development is programmed directly by genes. Much reliable information in the world guides development down adaptive trajectories. Genes may in fact affect developmental outcomes by leading people to be sensitive to particular information in the world, thereby exerting their effects through epigenetic developmental processes. The adaptive design that results from selection for these outcomes and associated developmental processes still fits with biologists' notion of what an adaptation is. Accordingly, the facts that neural development is not precisely programmed, and that it occurs over extended periods of time do *not* necessarily invalidate many evolutionary psychologists' claims about adaptations. Though maladaptive developmental outcomes can be produced by novel environments, selection usually shapes developmental processes toward adaptive outcomes in the developmental environments most commonly experienced by the population under selection. Indeed, the fact that many human psychological universals exist suggests that development typically does lead to specific robust outcomes, regardless of the processes through which those developmental outcomes are achieved.

THE HISTORY AND STRUCTURE OF THIS BOOK

Human evolutionary behavioral science is still undergoing a formative process. Several metatheories and methodologies have been put forward. Many paradigmatic exemplars of how these metatheories and methodologies can and should be applied to investigate and explain myriad human preferences and behaviors now exist. During the growth of a science, these paradigmatic exemplars—success stories—begin to anchor new approaches (Kuhn, 1962). Over time, however, critical self-evaluation, debate, and discussion start to shape or revise explicit assumptions that are necessary to, and still coherent with, the metatheories developed to explain certain phenomena. This process of critical evaluation does not reflect that a field is undergoing a "crisis" (Kuhn, 1962) or "degeneration" (Lakatos, 1970). Rather, it is part of normal, progressive science.

This book is intended to foster this process and, we hope, nudge human evolutionary science in fruitful directions. As is evident from our brief history of the field, several pressing issues involving the nature and study of human behavior remain matters of heated debate. Some of these fundamental issues arise from the fact that different theoretical and methodological approaches for studying evolution and human behavior exist—human behavioral ecology, evolutionary psychology, and gene–culture coevolutionary approaches. Although these approaches might be integrated, they have not been well-synthesized to this point. Other fundamental debates have centered on critiques from the developmental sciences. Still others involve specific proposals about certain core facets of human evolution (e.g., the nature of culture, the role of group selection, the evolution of human intelligence, the features of mating systems that distinguish humans from other species).

When planning this book, we identified 12 fundamental controversies. We then formulated each controversial issue in the form of a general question. We asked three to six major theoretical and empirical contributors to the study of evolution and human behavior to address each question in a short essay (approximately 2,000 words). Thus, authors had to focus on only a few aspects of the pertinent issues, which were of their choosing and defining, and were told that they did not need to answer each question fully.

When choosing contributors, we attempted to represent multiple perspectives, identifying authors who had expressed their views on a given topic or issue in earlier writings. Thus, we explicitly tried to solicit a diverse set of viewpoints, each one offered by a highly regarded expert in his or her specific field. Authors were also asked to limit their references, choosing exemplars of important points or principles. In most cases, individual authors were asked to address a single question. In cases in which certain authors were particularly well-known for holding views on multiple issues, we requested more than one chapter.

The 12 fundamental issues that we identified fall into three broad categories:

Methodological Issues

Four major issues center on the utility of using particular methodologies to study human behavior from an evolutionary perspective:

1. What methodologies can or should be used to reconstruct the evolution of the human mind?
2. What is the utility of tracking current fitness outcomes?
3. How is it useful to understand our closest ancestors (other primates) to comprehend human evolutionary outcomes?
4. What is the proper role of examining costs and benefits of behaviors or using quantitative modeling with respect to evolutionary outcomes?

Although all of these issues address the utility of applying different methodologies, different answers are likely to reflect different theoretical or metatheoretical assumptions. Indeed, as the reader will see, specific theoretical assumptions tend to be closely aligned with views about the utility of certain methodological approaches.

Metatheoretical Issues

Three issues involve metatheoretical themes:

5. Should the mind or psychological functions be thought of as modular and, if so, in what specific ways?
6. What are the implications of the developmental systems perspective—the idea that entire developmental systems, not simply genes, are targets of selection—for advancing our understanding of psychological adaptations?
7. What role, if any, did group selection assume in human evolution?

Issues Pertaining to Important Evolutionary Outcomes

Five issues reflect current debates over key evolutionary outcomes:

8. What major changes in selection pressures drove human evolution and led humans to be distinct from our closest ancestors?
9. What evolutionary processes contributed to the evolution of large brains in humans?
10. What is the significance of general abstractive abilities in understanding the evolution of humans?
11. How should culture be understood from an evolutionary perspective?
12. What are the most important features of hominid mating systems that have shaped how women and men relate to each other?

Admittedly, our division of questions and issues into these three categories is somewhat arbitrary. As mentioned earlier, many methodological issues are closely related to specific metatheoretical positions or assumptions. Answers to one question or issue (e.g., the role of understanding close ancestors) may be informed by views on other, key evolutionary outcomes in the hominid line. Similarly, whereas views of group selection might be more theoretical than metatheoretical, views on the role of culture might be more metatheoretical than theoretical. The organization of this book, therefore, is partly pragmatic.

We solicited and assembled this collection of essays to facilitate critical self-evaluation and to promote greater synthesis across the human evolutionary behavioral sciences. To date, debates have often resulted in greater polarization of viewpoints rather than integration or synthesis. We did not dictate how authors expressed their views on particular questions or issues. Close comparison of individual essays may reveal some polarization or entrenched views. We reasoned, however, that greater self-evaluation and synthesis might be fostered in two ways. First, by being able to compare and contrast specific positions directly, readers can discern for themselves where lingering questions and issues remain in major debates and perhaps new ways in which they might be resolved. Second, we (the editors) provide an integrative capstone chapter at the conclusion of the volume. Admittedly, this final chapter reflects some of our own views on where consensus may or may not be emerging with regard to certain questions and issues, points where important debate remains, and possible ways of clarifying or resolving certain debates. Though we tried not to express our personal views on various issues, we acknowledge that our own theoretical and empirical perspectives influenced how we addressed different responses each question/issue.

WHO SHOULD READ THIS BOOK

Several audiences should find this book particularly interesting. First, anyone who is interested in understanding the broad field of human evolutionary behavioral science—whether professionals, graduate students, or interested laypersons—will learn a great deal from this volume. Our primary intention was not to create a book that introduces major issues, perspectives, and assumptions in the human evolutionary behavioral sciences; several textbooks and primers already serve that function. This book attempts to be dialectical, describing, comparing, and contrasting different theoretical and metatheoretical views on important issues presented by respected scholars from different disciplines. Readers will learn much about how proponents of different perspectives think, and the different viewpoints can be directly compared and contrasted.

Second, we hope that this volume will also be read by persons who are invested in the future of human evolutionary behavioral science, those on whom the future of the field rests. Although we hope that it will be read and discussed by major scholars in the field, we also hope that it will reach graduate students and advanced undergraduates who are interested in evolutionary behavioral science, particularly those in the disciplines of psychology, biology, and anthropology. If this book succeeds at its primary task, it will lead scholars and students to gain a deeper appreciation of other views and perspectives, to understand the core assumptions and foundations of their own disciplines better, and to develop a clearer and more detailed "road map" outlining where the field needs to head in the future. In summary, the function of this book is to *provoke* critical analysis and *stimulate* new and creative thinking. Enjoy the intellectual ride.

REFERENCES

Alcock, J. (2001). *The triumph of sociobiology*. New York: Oxford University Press.
Barrett, L., Dunbar, R., & Lycett, J. (2002). *Human evolutionary psychology*. Princeton, NJ: Princeton University Press.
Boyd, R., & Richerson, P. J. (1985). *Culture and evolutionary process*. Chicago: University of Chicago Press.

Buller, D. J. (2005). *Adapting minds: Evolutionary psychology and the persistent quest for human nature.* Cambridge, MA: MIT Press.

Buss, D. M. (1999). *Evolutionary psychology: The new science of the mind.* Boston: Allyn & Bacon.

Buss, D. M. (Ed.). (2005). *The handbook of evolutionary psychology.* New York: Wiley.

Cartwright, J. (2000). *Evolution and human behavior.* Cambridge, MA: MIT Press.

Cavilli-Svorza, L. L., & Feldman, M. W. (1981). *Cultural transmission and evolution: A quantitative approach.* Princeton, NJ: Princeton University Press.

Chagnon, N. A., & Irons, W. (Eds.). (1979). *Evolutionary biology and human social behavior: An anthropological approach.* Scituate, MA: Duxbury Press.

Cole, L. C. (1954). The population consequences of life history phenomena. *Quarterly Review of Biology, 29,* 103–137.

Cosmides, L. (1989). The logic of social exchange: Has natural selection shaped how humans reason?: Studies with the Wason selection task. *Cognition, 31,* 187–276.

Crawford, C. B., & Krebs, D. L. (1998). *Handbook of evolutionary psychology: Ideas, issues, and applications.* Mahwah, NJ: Erlbaum.

Dawkins, R. (1976). *The selfish gene.* Oxford, UK: Oxford University Press.

Dennett, D. C. (1995). *Darwin's dangerous idea: The evolution and meanings of life.* New York: Simon & Schuster.

Dobzhansky, T. (1973). Nothing in biology makes sense except in the light of evolution. *American Biology Teacher, 3,* 125–129.

Dunbar, R. I. M., & Barrett, L. (2007). *The Oxford handbook of evolutionary psychology.* Oxford, UK: Oxford University Press.

Hamilton, W. D. (1964). The genetical evolution of social behavior. *Journal of Theoretical Biology, 7,* 1–52.

Hrdy, S. B. (1999). *Mother Nature: A history of mothers, infants, and natural selection.* New York: Pantheon.

Gangestad, S. W., & Simpson, J. A. (2000). The evolution of human mating: Trade-offs and strategic pluralism. *Behavioral and Brain Sciences, 23,* 573–587.

Gaulin, S. J. C., & McBurney, D. H. (2001). *Psychology: An evolutionary approach.* Upper Saddle River, NJ: Prentice-Hall.

Gould, S. J., & Lewontin, R. C. (1979). The spandrels of San Marco and the Panglossian paradigm: A critique of the adaptationist programme. *Proceedings of the Royal Society of London B, 205,* 581–598.

Kaplan, H., Hill, K., Lancaster, J., & Hurtado, A. M. (2000). A theory of human life history evolution: Diet, intelligence, and longevity. *Evolutionary Anthropology, 9,* 156–185.

Krebs, J. R., & Davies, N. B. (1997). *Behavioural ecology: An evolutionary approach* (4th ed.). Oxford, UK: Blackwell.

Kuhn, T. S. (1962). *The structure of scientific revolutions.* Chicago: University of Chicago Press.

Lack, D. (1966). *Population studies of birds.* London: Oxford University Press.

Lakatos, I. (1970). Falsification and the methodology of scientific research programmes. In I. Lakatos & A. Musgrave (Eds.), *Criticism and growth of knowledge* (pp. 91–96). Cambridge, UK: Cambridge University Press.

Laland, K. N., & Brown, G. (2002). *Sense and nonsense: Evolutionary perspectives on human behaviour.* London: Oxford University Press.

Lickliter, R., & Honeycutt, H. (2003). Developmental dynamics: Toward a biologically plausible evolutionary psychology. *Psychological Bulletin, 129,* 819–835.

Lumsden, C. J., & Wilson, E. O. (1981). *Genes, mind, and culture: The coevolutionary process.* Cambridge, MA: Harvard University Press.

Miller, G. F. (2000). *The mating mind: How sexual choice shaped the evolution of human nature.* New York: Doubleday.

Oyama. S., Griffiths, P. E., & Gray, R. D. (Eds.). (2001). *Cycles of contingency: Developmental systems and evolution.* Cambridge, MA: MIT Press.

Palmer, J. A., & Palmer, L. K. (2002). *Evolutionary psychology: The ultimate origins of human behavior.* Boston: Allyn & Bacon.

Pinker, S. (1994). *The language instinct.* New York: Morrow.

Pinker, S. (1997). *How the mind works.* New York: Norton.

Pinker, S. (2003). *The blank slate: The modern denial of human nature.* New York: Penguin.

Quartz, S. R., & Sejnowski, T. J. (2002). *Liars, lovers, and heroes: What the new brain science reveals about how we become who we are.* New York: HarperCollins.

Richerson, P. J., & Boyd, R. (2005). *Not by genes alone: How culture transformed human evolution.* Chicago: University of Chicago Press.

Ridley, M. (1993). *The red queen.* New York: Penguin.

Ridley, M. (1996). *The origins of virtue.* New York: Penguin.

Ridley, M. (2003). *Nature via nurture.* New York: HarperCollins.

Smith, E. A., Borgerhoff Mulder, M., & Hill, K. (2001). Controversies in the evolutionary social sciences: A guide to the perplexed. *Trends in Ecology and Evolution, 16,* 128–135.

Smith, E. A., & Winterhalder, B. (Eds.). (1992). *Evolutionary ecology and human behavior.* New York: de Gruyter.

Sober, E., & Wilson, D. S. (1998). *Unto others: The evolution and psychology of unselfish behavior.* Cambridge, MA: Harvard University Press.

Sperber, D. (1996). *Explaining culture: A naturalistic approach.* Oxford, UK: Blackwell.

Sulloway, F. (1996). *Born to rebel.* New York: Pantheon.

Symons, D. (1987). If we're all Darwinians, what's the fuss about? In C. Crawford, M. Smith, & D. Krebs (Eds.), *Sociobiology and psychology: Ideas, issues, and applications* (pp. 121–146). Hillsdale, NJ: Erlbaum.

Symons, (1990). Adaptiveness and adaptation. *Ethology and Sociobiology, 11,* 427–444.

Thornhill, R. (1997). The concept of an evolved adaptation. In M. Daly (Ed.), *Characterizing human psychological adaptations* (pp. 4–13). New York: Wiley.

Tooby, J., & Cosmides, L. (1989). Evolutionary psychology and the generation of culture: Part I. Theoretical considerations. *Ethology and Sociobiology, 10,* 29–49.

Tooby, J., & Cosmides, L. (1990). The past explains the present: Emotional adaptations and the structure of ancestral environments. *Ethology and Sociobiology, 11,* 375–424.

Tooby, J., & Cosmides, L. (1992). Psychological foundations of culture. In J. H.

Barkow, L. Cosmides, & J. Tooby (Eds.), *The adapted mind: Evolutionary psychology and the generation of culture* (pp. 19–136). New York: Oxford University Press.

Tooby, J., & Cosmides, L. (2000). Toward mapping the evolved functional organization of the mind and brain. In M. S. Gazzaniga (Ed.), *The new cognitive neurosciences* (pp. 1167–1178). Cambridge, MA: MIT Press.

Trivers, R. (1971). The evolution of reciprocal altruism. *Quarterly Review of Biology, 46*, 35–57.

Trivers, R. (1972). Parental investment and sexual selection. In B. Campbell (Ed.), *Sexual selection and the descent of man: 1871–1971* (pp. 136–179). Chicago: Aldine.

Trivers, R. (1974). Parent–offspring conflict. *American Zoologist, 14*, 249–264.

Trivers, R., & Willard, D. E. (1973). Natural selection of parental ability to vary the sex ratio of offspring. *Science, 179*, 90–92.

Williams, G. C. (1966). *Adaptation and natural selection*. Princeton, NJ: Princeton University Press.

Wilson, E. O. (1975). *Sociobiology: The new synthesis*. Cambridge, MA: Belknap Press.

Wilson, E. O. (1978). *On human nature*. Cambridge, MA: Harvard University Press.

Wright, R. (1994). *The moral animal: The new science of evolutionary psychology*. New York: Random House.

PART I

Methodological Issues

The Means of Darwinian Behavioral Science

Editors' Introduction

Darwinian biology is a historical science. The past explains the present. The field seeks to explain current distributions of behavioral traits and other features. But current distributions of features are the result of evolutionary phenomena that occurred in the distant past. Ancestral selection pressures that shaped traits are historical events of particular interest. We cannot go back and revisit history to observe these events directly. How, then, can we "know" distant past events and thereby explain current features? Perhaps no question is more foundational to the evolutionary behavioral sciences than this one.

Evolutionary scientists typically adopt several tacks to address this question. One tack is phylogenetic: We know which extant species are our closest living relatives and, based on genetic and paleontological data, can infer when we shared common ancestors with these species. Comparisons between modern humans and our closest living relatives can reveal a great deal about where we came from and the evolutionary paths we have taken. A second tack is archeological: We can piece together much of human history by examining the nature of historical artifacts. Bones, teeth, tools, housing ruins, and other residues of past human existences are important "documents" from which we can read the past. A third tack is argument from design: The most important artifacts that resulted in effective selection from which we can "read" evolutionary history are the features that past evolutionary history produced—our own features. Just as bird wings constitute critical evidence that birds were selected for flight, design features of modern humans constitute critical evidence of the selection pressures that gave rise to modern humans. A fourth tack is current adaptiveness: Darwin's theory leads us to expect that individuals will be shaped to be adapted to their environments. Are humans adapted to their environments? If so, in what specific ways?

These approaches, of course, are not mutually exclusive. Scientists can and often do use all of them. However, scientists must formulate the proper roles of each tack, and the proper roles have been vigorously debated. On the one hand, Thornhill (1997) claimed that even though archeological artifacts can provide hints about our evolutionary past, the only truly relevant evidence for past selection is found in the functional design of an organism. Some behavioral ecologists, on the other hand, have questioned whether functional design is revealing (e.g., Smith, Borgerhoff Mulder, & Hill, 2001). How can functional design be recognized? And how can one appreciate how it operated in ancestral environments if the nature of those environments is largely unknown?

We posed four different methodological issues to leading scholars.

HOW THE EVOLUTION OF THE HUMAN MIND MIGHT BE RECONSTRUCTED

Human evolution occurred across a vast span of time. We cannot directly observe what happened during the course of human evolutionary history. Yet evolutionary understandings of human psychology, if they are to be more than fanciful storytelling, must reflect what most likely occurred in our ancestral past; that is, they must satisfy conditions of truth.

"How can we accurately infer what transpired during evolutionary history that shaped the minds of humans?"

We solicited five answers to this fundamental question. Randy Thornhill is an evolutionary biologist who has firmly argued that functional design is crucial to inferring and understanding our evolutionary past. In this essay, he also emphasizes the importance of phylogenetic analyses. Edward H. Hagen and Donald Symons also address this question from a similar perspective. Paul W. Andrews has written on the nature of evidence needed to build a cogent argument for design. Representing a different perspective, Eric Alden Smith, a behavioral ecologist who questions whether we can know the past, therefore argues that evolutionary scientists should look for adaptations in current environments. Steven Mithen, an archaelogist, argues for the relevance of archaelogical data.

THE ROLE OF TRACKING CURRENT EVOLUTION

Evolution via natural selection occurs because of different rates of repro- duction. Evolutionary biologists and behavioral ecologists sometimes in- vestigate the nature of evolution by measuring reproductive outcomes ("counting babies"), then correlating those outcomes with the characteris- tics of particular individuals. Evolutionary psychologists have proposed that current reproduction, even in populations not using birth control, is ir- relevant to understanding current psychological adaptations, which evolved in distant ancestral environments.

"What is the use, if any, of measuring reproductive success in current envi- ronments?"

This question involves an issue that was central to a debate between evo- lutionary psychologists and evolutionary anthropologists in the late 1980s and early 1990s—the adaptationist versus adaptivist debate. We posed this question to Charles B. Crawford, an evolutionary psychologist who has taken a strong "adaptationist" stance, to Monique Borgerhoff Mulder, an anthropol- ogist who has defended the method of measuring current fitness to test evolu- tionary theories, and to H. Kern Reeve and Paul W. Sherman, evolutionary bi- ologists who wrote an influential article (1993) defining adaptation in terms of current utility and offer a justification for measuring current fitness.

OUR CLOSEST ANCESTORS

Humans diverged from our closest relatives, chimpanzees and bonobos, about 8 million years ago. These species in turn diverged from other apes several million years before that time period. Some scholars have argued that an understanding of our closest ancestors provides a window into hu- man evolution. Others have countered that studies of other species help us understand those particular species, but because key aspects of human evolution occurred after our divergence from our closest ancestors, com- parative information has little relevance to explaining and understanding human psychological adaptations.

"What is the utility of studying primates and other species for understand- ing human psychological evolution?"

We solicited answers to this question from three leading primatolo- gists, all of whom have extensive field experience working with nonhuman primates: Craig B. Stanford, Joan B. Silk, and Jane B. Lancaster (coauthored with Hillard S. Kaplan).

THE ROLE OF EXAMINING THE COSTS
AND BENEFITS OF BEHAVIORS

Evolutionary biologists and behavioral ecologists often use mathematical analyses to quantify the costs and benefits of specific behaviors, tactics, or strategies in terms of their effects on biological fitness or reproductive success. This includes optimality analyses and game theoretical modeling. Evolutionary psychologists, in contrast, use these tools much less frequently. Instead, they attempt to understand adaptations as solutions to "adaptive problems" posed by ancestral environments

"What is the proper role of formal optimality or game theoretical modeling in the study of human behavioral adaptations?"

We posed this question to three sets of authors. Hillard S. Kaplan and Steven W. Gangestad, an anthropologist and a psychologist, argue that optimality analyses are useful and indeed sometimes necessary to understand the ancestral selection pressures that forged certain current adaptations. Peter DeScioli and Robert Kurzban, both psychologists, present a framework for applying game theoretical analyses to understanding adaptation in social interactions. Douglas T. Kenrick and Jill M. Sundie, also both psychologists, suggest ways in which dynamical systems approaches to understanding group outcomes, combined with theories about evolved strategies, might be employed to reveal how evolved psychologies generate different outcomes depending on group composition and the spatial distribution of strategies.

REFERENCES

Reeve, H. K., & Sherman, P. W. (1993). Adaptation and the goals of evolutionary biology. *Quarterly Review of Biology, 68,* 1–32.

Smith, E. A., Borgerhoff Mulder, M., & Hill, K. (2001). Controversies in the evolutionary social sciences: A guide to the perplexed. *Trends in Ecology and Evolution, 16,* 128–135.

Thornill, R. (1997). The concept of an evolved adaptation. In M. Daley (Ed.), *Characterizing human psychological adaptations* (pp. 4–13). New York: Wiley.

How the Evolution of the Human Mind Might Be Reconstructed

1

Comprehensive Knowledge of Human Evolutionary History Requires Both Adaptationism and Phylogenetics

RANDY THORNHILL

Two methods—adaptationism and phylogenetics—are distinct, complementary, noncompetitive procedures for comprehensively understanding a biological trait's ultimate causation, that is, causation in evolutionary history. Science is the study of the causes of effects that exist in nature. A cause is something without which an effect or phenomenon could not have occurred. If a primordial mammary gland had not arisen initially from a sweat gland as a result of some developmental process in the species that was ancestral to all three of the major mammalian taxa (monotremes, marsupials, and placentals), modern mammary glands would not now exist across females of all mammalian taxa (for the origin of lactation, see Cowen, 1990). If this initial mammary gland trait had not been maintained by selection in all branches of the portion of the Tree of Life comprising Mammalia, then mammary glands would not exist now in these animals either. Evolutionary origin and maintenance are different, partial evolutionary ultimate causes; each is necessary, but neither alone is sufficient to explain fully a trait's evolutionary history. As West-Eberhard (2003, p. 197)

31

put this point, "research on selection and adaptation may tell why a trait persisted and spread, but it will not tell us where the trait came from." By "came from," she means the causal origin of the ancestral trait via some developmental process in the evolutionary history of life. Because origin and maintenance are complementary, ultimate causes, a trait's origin can be studied scientifically without simultaneously applying adaptationism to study the trait's persistence after its origin, and vice versa, but the complete understanding of the trait's evolutionary history requires knowledge of both.

The study of human mental and behavioral features by behavioral ecologists and evolutionary psychologists has focused almost exclusively on one component of evolutionary causation—maintenance, especially by selection during the last few to several million years—and generally has ignored the phylogenetic origins of features. Although this focus has delivered an impressive collection of discoveries about human functional design and hence human evolutionary history, it can provide only partial knowledge of that history. Hauser, Tsao, Garcia, and Spelke (2003) show the importance of analysis-of-origin issues that incorporate comparative data from early-appearing primate taxa and even other mammals in understanding the evolutionary history of human language. I suggest in my essay on women's sexuality that phylogenetic analysis of estrus across vertebrates validates the application of the term "estrus" to women's sexuality at peak fertility in the menstrual cycle (Chapter 43, this volume). Human behavior and related physiology (e.g., hormones) do not fossilize, but this is no problem for the study of trait origins, because appropriate comparative data alone can yield strong causal inferences.

The study of human evolutionary history will become comprehensive only when both adaptationism and phylogenetics are recognized widely as the two distinct and equally important tools for fully understanding that history. There is no scientific justification for the popular idea that the study of nonhuman primates alone can provide the most salient answers to questions about human evolutionary history (see de Waal, 2001, for examples). Nor is there validity in the view that the study of selection and functional design gives all the answers, which is implied by the emphasis on adaptationism by researchers in human evolutionary psychology, behavioral ecology, and related fields. Nonhuman primates sometimes tell us everything about the phylogenetic origin of human behavior but nothing about the hominin-lineage-specific selection that subsequently elaborated it. That selection will be stamped in the functional design of *human* psychological and behavioral adaptations. Many features of human behavior, however, are much older than the first primate and, in such cases, phylogenetic comparisons appropriately extend beyond primates. As I suggest in another essay (Chapter 43, this volume), estrus is one of these features. There is no scientifically legitimate reason to argue for one method over the other when the goal is to illuminate the ultimate causes of the features of humans.

The origin of each and every phenotypic trait on the Tree of Life is caused by the developmental transformation of an ancestral phenotype. As West-Eberhard (2003) has emphasized, biologists erroneously have restricted ontogenetic causes to the proximate causal domain. When development causes a trait or feature within an individual's lifetime, it is a proximate cause, but the ontogenetic, phylogenetic origin of a novel trait or feature is ultimate causation. (See my Chapter 21, this volume, on development and evolution.)

Evolutionary maintenance of a newly arisen trait, that is, persistence, and sometimes its spread through many descendant phylogenetic branches involves the process of either drift or selection, depending upon the trait. Maintenance of a trait by selection in the Tree of Life involves either direct or indirect selection. Contrary to the claims of some commentators, adaptationism is not a research program that claims every trait is an evolved adaptation (i.e., a product of direct selection for a function). Rather, it is a much broader method that can distinguish traits that have been selected from traits that have not, and whether the selected traits were selected directly or indirectly. Indirectly selected traits are incidental effects or by-products of adaptations.

An important component in the evolutionary persistence of traits is what Darwin called "descent with modification"; that is, the original trait is modified by the evolutionary process after its appearance, such that it is adaptive in relation to lineage-specific problems. For example, the designs of mammary glands differ among the three major mammalian taxa, as well as among more specific taxa of mammals, explaining why whale milk and human milk adaptively differ in composition. Hence, lineage-specific mammary gland adaptation is the result of lineage-specific selection. Aspects of the original gland machinery from the ancestral species still exist across all mammals, but a great deal of subsequent evolutionary modification has occurred, leading to different designs in mammary adaptations that are lineage-specific. Each of these different designs has an origin point on the mammalian phylogenetic tree, and at each of these points, phenotypic novelty was created by development.

Mammary glands are homologous across all mammals; that is, all mammals derive from a common ancestral species with mammary gland machinery. Homology means *similarity* in a feature across different kinds of organisms that is caused by common ancestry. An identical form of a trait across kinds of organisms is not the criterion for homology, because traits evolve. In contrast, analogy or convergence is similarity in a feature across different kinds of organisms that is caused by independent evolution (i.e., by independent processes of origin and maintenance). Adaptationism is a fundamental and necessary tool for phylogenetic reconstruction, because all phylogenetic evidence is evidence of homology. Adaptationism's analysis of traits provides the understanding of the basis of similarity among traits of different kinds of organisms.

The deduction that mammary glands first arose in the species that was ancestral to all mammals applies the routine phylogenetic *principle of parsimony*. All mammals have homologous mammary machinery; thus, aspects of the same machinery existed in their common ancestral species. The retention of the mammary gland by descent after its origin is far more likely than the independent evolution of glands in each of the many mammal lineages. By descent, I do not mean inheritance alone (the transmission of the phenotype between generations; see Chapter 21, this volume, on development and evolution). The action of some evolutionary agent in concert with inheritance is necessary to explain the maintenance of mammary glands throughout the history of the mammals. Inheritance alone is insufficient, because it is a different process than the differential reproductive success of individuals, which affects which traits are transmitted by inheritance and thereby fuels a trait's phylogenetic descent. The differential reproduction of individuals involved in descent may arise from chance, in which case it is caused by drift, or derives from trait differences (i.e., from selection).

It is common to read in the evolutionary literature the erroneous notion that traits persist in the Tree of Life as a result of so-called "phylogenetic inertia," also called, simply, "phylogeny." Retention of traits in the Tree of Life must be the result of drift, or direct or indirect selection. Genetic correlation also is sometimes claimed to explain the maintenance of a trait in the Tree of Life, but this, too, is erroneous, because the correlation itself does not account for the maintenance. A phylogenetically retained trait that is correlated genetically with a directly selected trait persists through its indirect selection. "Developmental constraint" is another popular explanation for phylogenetic trait retention. It is similar, if not identical, to phylogenetic inertia and reflects the same misunderstandings (see also Reeve & Sherman, 2001; West-Eberhard, 2003).

Adaptationism figuratively carves the organism's phenotype to separate empirically its evolved adaptations from its by-products and other traits. George Williams, a pioneer of the modern study of adaptation in biology, emphasized 40 years ago that adaptation is an onerous concept in biology and should be applied only when there is evidence that a feature has functional design. Hence, the necessary and sufficient evidence for identifying evolved adaptation is a demonstration of a sufficient fit or coordination between a trait and a problem faced by an organism to rule out chance association that can arise from by-product effects, mutation, or drift. Selection does not cause the appearance of novel, adaptive phenotypes— development does. Selection is the separate, causal process that arises after ontogenetic origin and with accompanying heritability of trait variation may lead to an evolutionary response. Cumulative evolution by selection produces features that are functionally designed unambiguously. An evolved adaptation, then, contains in its functional design the evidence of the kind of historical selection that made it (Thornhill, 1997).

Reeve and Sherman (1993) define an "adaptation" as any trait that is adaptive currently (i.e., when variation in the trait across individuals covaries with reproductive success in a contemporary population). Their concept of adaptation is different from that of an evolved adaptation. Current adaptiveness is not a criterion for identifying an evolved adaptation; the only criterion is functional design. An evolved adaptation may be currently nonadaptive and even maladaptive, because the current ecological setting in which it occurs differs importantly from the evolutionary historical setting that selected it. Also, an incidental effect may be adaptive currently (Thornhill, 1997).

The distinction between evolved adaptation and current adaptiveness is not always recognized. For example, Setchell and Kappeler (2003) advise caution in interpreting David Buss's and Steven Gangestad's and my research on human sexual behavior, because it does not include paternity analysis and data on lifetime reproductive success. The research they criticize is focused on the functional design of men's and women's sexuality, not on its current adaptiveness. Hence, the studies they call for address fundamentally different questions than those examined in the research they criticize.

Martins (2000) suggests that an adaptation is any trait that persists in the Tree of Life. Phylogenetic persistence, however, does not distinguish adaptation from nonadaptation in organisms for three reasons. First, by-products may persist phylogenetically (e.g., the color of bones across vertebrates) through their indirect selection. Second, traits can be conserved phylogenetically by drift. Third, an evolved adaptation may not persist phylogenetically, due to lineage extinction.

When phylogenetics and adaptationism are combined and properly applied, they can give a full understanding of ultimate causation. Their validity for determining the true evolutionary history of life relies on Darwin's general method of historical science that has "triumphed," as Ghiselin (1969) put it. The method is used routinely and respectfully in all sciences that are charged with understanding the distant past, including biology, geology, and astronomy, because of its scientific power. A "scientific hypothesis" is a statement of possible causation that is tested by empirical evaluation of its predictions or consequences (i.e., those things that must be true if the hypothesized cause is reality). An "evolutionary historical hypothesis" is a statement of possible causation that acted in the deep-time past. Actual deep-time historical causes will have left consequences, which are the predictions of an evolutionary historical hypothesis. The empirical absence of these consequences falsifies the hypothesis. Empirical proof of the consequences is the definitive evidence for past causation that cannot be observed directly. Darwin's method can penetrate vast stretches of deep-time history to identify causation as seen, for example, in scientific knowledge that all life is the result of descent with modification from an ancestral species with nucleic acid, a fact demonstrated by the phylogenetic principle of parsimony that, in this case, takes causal understanding back more than 3 billion years.

ACKNOWLEDGMENT

Rosalind Arden, Steve Gangestad, Jeff Simpson, and Paul Watson provided useful comments on the manuscript.

REFERENCES

Cowen, R. (1990). *History of life*. Boston, MA: Blackwell.

de Waal, F. F. M. (2001). *Tree of origin: What primate behavior can tell us about human social evolution*. Cambridge, MA: Harvard University Press.

Ghiselin, M. T. (1969). *The triumph of the Darwinian method*. Berkeley: University of California Press.

Hauser, M. D., Tsao, F., Garcia, P., & Spelke, E. S. (2003). Evolutionary foundations of number: Spontaneous representation of numerical magnitudes by cotton-top tamarins. *Proceedings of the Royal Society of London B, 270*, 1441–1446.

Martins, E. P. (2000). Adaptation and the comparative method. *Trends in Ecology and Evolution, 15*, 296–299.

Reeve, H. K., & Sherman, P. W. (1993). Adaptation and the goals of evolutionary research. *Quarterly Review of Biology, 68*, 1–32.

Reeve, H. K., & Sherman, P. W. (2001). Optimality and phylogeny: A critique of current thought. In S. Orzack & E. Sober (Eds.), *Adaptationism and aptimality* (pp. 64–113). Cambridge, UK: Cambridge University Press.

Setchell, J. M., & Kappeler, P. M. (2003). Selection in relation to sex in primates. *Advances in the Study of Behavior, 33*, 87–173.

Smith, E. A., Borgerhoff Mulder, M., & Hill, K. (2001). Controversies in the evolutionary sciences: A guide to the perplexed. *Trends in Ecology and Evolution, 16*, 128–135.

Thornhill, R. (1997). The concept of an evolved adaptation. In M. Daly (Ed.), *Characterizing human psychological adaptations* (pp. 4–13). London: Wiley.

West-Eberhard, M. J. (2003). *Developmental plasticity and evolution.* New York: Oxford University Press.

🙰 2

Natural Psychology

The Environment of Evolutionary
Adaptedness and the Structure of Cognition

EDWARD H. HAGEN
DONALD SYMONS

The modern materialist conception of nature was born in the first half of the 17th century with major works by Bacon, Harvey, Galileo, and Descartes. In its current form, the universe comprises fundamental particles and forces that obey precise laws; more complex entities such as nuclei, atoms, molecules, gases, stars, and galaxies are explicable, it is believed, solely in terms of these fundamental particles and forces. Given a precise description of the state of even a very complex system at one point in time, its properties at any future point in time are determined by the operation of physical law. The universe, in short, is a big machine. (Quantum mechanics does not really change this view, nor do recent ideas on chaos, complexity, and emergent properties; see Bricmont, 2004.)

If materialism is correct, everything in the universe, including life, brains, thoughts, and feelings, has a material explanation. Providing these explanations has been a formidable and ongoing challenge. Two challenges are particularly important to cognitive science: the origins and nature of life, and, of course, cognition itself. In this essay, we sketch an idealized history of the successful surmounting of the first challenge, and the current state of efforts to surmount the second. We see these two challenges as essentially one and the same. Evolutionary psychology is an attempt to apply to the brain the model that has worked so well for the rest of the body. Yet it has failed to embrace fully a key lesson from anatomy and physiology: our detailed understanding of the body is grounded in an equally detailed understanding of the world with which the body has interacted.

Following Harvey's discovery that the heart is a pump, there was an explosion of research in anatomy and physiology that adopted not merely a materialist but a distinctly functional approach; bodies were increasingly understood as machines. This idea, however, is fundamentally different from the idea of the universe as a machine. Unlike nonliving systems, hearts, lungs, and eyes have a purpose or function. Like human artifacts, they show clear evidence of *design*—of having been engineered to perform specific functions that benefit the organism. Body parts are not only physical entities that obey physical laws, they are *functional*. The latter property raised one of the most important questions ever asked in science: Who or what designed the functions evident in living organisms?

We are not sure when the critical distinction between living systems as functional, and nonliving systems as nonfunctional, was first appreciated. It is clear, however, that natural theology, brilliantly synthesized in William Paley's 1809 book of the same name, played a decisive role in making this distinction and, thus, in framing a core problem for Darwin and Wallace. Whereas revealed theology was based on scripture and religious experience, natural theology sought evidence for God in the natural world: God is not merely a matter of faith, but can be demonstrated using logic and commonly observed facts. That "things of different natures [fall] into harmonious order, not rarely and fortuitously, but always or for the most part" was for Aquinas (1905) evidence of "some Power by whose providence the world is governed; and that we call God." In this form, natural theology would have been of little use to Darwin. Much of the order and harmony of the physical world was rapidly being explained in materialist terms and, in any case, Darwin was not a physicist.

Paley's *Natural Theology* (1809), however, is rich with keen observations of the living world. In the structure of organisms, unlike most of the physical world, Paley saw not only order but also purpose or function.[1] An

---

[1] In his chapter on astronomy (Ch. 22) Paley does argue that the order of the heavens is evidence for a designer.

organism was a "cluster of contrivances . . . for nourishment . . . for generation" (Paley, 1809, p. 185). Critically, each "contrivance" was exquisitely
matched to the organism's environment. Darwin took from Paley a superbly
well-defined problem, which he and Wallace then solved. Their theory of
natural selection explained in materialist terms how such "contrivances"
could arise without a designer, why their purposes would be limited to
those that could be linked to the reproduction of the organism, and why
they would closely reflect the organism's environment.

The successful explication of most of the body's "contrivances" is a
pinnacle of science. Remarkably, reaching this pinnacle required little, if
any, Darwinian theory. The simple, almost atheoretical heuristic that body
functions serve survival or reproduction captures much of the content of
the theory of natural selection, usually rendering a formal appeal to the theory unnecessary.

Despite the amazing achievements of physiology, no materialist theory
of thoughts, feelings, and consciousness—which we refer to as *cognition*—
has produced anything approaching a scientific consensus. Although it has
long been recognized that cognition is somehow a product of the brain,
forging each link in the chain from brain to cognition has been extremely
difficult. Some early, influential psychologists such as Watson and Skinner
even believed that behavior must be explained without reference to cognitive properties such as mental events, states, or processes. This so-called
behaviorism, popular during the first half of the 20th century, rapidly col-
lapsed when Chomsky showed that language could be explained only with
recourse to mental states and processes.

Equally important in behaviorism's demise was the midcentury invention and commercialization of the electronic computer, a machine with
properties heretofore only possessed by brains. Computers could do things,
such as playing chess, that required something like "thought," and this behavior could only be explained with reference to the computer's internal
states—its program and memory. Chomsky's (1959) critique of behaviorism, his views on language, and the invention of the computer launched the
cognitive revolution: Mental states cause behavior and can be scientifically
studied by making inferences from that behavior, and these states can be
rigorously modeled as the states of one or more computational devices.

Recognizing that the brain could be modeled as a computer was a tremendous step toward a materialist explanation of cognition. In and of
themselves, however, computers are far too general machines to serve as
useful models of nervous systems. The state of a computer's memory can
characterize just about any physical system; sequences of computer in-

structions (algorithms) can transform this state into any other state. Thus, computers can model almost anything, including the weather, fires, automobiles, and the postal service. Nothing in the idea of a computer per se is specific to nervous systems. To create a computational model of nervous systems in general, and the human nervous system in particular, additional principles are needed.

Our current model of body organs and tissues is that (1) they are machines (or parts thereof), and (2) these machines serve survival or reproductive functions. The computer model of cognition, on the other hand, claims only that the brain comprises one or more computational devices, akin to (1). But there is no part (2), no explicit requirement that these computational devices serve the survival or reproduction of the organism! It is as if scientists were demonstrating how body parts could be conceptualized as machines—a lever-arm here, a fulcrum there—but had little idea what kinds of machines they were a part of, or what these machines were for. Cognitive science has mostly focused on how the brain could support computation (as we noted, a much too general model), but it has paid too little attention to what, exactly, should be computed (the popular idea that the brain is simply a general learning machine is a nonstarter; see Gallistel, 1999; Pinker, 2002).

The prime contribution that evolutionary psychology (EP) has made to the cognitive revolution is to provide key principles that were missing from the computational model. The brain is not merely a collection of one or more computational devices, but a collection of computational devices that evolved to facilitate or enable reproduction in ancestral environments by manipulating aspects of those environments. The aspects of the environment that a mechanism evolved to manipulate are referred to as the "environment of evolutionary adaptedness" (EEA) of that mechanism (although the EEA is adaptation-specific, the term is also used as shorthand to refer to the EEAs of all a species' adaptations; for more details, see Hagen, 2005; Salmon & Symons, 2003; Tooby & Cosmides, 1990). Embedded in any functional hypothesis for a body structure is a hypothesis about the environment that structure is designed to manipulate. The hypothesis that the immune system identifies and eliminates pathogens from the body, for example, entails numerous assumptions about the nature of pathogens.

EP has, in essence, aligned the computational model of the brain with the functional model used for all other body tissues and organs. But instead of just adding the simple heuristic that brain mechanisms serve survival or reproduction, EP has brought the full power of evolutionary theory to bear: Cognitive mechanisms are adaptations.

Research in many domains of psychology and neuroscience were already in line with research on other body functions, of course. Researchers studying vision and the other senses would certainly agree that the senses serve survival or reproductive functions by enabling the organism to obtain a more or less accurate model of its physical surroundings. Furthermore, to understand these mechanisms, these researchers paid extremely close attention to the properties of the EEA, the nature of sunlight and acoustic vibrations, for example. Yet this has been more the exception than the rule in the various cognitive sciences. Too many cognitive science research programs, including EP, have focused almost all of their attention on cognitive mechanisms, and virtually none on the structure of the environments with which those mechanisms were designed to interact.

Understanding the design and function of the eye requires a deep understanding of the properties of light and its interaction with matter, as well as a precise description of how the eye should transform incident light. Our understanding of the immune system is founded on a truly massive research effort that has revealed the nature of infections and proteins, as well as the recognition that the goal of the immune system is to kill and remove pathogens from the body. An understanding of the logic of any mechanism almost always requires a thorough knowledge of the physical system that the mechanism was designed to manipulate, and the ways in which it should be manipulated.

Although EP has long argued that evolved functions can only be understood in relation to their EEA (e.g., Symons, 1979), by adopting the traditional methods of cognitive and social psychology, EP has inherited some of the intrinsic limits of these methods. These methods were designed to investigate cognitive mechanisms, *not* the properties of the mechanisms' EEA. As the examples of the senses and immune system make clear, however, it may be extremely difficult to elucidate cognitive mechanisms without a detailed understanding of the EEA. Imagine trying to investigate the structure of the eye with only a vague understanding of optics.

An important exception to the foregoing is what has come to be known as *ecological rationality* (e.g., Gigerenzer & Todd, 1999; Simon, 1956), an approach in psychology that emphasizes that decision-making heuristics will correspond closely to the information structure of the environment, and that actively investigates this information structure. Not surprisingly, EP and the ecological rationality school have become closely aligned.

The EEA concept is central to the scientific study of organism structure. If one knew the theory of natural selection but *nothing* else, one could say little, if anything, about the nature of organisms. Organisms evolved to reproduce in a particular environment; if nothing is known about that environment, almost nothing can be said about what it takes to reproduce in it. The structure of the organism itself, of course, contains much information about its EEA. Via natural selection, a gene pool gradually accumulates information on how to transform its EEA. Functional organism structures (i.e., adaptations), as products of the genome, reflect this accumulated information in intricate detail. Adaptations can often be recognized, in fact, by the information they contain about their target EEA. The eye contains tremendous amounts of information about light, and how to transform it to the organism's benefit. The embodiment by one system—the adaptation—of detailed information about useful transformations of another system—the target EEA—serves as a clear marker of natural selection.

One of the most famous such examples is the Star-of-Bethlehem orchid, whose nectar-producing organ lies 30 centimeters inside it. Darwin predicted that an insect with a proboscis at least 30 cm long would be discovered that pollinated the orchid. In 1903, 21 years after Darwin's death, a moth with a proboscis 30–35 cm in length was discovered that pollinated the orchid. It was christened *Xanthopan morgani praedicta*, in honor of Darwin's prediction.

Interpreting the information exhibited by adaptations about their EEAs, however, can be a formidable challenge. Without many background facts, it will often be difficult, if not impossible, to correctly infer an adaptation's function. Darwin's prediction required considerable knowledge of plant pollination and the role of insects therein. Elucidating adaptations and their EEAs is an iterative process. Like keys and locks, the more that is known about one, the more that can be known about the other.

It follows, then, that EP must pay as close attention to the EEA of each psychological mechanism as physiology and anatomy do to the EEA of physiological mechanisms. To predict and explore cognitive structures, most EP studies rely on assumptions derived from abstract theories, such as reciprocal altruism and parental investment theory. Yet virtually none of these studies actually investigate the putative EEA of those cognitive structures. EP has been trying to study keys (adaptations) without studying the matching locks (the adaptation's EEA).

Countless EP studies, for example, have examined human mate choice cognition, yet almost none have investigated patterns of human mate choice in the EEA. Arranged marriages are one of the best-documented and important aspects of mating in the small-scale traditional societies that are most likely to resemble EEA societies. The close involvement of parents and other family members in many marriages implies, at the very least, constraints on individual mate choice, and evolved mating psychology should reflect this fact.

In summary, EP has provided the principles lacking in the computation model of cognition. Similar to other body mechanisms, cognitive mechanisms evolved to manipulate specific aspects of the EEA, enabling and facilitating reproduction. With EP, cognitive science has almost, but not quite, all of the conceptual tools that guaranteed the success of anatomy and physiology. The next steps, we believe, will involve detailed studies of not only cognitive mechanisms but also the EEA of those mechanisms.

REFERENCES

Aquinas, T. (1905). Reasons in proof of the existence of God. In *An annotated translation (with some abridgement) of the Summa Contra Gentiles of Saint Thos Aquinas by Joseph Rickaby, S.J., M.A. Lond: B.Sc. Oxon., Author of "Aquinas Ethicus* (Book I, Chapter 13). London: Burns & Oates. Available at http://www2.nd.edu/Departments/Maritain/etext/gc.htm

Bricmont, J. (2004). *Determinism, chaos and quantum mechanics.* Available at www.fyma.ucl.ac.be/files/Turin.pdf

Chomsky, N. (1959). A review of B. F. Skinner's *Verbal Behavior. Language, 35,* 26–58.

Gallistel, C. R. (1999). The replacement of general-purpose learning models with adaptively specialized learning modules. In M.S. Gazzaniga (Ed.), *The cognitive neurosciences* (2nd ed, pp. 1179–1191). Cambridge, MA: MIT Press.

Gigerenzer, G., & Todd, P. M. (1999). *Simple heuristics that make us smart.* New York: Oxford University Press.

Hagen, E. H. (2005) Controversial issues in evolutionary psychology. In D. M. Buss (Ed.), *The handbook of evolutionary psychology* (p. 145–174). New York: Wiley.

Paley, W. (1809). *Natural theology; or, evidence of the existence and attributes of the deity* (12th ed.). London: J. Faulder. Available at http://www.hti.umich.edu/cgi/p/pd-modeng/pd-modeng-idx?type=HTML&rgn=TEI.2&byte=53049319

Pinker, S. (2002). *The blank slate.* New York: Penguin Putnam.

Salmon, C., & Symons, D. (2003) *Warrior lovers: Erotic fiction, evolution and female sexuality.* New Haven, CT: Yale University Press.

Simon, H. A. (1956). Rational choice and the structure of the environment. *Psychological Review, 63,* 129–138.

Symons, D. (1979). *The evolution of human sexuality.* Oxford, UK: Oxford University Press.

Tooby, J., & Cosmides, L. (1990). The past explains the present: Emotional adaptations and the structure of ancestral environments. *Ethology and Sociobiology, 11,* 375–424.

3

Reconstructing the Evolution of the Mind Is Depressingly Difficult

PAUL W. ANDREWS

One of the important goals of the evolutionary psychologist is to elucidate the evolutionary history of psychological traits, including the forces that generated and shaped them. This task is complicated by the fact that the "shapes" of psycyhological traits are not directly observable, nor are the forces that shaped them.

Selection contributes to the shaping of the phenotype when a new allele modifies a trait in a way that has a gene-propagating effect. Under such circumstances, the trait has been *adapted* for the effect, and the effect is a *function* of the trait (Williams, 1966).

A "constraint" is something that opposes the modifying influence of selection on a trait so that there exists a more optimal (fitness enhancing) phenotype that it cannot reach (Andrews, Gangestad, & Matthews, 2002a). Constraints contribute to the shaping of a trait by inhibiting the influence of selection.

Exaptation is not usually viewed as a force that influences trait design, because a trait that has been *exapted* takes on a new, beneficial effect without being modified by selection for that effect (Gould & Vrba, 1982). It is possible, however, for *exapted learning mechanisms* (ELMs) to influence the design of psychological traits (Andrews et al., 2002a). Learning is a process by which feedback from the environment modifies the neurological structures that give rise to behavior and cognition. Learning mechanisms are adaptations that allow the organism to modulate behavior with changing environments. As adaptations, they have functions (e.g., learn a language, fear a predator), but they are somewhat flexible with respect to outcome. A learning mechanism can be so flexible that it produces useful behavioral and cognitive traits that are not the function of the mechanism. The ability to read, to perform abstract mathematics, or to play the stock market must represent the output of ELMs. In this sense, exaptation is able to influence the shape of psychological traits.

A "spandrel" is a trait that evolved, not because it was selectively advantageous, but because it was tied to another trait (e.g., by linkage disequilibrium or pleiotropy) that was selectively advantageous (Gould & Lewontin, 1979). Some species of snail have a space in their shell that they use to brood their eggs but that probably evolved as a consequence of a shell developmental plan that was the outcome of selection (Gould, 1997).

A common complaint is that evolutionary psychology focuses on adaptationist hypotheses for trait design and ignores nonadaptationist hypotheses (Gould & Lewontin, 1979; Gould & Vrba, 1982). Traits can be complex mixtures of adaptation, exaptation, spandrel, and constraint (Andrews et al., 2002a). In this sense, adaptationist and nonadaptationist hypotheses are not mutually exclusive. But critics often ask evolutionary scientists to consider and test exaptation, spandrel, and constraint as *alternatives* to adaptationist hypotheses.

How are evolutionary psychologists to parse among adaptation, constraint, exaptation, and spandrel as influences on trait design? Adaptationist and nonadaptationist hypotheses are epistemologically entwined together (Andrews et al., 2002a; Andrews, Gangestad, & Matthews, 2002b). Before accepting a particular hypothesis, the scientist must first show that alternative hypotheses fare worse as explanations. Evidence shows that a trait's features are best explained by adaptation only to the extent that it weakens the case for nonadaptationist hypotheses. Similarly, evidence that strengthens the case for exaptation, spandrel, or constraint must weaken the case for adaptationist hypotheses. For this reason, the rigorous search for evidence of adaptation, and the failure to find it, is a crucial criterion for demonstrating nonadaptationist hypotheses.

My colleagues and I have discussed this, and related issues, at length elsewhere (Andrews et al., 2002a, 2002b). For this essay, I focus on depression to exemplify this point. Depression is an unpleasant state of low affect in which the sufferer experiences a loss in the ability to derive pleasure from otherwise pleasurable things ("anhedonia"). Depression is often assumed to be categorical, with severe, chronic depression being qualitatively different from subclinical depression or transient sadness. Although support for a categorical approach comes from evidence that different kinds of life stressors elicit different depression symptom profiles (Keller & Nesse, 2006), the symptoms themselves are distributed continuously over the population (Hankin, Fraley, Lahey, & Waldman, 2005). Moreover, the degree of cognitive and psychosocial impairment both covary continuously with the number of depressive symptoms, and liability to depression is better predicted by continuous models than categorical models (Aggen, Neale, & Kendler, 2005; Elderkin-Thompson et al., 2003; Kessler, Zhao, Blazer, & Swartz, 1997). Because there is little evidence that clinical depression is qualitatively different in subclinical forms, I use the term *depression* to refer to a continuum that includes both transient sadness and severe, chronic depression.

The medical view is that depression is a neurochemical disorder, at least in its extreme forms. The origin of this view was not firmly rooted in scientific evidence, but is largely attributable to economic and political forces (Valenstein, 1998). Subsequent research has reified the medical view by cataloguing numerous detrimental and costly aspects of depression, including cognitive deficits (Austin, Mitchell, & Goodwin, 2001), a loss of hippocampal brain tissue (Duman, 2004), a reduced motivation or ability to care for oneself and one's social obligations, social rejection (Segrin & Dillard, 1992), an enhanced risk of suicidal behavior, and many others.

Does the fact that depression is costly prove that it is a disorder? Adaptations are often costly to operate, construct, or maintain. Fever evolved to fight off pathogens by providing a nonoptimal temperature for the growth of pathogens and activating elements of the immune system (Nesse & Williams, 1994). Fever has high operational costs—it causes the body to utilize resources at a 20% faster rate, it causes temporary sterility in males, and high fever can cause delirium and tissue damage. The costs of depression may suggest dysfunction, but, like fever, they may also suggest the existence of compensatory benefits. Even the fact that depression plays a causal role in suicidal behavior is not proof of dysfunction. Adaptations for suicide exist in other species (Alcock, 1998), and there is some evidence of adaptive modulation of suicidal behavior in human beings (Andrews, 2006; Joiner et al., 2002).

Only a limited number of hypotheses can explain depression's existence. First, depression may be a novel reaction of the nervous system to modern environments, so that selection has not yet had time to act against depression and its costs. One reason to doubt this hypothesis is that much of our understanding of the neurobiology of depression comes from research in other animals (e.g., rodents, cats, primates), suggesting that depression may be phylogenetically old. Second, depression could be a maladaptive spandrel that evolved because it was tied to another trait that was so adaptive that it compensated for the costs of depression. Finally, depression could have evolved because it had a useful function that compensated for its costs (i.e., depression could be an adaptation). This hypothesis does not require that depression must always produce adaptive outcomes. Adaptations need only be adaptive on average to evolve; they can malfunction, and they need not produce adaptive outcomes in evolutionarily novel environments.

Why should the adaptationist hypothesis be treated seriously? Imagine the newspapers and news shows abuzz tomorrow about a new study demonstrating that depression does something extraordinarily useful. All of a sudden, the hypothesis that depression is an adaptation would appear much more plausible. This thought experiment reveals that the current research on depression has a huge hole in it. Unless we look for and fail to find evidence of adaptation, we cannot be sure that a trait is not an adaptation, because it is possible that evidence of adaptation will eventually be found. Most of the existing research on depression has not been designed to search for evidence of function. It has been designed to search for evidence that it is costly.

Because the absence of adaptation is a crucial part of building a case for nonadaptationist hypotheses, the scientist must recognize its presence. An adaptation must have had a beneficial effect that helped shape the trait over evolutionary time. But the fact that a trait has a beneficial effect is insufficient to establish adaptation or evolved function: Traits can be exapted to new beneficial effects. But clearly the search for beneficial effects is crucial to building a case for either adaptation or exaptation.

Despite little research directed toward the issue, there is evidence that depression has some beneficial effects. First, although depression elicits negative emotions in others that can lead people to reject the depressive (Segrin & Dillard, 1992), it may still prompt solicitous behavior from close social partners (e.g., spouses or parents; Sheeber, Hops, Andrews, Alpert, & Davis, 1998). Indeed, some evolutionary psychologists have hypothesized that depression may have evolved to pressure close social partners to provide help or make concessions (Hagen, 2003; Watson & Andrews, 2002). Second, depressed affect seems to promote an analytical cognitive style (Ambady & Gray, 2002; Forgas, 1998; Schwarz & Bless, 1991). This suggests the hypothesis that depression may have evolved to promote the analysis of complex problems (Watson & Andrews, 2002). Many other candidate functions for depression have been proposed (Nesse, 2000), which include minimizing social risks when one's net value to others is low (Allen & Badcock, 2003), and facilitating the disengagement from unrewarding environments (Nesse, 2000).

To rule out exaptation as an explanation for a beneficial effect, the scientist must build an empirical argument that selection helped shape the trait for the effect. If the trait has multiple effects and produces them equally well, it may be difficult to show that the trait has features that have been specifically designed for promoting any of the effects (Andrews et al., 2002a). Thus, if a trait has features suggesting that it has been specifically shaped to promote a particular effect, that may strengthen the case that the effect is an evolved function of the trait (Andrews et al., 2002a; Williams, 1966).

For a beneficial effect to be an evolved function, it must also solve some evolutionarily relevant problem or opportunity in the environment. Evidence that a beneficial effect is elicited by an environmental precipitant may help build a case that the precipitant is a candidate problem or opportunity that the trait may have evolved to solve. Evidence that it is *preferentially* elicited by some precipitants and not others may provide further evidence of special design. For a trait such as depression, another way to identify possible problems that it may have evolved to solve is by assessing treatment efficacy. Although antidepressants alleviate acute depression, they do not prevent relapse, whereas talking therapies do (Hollon, Thase, & Markowitz, 2002). Moreover, talking therapies that attempt to address social problems (e.g., behavioral activation and interpersonal therapy) are often the most effective (Hollon et al., 2002; Jacobson, Martell, & Dimidjian, 2001). Because treating the cause should be more effective than treating the symptom, the fact that social interventions are better than medications at preventing relapse suggests that the cause of depression resides more in the social environment than in a malfunctioning nervous system.

As noted earlier, ELMs can influence the design of psychological traits. We can probably rule out an ELM explanation for depression. First, emotions are basic psychological phenomena with long evolutionary histories. Learning can play a role in the kinds of stimuli that elicit an emotion, and in regulating emotional states, but it is not clear how someone could learn the basic capacity to feel an emotion. One either has that capacity or not. Second, the capacity to feel sad or depressed is cross-culturally universal (Nesse & Williams, 1994), and the fact that animal models have played a large role in understanding the mechanisms involved in human depression suggests that it is evolutionarily old. Since it appears that the capacity for depression is the product of ancient developmental processes, it is probably not the outcome of an ELM.

Other kinds of evidence—including optimization, phylogenetic, neurobiological, molecular, and genetic analyses—can also be used to help identify adaptation (Andrews et al., 2002a, 2002b). The systematic failure to find evidence that a trait has undergone adaptation for a particular beneficial effect will enhance the case that it has been exapted to it.

Even if a trait is an adaptation, it can still malfunction. Many hypotheses propose, for instance, that subclinical depression may be an adaptation, but severe depression is the product of malfunctioning neurological machinery (for a review, see Nesse, 2000). This hypothesis for depression cannot be assumed without first ascertaining whether it is an adaptation and what its evolved function is. Elucidating the problem that depression evolved to solve, and how it solved it, is crucial to ascertaining whether it is functioning properly.

On the basis of a review of depression's costs, it has recently been claimed that "we don't have a clear reason for assuming that depression is anything other than a spandrel" (Kramer, 2005, p. 253). But this conclusion is premature. Evidence of cost is not evidence of the absence of adaptation. The spandrel hypothesis also requires evidence that depression is linked to some other trait that compensated for the costs of depression, and it is not clear what this trait could be. Finally, this hypothesis supposes that there was a constraint that prevented the organism from reaching a more optimal place in phenotypic space. None of these things have yet been demonstrated.

Neither adaptationist or nonadaptationist hypotheses for depression should be accepted without sufficient empirical justification. The task of parsing between them requires, among other things, the rigorous search for evidence of adaptation and evolved function, and success or failure in finding it. Because little research on depression has been designed to search for evidence of adaptation, the widespread belief that depression is a disorder could be wrong.

ACKNOWLEDGMENTS

Thanks to Matt Keller for reading and commenting on an earlier draft of this essay. This work was completed with support from a Research Training Grant in Psychiatric and Statistical Genetics from the National Institutes of Health (Grant No. 2T32MHT0030).

REFERENCES

Aggen, S. A., Neale, M. C., & Kendler, K. S. (2005). DSM criteria for major depression: Evaluating symptom patterns using latent-trait item response models. *Psychological Medicine, 35,* 475–487.

Alcock, J. (1998). *Animal behavior: An evolutionary approach* (6th ed.). Sunderland, MA: Sinauer.

Allen, N. B., & Badcock, P. B. T. (2003). The social risk hypothesis of depressed mood: Evolutionary, psychological and neurobiological perspectives. *Psychological Bulletin, 129,* 887–913.

Ambady, N., & Gray, H. M. (2002). On being sad and mistaken: Mood effects on the accuracy of thin-slice judgments. *Journal of Personality and Social Psychology, 83,* 947–961.

Andrews, P. W. (2006). Parent–offspring conflict and cost–benefit tradeoffs in adolescent suicidal behavior: The effects of birth order and maternal conflict on attempt incidence and severity. *Human Nature, 17*(2), 190–211.

Andrews, P. W., Gangestad, S. W., & Matthews, D. (2002a). Adaptationism—how to carry out an exaptationist program. *Behavioral and Brain Sciences, 25,* 489–504.

Andrews, P. W., Gangestad, S. W., & Matthews, D. (2002b). Adaptationism, exaptationism, and evolutionary behavioral science. *Behavioral and Brain Sciences, 25,* 534–553.

Austin, M. P., Mitchell, P., & Goodwin, G. M. (2001). Cognitive deficits in depression: Possible implications for functional neuropathology. *British Journal of Psychiatry, 178,* 200–206.

Duman, R. S. (2004). Depression: A case of neuronal life and death? *Biological Psychiatry, 56,* 140–145.

Elderkin-Thompson, V., Kumar, A., Bilker, W. B., Dunkin, J. J., Mintz, J., Moberg, P. J., et al. (2003). Neuropsychological deficits among patients with late-onset minor and major depression. *Archives of Clinical Neuropsychology, 615,* 1–21.

Forgas, J. P. (1998). On being happy and mistaken: Mood effects on the fundamental attribution error. *Journal of Personality and Social Psychology, 75,* 318–331.

Gould, S. J. (1997). The exaptive excellence of spandrels as a term and prototype. *Proceedings of the National Academy of Sciences of the United States of America, 94,* 10750–10755.

Gould, S. J., & Lewontin, R. C. (1979). The spandrels of San Marco and the Panglossian paradigm: A critique of the adaptationist programme. *Proceedings of the Royal Society of London B, 205,* 581–598.

Gould, S. J., & Vrba, E. S. (1982). Exaptation: A missing term in the science of form. *Paleobiology, 8,* 4–15.

Hagen, E. H. (2003). The bargaining model of depression. In P. Hammerstein (Ed.), *Genetic and cultural evolution of cooperation* (pp. 95–103). Cambridge, MA: MIT Press.

Hankin, B. L., Fraley, R. C., Lahey, B. B., & Waldman, I. D. (2005). Is depression best viewed as a continuum or discrete category?: A taxonomic analysis of childhood and adolescent depression in a population-based sample. *Journal of Abnormal Psychology, 114*, 96–110.

Hollon, S. D., Thase, M. E., & Markowitz, J. C. (2002). Treatment and prevention of depression. *Psychological Science in the Public Interest, 3*, 39–77.

Jacobson, N. S., Martell, C. R., & Dimidjian, S. (2001). Behavioral activation treatment for depression: Returning to contextual roots. *Clinical Psychology: Science and Practice, 8*, 255–270.

Joiner, T. E., Petit, J. W., Walker, R. L., Voelz, Z. R., Cruz. J., Rudd, M. D., et al. (2002). Perceived burdensomeness and suicidality: Two studies on the suicide notes of those attempting and those completing suicide. *Journal of Social and Clinical Psychology, 21*, 531–545.

Keller, M. C., & Nesse, R. M. (2006). The evolutionary significance of depressive symptoms: Different adverse situations lead to different depressive symptom patterns. *Journal of Personality and Social Psychology, 91*(2), 316–330.

Kessler, R. C., Zhao, S., Blazer, D. G., & Swartz, M. (1997). Prevalence, correlates, and course of minor depression and major depression in the national comorbidity survey. *Journal of Affective Disorders, 45*, 19–30.

Kramer, P. D. (2005). *Against depression*. New York: Viking.

Nesse, R. (2000). Is depression an adaptation? *Archives of General Psychiatry, 57*, 14–20.

Nesse, R. M., & Williams, G. C. (1994). *Why we get sick: The new science of Darwinian medicine*. New York: Vintage Books.

Schwarz, N., & Bless, H. (1991). Happy and mindless, but sad and smart?: The impact of affective states on analytic reasoning. In J. P. Forgas (Ed.), *Emotion and social judgment* (pp. 55–72). New York: Pergamon.

Segrin, C., & Dillard, J. P. (1992). The interactional theory of depression: A meta-analysis of the literature. *Journal of Social Clinical Psychology, 11*, 43–70.

Sheeber, L., Hops, H., Andrews, J., Alpert, T., & Davis, B. (1998). Interactional processes in families with depressed and non-depressed adolescents: Reinforcement with depressive behavior. *Behaviour Research and Therapy, 36*, 417–427.

Valenstein, E. S. (1998). *Blaming the brain: The truth about drugs and mental health*. New York: Free Press.

Watson, P. J., & Andrews, P. W. (2002). Toward a revised evolutionary adaptationist analysis of depression. *Journal of Affective Disorders, 72*, 1–14.

Williams, G. C. (1966). *Adaptation and natural selection*. Princeton, NJ: Princeton University Press.

✿ 4

Reconstructing the Evolution of the Human Mind

ERIC ALDEN SMITH

I approach this topic as an anthropologist who draws primarily on behavioral ecology for my theoretical and methodological inspiration. I study contemporary hunter-gatherer societies with an eye toward understanding decision making and ecological adaptation in small-scale social systems, which would include those of our human ancestors. However, I do not frame my research as an attempt to reconstruct remote (e.g., Pleistocene Epoch) selective environments or social behavior. Indeed, I am somewhat skeptical of such an endeavor, for reasons that I make clear in this chapter. Nevertheless, if the endeavor is to be undertaken, I believe it is best to grapple directly with the complexities and limitations we face.

There are at least three distinct and complementary empirical sources of information on the evolution of the human mind. First, there is the prehistoric record, consisting of archaeological, paleontological, and paleoecological components. This source is the only one approximating a direct record of past selective environments and evolutionary processes, but it is inherently incomplete.

A second source of evidence is the study of mental faculties in the artificially constructed situations utilized by laboratory psychologists, neuroscientists, experimental economists, and the like. These *in vitro* studies allow for considerable control over variables that might confound the investigation at hand, but at some (usually unknown) cost in loss of realism or "ecological validity."

A third source of evidence is behavioral data gathered *in vivo*, through ethnographic or ethological study of functioning social systems, be they contemporary hunter-gatherers, urban dwellers, or chimpanzees. This produces the most fine-grained and contextually rich kinds of data, but to the extent that present environments differ importantly from ancestral ones in features relevant to evolved cognitive abilities, it also raises issues of ecological validity.

Each of these data sources or research foci, then, has strengths and corresponding weaknesses. Archaeologists and others who directly study records of the past necessarily engage in a great amount of inference in going from stones and bones to statements about cognition, evolution, and behavior. They literally cannot observe past human behavior or environments, but only their residues. Those who study contemporary humans (or their primate relatives), either *in vitro* or *in vivo*, can study behavior and its environmental context directly, but can only inferentially address the relation of these to ancestral humans and environments. Thus, each body of data and form of inquiry is seriously incomplete, and on some topics, we must either remain silent or engage in unreliable speculation. Obviously, an integrated approach that constrains inference from one evidentiary source with reference to findings from the others offers the best hope of advancing our understanding. At present, however, those who specialize in one of the three approaches just outlined rarely know much about the other two.

WHAT ARE WE STUDYING?

I assume that the primary object of explanation is human behavior in its adaptive context. The study of "mind" is of interest only because minds (cognitive processes) interact with environmental information to produce behavior. Philosophers and novelists may be interested in mind in the sense of inner thoughts, but scientists qua evolutionists are interested in its observable products (behavior), because that is what produces effects in the world that translate into adaptive consequences and allow natural selection to act on heritable variation.

There seem to be at least three ideal types of mind–behavior processes that interest evolutionists. Type I consists of relatively unconscious cognitive processes that produce behavioral tendencies—for example, preference for individuals who have high levels of facial symmetry. Type II involves forms of decision making that are conscious and deliberative, involving either individual or social learning—for example, selection of which prey to pursue or how reliable an ally someone is. Type III includes patterns of behavior that appear to be primarily a product of cultural traditions, such as the forms of subsistence technology or which offspring will inherit the family estate. Type I is the favored domain of evolutionary psychologists; Type II, of behavioral ecologists; and Type III is the special focus of cultural evolutionists.

Despite my heuristic examples, I doubt that much human behavior can be classified into one of these pure types. Rather, any given behavioral pattern is likely to be generated by a mixture of two or three of these processes. Take the prey choice example: Hunter-gatherers clearly engage in cost–benefit decision making in the course of foraging trips, sometimes deciding to settle for low-return prey when higher-return prey prove scarce (Kaplan & Hill, 1992); but these prey rankings are guided by unconscious algorithms for calibrating time expenditure and nutritional value, and they also depend on extensive cultural transmission of knowledge concerning prey behavior, foraging methods and technology, dietary traditions and taboos, and so on.

If my general argument against purity of process is correct, it follows that there is no single path to understanding the adaptive function of the human mind. Particular claims of evolutionary psychologists, behavioral ecologists, and cultural evolutionists may be erroneous or misguided, but we cannot afford to dismiss any framework categorically. They are complementary, and we need all three to understand human behavioral evolution (Smith, 2000).

ADAPTIVE NOVELTY

The question of adaptive novelty is one that dominates many debates among evolutionary social scientists. According to one influential view, our cognitive systems evolved under a specific set of selective conditions—the "environment of evolutionary adaptedness," or EEA—and may routinely produce maladaptive output under modern conditions (see Symons, 1989, among others). Along with other critics (e.g., Foley, 1996; Irons, 1998; Strassmann & Dunbar, 1999), I find the EEA/adaptive lag thesis not so much wrong as ambiguous and oversimplified (Smith, 1998; Smith, Borgerhoff Mulder, & Hill, 2001). Because I have addressed this and related issues at length in the cited articles, I will be very brief.

People regularly solve adaptive problems that their ancestors never had to solve—how to deal with neighbors who have nuclear weapons, how to apportion access rights to a declining fishery, whether to try and lose weight by joining a health club. Our ancestors also solved many novel adaptive problems—whether (and how) to hunt woolly mammoths, what to do about neighbors who possess novel weapons or trade goods, whether to abandon an area and travel to new lands. No doubt there are problems whose resolution lies outside our evolved capabilities and that are also resistant to adaptive solution via cultural evolution. But the widely propounded view that we possess "stone-age minds," ill-suited to the novelties of the modern world, that we endlessly replay Pleistocene scripts in urban jungles regardless of their maladaptive consequences—that we are, in effect, prisoners of our evolved adaptations to past environments—strikes me as a fundamental misconstrual of human adaptation.

Our genus evolved in the context of radically fluctuating environments driven by the stochastic nature of Pleistocene climate. Our ancestors, even at the *Homo erectus* stage, managed to colonize a far broader range of habitats than any other primate species. By the time modern forms of *Homo sapiens* emerged, but long before the development of agriculture, we were able to flourish in every major terrestrial habitat on the planet, from Amazonia to the Arctic. To accomplish this, our ancestors must have been able to refashion radically their diets, technologies, social organizations, mating systems, and cosmologies to adapt to each new environment. In fact, the ethnographic and archaeological evidence makes clear that they did so rapidly and repeatedly, creating preagricultural societies as diverse as Northwest Coast chiefdoms stratified into three distinct classes (including slaves), small bands of arctic hunters that moved every few weeks and lived in snowhouses built on sea ice, and wild grain-gathering sedentary villagers in the Zagros foothills.

Human behavioral diversity is immense, and utterly dwarfs that of other species. The spatiotemporal patterning of this variation, plus the ease with which people adopt the norms, beliefs, and practices of others, make it abundantly clear that very little of it is due to varying genetic endowments (with obvious exceptions, such as adult lactose tolerance). Instead, this behavioral diversity is due to evolved capacities of the human psyche to generate novel responses to adaptive problems. This set of capacities has been termed "open programs" (Mayr, 1974) and "the cognitive niche" (Tooby & DeVore, 1987). Though recognizing the complex and specialized set of cognitive mechanisms that must be implicated in human behavioral ontogeny, like most social scientists, I ascribe much of the generation of human behavioral variation to language and culture.

It is impossible to explain the evolutionary success of *Homo sapiens* without reference to culture (i.e., socially acquired information). Indeed, cultural transmission is necessary to complete the human mind. Without cultural input, a human organism is not, and cannot become, a functioning and competent person. It follows that the search for a human nature in the form of a set of algorithms that produce human behavior without any culturally specific input is quixotic (Richerson & Boyd, 2005).

WHAT METHODS?

If (as I have argued) there are several valid and complementary frameworks for studying the evolution of the human mind, then there are multiple useful methods for conducting such study. I am partial to the methods employed in behavioral ecology, suitably modified for the special attributes of human subjects (e.g., linguistic communication, ethical restraints). The overall research strategy in behavioral ecology can be described as hypotheticodeductive: Formal models are developed, they are manipulated to generate hypotheses, and these hypotheses are then subjected to empirical test. Such a schematic summary does little to convey the particulars of the research strategy, but it does highlight the use of formal theory to deductively generate testable hypotheses, an approach that is surprisingly rare in other branches of evolutionary social science (in which hypotheses are either generated in a more informal manner only loosely linked to theory, or formal theory is developed but rarely tested).

The models that are most useful for understanding adaptive variation in human behavior are ones that (1) specify a few key parameters that (2) vary across social or natural environments and (3) are likely to have important fitness effects. For example, a simple model of mating systems (the "polygyny threshold" model; Orians, 1969) specifies the degree to which members of one sex (usually males) can monopolize resources needed by members of the other sex as the key parameter that will determine the degree of polygyny versus monogamy. Although obviously insufficient, this model is a very useful starting point for more sophisticated explorations of adaptive variation in human mating systems (Borgerhoff Mulder, 1992; Voland, 1998). The focus of models such as these—using socioecological factors to explain behavioral variation—turns us away from any attempt to specify a single "ancestral form" of human mating systems.

Formal models are useful for at least two reasons. First, they force us to make our assumptions explicit (thus, subject to critical scrutiny). Second, they generate predictions that we might not arrive at via intuition. Even though many of these predictions might be wrong, at least we know that they follow directly from our assumptions. This allows us to make more rapid progress in falsifying hypotheses that do not pan out, increasing the chances of generating hypotheses that will be supported. Although the hypotheticodeductive method is neither foolproof nor universally applicable, it has proven far more productive than unsystematic and informal methods of studying nature, including human nature. It is much needed in a field that has been too enamored of plausibility arguments and intuitions about selective pressures.

Although formal theory and deductive hypotheses are useful elements of a research strategy, careful attention to empirical evidence (including the archaeological and ethnographic record) is indispensable. My main caution would be to avoid the common view that knowledge of one or two societies (e.g., the !Kung San and the Yanomamo) is sufficient to generate empirical constraints on evolutionary hypotheses. As I argued earlier, the record of preagricultural societies indicates a remarkable amount of variation, some ecologically correlated and some apparently not (Kelly, 1995). Systematic attention to this variation is necessary to avoid a blinkered view of the range of behavioral patterns and social systems generated by our ancestors. In this endeavor, various forms of the comparative method (Borgerhoff Mulder, 2001) will prove indispensable.

REFERENCES

Borgerhoff Mulder, M. (1992) Women's strategies in polygynous marriage: Kipsigis, Datoga, and other East African cases. *Human Nature, 3,* 45–70.

Borgerhoff Mulder, M. (2001) Using phylogenetically based comparative methods in anthropology: More questions than answers. *Evolutionary Anthropology, 10*(3), 99–111.

Foley, R. (1996). The adaptive legacy of human evolution: A search for the environment of evolutionary adaptedness. *Evolutionary Anthropology, 4*(6), 194–203.

Irons, W. G. (1998). Adaptively relevant environments versus the environment of evolutionary adaptedness. *Evolutionary Anthropology, 6*(6), 194–204.

Kaplan, H., & Hill, K. (1992). The evolutionary ecology of food acquisition. In E. A. Smith & B. Winterhalder (Eds.), *Evolutionary ecology and human behavior* (pp. 167–201). Hawthorne, NY: Aldine de Gruyter.

Kelly, R. L. (1995). *The foraging spectrum: Diversity in hunter-gatherer lifeways.* Washington, DC: Smithsonian Institution Press.

Mayr, E. (1974). Behavior programs and evolutionary strategies. *American Scientist, 62,* 650–659.

Orians, G. H. (1969). On the evolution of mating systems in birds and mammals. *American Naturalist, 103*, 589–603.

Richerson, P. J., & Boyd, R. (2005). *Not by genes alone: How culture transformed human evolution.* Chicago: University of Chicago Press.

Smith, E. A. (1998). Is Tibetan polyandry adaptive?: Methodological and metatheoretical analyses. *Human Nature, 9*(3), 225–261.

Smith, E. A. (2000). Three styles in the evolutionary study of human behavior. In L. Cronk, N. Chagnon, & W. Irons (Eds.). *Human behavior and adaptation: An anthropological perspective* (pp. 27–46). Hawthorne, NY: Aldine de Gruyter.

Smith, E. A., Borgerhoff Mulder, M., & Hill, R. (2001). Controversies in the evolutionary social sciences: A guide for the perplexed. *Trends in Ecology and Evolution, 16*, 128–135.

Strassmann, B. I., & Dunbar, R. I. M. (1999). Human evolution and disease: Putting the Stone Age in perspective. In S. C. Stearns (Ed.), *Evolution in health and disease* (pp. 91–101). New York: Oxford University Press.

Symons, D. (1989). A critique of Darwinian anthropology. *Ethology and Sociobiology, 10*, 131–134.

Tooby, J., & DeVore, I. (1987). The reconstruction of hominid behavioral evolution through strategic modeling. In W. G. Kinzey (Ed.), *The evolution of human behavior: Primate models* (pp. 183–237). Albany: State University of New York Press.

Voland, E. (1998) Evolutionary ecology of human reproduction. *Annual Review of Anthropology, 27*, 347–374.

✍ 5

How the Evolution of the Human Mind Might Be Reconstructed

STEVEN MITHEN

> Human evolution occurred across vast amounts of time. We
> cannot directly observe what happened during human
> evolutionary history. Yet evolutionary understandings of human
> psychology, if they are to be more than fanciful storytelling, must
> reflect what probably occurred in the past. That is, they must
> satisfy conditions of truth.
> —S. W. GANGESTAD AND J. A. SIMPSON (personal communication)

The key answer to the question of how the evolution of the human mind might be reconstructed is quite simple: Pay substantial and serious attention to the evidence from paleoanthropology, the fossil and archaeological records. Not just the data themselves, but the theories and methods that paleoanthropologists bring to bear upon its interpretation. In a very real sense, this evidence does allow us to "directly observe what happened during human evolutionary history." Not "observe" in the behavioral sense of witnessing specific actions taking place, but in terms of the material products of that behavior, whether it is debris from manufacture of stone artifacts or paintings on cave walls.

The analysis of how the stone artifacts were manufactured at Lokalalei 2c in East Africa 2.34 million years ago by the refitting of stone flakes (Roche et al., 1999) epitomizes the detail with which such reconstructions can be made. In addition, reconstructions can be produced for archaeological sites as a whole. At Boxgrove in Southern England, for instance, detailed insights have been gained into not only the manner in which stone tools were made but also how carcasses were butchered 0.5 million years ago. The excavated evidence also indicates how the Boxgrove occupants (*Homo heidelbergensis*) had arranged themselves in space and moved around the site, and informs us about the local and regional landscapes in which they lived (Roberts & Parfitt, 1999).

Such evidence allows archaeologists to reconstruct specific events that occurred in the past. Of equal interest, however, is that archaeologists can reconstruct long-term patterns of change, such as how the techniques of tool manufacture changed over millennia (and in some cases did not change), how brain size and skeletal morphology evolved, and how environments developed. So the evidence from Lokalalei 2c, most likely produced by *H. habilis*, can be compared with that from Mastricht-Belvedere, where stone tools manufactured by a Neanderthal 125,000 years ago have also been meticulously reconstructed (Schlanger, 1996), and that from Les Etiolles or Trollesgrave, where equivalent reconstructions of blade core technology by *H. sapiens* 11,000 years ago have been made (Fischer, 1990; Pigeot, 1987). The contrast in methods used by *H. habilis*, *H. neanderthalensis*, and *H. sapiens* may partly reflect different cognitive capacities. One challenge faced by paleoanthropologists is to tease these out from the other factors that influence knapping activities, such as raw materials and functional requirements. Another challenge is to infer what cognitive characteristics would have been required to manufacture tools in the observed manner.

The fossil and archaeological evidence requires interpretation. It does not simply provide a set of ready-to-read facts about the past. One might draw an analogy between an archaeologist interpreting a cave painting and a neuroscientist interpreting a brain scan. The latter must bring a theory of how the brain works and a detailed understanding of the methodology used to generate the scan to the image being inspected. This is, in principle, no different than how the archaeologist must interpret the cave painting, or indeed a fossil skull, a stone artifact, a human burial site, a carved figurine, the archaeological record of an entire settlement, or even that of an entire landscape. In all of these cases, robust bodies of theory and methodology are required.

Paleoanthropologists must also pay attention to how their evidence is formed, with particular regard to differential biases of preservation and discovery, and the specific methods used during excavation and analysis. Just like neuroscientists, paleoanthropologists have an ever-increasing range of methods for extracting ever-increasing amounts of detail from the material they study. Two of the most important recent developments have been advances in the use of stable isotopes to make inferences about past diet from skeletal evidence and the extraction of ancient DNA to make inferences about evolutionary relationships and patterns of dispersal.

The neglect of the paleoanthropological record by numerous evolutionary psychologists has led to severe weaknesses in their work (e.g., Pinker, 1997; Tooby & Cosmides, 1992). Particularly poor work has been done by psychologists who compare chimpanzee behavior with that of modern humans, then claim that the addition of one new ingredient to the chimpanzee mind would create the modern human mind, such as the capacity for imitation (e.g., Boyd & Richerson, 1996; Tomasello, Kruger, & Ratner, 1993). By neglecting the paleoanthropological record, such psychologists fail to appreciate that the one "ingredient" may have evolved earlier in the *Homo* lineage, quite independently from the other qualities of the modern human mind, as might be true of imitation (Mithen, 1999).

Just as evolutionary scientists need to engage with the archaeological and fossil evidence, so too do the paleoanthropologists need to engage with the theories, methods, interpretations, and debates in evolutionary psychology and, indeed, the cognitive sciences in general. The last decade has seen a considerable growth in "cognitive archaeology" (e.g., see Mellars & Gibson, 1996; Nowell, 2001; Renfew & Scarre, 1998). Unfortunately, much of this work fails to engage with ongoing debates in cognitive science, and some of it neglects to adopt an explicitly evolutionary perspective.

The latter is, by definition, essential. Those addressing the evolution of human cognition need to adopt an explicitly Darwinian approach based on the principles of natural and sexual selection. That said, the precise nature of this approach when dealing with both *H. sapiens* today and hominin ancestors remains unclear. The complicating factor is that we have multiple processes operating simultaneously and in conjunction with each other, including cognitive development during ontogeny, cognitive evolution, cultural learning, and cultural evolution. Various forms of gene–culture coevolutionary models have been proposed, as reviewed by Shennan (2002), but none have been entirely satisfactory. The key problem is to understand how Darwinian principles can be applied to a species that is profoundly reliant on material culture and learning for its interactions with the natural world.

The most demanding challenge is with species such as *H. ergaster, heidelbergensis,* and *neanderthalensis*—those I term Early Humans and date within the past 2 million years. Whereas research on australopithecines can draw productively on studies of living primates, and those of prehistoric *H. sapiens* on historically documented hunter-gatherers, there are no adequate analogues in the modern world for Early Humans. In terms of their cognition, behavior, and material culture, they are quite different from both modern humans and the great apes. And so we must recognize another key requirement for reconstructing the evolution of the human mind: A creative imagination on the part of academics trying to conceive of types of large-brained, terrestrial, bipedal, tool-using primates that are distinctly different from any primate alive today.

The challenge we all face is with the breadth of expertise required to produce any meaningful inferences about the course of human cognitive evolution. We may be aware of the debates that exist within our own disciplinary fields, but no one can be a true expert in more than a narrow subfield within one's own discipline. Yet we need to have at least an awareness of the relevant data, theories, and issues coming from numerous other disciplines, in addition to those of our own. So, in my own recent work on the evolution of the human capacity for music (Mithen, 2005), my focus has been on the paleoanthropological evidence. To interpret it, I was required to draw on research in cognitive, developmental, and evolutionary psychology; primate studies; neuroscience; linguistics; musicology, ethnomusicology, music therapy; and so forth. The extent to which any single academic can undertake such work in a sufficiently comprehensive fashion is questionable. Academic collaborations are likely to become increasingly important, such as that between the archaeologist Thomas Wynn and the psychologist Fred Coolidge on the nature of Neanderthal intelligence and memory (Wynn & Coolidge, 2004a, 2004b).

A constraint on both the interdisciplinary studies by a single academic and the development of collaborations is the nature of the institutions within which we work and, to some extent, the wider academic agenda. Within the United Kingdom, for example, Departments of Archaeology and Psychology are usually located in different Faculties, often positioned on entirely different parts of the campus, and with no academic structures in place for developing collaboration. Indeed, there are structural constraints on developing collaborations, owing to the academic traditions in which archaeology is related to history and classics (because these are the disciplines from which the field emerged during the 19th century in the United Kingdom, in contrast to its anthropological basis in the United States). Moreover, for the last 15 years, university-based research in the United Kingdom has been conditioned by what is known as the "research assessment exercise" (RAE), which constrains interdisciplinary research, or at least inhibits universities and staff from supporting such research. The next RAE assessment is in 2008, at which time each individual will be assessed as to academic contribution toward his or her own specific discipline—an appallingly archaic exercise at a time when teamwork and interdisciplinarity should be encouraged. Moreover, given the level of government funding that departments receive will be based on those assessments, academics effectively have no option but to "play the game."

The problems extend to the nature of funding agencies, very few of which are able to support interdisciplinary research of the nature required to reconstruct human cognitive evolution. The consequence of these institutional and funding situations is that those academics who wish to develop the necessary collaborations for reconstructing cognitive evolution will have to work that much harder than those who are pursuing traditional forms of interdisciplinary research, or those who remain within the traditional confines of their disciplinary boundaries.

It is not all bleak. Funding agencies are increasingly realizing the need for new types of interdisciplinary collaboration. I recently secured a grant from the Standing Committee for the Humanities of the European Science Foundation from a program specifically designed to bring academics from the humanities and the sciences together for exploratory workshops. This enabled the Music, Language and Human Evolution workshop to take place at the University of Reading in October 2004, which bought together a unique collection of archaeologists, anthropologists, psychologists, neuroscientists, and musicologists (Balter, 2004). Similarly, The Templeton Foundation recently funded a workshop on the evolution of religious thought that brought theologians and paleoanthropologists together. Other bodies, such as the Fyssen Foundation, have a specific remit to fund work on cognitive evolution. Moreover, the European Union has now provided some major research grants to fund programs for interdisciplinary collaboration involving institutions from across Europe on specific aspects of cognitive evolution, such as that on the origin of referential language.

It is not only interdisciplinary research that requires development but also teaching. Even though many undergraduates are interested in the "big" questions about human cognitive evolution, and some may have opportunities to take courses or write dissertations on this topic, their studies must inevitably be focused on core disciplinary materials, whether that is archaeology, psychology, or linguistics. But for progress to be made on understanding cognitive evolution, we need a new generation of researchers who begin their research on cognitive evolution with some awareness of the theories, data, issues, and debates in more than one specific discipline. In the United Kingdom, the most appropriate vehicle for acquiring such awareness is a 1-year Master's degree, which now is compulsory prior to the start of a 3-year PhD degree.

To this end, the University of Reading devised and ran a MA degree in Cognitive Evolution between 1996 and 2001. This required students to study human evolution, the philosophy of mind, primate cognition, and evolution of language, each taught by experts in those fields, and to then participate in training that explored the potential and challenges of integrating material from these fields. The degree attracted students from a wide range of disciplines, and many have now undertaken PhD studies on aspects of cognitive evolution.

As the instigator and convenor of that degree, I can testify to the challenge of establishing cooperation between four separate departments located in three Faculties to provide it, and the vast amount of administrative effort needed to ensure its success. I can also testify to the remarkable intellectual experience it provided to both students and staff. Although convening and teaching this degree reduced my own time for research, that research moved forward far more swiftly than would have otherwise been the case.

To conclude, let me summarize my response to the question: *How might the evolution of the human mind be reconstructed?*

- Pay serious and sufficient attention to the evidence from the archaeological and fossil record, as well as the theories and methods that paleoanthropologists use to interpret this evidence.
- Paleoanthropolgists must similarly engage with the evidence, methods, and theories from the cognitive sciences.
- Develop Darwinian-based theories of evolution that are appropriate for large-brained, bipedal, and culture-bearing hominins.
- Develop collaborative, interdisciplinary research programs and influence funding agencies to support such research.
- Develop interdisciplinary teaching at an advanced undergraduate and postgraduate levels to produce a new generation of researchers who begin their studies with an interdisciplinary perspective.
- Be imaginative in one's ideas and humble in the face of what we do not know about human cognition in both the present and the past.

REFERENCES

Balter, M. (2004). Seeking the key to music. *Science, 306,* 1120–1122.

Boyd, R., & Richerson, P. (1996). Why culture is common but cultural evolution is rare. *Proceedings of the British Academy, 88,* 73–93.

Fischer, A. (1990). On being a pupil of a flintknapper 11,000 years ago: A preliminary analysis of settlement organization and flint technology based on conjoined flint artefacts from the Trollesgave site. In E. Cziesla, S. Eickhoff, N. Arts, & D. Winter

(Eds.), *The big puzzle: International Symposium on Refitting Stone Artefacts* (pp. 447–464). Bonn: Holos.

Mellars, P., & Gibson, K. R. (Eds.). (1996). *Modelling the early human mind.* Cambridge, UK: McDonald Institute for Archaeolgical Research.

Mithen, S. J. (1999). Social learning and cultural change: a view from the stone age. In H. Box & K. Gibson (Eds.), *Mammalian social learning: Comparative and ecological perspectives* (pp. 389–399). Cambridge, UK: Cambridge University Press.

Mithen, S. J. (2005). *The singing Neanderthals: The origin of music, language, mind and body.* London: Weidenfeld & Nicolson.

Nowell, A. (Ed.). (2001). *In the mind's eye: Multidisciplinary approaches to the evolution of human cognition.* Ann Arbor, MI: International Monographs in Prehistory.

Pigeot, N. (1987). *Magdalniens d'Etiolles: fconomie de D bitage et Organisation Sociale.* Centre National de la Recherche Scientifique. Paris: CNRS.

Pinker, S. (1997). *How the mind works.* New York: Norton.

Renfrew, C., & Scarre, C. (Eds.). (1998). *Cognition and material culture: The archaeology of symbolic storage.* Cambridge, UK: McDonald Institute of Archaeological Research.

Roberts, M. B., & Parfitt, S. A. (1999). *Boxgrove, a Middle Pleistocene hominid site at Eartham Quarry, Boxgrove, West Sussex* (Report No. 17). London: English Heritage Archaeological Report.

Roche, H., Delagnes, A., Brugal, J.-P., Feibel, C., Kibunjla, M., Mourre, V., et al. (1999). Early hominid stone tool production and technical skill 2.34 Myr ago in West Turkana, Kenya. *Nature, 399,* 57–60.

Schlanger, N. (1996). Understanding levallois–lithic technology and cognitive archaeology. *Cambridge Archaeological Journal, 6,* 231–254.

Shennan, S. (2002). *Genes, memes and human history; Darwinian archaeology and cultural evolution.* London: Thames & Hudson.

Tomasello, M., Kruger, A. C., & Ratner, H. H. (1993). Cultural learning. *Behavior and Brain Sciences, 16,* 495–552.

Tooby, J., & Cosmides, L. (1992). The psychological foundations of culture. In J. H. Barkow, L. Cosmides, & J. Tooby (Eds.), *The adapted mind: Evolutionary psychology and the generation of culture* (pp. 19–136). New York: Oxford University Press.

Wynn, T., & Coolidge, F. L. (2004a). A cognitive and neuropsychological perspective on the Chatelperonian. *Journal of Anthropological Research, 60,* 55–73.

Wynn, T., & Coolidge, F. L. (2004b). The expert Neanderthal mind. *Journal of Human Evolution, 46,* 467–487.

The Role of Tracking Current Evolution

✿ 6

Reproductive Success

Then and Now

CHARLES B. CRAWFORD

I write from the perspective of an evolutionary psychologist. As I see it, evolutionary psychology is concerned with the relationship among three things: (1) the environmental challenges that our hominid and primate ancestors encountered as they went about their daily lives; (2) the psychological adaptations that natural selection shaped to help them deal with those challenges; and (3) the way that the resulting evolved adaptations function in the infinitesimal slices of evolutionary time in which we live (Crawford & Anderson, 1989). I define an "adaptation" as a set of genetically organized decision processes that embody the costs and benefits of the functioning of the decision processes across evolutionary time, and that organized the effector processes for dealing with those contingencies in such a way that the gene(s) producing the decision processes were reproduced better than alternate gene(s) (modified from Crawford, 1998).

I distinguish between innate and operational adaptations, between ancestral and current developmental environments, between ancestral and current immediate environments, and between ancestral expected and current realized reproductive success (Crawford, 1993, 2000). I use the example of the putative brother–sister incest avoidance adaptation to illustrate how I see the relation between these concepts. My arguments are illustrated using Figure 6.1. I conclude (1) that studies of reproductive success in current environments may sometimes be useful in the study of psychological adaptations, and (2) that if reproductive data are used they must be integrated with other data. It this is done reproductive data may help provide a more compete picture of how evolved adaptations evolved and function.

ADAPTATIONS: THEN AND NOW

The lower part of Figure 6.1 represents a particular infinitesimal slice of evolutionary time in which an organism is born, grows, reproduces, senesces, and dies. The upper part represents the evolutionary time required for an adaptation to evolve. The "innate adaptation" is the genotype of an adaptation. It is the genetic information about an ancestral problem and its solution(s) that can be encoded in DNA by natural selection. It comes into being because it contributed to *ancestral expected reproductive success* (i.e., ancestral reproductive success across a significant period of evolutionary time). For the purposes of much work in evolutionary psychology, we can assume that the innate adaptation is identical in ancestral and current environments. Note that in Figure 6.1 it is represented as being identical in these environments. The information-processing definition of adaptation given earlier refers to the operational adaptation. It develops as the information about ancestral environments encoded in genes interacts with information from the current developmental environment during development. Because developmental change occurs continually throughout an organism's life, the operational adaptation is dynamic and changes as the organisms matures.

The "immediate environment" is the conditions in the present environment, whether ancestral or current, that activate the operational adaptation to enable an organism to deal with conditions in its present environment. Current, "realized reproductive success" refers to reproductive success in the immediate environment. Evolutionary psychology in its fullest sense is concerned with the formation of the innate adaptation by natural selection, the interactions between the innate adaptation and environmental conditions during development (the developmental environment) to form the operational adaptation, and the way the operational adaptation works with conditions in the immediate environment to produce ongoing behavior.

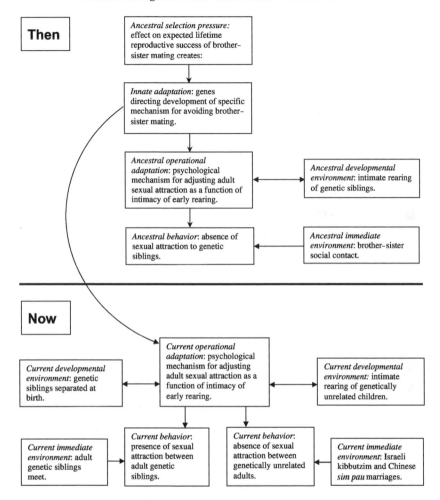

Intimate Rearing and Brother–Sister Incest: Then and Now

FIGURE 6.1. The evolutionary psychologist's perspective on how an evolved, innate adaptation in conjunction with the developmental and immediate environments can produce different behaviors in ancestral and current environments. Note that the innate adaptation that prevented brother–sister incest in ancestral environments can produce either sexual attraction between genetic siblings or absence of sexual attraction between genetically unrelated individuals, depending on the conditions of rearing in the current environment. Because there is a clear distinction between ancestral and current environments, and between ancestral and current operational adaptations (although not between ancestral and current innate adaptations), ancestral and current behavior may differ considerably. Although ancestral behavior contributed to ancestral fitness and, hence, to the evolution of the innate adaptation, current behavior need not contribute to current fitness.

THE WESTERMARK EFFECT

Close inbreeding is detrimental to reproduction and survival because it brings deleterious recessive alleles, such as the allele causing phenylketonuria, together in the same individuals. Several researchers (Mealey, 2000) have argued that natural selection has produced a variety of mechanisms in different species for reducing its likelihood. Intimate rearing of brothers and sisters during their first few years, which reduces or eliminates adult sexual attraction between them, may reflect a mechanism that humans evolved to help avoid it (Westermark, 1891). Evidence from (1) boys and girls reared in the same Children's Houses in Israeli kibbutzim, who rarely find each other sexually attractive as adults (Shepher, 1983); (2) the reduced success of Chinese *sim pau* marriages, in which a genetically unrelated baby girl is adopted into a family at birth, with the expectation that she will marry a son of the family at their sexual maturity (Wolf, 1995); and (3) sexual attraction between adult genetic siblings separated at birth (Bevc & Silverman, 2000) suggests that natural selection may have produced an adaptation that produces an aversion to sexual contact in individuals that are reared together intimately.

In the upper part of Figure 6.1, the assumption is that brothers and sisters who avoided incest had greater expected lifetime reproductive success across evolutionary time than those who did not. Hence, natural selection likely shaped one or more mechanisms for avoiding incest. Here we are concerned with a mechanism for avoiding sexual contact between siblings through adult sexual aversion to childhood intimates, who in an ancestral environment would most likely have been genetic siblings. The ancestral developmental environment, being intimately reared with genetic siblings, produces the ancestral operational adaptation, which in turn produces the adult aversion to sexual contact with adult childhood intimates. Note the assumption that the mechanism was designed for a specific purpose—to reduce the likelihood of mating between genetic brothers and sisters. Its operation can be described in terms of decision rules, such as "Store information about the physical features of childhood intimates," and "Use this information as one of the decision processes for choosing the objects of adult sexual attraction." The ancestral immediate environment refers to particular instances of contact with sexually mature, ancestral, opposite-sex individuals. The functioning of the ancestral operational adaptation reduces the likelihood of brothers and sisters mating and contributes to their reproductive success over evolutionary time.

REPRODUCTIVE SUCCESS

Note also, however, that in any particular short segment of evolutionary time, the adaptation may not have contributed to the actual lifetime realized reproductive success of brothers and sisters. For example, there may have been times in our evolutionary history, say, when group size was very small and groups were widely dispersed, that would have made mates difficult to find. In such cases, avoiding mating between brothers and sisters would have been detrimental to their lifetime reproductive success. Hence, it is necessary to distinguish between *ancestral expected lifetime reproductive success* measured across many lifetimes in evolutionary time and *realized lifetime reproductive success* measured on the lifetimes of individuals in one or possibly a few generations. We are concerned with ancestral expected reproductive success when considering the evolution of adaptations.

Now consider the lower part of Figure 6.1, which represents an infinitesimal segment of evolutionary time—a few years in an Israeli kibbutz, a Chinese *sim pau* marriage, or the meeting of an adult brother and sister separated at birth and reared in different homes. In all three cases, the putative adaptation processes information about intimate rearing and adjustment of adult sexual attraction, as it was designed to do. However, because it is functioning in novel environments, it produces potentially fitness-reducing behavior. In the case of the Israeli kibbutzniks, its malfunction likely has little effect on reproductive success, because there are many opportunities for finding mates in modern Israel. In the case of the *sim pau* marriages, Wolf (1995) has shown that these marriages have lower than average reproductive success. Studies of incest have shown that, in most cases, the effect of close inbreeding is detrimental on reproductive success (Cavalli-Sforza, 1977). Hence, it is likely that brother–sister matings will have lowered reproductive success. These examples illustrate that it is not easy to see how studies of reproductive success in current environments, whether in current hunter-gatherer or modern urban environments, can tell us much about what evolutionary psychologists are interested in, namely, the functioning of evolved psychological adaptations. Similar reasoning has led many evolutionary psychologists to conclude that studies of reproductive success in current environments are not useful in elucidating the functioning of psychological adaptations (Symons, 1987, 1989).

Although these arguments may be valid, I do not believe they obviate the use of reproductive data when studying how adaptations function. Adaptations evolved because they promoted their genetic basis better than alternative adaptations by enhancing the reproductive success of their possessors, or of their possessors' genetic relatives, more than alternative adaptations (Tooby & Cosmides, 1990). If an adaptation malfunctions because it systematically encounters environmental conditions different from those in which it evolved, there must be some impact on expected reproductive success in the changed environment. If there were no impact on reproductive fitness when an adaptation encountered conditions different from those in which it evolved, the adaptation could not have evolved through natural selection, because it could not have contributed to the ancestral differential reproductive success necessary for an adaptation to evolve.

In many cases, the changed environment, similar to most mutations, will have a negative impact on fitness. The information-processing, cost–benefit structure of an adaptation evolved to respond to ancestral conditions in such a way that it contributed to ancestral expected reproductive success better than an alternative adaptation. Hence, any change in the environment is likely to detract from reproductive success in the changed environment. However, changes in living conditions may short-circuit the functioning of an adaptation. For example, although current foragers have a total fertility of from five to eight births (Kelly, 1995), the average number of live births for Canadian Hutterite women is 10.4 (Short, 1983). There are apparently two reasons for Hutterites' high birthrate. First, Hutterite women nurse their babies on a very rigid pattern—once every 4 hours— that reduces the effectiveness of ancestral nursing adaptations for spacing children. Second, the Hutterite way of life provides the resources for rearing large families.[1] Finally, one indication that an adaptation is functioning in an environment different from the one in which it evolved is unusual reproductive patterns. If a putative adaptation contributes to reproductive patterns that differ markedly from ancestral patterns, we have evidence that ancestral and current environments differ with respect to its functioning. This is valuable knowledge for anyone interested in evolutionary studies of human and animal behavior. Hence, realized reproductive success can be a useful dependent variable in some research studies.

As I see it, however, a key issue with using reproductive success as a dependent variable in studies of psychological adaptations is that it is not

---

[1] Interestingly, the birthrate in many Canadian Hutterite colonies has fallen from around 10 to around five births in the last few years, because many Hutterite women are having hysterectomies (K. Peter, personal communication, Fall 1990). Apparently, when Hutterite women have the option of acting on their reproductive preferences, they prefer to have about the same number of live births as our hunter-gatherer ancestors. This finding suggests that personal preferences may be another source of evidence that reproductive patterns differ from the ancestral norm.

specific to any particular adaptation; that is, unusual realized reproductive success in a novel environment may be caused by changed functioning in one or more of a number of adaptations. The unusual reproductive success of Hutterite woman and *sim pau* marriages, for example, may suggest that one or more adaptations in these populations is functioning in an unusual environment, but it does not tell us much about which one. How are we to discover the real culprit?

A possible solution to this problem would be to include reproductive success measures in long-term experimental studies of variables thought to affect a particular adaptation. For example, one might develop hypotheses about a variety of causes for the unusual reproductive patterns of *sim pau* and Hutterite marriages, and carry out experiments to discover the crucial causal variables. There are two problems with this approach. First, such manipulations could not ethically be applied to human beings in most current societies. Second, even if they could, current reproductive success would not necessarily be the best dependent variable. Measures of sexual attraction and motivation, for example, might be better variables for measuring the functioning of putative adaptations in kibbutzim, *sim pau*, and reared apart brother–sister marriages than measures of current reproductive success. Nevertheless, given that adaptations evolved because they contributed to ancestral differential expected reproductive success, integrating measures of expected reproductive success into studies of the validity of evolutionary hypotheses about adaptations can be valuable.

Evolutionary psychologists could improve the plausibility of their hypotheses if they found ways of incorporating estimates of expected ancestral reproductive success into their research. Perusse (1993) attempted to do this by developing a measure of potential male reproductive success in his study of reproductive success and male status in a current environment. Anderson and Crawford (1992) attempted to model the ancestral costs and benefits of reproduction suppression in their studies of the evolutionary significance of anorexic behavior, as well as the ancestral reproductive costs and benefits of sex-biased parental investment in their studies of parental investment in sons and daughters (Anderson & Crawford, 1993). More work along these lines is needed.

CONCLUDING THOUGHTS

Using measures of current reproductive success in developing evolutionary explanations of human behavior is not easy. We can only study the functioning of evolved psychological mechanisms in the infinitesimal slices of evolutionary time where they occur. A mechanism that evolved because it contributed to reproduction across eons of evolutionary time may not contribute to it in any particular segment of that time. Hence, studies of realized reproductive success are ambiguous. Moreover, because reproductive success is not specific to any particular adaptation, its measures are difficult to interpret. Nevertheless, measures of realized reproductive success in a particular environment can provide useful indicators of whether individuals are living in an unusual environment from an evolutionary perspective. Moreover, since adaptations evolved because they contributed to ancestral differential reproduction, including some type of measures of current reproductive success in the study of adaptations would contribute to the plausibility, and, hence, the acceptance of evolutionary hypotheses.

REFERENCES

Anderson, J. L., & Crawford, C. B. (1992). Modeling costs and benefits of adolescent weight control as a mechanism for reproduction suppression. *Human Nature, 3,* 299–334.

Anderson, J. L., & Crawford, C. B. (1993). Trivers-Willard rules for sex allocation: When are they adaptive in humans? *Human Nature, 4,* 137–174.

Bevc, I., & Silverman, I. (2000). Early separation and sibling incest: A test of the revised Westermark theory. *Evolution and Human Behavior, 21,* 151–161.

Cavalli-Sforza, L. L. (1977). *Elements of human genetics* (2nd ed.). Menlo Park, CA: Benjamin.

Crawford, C. B. (1993). The future of sociobiology: Counting babies or studying proximate mechanisms. *Trends in Ecology and Evolution, 8*(5), 183–186.

Crawford, C. B. (1998). The theory of evolution in the study of human behavior: An introduction and overview. In C. Crawford & D. Krebbs (Eds.), *Handbook of evolutionary psychology* (pp. 3–41). NJ: Earlbaum.

Crawford, C. B. (2000). Evolutionary psychology: Counting babies or studying information-processing mechanisms. *Annals of the New York Academy of Sciences, 44,* 21–38.

Crawford, C. B., & Anderson, J. L. (1989). Sociobiology: An environmentalist discipline? *American Psychologist, 44,* 1449–1459.

Kelly, R. L. (1995). *Foraging spectrum: Diversity in hunter-gatherer lifeways.* Washington, DC: Smithsonian Institution Press.

Mealey, L. (2000). *Sex differences: Developmental and evolutionary strategies.* San Diego, CA: Academic Press.

Perusse, D. (1993). Cultural and reproductive success in industrial societies: Testing the relationship at the proximate and ultimate levels. *Behavioral and Brain Sciences, 16,* 267–322.

Shepher, J. (1983). *Incest: A biosocial view.* New York: Academic Press.

Short, R. V. (1983). The biological basis for the contraceptive effects of breast-feeding. In D. B. Jelliffe & E. F. P. Jelliffe (Eds.), *Advances in international maternal and child health* (Vol. 3, pp. 27–39). New York: Oxford University Press.

Symons, D. (1987). If we're all Darwinians, what's the fuss about? In C. B. Crawford, M. Smith, & D. Krebs (Eds.), *Sociobiology and psychology: Ideas, issues, and applications* (pp. 121–146). Hillsdale, NJ: Erlbaum.

Symons, D. (1989). A critique of Darwinian anthropology. *Ethology and Sociobiology, 10,* 131–144.

Tooby, J., & Cosmides, L. (1990). The past explains the present: Emotional adaptations and the structure of ancestral environments. *Ethology and Sociobiology, 11,* 375–424.

Westermark, E. A. (1891). *The history of human marriage.* New York: Macmillan.

Wolf, A. (1995). *Sexual attraction and childhood association: A Chinese brief for Edward Westermark.* Stanford, CA: Stanford University Press.

7

On the Utility, Not the Necessity, of Tracking Current Fitness

MONIQUE BORGERHOFF MULDER

To determine the role that evolution has played in shaping the minds and behavior of humans, should we be measuring current fitness differentials, "counting babies," in Crawford's (1993) terminology, and then correlating these measures with the characteristics of individuals? I begin my commentary by drawing attention to the fact that this question is part of a much broader epistemological discussion within the evolutionary sciences regarding the role of history in the definition of adaptation. I emphasize the sterility of the debate over baby counting and its divisive properties, pointing out that appropriate methods and evidentiary procedures depend critically on the question at hand. Given that a key goal of the evolutionary social sciences is to explain human behavioral variation and diversity, I devote the remainder of the commentary to elucidating the reasons why studies of current fitness differentials are useful in this respect, updating the reader on recent conceptual and methodological improvements.

Should we be measuring current fitness differentials in human populations? The answer to this question depends quite simply on whether the investigator uses a definition of adaptation that focuses primarily on current function, or one that entails assumptions about the history of the trait. Investigators interested in current function look at the relative reproductive success of existing behavioral variation in particular environmental and

social contexts to determine the *selective context* of variation; they largely
ignore questions about whether the trait evolved for the currently observed
function, and whether key environmental conditions favoring the trait existed for a selectively significant span of time (Clutton-Brock & Harvey,
1979; Smith, Borgerhoff Mulder, & Hill, 2001). Investigators favoring historical definitions of adaptation give prominence to determining a trait's
function in its ancestral environment (Thornhill, 1990; Williams, 1966),
viewing analyses of current function as superfluous (indeed, irrelevant) evidence of adaptation on the grounds that present phenotypes reflect past
selection pressures (Tooby & Cosmides, 1990; Symons, 1990). Their evidence for adaptation lies primarily with the perfection of the design of a
trait, on the assumption that an intricate fit between form and function can
only arise through natural selection (Williams, 1966). This methodological
procedure is often referred to as "reverse engineering"—using the design of
the trait to figure out for what natural selection designed it (Dennett,
1995). A tension between nonhistorical definitions and what Reeve and
Sherman (1993) call "history laden definitions" threads throughout modern biology, most notoriously in the debates sparked by Gould and
Lewontin's (1979) critique of adaptationism; it has major implications for
the distinction between adaptations and exaptations, the relevance of
phylogenetic control in comparative studies, the significance of derived
traits, and the need for identifying complex design in behavior.

Both historical and nonhistorical approaches to the study of adaptation offer valuable insights into how natural selection has shaped variations
in human behavior. Furthermore, the epistemological debate over whether
and how to incorporate history into the study of adaptation has served to
sharpen definitions and logic regarding evidential standards (Andrews,
Gangestad, & Matthews, 2002; Reeve & Sherman, 1993). It is only the more
extreme pronouncements provoked by this debate that are problematic—
most pertinently the claim that current fitness measures are irrelevant to
the study of adaptation. This claim has divided evolutionists engaged with
different questions, different timescales, and different kinds of data into
mutually suspicious camps, when their efforts would be better spent ex-
ploring the intersections and compatibilities of their findings (Borgerhoff
Mulder, Richerson, Thornhill, & Voland, 1997; Laland & Brown, 2002).
Most critically, it overlooks the need to study adaptation in a manner
appropriate to the problem under investigation. In my view the "right" approach depends crucially on the question at hand.

The most unique feature of our species is its extraordinary phenotypic
flexibility, as indicated by the vast behavioral repertoire of our species and

its deep patterning both across and within different populations. A key question for the evolutionary social scientist is how to account for this variability. As a hypothesis, we might predict that some proportion of behavioral variability (both within and between populations) can be explained as facultative responses of an evolved organism to social and ecological conditions. There are several avenues to test this hypothesis. One is to examine design—to look at whether decisions and values are primed by different developmental and ecological circumstances in a manner consistent with formal models (e.g., McElreath, 2004). Another is to use the comparative method to test evolutionary hypotheses for the diversity of cultural traits across human populations (Borgerhoff Mulder, 2001). A third avenue is to examine the relative fitness of a set of traits within a given socioecological setting through empirical work and modeling typical of human behavioral ecology (reviewed in Winterhalder & Smith, 2000). Determination of current function is integral to this latter route, even though fitness optimization is neither a necessary nor sufficient criterion for identifying adaptations.

I use the remainder of this commentary to expand on some of the reasons why studies of current function are useful, but first I offer some definitions and provisos. Studies of current function examine correlations between traits and fitness outcomes, with the goal of determining whether a specific phenotypic variant results in higher fitness in a given environment compared to other specified variants. Traits are the underlying decision rules and information-processing algorithms, and are most usefully identified (and studied) as behavioral strategies or other phenotypes. As regards measuring the fitness outcome, it is worth clarifying that this need not entail "baby counting." Appropriate currencies depend on the behavior under investigation. Though a researcher examining a set of foraging decisions might ultimately be interested in the fitness consequences of different search strategies, he or she would necessarily design a study around more proximate outcomes such as foraging returns (see Winterhalder & Smith, 2000). Similarly, studies of reproductive decision making can often more usefully focus on nutritional or health outcomes for children and mothers than on distal measures of fitness (Sellen, 1999).

Let us now turn to the utility of studies of current function, so defined.

1. Studies of current function shed light on the selective contexts in which certain traits may or may not be favored. For instance, Lummaa, Haukioja, Lemmetyinen, and Pikkola (1998) demonstrated the role of current selection pressures in historically isolated populations by showing

that, in the Finnish archipelago, mothers who produce twins obtain higher fitness than mothers who produce singletons, whereas the opposite is true on the mainland. Given the ecological differences between these regions, and the preponderance of twin births in the ecologically more productive archipelago communities, this study provides evidence that twinning frequency is maintained by natural selection, and points to the ecological conditions in which twin births may be maintained as a trait. Traits, like twinning, are not inherently adaptive or maladaptive. It is their greater probability of expression in appropriate conditions (here, in high-quality environments) that constitutes the adaptation.

2. Studies of current function play a critical role in the evaluation of hypotheses for the evolution of specific traits. For instance, one hypothesis for the evolution of the human female postreproductive lifespan is that longevity was favored under conditions where coresident older women could contribute to the foraging of food, thereby subsidizing the costs of repro duction for their daughters (Hawkes, O'Connell, Jones, Alvarez, & Charnov, 1998). Situations in which grannies do and do not affect fitness outcomes need closer quantitative comparative analyses to refine hypotheses (or to point to alternative selective pressures) for postreproductive lifespans (Leonetti, Nath, Hemam, & Neill, 2005). Similar arguments can be made regarding the evolution of human mate choice preferences, on the evidence that favored waist-to-hip ratios vary with ecological context (Pawlowski & Dunbar, 2005).

3. Studies of current fitness differentials can also reveal conflicting selective pressures on a trait in a given population. Observed trait values are often intermediary values, resulting from trade-offs between different selective factors; thus, offspring number may be traded for offspring quality, for lower food intake, or for predator protection. Birthweight is likely a trade-off given that heavy babies are relatively protected against infectious and somatic assaults but are costly to their mothers at parturition. This suggests the hypothesis that global variation in birthweight reflects disease prevalence in different regions (Thomas et al., 2004). Only with detailed studies of the correlation between a trait (e.g., birthweight) and fitness (e.g., maternal mortality in childbirth, child survival) in different disease environments can specific evolutionary hypotheses for how birthweight (or any other trait) is shaped by natural selection be critically evaluated.

4. Studies of fitness outcomes in rapidly changing environments provide a natural laboratory for looking at phenotypic flexibility, for predicting how shifts in the environment might impact trait values, and for evaluating the scope and limits of human adaptation. Indeed, without studies of cur-

rent function, the commonly made assumption that behavior in rapidly changing environments is maladaptive cannot be confirmed or rejected. Thus, investigators have usefully examined the notion that fertility limitation is maladaptive in modern environments (reviewed in Borgerhoff Mulder, 1998). Situations in which behavioral responses fail to track a rapidly changing environment have been termed "ecological (or evolutionary) traps" (Schlaepfer, Runge, & Sherman, 2002). Although the "trap" concept is primarily of significance for conservationists concerned with understanding how to "engineer" appropriate responses in animals or plants facing radically altered environments, it has potential for addressing issues of social pathology (Somit & Peterson, 2003).

5. Finally, it is worth stressing that just as the old-style adaptationism attacked by Gould and Lewontin (and characterized here as "baby counting") has been in decline for many years (e.g., Rose & Lauder, 1996), so have the methods of identifying adaptation among humans grown in sophistication. First, statistical standards for evaluating correlations and excluding null hypotheses are undergoing close scrutiny (for evolutionary anthropological applications, see Towner & Luttbeg, under review). Second, fitness outcomes can productively be incorporated into optimization models to evaluate the conditions under which particular behavior patterns may have evolved. For example, we examined (and excluded) the possibility of rape as an adaptive reproductive strategy by calculating the payoffs to alternative strategies, using as parameters fitness measures taken from the contemporary Aché (Smith et al., 2001). Third, evidentiary standards increasingly require that studies of current function be supplemented by additional methods, such as experimental work teasing out the specific conditions (design) needed to generate a behavioral response (Henrich et al., 2001). Fourth, although studies of current function permit identification of the selective factors responsible for variation and change in traits, they do not directly address the reasons why a particular trait arose in the first place (although under conditions in which environmental stability can be assumed, the method allows for such inferences). Accordingly, studies of current function are now being supplemented by historically informed comparative analyses (Holden, 2002), building on new developments within comparative biology. Such analyses use phylogenies (based on linguistic or genetic data) to determine the independent emergence of trait correlations in ancestral populations (Borgerhoff Mulder, Nunn, & Towner, 2006).

In conclusion, studies of current function yield an understanding of context dependency critical to evolutionary explanation. Although we cannot rashly generalize the contingencies shown in one study to an entirely different context, we can use the insights they generate to piece together the selective architecture of human variation and its intricate relations with the environment with empirically derived information on the trait's history. I see this as vastly preferable to arguments based solely on reverse engineering for two reasons. First, studies of current function do not rely on reconstructing past environments or selective pressures. (Much has been written about the weak plausibility of such reconstructions under the rubric of the environment of evolutionary adaptedness, or EEA.) Second, studies of current function do not depend on assumptions about the specificity of the evolved psychological mechanism underlying an adaptation, a topic over which psychologists are bitterly divided (Smith et al., 2001). I emphasize in closing, however, the point made at the outset of this commentary—that the various definitions of adaptation are mere intellectual concepts, and that the relative utility of any one variant depends entirely on the job (and the data) at hand. I have presented the evolutionary anthropologists' argument for the study of current function. I do not argue that other approaches are neither complementary nor useful, only that studies of current function throw considerable light on our understanding of human cultural diversity.

REFERENCES

Andrews, P. W., Gangestad, S. W., & Matthews, D. (2002). Adaptationism: How to carry out an exaptationist program. *Behavioral and Brain Sciences, 25*, 489–553.

Borgerhoff Mulder, M. (1998). Demographic transition: Are we any closer to an evolutionary explanation? *Trends in Ecology and Evolution, 13*(7), 266–270.

Borgerhoff Mulder, M. (2001). Using phylogenetically based comparative methods in anthropology: More questions than answers. *Evolutionary Anthropology, 10*(3), 99–111.

Borgerhoff Mulder, M., Nunn, C. L., & Towner, M. (2006). Macroevolutionary studies of cultural trait variation: The importance of transmission mode. *Evolutionary Anthropology, 15*, 52–64.

Borgerhoff Mulder, M., Richerson, P. J., Thornhill, N., & Voland, E. (1997). The place of behavioural ecology in the evolutionary social science. In P. Weingart, S. D. Mitchel, P. J. Richerson, & S. Maasen (Eds.). *Human by nature: Between biology and the social sciences* (pp. 253–282). Mahwah, NJ: Erlbaum.

Clutton-Brock, T. H., & Harvey, P. H. (1979). Comparison and adaptation. *Proceedings of the Royal Society of London B, 205*, 547–565.

Crawford, C. B. (1993). The future of sociobiology: Counting babies or studying proximate mechanisms. *Trends in Ecology and Evolution, 8*(5), 183–186.

Dennett, D. C. (1995). *Darwin's dangerous idea: Evolution and the meaning of life*. New York: Simon & Schuster.

Gould, S. J., & Lewontin, R. C. (1979). The spandrels of San Marco and the Panglossian paradigm: a critique of the adaptationist programme. *Proceedings of the Royal Society of London B, 205*, 581–598.

Hawkes, K., O'Connell, J. F., Jones, N. G., Alvarez, H., & Charnov, E. L. (1998). Grandmothering, menopause, and the evolution of human life histories. *Proceedings of the National Academy of Sciences of the United States of America, 95*, 1336–1339.

Henrich, J., Boyd, R., Bowles, S., Camerer, C., Fehr, E., Gintis, H., et al. (2001). In search of *Homo economicus*: Behavioral experiments in 15 small-scale societies. *American Economic Review, 91*(2), 73–78.

Holden, C. J. (2002). Bantu languages reflect the spread of farming across sub-Saharan Africa: A maximum-parsimony analysis. *Proceedings of the Royal Society of London B, 269*, 793–799.

Laland, K. N., & Brown, G. R. (2002). *Sense and nonsense: Evolutionary perspectives on human behaviour*. Oxford, UK: Oxford University Press.

Leonetti, D. L., Nath, D. C., Hemam, N. S., & Neill, D. B. (2005). Kinship organization and the impact of grandmothers on reproductive success among the matrilineal Khasi and patrilineal Bengali of Northeast India. In E. Voland, A. Chasiotis, & W. Schiefenhoevel (Eds.), *Grandmotherhood—the evolutionary significance of the second half of female life* (pp. 194–214). Piscataway, NJ: Rutgers University Press.

Lummaa, V., Haukioja, E., Lemmetyinen, R., & Pikkola, M. (1998). Natural selection on human twinning. *Nature, 394*, 533–534.

McElreath, R. (2004). Social learning and the maintenance of cultural variation: An evolutionary model and data from East Africa. *American Anthropologist, 106*(2), 308–321.

Pawlowski, B., & Dunbar, R. I. M. (2005). Waist-to-hip ratio versus body mass index as predictors of fitness in women. *Human Nature, 16*(2), 164–177.

Reeve, H. K., & Sherman, P. W. (1993). Adaptation and the goals of evolutionary research. *Quarterly Review of Biology, 68*, 1–32.

Rose, M. R., & Lauder, G. V. (1996). *Adaptation*. San Diego, CA: Academic Press.

Schlaepfer, M. A., Runge, M. C., & Sherman, P. W. (2002). Ecological and evolutionary traps. *Trends in Ecology and Evolution, 17*(10), 474–480.

Sellen, D. W. (1999). Polygyny and child growth in a traditional pastoral society: The case of the Datoga of Tanzania. *Human Nature, 10*, 329–371.

Smith, E. A., Borgerhoff Mulder, M., & Hill, K. (2001). Controversies in the evolutionary social sciences: A guide for the perplexed. *Trends in Ecology and Evolution, 16*(3), 128–135.

Somit, A., & Peterson, S. (Eds.). (2003). *Human nature and public policy: An evolutionary approach*. New York: Palgrave Macmillan.

Symons, D. (1990). Adaptiveness and adaptation. *Ethology and Sociobiology, 11*, 427–444.

Thomas, F., Teriokhin, A. T., Budilova, E. V., Brown, S. P., Renaud, F., & Guegan, J. F.

(2004). Human birthweight evolution across contrasting environments. *Journal of Evolutionary Biology, 17*(4), 542–553.

Thornhill, R. (1990). The study of adaptation. In M. Beckoff & D. Jamieson (Eds.), *Interpretation and explanation in the study of behavior* (pp. 31–62). Boulder, CO: Westview Press.

Tooby, J., & Cosmides, L. (1990). The past explains the present: Emotional adaptations and the structure of ancestral environments. *Ethology and Sociobiology, 11*(4–5), 375–424.

Towner, M. C., & Luttbeg, B. (under review). Alternative statistical approaches to the use of data as evidence for hypotheses in human behavioral ecology. *Evolutionary Anthropology.*

Williams, G. C. (1966). *Adaptation and natural selection.* Princeton, NJ: Princeton University Press.

Winterhalder, B., & Smith, E. A. (2000). Analyzing adaptive strategies: Human behavioral ecology at twenty-five. *Evolutionary Anthropology, 9*(2), 51–72.

8

Why Measuring Reproductive Success in Current Populations Is Valuable

Moving Forward by Going Backward

H. KERN REEVE
PAUL W. SHERMAN

Any test of a selectionist hypothesis about the adaptive significance of human behavior must specify three components (Sherman &
Reeve, 1997): (1) a set of behavioral variants ("strategies"), (2) a selective
context in which those strategies compete (e.g., the marriage system of a
society), and (3) a fitness value ("payoff") attached to each of those strategies under the assumed selective context. In *forward tests*, the investigator
identifies a strategy set based on the problem of interest and knowledge of
human behavior and, from the specified context, theoretically derives the
relative fitness values for each strategy in the set. Data are then gathered to
determine the frequencies of occurrence of the various strategies, either directly, by observing individuals' behaviors, or indirectly, by synthesizing
previously published reports of those behaviors, or by conducting ques-
tionnaire surveys and summarizing the resulting retrospective self-reports.
Finally, the investigator conducts the test by determining whether the strat-

egy with the highest predicted fitness value actually is the one that predominates in the specified context (or if a predicted stable mixture of strategies occurs in that context). If so, the test outcome supports the selectionist hypothesis.

Evolutionary psychologists generally use the forward approach to test selectionist hypotheses. To do so, they assign fitness values to alternative strategies by hypothesizing that the evolutionarily relevant context is the "environment of evolutionary adaptedness" (EEA). This is the presumed environment in which our psychological mechanisms evolved the characteristics that exist today—that is, the environment in which our neural machinery (brain "hardware") and Darwinian algorithms (brain "software," or decision rules) were last in selective competition with alternative brain structures and algorithms. Most evolutionary psychologists (e.g., Cosmides & Tooby, 1987) believe that it is pointless to investigate how the behaviors of modern humans affect fitness values today, because modern environments are, superficially at least, so different from the environments in which our neural mechanisms and Darwinian algorithms evolved that fitness comparisons would be meaningless.

But what was our EEA? This is a tough question because, according to many evolutionary psychologists, the EEA no longer exists, having presumably disappeared some time between the Pleistocene and the present (i.e., during the past 1.8 million years). Moreover, there must have been a series of different EEAs rather than just one, and how to delineate their chronology or pick the "correct" one to investigate the adaptive significance of the psychological mechanism underlying a specific behavior is unknown. In an attempt to circumvent these problems, evolutionary psychologists have sometimes used the behaviors and social structures of existing hunter-gatherer societies as guides to constructing an EEA. Adopting this approach, the investigator determines the attributes of the selective context based on field studies and uses that information to develop a payoff matrix for presumed neural mechanisms or Darwinian algorithms controlling behaviors that resemble, at least superficially, those occurring in modern industrialized societies.

Obviously, however, the critical assumption behind use of the forward approach to study modern humans—that the appropriate EEA has been identified—is shaky. Luckily, a second approach is available, one that often has been used in studies of nonhuman animals. In this *backward test* (Sherman & Reeve, 1997), an investigator begins by determining the relative frequencies of behaviors or social structures in present-day environments, then quantifies the fitness values of the alternative behavioral strategies in those same environments, and finally checks to see whether, as predicted under a selectionist hypothesis, the predominant strategy is the one that has the highest fitness (or that the strategies in a mix have equal, negatively frequency-dependent fitness values). An important submethod of this approach involves measuring different components of fitness separately to determine whether the component accounting for the principal advantage of the favored behavioral strategy is the one predicted by the specific selectionist hypothesis being tested. Of course, successful use of the backward approach requires the natural co-occurrence or successful experimental creation of alternative behavioral strategies whose relative fitness values can be measured.

Behavioral ecologists have used both forward and backward approaches productively in numerous tests of selectionist hypotheses (Alcock, 2005; Sherman & Reeve, 1997). They have even done so when there was evidence of current maladaptation. The predominance of a suboptimal strategy in a population (assessed through the backward method) can enable one to hypothesize an environment in which the predominant strategy would have been adaptive (the forward method). One can then attempt to determine whether the population's native habitat and environment is the same as the hypothesized one.

This essay has two foci. First, we critically analyze the assumption made by evolutionary psychologists that the EEA is an ancient environmental context that is so unlike any current environment that use of the backward approach is essentially precluded. The reason we focus on this assumption is that it has caused a major methodological rift between evolutionary psychology and Darwinian anthropology, a divide that has persisted (Crawford, 1993; Sherman & Reeve, 1997). We believe the assumption that the EEA is defunct is not only suspect, but that it also belies a commitment to a particular view about the relation between genes and behavior, one that is unsupportable theoretically and empirically. Second, we discuss difficulties in measurement of human fitness values, and conclude that it is not as straightforward as believed by some Darwinian anthropologists. In particular, counting offspring is unlikely to adequately measure fitness in evolutionary analyses of many behaviors of modern humans.

DOES THE EEA REFER TO A REMOTE TIME PERIOD?

The assumption that the EEA refers to some specific epoch in human history, such as the Pleistocene, has never been and probably cannot be tested.

Moreover, it does not flow from a rigorous theoretical argument. Consider an allele (call it "A") that causes the context-specific expression of some behavior or social structure in a modern population. The period during which this imaginary allele was spreading extends from its origin as a mutation to the time when it reached fixation within that population. It is the ecological and social conditions that prevailed during this "spreading period" that is the *true* EEA for the target behavior.

However, it is not clear that the prevailing conditions during the period when "A" was spreading were specific only to some particular epoch. The spreading periods for different alleles vary depending on the time when they initially appeared and the strength of selection favoring each variant. Different alleles undoubtedly spread at different intervals in evolutionary time. And, probably, the spreading period for alleles underlying at least some human behavioral strategies (e.g., mate choice or reciprocal exchange) occurred even earlier in evolutionary time than the Pleistocene. Because humans lived as hunter-gatherers long before the Pleistocene, our ancestors undoubtedly did not suddenly begin behaving socially 1.8 million years ago.

Persistence until the present time of "As" that spread under distantly prehistoric socioecological circumstances would imply that selection pressures were constant enough to maintain "A" against the invasion of alternative strategies, despite changes in many aspects of our physical, social, and economic environments. If so, it would be reasonable to hypothesize that the selection pressures maintaining "A" today are similar to what they were at the end of Pleistocene, just as they were similar between the time when "A" arose and spread, and the start of the Pleistocene.

This argument implies that the backward approach, which involves measuring fitness values in contemporary human societies, is a legitimate way of testing selectionist hypotheses, because, for at least some behaviors and social structures, the critical features of the environment in which they spread (i.e., their real EEAs) may be similar enough to today's environments that backward tests can be utilized. Thus, it is incorrect to make the blanket claim that current utility is irrelevant because the spreading period occurred in the past. If one or more "As" have persisted from the Pleistocene or even longer, the implication is that the real EEA for those alleles is *not* defunct; otherwise they would have been replaced by a fitter alternative sometime within the past 1.8 million years.

Indeed, the backward approach has been used productively to study contemporary human societies (Bereczkei & Csanaky, 1996; Lahdenpera, Lummaa, Helle, Tremblay, & Russell, 2004; Perusse, 1993). For example,

Perusse (1993) reported a strong positive correlation between mating success and social status (based on income, education, and occupational prestige) among Canadian men, but no association between status and the number of children the men acknowledged siring. Perusse argued that the number of potential conceptions (estimated from self-reported copulatory frequencies and numbers of different sex partners) is the best measure of fitness under the novel social conditions imposed by social monogamy and widespread contraception. Perusse's results imply that status-seeking behavior was, and probably still is, selectively favored among men (depending on the veracity of the self-reports about paternity). The point at which status seeking apparently becomes disconnected from offspring production is proximal to copulatory frequency. This suggests that status-seeking behavior was favored until recent cultural forces uncoupled copulation from reproduction. The critical point is that the backward approach proved useful for understanding the behavior of modern-day Canadian men, with copulatory frequency as the fitness measure.

GENES ARE ROOTED IN THE PAST, BUT THE BRAINS THEY BUILD ARE NOT

In the previous section, we imagined that natural selection was operating on an allele "A" that predisposed its bearer to behave in a particular way. We assumed a tight connection between the genotype and phenotype, namely, that there is essentially a one-to-one mapping between alleles and the behaviors that they promote (note that this is *not* to say that one allele by itself is sufficient for the full-blown expression of the behavior it promotes). This one-to-one view of gene–behavior connections is implied by the evolutionary psychologist's rejection of backward tests because, according to this view, to know why we observe certain behaviors today requires knowing the selection pressures that prevailed when the genes promoting those behaviors originally spread. Undoubtedly, a one-to-one relation between genes and behavior is overly simplistic. Despite growing evidence from molecular genetics that specific genes influence specific behaviors, it has become abundantly clear that most phenotypes (even "genetic diseases" such as sickle-cell anemia and prostate cancer) are strongly affected by gene–environment interactions, and most genes have pleiotropic effects on many aspects of phenotypes.

So, let us imagine instead that genes work together to build a computer (i.e., the nervous system) that flexibly and continually computes the

expected fitness outcomes of alternative strategies (i.e., Darwinian algorithms), then selects the strategy (behavior) that maximizes fitness. Selection
would have inexorably favored nervous systems that, on average, accurately computed the anticipated present-plus-future fitness consequences
of alternative possible actions in each social environment and caused the
individual to choose the behavior that maximized projected fitness. Such
fitness-projecting brains would be capable of dealing with changing envi
ronmental and social situations. Hominids spread across the world throughout an incredible diversity of habitats, then proceeded to modify their environments extensively, so there probably has been a consistent premium on
our ability to project fitness consequences in novel circumstances. As a
result, flexible brain "hardware" and "software" would consistently be favored by selection relative to brains that were locked repositories of adaptive actions in past environments.

This scenario is not far-fetched. Indeed, Edelman (1987), on the basis
of extensive neurophysiological evidence, has suggested that the human
brain works according to a Darwinian analogy, with an internal selection
process leading to the emergence of a specific behavioral output from a
suite of possible outputs. We add a new element to Edelman's metaphor,
namely, that the selected behavior should have a very specific, mathematically determinate property: It should maximize the organism's projected
"inclusive fitness," defined as the sum of an individual's own fitness and the
fitnesses of relatives, weighted by the coefficients of genetic relatedness to
those relatives (Hamilton, 1964). To put the latter point another way: *Genes
that built brains basing their choice of behaviors on inclusive fitness maximization inevitably would have been favored by natural selection over genes promoting alternative behavioral choice criteria.* The crucial consequence is that
how people will behave is, in principle, predictable for any given context,
even in novel environments.

This view of the human brain as an *active fitness projector* is one that
we and our behavioral ecologist colleagues have arrived at based on numerous studies of adaptive behavioral flexibility in multiple vertebrate and in-
vertebrate species (see Alcock, 2001, 2005). Virtually everywhere that they
have looked, behavioral ecologists have found that animals modify their behaviors in ways that suggest they are constantly updating and attending to
the projected inclusive fitness consequences of alternative actions, whether
the context is foraging, mating, cooperation, competition, or communication. A dramatic example is presented by species that live in family groups
containing normally nonreproductive "helpers" that are capable of revers-
ing their social behavior when the fitness payoffs for alternative actions

change. Thus, social wasp, termite, acorn woodpecker, and naked mole-rat workers facultatively pursue the option of becoming a breeder according to their size and age (which determine relative dominance), their relatedness to the breeding female (or male), and the value of their help in raising the resident's offspring, all of which determine the future fitness payoffs for attempting to breed versus remaining a helper.

Many evolutionary psychologists have promoted the view that the brain is composed of specialized (domain-specific) modules that are essentially hardwired behavioral subprograms established by natural selection in ancestral environments. A consequence of this view is that behaviors triggered by these programs under novel, present-day, contextual stimuli probably are no longer adaptive. This view is often pitted against the notion in cognitive psychology that brains can be regarded as general-purpose, open-ended, computer-like structures, albeit computers subjected to specific, built-in biases.

Our "fitness projector" view melts this dispute. We believe that brains *are* flexible computers, but ones whose outputs are always designed to maximize one thing: projected (inclusive) fitness. The fitness projector view disposes of the innatism of simplistic views of behavior, because genes are not seen as mapping onto behavioral outputs in a rigid, one-to-one fashion but are instead considered to be working together to build fitness-maximizing computers with flexible outputs. These computers can take as inputs various aspects of the environment, including learning through social observation (Flinn & Alexander, 1982). And if genes build computers that can flexibly choose projected fitness-maximizing behavioral options that can be learned, behavioral adaptation is no longer leashed to a bygone EEA.

WHAT IS THE BEST FITNESS MEASURE IN HUMANS?

We have argued that measuring fitness in modern human populations may provide useful tests of the adaptive significance of some human behaviors and social structures. However, measuring fitness can be tricky (e.g., Strassmann & Gillespie, 2003). In particular, strictly "counting babies" (Crawford, 1993) will usually not work for at least four reasons, the last being peculiar to humans:

1. Because natural selection favors behavioral strategies that maximize inclusive fitness, fitness measurements must take into account the effect of

a behavior on the spread of the actor's genes. This means one must assess not only the actor's reproduction but also the offspring production of all relatives affected by the actor, including descendant and collateral kin.

2. Not only offspring number but also offspring quality (survival and mating success) have to be accounted for in any fitness measure.

3. The ultimate fitness effect of a strategy often does not manifest itself for two or more generations of descendant kin. For example, to understand the evolution of the equilibrium sex ratio or how sexual selection can sometimes "run away," the mating success of sons is the critical factor. Moreover, to understand the evolution of menopause, it is the positive effect of a postreproductive woman on the reproduction of her daughters and the survival of grandchildren that favors termination of reproduction and prolonged postreproductive life (Lahdenpera et al., 2004). In these and probably many other human examples, numbers of grand-offspring or later generations of descendant kin becomes the relevant fitness measure.

4. Humans transmit to the next generation not only genes in descendant and collateral kin but also resources that can ultimately affect the survival of their entire lineage. One might think that these resources simply feed into the aforementioned offspring "quality." However, if resources given to offspring can be invested to generate additional resources, which can then be passed to grand-offspring and beyond, it is appropriate to think of resources almost as a second "kind" of offspring that combines with number of biological offspring to determine ultimate fitness.

This approach may yield a novel solution to the puzzle of the "demographic transition" (i.e., why wealth and fertility are negatively correlated across human societies). In wealthier societies, the potential for resources to "snowball"—in essence, to generate compound "interest" across generations—means that the optimal strategy may be to increase effort in resource generation now, even at the expense of current offspring production, to reap bigger reproductive rewards in subsequent generations (Hill & Reeve, 2005). This explanation suggests that the demographic transition is not evidence of human maladaptation (as has been argued, because traditional "offspring quality" models predict a positive relation between wealth and fertility [Perusse, 1993]), but rather reflects adaptive life-history decision making by fitness-projecting brains with respect to the correct fitness measure.

In conclusion, we have argued that it is time for evolutionary psychologists to discard the assumptions that underlie their wholesale dismissal of the backward approach to studying adaptations of modern humans. Likewise, it is also time for Darwinian anthropologists to revise and update ways of measuring fitness in contemporary societies. If brains are indeed inclusive fitness projectors, the backward approach is empowered, and its use may result in discoveries that would have remained hidden to traditional methods of evolutionary psychology. To use this approach effectively, however, we must develop more complete and accurate measures of fitness under modern socioeconomic and political conditions. We believe that this is imminent, so we are optimistic that our understanding of modern human social behavior can continue moving forward by going backward.

REFERENCES

Alcock, J. (2001). *The triumph of sociobiology.* New York: Oxford University Press.

Alcock, J. (2005). *Animal behavior* (8th ed). Sunderland, MA: Sinauer.

Bereczkei, T., & Csanaky, T. (1996). Mate choice, marital success, and reproduction in a modern society. *Ethology and Sociobiology, 17,* 17–35.

Cosmides, L., & Tooby, J. (1987). From evolution to behavior: Evolutionary psychology as the missing link. In J. Dupre (Ed.), *The latest on the best: Essays on evolution and optimality* (pp. 277–306). Cambridge, MA: MIT Press.

Crawford, C. B. (1993). The future of sociobiology: Counting babies or proximate mechanisms? *Trends in Ecology and Evolution, 8,* 183–186.

Edelman, G. (1987). *Neural Darwinism: The theory of neuronal group selection.* New York: Basic Books.

Flinn, M. V., & Alexander, R. D. (1982). Culture theory: The developing synthesis from biology. *Human Ecology, 10,* 383–400.

Hamilton, W. D. (1964). The genetical theory of social behavior, I and II. *Journal of Theoretical Biology, 7,* 1–52.

Hill, S. E., & Reeve, H. K. (2005). Low fertility in humans as the evolutionary outcome of snowballing resource games. *Behavioral Ecology, 16,* 398–402.

Lahdenpera, M., Lummaa, V., Helle, S., Tremblay, M., & Russell, A. F. (2004). Fitness benefits of prolonged post-reproductive lifespan in women. *Nature, 428,* 178–181.

Perusse, D. (1993). Cultural and biological success in industrial societies. *Behavioral and Brain Sciences, 9,* 267–322.

Sherman, P. W., & Reeve, H. K. (1997). Forward and backward: Alternative approaches to studying human social evolution. In L. Betzig (Ed.), *Human nature: A critical reader* (pp. 147–158). Oxford, UK: Oxford University Press.

Strassmann, B. I., & Gillespie, B. (2003). How to measure reproductive success? *American Journal of Human Biology, 15,* 361–369.

Our Closest Ancestors

9

What Nonhuman Primates Can and Can't Teach Us about the Evolution of Mind

CRAIG B. STANFORD

We didn't evolve from chimpanzees. This is something I tell my undergraduate students in introductory classes in human evolution. Current molecular and fossil evidence indicate that chimpanzees, bonobos, and humans shared a common ancestor approximately 6 million years ago. But many human evolutionary scientists seem to accept the "human-from-chimpanzee" paradigm, at least implicitly. We look to great apes to extrapolate particular social behaviors, from mate choice (Stumpf & Boesch, 2004) to murder (Wrangham, 1999). A sound approach should consider the range of social behaviors seen in the four living great apes, and infer the probable range of behaviors in early hominids (e.g., Wrangham, 1987). We should, in effect, bracket the range of social behaviors rather than pick and choose among them, bearing in mind the great degree of behavioral plasticity living or extinct hominoid taxa would have exhibited. For example, we could infer from the meat-eating behavior of modern chimpanzees that early humans both hunted and scavenged carcasses, that the pattern of meat foraging varied widely over their geographic range, and that even between two nearby sites, early hominids might have hunted or scavenged for meat in very different ways. These inferences are all reasonable given the range of meat-eating behavior exhibited by modern chimpanzees (Boesch & Boesch-Achermann, 2000; Stanford, 1998)

Primatologists studying cognition differ on the likeliest set of socio-ecological factors that promoted the evolution of intelligence in our nonhuman primate ancestors and, therefore, in our own species. The traditional view was Darwin's, that intelligence, tool use, and bipedalism evolved in a positive feedback loop, with upright posture allowing the use of the hands, which put a premium on toolmaking abilities and, therefore, intelligence (Darwin, 1871). Modern dating of fossils has shown that these evolutionary events actually occurred millions of years apart: bipedalism before 5 million years ago (mya), tool use at 2.5 mya, and the rapid expansion of homind brain size only in the past few hundred thousand years.

A second school of thought has focused on intelligence required to solve survival puzzles in the natural world (e.g., Milton, 1981). Primates may have evolved complex brains to navigate through a complicated tropical forest environment full of ephemeral, hard-to-find food resources. Diets that are rich in fruits, an ephemeral and patchy resource, are especially likely to place a premium on excellent spatial reasoning skills, memory, and associative abilities. This school of thought fails to explain, however, why other animals, from rodents to birds, manage to survive in the same forest habitat without the benefits of higher cognition.

The prevailing wisdom among primatologists in recent years has been that intelligence evolved when a premium was placed on the ability to remember and use an increasingly large and complex web of social relationships. The rise of highly detailed studies of the social dynamics (de Waal, 1989), vocalizations (Cheney & Seyfarth, 1991), and social manipulation of group mates (Byrne & Whiten, 1988a, 1988b) brought "social intelligence" to the fore as the cause of increased brain size and intelligence in nonhuman primates. As social groups grew larger, so did the reproductive advantages of those individuals who were able to recall social debts, favors owed, and manipulate others in pursuit of their own mating agendas. This school of thought is appealing to the current generation of primatologists, because it places social behavior squarely at the core of the suite of adaptive traits that characterize primates.

The study of social behavior as a phenotype on which natural and sexual selection may act figures prominently in modern behavioral primatology. Researchers would like to know whether behaviors such as aggression, mate choice, dominance, and infanticide are evolved strategies. By collecting reproductive data on offspring survival, we can infer with some confidence the adaptive value of particular traits (e.g., Cheney, Seyfarth, Andelman, & Lee, 1988; Silk, Alberts, & Altmann, 2003). Testing hypotheses about such behaviors is difficult, because the primate lifespan is long and its reproductive rate low. But testing is possible. Such an approach may not be amenable to a graduate student with a year or two of field data, but scientific careers are being made today that use decades of correlations of behavior and survivorship to investigate the evolutionary forces that have molded primate societies.

If we begin with the view that apes can teach us the range of likely early human adaptations, we may be able to infer aspects of the evolution of mind as well. Chimpanzees employ Machiavellian tactics to pursue reproductive agendas. Low-ranking males distract the attention of alphas in order to mate furtively with females. Females actively pursue such males despite mate-guarding behavior by alphas. Males use captured prey carcasses as social currency to influence their social interactions with other members of the community. We know that nonhuman primates are better at social-cognitive tasks than at nonsocial associative cognition. For instance, wild vervet monkeys understand the kin network within their group and use alarm calls to warn kin more than nonkin (Cheney & Seyfarth, 1991). They also "lie," employing alarm calls to deceive food competitors into fleeing food sources, by uttering predator-specific alarms at inappropriate times. The use of such calls improves as vervets mature. But despite their social intelligence, vervets do not learn to associate the obvious tracks of potential predators, such as pythons or lions, with the possible presence of danger nearby. Nor do they associate the presence of a freshly killed carcass with the possible proximity of danger.

The starting point for reconstructing human cognitive mechanisms must be the continuum of such adaptations from nonhuman primate ancestors. Based on the brief sampling of cognitive adaptations cited earlier, we can infer reasonably that the evolution of mind involved the development of sophisticated levels of tactical deceit, tactical manipulation of group mates, and social bargaining. These are all cognitive traits that likely existed in the earliest hominids as well, behaviors seen in nonhuman primates whose underlying cognitive mechanisms appear, in form and function, to be very similar to those found in humans. The most parsimonious explanation for this is that many human cognitive adaptations are inherited baggage from nonhuman primate ancestors.

The idea that human cognition was inherited from selective pressures that occurred during ancient, prehuman evolution sounds logical to most human evolutionary scholars. Cognitive adaptations should be interpreted in much the same way as morphological ones. Humans inherited their general anatomy—five-digit limbs, forward-facing eyes, large brains, and so on—from their immediate primate ancestors. But many evolutionary psychologists do not extend the evolutionary continuity argument from anatomical to cognitive evolution. In their quest to understand what is uniquely human about the mind, many evolutionary psychologists take an implicitly creationist approach, arguing that the human cognitive mechanisms seen in *Homo sapiens* arose anew in our own lineage. This is extremely unlikely to be the case viewed from the broader perspective of human evolution. No one would argue that the femur in a modern human leg has a different deep evolutionary past than the femur in a gorilla. In the same way, it should be evident that human incest avoidance or mate choice share the same ancestral cognitive adaptive foundations and the same cognitive mechanisms as witnessed in the great apes.

Some evolutionary psychologists, however, claim that the entire endeavor of reconstructing human behavior based on modern primate behavior is at best irrelevant, and at worst misleading (Barkow, Cosmides, & Tooby, 1991). They argue that primate behavior has little insight to offer into the evolutionary history of the human mind. They argue that primatologists, thinking they are watching the workings of the mind when they see two male baboons vying for the opportunity to mate with a female, are not making valid inferences. Because cognitive mechanisms of the mind are the ultimate objects of selection, the behavior itself is at best not highly relevant, and at worst utterly misleading.

As a field primatologist, I agree with this view to some extent. We have made enormous strides in parsing out the whys and wherefores of primate social behavior, even creating an entirely new discipline of cognitive ecology devoted to getting inside the primate mind (see Cheney & Seyfarth, 1991; Garber & Paciulli, 1997; Janson, 1998). But we are still a long way from being able to address the fundamental questions of whether and how individual behaviors are adaptations that may separate—or link—the minds of human and nonhuman primates.

But one fundamental difference in the way that evolutionary psychologists address hypotheses relative to the way that primatologists do so, in my view, renders evolutionary psychology problematic. Despite evolutionary psychologists' contention that adaptation occurs at the level of the cognitive mechanism, the only valid test of the hypothesis that the mind is an adaptive organ is whether a given impulse—incest avoidance or competitive striving for social standing—translates into reproductive success. Even if we accept the premise that a human research participant who claims to be less sexually attracted to a sibling than to a nonrelative is verbalizing the output of an evolved cognitive mechanism, evolutionary psychology does not test this hypothesis. The primatologist can test such a hypothesis directly by measuring mate choice and reproductive success over subsequent generations.

Evolutionary psychologists have argued that the use of the cognitive domain paradigm can lead to reconstructions of the last common ancestor of apes and hominids that are more realistic than analogic models, such as the "chimp model," used by primatologists. Tooby and DeVore (1987) presented a case for "strategic modeling" replacing the chimpanzee model with a conceptual model drawn from a variety of empirical evidence. However, their reconstruction resembles a chimpanzee model, which suggests they are as bound by the limitations of primate behavioral data as any other scholars (Stanford & Allen, 1991).

Reconstructing the evolutionary history and nature of the human mind using a Darwinian approach is a highly worthwhile venture. I would argue, however, that the approach often favored by evolutionary psychologists tends to ignore the value of primate behavior in favor of hypotheses about human social behavior that, while important and intriguing, are frequently untestable. Evolutionary scientists of all specialties are familiar with the premise that important results sometimes begin with stories. Unless the ideas behind the stories are testable with long-term reproductive data, however, they will remain only stories.

REFERENCES

Barkow, J., Cosmides, L., & Tooby, J. (Eds.). (1991). *The adapted mind: Evolutionary psychology and the generation of culture.* New York: Oxford University Press.

Boesch, C., & Boech-Achermann, H. (2000). *The chimpanzees of the Taï forest.* Oxford, UK: Oxford University Press.

Byrne, R. W., & Whiten, A. (1988a). (Eds.). *Machiavellian intelligence.* Oxford, UK: Clarendon Press.

Byrne, R. W., & Whiten, A. (1988b). Towards the next generation in data quality: A new survey of primate tactical deception. *Behavioral and Brain Sciences, 11,* 267–273.

Cheney, D. L., & Seyfarth, R. M. (1991). *How monkeys see the world.* Chicago: University of Chicago Press.

Cheney, D. L., Seyfarth, R. M., Andelman, S. J., & Lee, P. C. (1988). Reproductive success in vervet monkeys. In T. H. Clutton-Brock (Ed.), *Reproductive success* (pp. 384–402). Chicago: University of Chicago Press.

Darwin, C. (1871). *The descent of man and selection in relation to sex.* London: Murray.

de Waal, F. B. M. (1989). Food sharing and reciprocal obligations among chimpanzees. *Journal of Human Evolution, 18,* 433–459.

Garber, P. A., & Paciulli, L. M. (1997). Experimental field study of spatial memory and learning in wild capuchin monkeys (*Cebus capucinus*). *Folia Primatologica, 68,* 236–253.

Janson, C. H. (1998). Experimental evidence for spatial memory in wild brown capuchin monkeys (*Cebus apella*). *Animal Behaviour, 55,* 1129–1143.

Milton, K. (1981). Distribution patterns of tropical food plants as a stimulus to primate mental development. *American Anthropologist, 83,* 534–548.

Silk, J. B., Alberts, S. C., & Altmann, J. (2003). Social bonds of female baboons enhance infant survival. *Science, 302,* 1231–1234.

Stanford, C. B. (1998). *Chimpanzee and red colobus: The ecology of predator and prey.* Cambridge, MA: Harvard University Press.

Stanford, C. B., & Allen, J. S. (1991). On strategic storytelling: Current models of human behavioral evolution. *Current Anthropology, 32,* 58–61.

Stumpf, R. M., & Boesch, C. (2004). The efficacy of female choice in chimpanzees of the Taï National Park, Côte d'Ivoire. *American Journal of Physical Anthropology, 123*(Suppl. 38), 190–191.

Tooby, J., & DeVore, I. (1987). The reconstruction of hominid behavioral evolution through strategic modeling. In W. G. Kinzey (Ed.), *The evolution of human behavior: Primate models* (pp. 183–238). Albany: State University of New York Press.

Wrangham, R. W. (1987). The significance of African apes for reconstructing human social evolution. In W. G. Kinzey (Ed.), *The evolution of human behavior: Primate models* (pp. 51–71). Albany: State University of New York Press.

Wrangham, R. W. (1999). The evolution of coalitionary killing. *Yearbook of Physical Anthropology, 42* 1–30.

🜊 10

Who Lived in the Environment of Evolutionary Adaptedness?

JOAN B. SILK

There can be no doubt that the difference between the mind of the lowest man and that of the highest animal is immense. An anthropomorphous ape, if he could take a dispassionate view of his own case, would admit that though he could form an artful plan to plunder a garden—though he could use stones for fighting or for breaking open nuts, yet that the thought of fashioning a stone into a tool was quite beyond his scope. Still less, as he would admit, could he follow out a train of metaphysical reasoning, or solve a mathematical puzzle, or reflect on God, or admire a grand natural scene. Some apes, however, would probably declare that they could and did admire the beauty of the colored skin and fur of their partners in marriage. They would admit, that though they could make other apes understand by cries some of their perceptions and wants, the notion of expressing definite ideas by definite sounds had never crossed their minds. They might insist that they were ready to aid their fellow-apes of the same troop in many ways, to risk their lives for them, and to take charge of their orphans; but they would be forced to acknowledge that disinterested love for all creatures, the most notable attribute of man, was quite beyond their comprehension.

Nevertheless, the difference in mind between man and higher animals, great as it is, certainly is one of degree and not of kind. We have seen that the senses and intuitions, the various emotions and faculties, such as love, memory, attention, curiosity, imitation, reason, &c., of which man boasts, may be found in incipient, or even sometimes in a well-developed condition, in the lower animals. . . . If it could be proved that certain higher mental powers, such as the formation of general concepts, self-consciousness &c., were absolutely peculiar to man, which seems extremely doubtful, it is not improbable that these qualities are merely the incidental results of other highly-advanced intellectual properties.

—DARWIN (1871, pp. 104–105)

When Darwin bravely conjectured that the differences between humans and "higher animals" were ones of "degree and not of kind," we knew almost nothing about the behavior of other primates or the origins of our own species. But Darwin, who was quite taken with Jenny, a lone orangutan on exhibit at the London Zoo (Keynes, 2002), would surely have been fascinated by the vast body of information about the behavior of nonhuman primates compiled in the last 25 years. And he would certainly have been gratified to discover that the evolutionary principles that he wrote about in *The Descent of Man and Selection in Relation to Sex* have illuminated our understanding of behavioral strategies that we observe in nature. (One can only imagine the lengthy correspondence he would have exchanged with Sarah Blaffer Hrdy on the topic of infanticide.) When Darwin scrawled in his notebook, "He who understands baboon does more to metaphysics than Locke" (1838/1980) he articulated a rationale that has motivated decades of research on the behavior of nonhuman primates.

Beginning in the 1960s and continuing to the present, Darwin's intuition was supported by a series of unexpected revelations about nonhuman primates: A number of species make tools (Panger, Brooks, Richmond, & Wood, 2002), make use of referential signals (Seyfarth & Cheney, 2003), understand causal reasoning (Cheney, Seyfarth, & Silk, 1995), maintain cultural traditions (Perry et al., 2003; van Schaik et al., 2003; Whiten et al., 1999; Whiten, Horner, & Marshall-Pescini, 2003), and have a rich repertoire of expressions and emotions (de Waal, 1982; Preston & de Waal, 2002). These observations emphasized the similarities between humans and other primates, and reinforced the notion that humans are quantitatively, but not qualitatively, distinct from other species.

But there is now a growing sense in evolutionary psychology that modern human social life is fundamentally tied to a set of cognitive traits and psychological capacities that evolved after humans diverged from the ape lineage 5–7 million years ago. These novel traits include the capacity for spoken language; cultural transmission of ideas, values, and beliefs; a well-developed theory of mind and perspective taking; and the development of moral sentiments. These traits, it is argued, represent "emergent properties" that make humans qualitatively different than other primates.

If modern human life is fundamentally tied to this set of emergent properties, what can we learn from studying animals that cannot produce them? Comparative data derived from studies of living primates are an invaluable resource for evolutionary psychologists for at least three reasons (see Byrne, 2000; Byrne et al., 2004; Maestripieri, 2003). First, they help us to identify the ways humans differ from other creatures. This task requires comparative data. Second, they give us insight about the historical origins of emergent properties of modern humans. By tracing the phylogeny of particular traits, we learn something about the selective forces that shaped them. Third, they provide a database that enables us to test adaptive hypotheses about the factors that shape the evolution of behavioral and cognitive traits.

According to the logic of evolutionary psychology, the human mind is designed to solve the kinds of ecological, technological, and social problems that our ancestors faced in the environment of evolutionary adaptedness (EEA). Unfortunately, the original occupants of the EEA are gone, leaving us few traces of their behavior and still less evidence of their thoughts and cognitive capacities. One thing is certain: They were not much like modern people, not even foragers such as the !Kung San, the Aché, the Hadza, or the Inuit. All modern peoples, including all contemporary foraging peoples, have complex languages, sophisticated technology, elaborate stores of cultural knowledge and beliefs, and well-developed understandings of others' thoughts, feelings, and intentions. Apes and other primates largely lack these traits, so it is likely that the first occupants of the EEA lacked them as well. These traits presumably evolved step-by-step over successive generations as the occupants of the EEA were slowly transformed from ape-like bipeds to people much like us.

We might debate (endlessly) about whether Kanzi's mastery of lexicons is qualitatively or quantitatively different than the human child's mastery of spoken language. We might also have a lively discussion about whether the cultural traditions of capuchins (or whales) are different in degree or kind from the cultural systems in modern human groups. But I think that we could all agree that there is a sizable gap between human and nonhuman primates in some of the products that our minds create: language, complex technology, elaborate culture, and systems of belief. And it makes sense to think that the minds that give rise to these products are also different, although we do not know precisely how different they are.

Comparative data are necessary to identify the distinctive features of human cognition. Knowledge of the cognitive abilities of monkeys and apes allows us to determine which cognitive capacities we share with other primates and which we don't. For example, even though many animal species are able to make and use tools, few acquire these skills by observing conspecifics (Fragaszy & Perry, 2003). Examples of learning by observation are much scarcer than we once believed, and there are even fewer example of cumulative cultural change (Richerson & Boyd, 2004). It seems likely that the ability to learn from others requires cognitive abilities that most animals do not possess. Similarly, carefully designed experimental studies are beginning to delineate differences between what humans and other primates know about others' minds.

Comparative studies allow us to develop testable hypotheses about the function of particular cognitive adaptations. For example, a considerable body of research over the last two decades has provided insights about the selective forces that have shaped increases in the size and configuration of the primate brain. Drawing on seminal work by Alison Jolly (1966) and Nick Humphrey (1976), Andrew Whiten and Richard Byrne (1988) formulated what has come to be known as the social intelligence hypothesis, according to which the social challenges that group-living primates faced as they navigated their daily lives favored increases in the size and changes in the configuration of primate brains (Byrne & Whiten, 1988). Researchers subsequently documented significant associations between measures of encephalization and the extent of social complexity (Byrne & Corp, 2004; Dunbar, 1991, 1992, 1995; Kudo & Dunbar, 2001). In addition, primatologists discovered that nonhuman primates had a range of cognitive abilities that could be applied in social situations, including knowledge of the kinship and rank relationships between other group members, skill in tactical deception, and implementation of complex coalitionary strategies (Tomasello & Call, 1997).

It did not take long for primatologists to realize, however, that apes are an embarrassment for the social intelligence hypothesis. Apes have very large neocortex ratios and seem to differ in some aspects of their cognition as well. Apes seem to be more adept than monkeys at manipulating rivals and devising deceptive tactics (Byrne & Whiten, 1988; Whiten & Byrne, 1988). They also seem to be better able than monkeys to anticipate what others will do in competitive situations (Hare, Addessi, Call, Tomasello, & Visalberghi, 2003; Hare, Call, Agnetta, & Tomasello, 2000; Tomasello, Call, & Hare, 2003), and are better at taking the perspective of others (Kummer, Anzenberger, & Hemelrijk, 1996; Povinelli, Nelson, & Boysen, 1992a; Povinelli, Parks, & Novak, 1992b). Tool use is also more common in apes than in monkeys (Byrne, 2000), and apes apparently learn some skills by observing others (Lonsdorf, Eberly, & Pusey, 2004; Whiten, 2005; Whiten, Horner, & de Waal, 2005). But despite their cognitive and technical prowess, apes live in relatively small groups.

Newer comparative analyses suggest that the selective advantages derived from the ability to innovate and to learn socially may contribute to the evolution of primate brains. Reader and Laland (2001, 2002; see also Reader, 2003) compiled field reports of innovation and social learning in wild primates. They tabulated the number of reports for each species, then corrected for the amount of time that the animals had been observed. They found that social learning and innovation are more common in species with larger brains, and most innovation is observed in the context of foraging. Moreover, the ability to innovate explains more of the variation in encephalization than does group size. One possible interpretation of these results is that the impressive social skills that primates display are a side effect of having large brains and a substantial capacity for learning, not the primary selective force driving cognitive evolution in primates.

These results mesh neatly with work on the evolution of life-history strategies within the primate order (Kaplan, Mueller, Gangestad, & Lancaster, 2003). Kaplan and his colleagues have focused on the evolutionary consequences of specialization on resources that are difficult to procure and process, such as buried roots and animal prey. Human foragers rely heavily on hunted foods and exploit a range of resources that require specialized skill and knowledge to obtain and to prepare. Complex foraging techniques such as these take a long time to master, and this in turn may have favored delays in sexual maturation, enhanced learning abilities, and extension of the human lifespan.

Great apes rely more on complex foraging techniques than do other nonhuman primates. For example, chimpanzees in West Africa use tools to pound open hard-shelled nuts and to extract insects from their nests (Boesch & Boesch, 1984; Sugiyama, Fushimi, Sakura, & Matsuzawa, 1993); orangutans at some sites in Sumatra use sticks to avoid painful stings from the spiny husks of *Neesia* fruits (van Schaik & Knott, 2001); and mountain gorillas in Rwanda follow elaborate routines as they process food items (Byrne, 2001). These foraging techniques take a considerable amount of time to master. Moreover, there is considerable variability in tool use and food-processing techniques across ape groups (van Schaik et al., 2003; Whiten et al., 1999). This suggests that social learning processes may play an important role in the acquisition of food-processing skills. Although there is very little evidence for observational learning in nonhuman primates, the best naturalistic example comes from a recent study of how young chimpanzees learn to fish for termites (Lonsdorf et al., 2004). Young females, who spend considerable amounts of time watching their mothers fish for termites, are likely to use tools in the same way as their mothers, whereas males, who spend considerably less time watching their mothers, do not consistently use tools the same way their mothers do.

These analyses suggest that ecological pressures may have played an important role in the evolution of the cognitive capacities that underlie social learning and innovation. Although apes flourished during the Miocene, only a few ape lineages have survived to the present (Begun, 2003). The apes' demise may have been linked to changes in the frequency and intensity of climatic fluctuations that marked the Late Miocene and Early Pliocene (Potts, 1996). These are the kinds of ecological conditions that favor phenotypic plasticity and learning. It seems plausible that members of ancient ape lineages that were able to create novel solutions to ecological problems, learn socially, and adjust their behavior in the face of environmental contingencies may have been more likely to survive in an unpredictable world.

It seems likely that the early occupants of the EEA shared these traits with their ape ancestors. At the same time, the modest technical accomplishments of apes and the relatively limited scope of variation in their local traditions suggest that some traits that apes lack, such as a more fully developed theory of mind and capacity for spoken language, may play a critical role in the acquisition, transmission, and elaboration of behavior, and shape the capacity for cumulative cultural change. If this scenario is correct, it may have been an enhanced capacity to learn from others that set our human ancestors apart from other primates and launched us on the path the led us here.

When Darwin wrote, "He who understand baboon would do more to metaphysics than Locke" (1838/1980), he could not have anticipated how much we would discover about the minds of other primates. But he would not have been surprised that the comparative approach that he championed has been a fruitful source of insight about ourselves.

REFERENCES

Begun, D. R. (2003). Planet of the apes. *Scientific American, 289*, 74–83.

Boesch, C., & Boesch, H. (1984). Possible causes of sex differences in the use of natural hammers by wild chimpanzees. *Journal of Human Evolution, 13*, 415–440.

Byrne, R. W. (2000). Evolution of primate cognition. *Cognitive Science, 24*, 543–557.

Byrne, R. W. (2001). Clever hands: The food processing skills of mountain gorillas. In M. M. Robbins, P. Sicotte, & K. Stewart (Eds.), *Mountain gorillas. Three decades of research at Karisoke* (pp. 293–313). Cambridge, UK: Cambridge University Press.

Byrne, R. W., Barnard, P. J., Davidson, I., Janik, V. M., McGrew, W.C., Miklósi, A., et al. (2004). Understanding culture across species. *Trends in Cognitive Sciences, 8*, 341–346.

Byrne, R. W., & Corp, N. (2004). Neocortex size predicts deception rate in primates. *Proceedings of the Royal Society of London, B, 271*, 1693–1699.

Byrne, R. W. & Whiten, A. (Eds.). (1988). *Machiavellian intelligence: Social expertise and the evolution of intellect in monkeys, apes and humans*. Oxford, UK: Oxford University Press.

Cheney, D. L., Seyfarth, R. M., & Silk, J. B. (1995). The responses of female baboons (*Papio cynocephalus ursinus*) to anomalous social interactions: Evidence for causal reasoning? *Journal of Comparative Psychology, 109,* 134–141.

Darwin, C. (1980). M notebook. In P. H. Barrett (Ed.), *Metaphysics, materialism, and the evolution of mind: Early writings of Charles Darwin.* Chicago: University of Chicago Press. (Original work published 1838)

Darwin, C. (1871). *The descent of man and selection in relation to sex.* London: Murray.

de Waal, F. B. M. (1982). *Chimpanzee politics.* Baltimore: Johns Hopkins University Press.

Dunbar, R. I. M. (1991). Functional significance of social grooming in primates. *Folia Primatologica, 57,* 121–131.

Dunbar, R. I. M. (1992a). Neocortex size as a constraint on group size in primates. *Journal of Human Evolution, 20,* 469–493.

Dunbar, R. I. M. (1995). Neocortex size and group size in primates: A test of the hypothesis. *Journal of Human Evolution, 28,* 287–296.

Fragaszy, D., & Perry, S. (Eds.). (2003). *The biology of traditions: Models and evidence.* Cambridge, UK: Cambridge University Press.

Hare, B., Addessi, E., Call, J., Tomasello, M., & Visalberghi, E. (2003). Do capuchin monkeys (*Cebus apella*) know what conspecifics do and do not see? *Animal Behaviour, 65,* 131–142.

Hare, B., Call, J., Agnetta, B., & Tomasello, M. (2000). Chimpanzees know what conspecifics do and do not see. *Animal Behaviour, 59,* 771–786.

Humphrey, N. (1976). The social function of intellect. In P. P. G. Bateson & R. A. Hinde (Eds.), *Growing points in ethology* (pp. 303–317). London: Faber & Faber.

Jolly, A. (1966). *Lemur behavior.* Chicago: University of Chicago Press.

Kaplan, H, Mueller, T., Gangestad, S., & Lancaster, J. (2003). Neural capital and lifespan evolution among primates and humans. In C. E. Finch, J.-M. Robine, & Y. Christen (Eds.), *The brain and longevity* (pp. 69–98). New York: Springer.

Keynes, R. (2002). *Darwin, his daughter, and human evolution.* New York: Penguin Putnam.

Kudo, H., & Dunbar, R. I. M. (2001). Neocortex size and social network size in primates. *Animal Behaviour, 62,* 711–722.

Kummer, H., Anzenberger, G., & Hemelrijk, C. (1996). Hiding and perspective taking in long-tailed macaques (*Macaca fascicularis*). *Journal of Comparative Psychology, 110,* 97–102.

Lonsdorf, E. V., Eberly, L. E., & Pusey, A. E. (2004). Sex differences in learning in chimpanzees. *Nature, 428,* 715–716.

Maestripieri, D. (Ed.). (2003). *Primate psychology.* Cambridge, MA: Harvard University Press.

Panger, M. A., Brooks, A. S., Richmond, B. G., & Wood, B. (2002). Older than the Oldowan?: Rethinking the emergence of hominin tool use. *Evolutionary Anthropology, 11,* 235–245.

Perry, S., Baker, M., Fedigan, L., Gros-Luis, J., Jack, K., MacKinnon, K. C., et al. (2003). Social conventions in wild white-faced capuchin monkeys: Evidence for traditions in a neotropical primate. *Current Anthropology, 44,* 241–268.

Potts, R. (1996). *Humanity's descent: The consequences of ecological instability.* New York: Morrow.

Povinelli, D. J., Nelson, K. E., & Boysen, S. T. (1992a). Comprehension of role reversal in chimpanzees: Evidence of empathy? *Animal Behaviour, 43,* 633–640.

Povinelli, D. J., Parks, K. A., & Novak, M. A. (1992b). Role reversal by rhesus monkeys, but no evidence of empathy. *Animal Behaviour, 43,* 269–281.

Preston, S. D., & de Waal, F. B. M. (2002). Empathy: Its ultimate and proximate bases. *Behavioral and Brain Sciences, 25,* 1–72.

Reader, S. M. (2003). Relative brain size and the distribution of innovation and social learning across the nonhuman primates. In D. M. Fragaszy & S. Perry (Eds.), *The biology of traditions: Models and evidence* (pp. 56–93). Cambridge, UK: Cambridge University Press.

Reader, S. M., & Laland, K. N. (2001). Primate innovation: Sex, age and social rank differences. *International Journal of Primatology, 22,* 787–805.

Reader, S. M., & Laland, K. N. (2002). Social intelligence, innovation, and enhanced brain size in primates. *Proceedings of the National Academy of Sciences of the United States of America, 99,* 4436–4441.

Richerson, P. J., & Boyd, R. (2004). *Not by genes alone: How culture transformed human evolution.* Chicago: University of Chicago Press.

Seyfarth, R. M., & Cheney, D. L. (2003). Signallers and receivers in animal communication. *Annual Review of Psychology, 54,* 145–173.

Sugiyama, Y., Fushimi, T., Sakura, O., & Matsuzawa, T. (1993). Hand preference and tool use in wild chimpanzees. *Primates, 34,* 151–159.

Tomasello, M., & Call. J. (1997). *Primate cognition.* New York: Oxford University Press.

Tomasello, M., Call, J., & Hare, B. (2003). Chimpanzees understand psychological states—the question is which ones and to what extent. *Trends in Cognitive Science, 7,* 153–156.

van Schaik, C. P., & Knott, C. D. (2001). Geographic variation in tool use on *Neesia* fruits in orangutans. *American Journal of Physical Anthropology, 114,* 331–342.

van Schaik, C. P., Ancrenaz, M., Borgen, G., Galdikas, B., Knott, C. D., Singleton, I., et al. (2003). Orangutan cultures and the evolution of material culture. *Science, 299,* 102–105.

Whiten, A. (2005). The second inheritance system of chimpanzees and humans. *Nature, 437,* 52–55.

Whiten, A., Horner, V., & de Waal, F. B. M. (2005). Conformity to cultural norms of tool use in chimpanzees. *Nature,* advance online publication, August 21, 2005.

Whiten, A., Horner, V., & Marshall-Pescini, S. (2003). Cultural panthropology. *Evolutionary Anthropology, 12,* 92–105.

Whiten A., Goodall J., McGrew W. C., Nishida T., Reynolds V., Sugiyama Y., et al. (1999). Cultures in chimpanzees. *Nature, 399,* 682–685.

Whiten, A., & Byrne, R. (1988). Taking (Machiavellian) intelligence apart: Editorial. In R. W. Byrne & A. Whiten (Eds.), *Machiavellian intelligence: Social expertise and the evolution of intellect in monkeys, apes and humans* (pp. 50–65). Oxford, UK: Oxford University Press.

11

Chimpanzee and Human Intelligence

Life History, Diet, and the Mind

JANE B. LANCASTER
HILLARD S. KAPLAN

Compared to our close living relative, the chimpanzee, humans have at least five distinctive life-history and behavior characteristics: (1) an exceptionally long lifespan; (2) an extended period of juvenile dependence and learning; (3) a pattern of food sharing, particularly between the sexes and from older to younger; (4) male support of reproduction through the provisioning of females and their offspring; and (5) a unique feeding niche based on food-sharing that exploits high-quality, difficult-to-acquire resources. This suite of characteristics is associated with a large brain and the psychological attributes of increased cognitive capacity and insight acquired through an extended period of learning and development.

These extraordinarily distinctive features are such that everywhere humans live, they are at the very top of the food hierarchy, whereas our close relatives live in highly restricted distributions and are nearing extinction. Nevertheless, there is so much shared history, biology, and behavior between humans and chimpanzees that it is often proposed that we can see and better understand ourselves by understanding them. The mapping of the chimpanzee genome suggests that we differ by approximately 1% of the functional genome, and that the separation of the two species is only 5 to 7 million years ago (Chimpanzee Sequencing and Analysis Consortium, 2005). Chimpanzee cognitive capacities and social behavior are also striking in their high levels of socially transmitted behavior, patterns of food procurement that include extractive foraging and the hunting and social exchange of meat, fission–fusion male-bonded social systems, similar patterns of social alliances and conflict resolution, and cognitive behaviors that suggest both a concept of the minds of others and quantitative representation. This impressive display of commonalities leads one to ask whether the differences between the two species are largely matters of degree. Conversely, when we explore the parameters of the two species' life courses, their feeding niches, and intelligent performances, we find major distinctions that set humans far apart.

CHIMPANZEE CULTURE, BEHAVIOR, AND COGNITION

The recognition and identification of socially transmitted, locally variable, adaptive behavior patterns among chimpanzees have been the focus of numerous recent books and publications (Boesch, Hohmann, & Marchant, 2002; McGrew, 2005; McGrew, Marchant, & Nishida, 1996). It is clear that chimpanzees use socially transmitted behavior patterns to solve many critical evolutionary challenges, such as finding food, acquiring mates, forming social alliances, and raising young. Furthermore, studies in captivity indicate that chimpanzee cognition and intelligence may combine features of learning processes, self-awareness, and ability to communicate, which are critical underpinnings to human culture. We also see striking continuities in diet, including food sharing, hunting, and tool use.

The foundation of the chimpanzee diet is collected plant parts and animals. Chimpanzees are notable for two features that link them to humans (Byrne, 1995). The first is their use of extractive foraging techniques and the hunting of meat. These behaviors involve acquisition of skilled performances during development, as well as variability from one study locale to the next. The second is their use of tools as aids to extractive foraging. Tool use has been well described at all the major study sites for chimpanzees. It includes sponging, fishing, probing, digging, and bashing behaviors, all of which give chimpanzees access to resources that are not accessible or are inefficiently extracted by bare hand. Although the calories gained from extractive foraging and hunting form a relatively small percentage of their total diet, this aspect of chimpanzee behavior indicates an interest in hard-to-acquire foods and is expressed in ecologically diverse habitats (Lancaster, Kaplan, Hill, & Hurtado, 2000).

Another feature of chimpanzee behavior that has attracted the attention of evolutionary socioecologists is their pattern of group formation, which is unusual among nonhuman primates (Boesch et al., 2002; McGrew et al., 1996). Chimpanzee social organization is characterized by male philopatry, female migration at puberty, bonding between male relatives, and the collaboration of bonded males in hunting and in the defense of resident females against other male-bonded groups. This complex is shared with humans, another species characterized by male bonding and collaboration for aggression and defense. The alliances formed by chimpanzees for the purpose of gaining and defending mates, social status, and feeding territories are supported by a repertoire of behaviors also shared with humans. Researchers have described social alliances and conflict resolution through reciprocity, retaliation when favors are not returned, reconciliation, and a form of negotiation through conflictive interactions. Even more interesting, field researchers have described chimpanzee adult males' use of hunted meat as a medium of social exchange for access to both sex and allies. Food sharing is such a critical feature of the human adaptive pattern, in which adults feed young, and men and women share collected and hunted foods, that any food sharing in chimpanzees arouses great interest in the scientific community. So far, food sharing has been reported for chimpanzee mothers to offspring for hard-to-process foods, for males to female partners for sex, and for possessors of meat to social allies and close kin, all of which are identifiable as typically human sharing behaviors.

The question of chimpanzee intelligence, cognitive abilities, the mode of transmission from one generation to the next of locally variable and adaptive behavior patterns, and the extent to which chimpanzees can interpret the behavior and understand the thinking processes of other chimpanzees can only be investigated fully in captivity (Bering & Povinelli, 2003; Byrne, 1995; Maestripieri, 2003; Povinelli, 2003). Byrne (1995) argues that great apes and humans stand apart from other primates in their ability to acquire novel behavior patterns through imitation—a quick way of acquiring a complex skill and, at the same time, avoiding time-consuming and potentially dangerous errors. The ability to imitate is especially significant for a species that depends on skills-based performances for extractive foraging and hunting. The intelligence of chimpanzee behavior in the laboratory also suggests a theory of the mind, the ability to manipulate numbers, and the use and manipulation of symbols (Maestripieri, 2003).

Bering and Povinelli (2003), however, argue that similarities in behavior such as the use of symbols can be very deceptive. They note that humans as a species attribute their own emotions, desires, thoughts, and feelings to a dramatic range of animals, plants, and even objects. This means that we are willing to attribute mental states to chimpanzees and to assume that chimpanzees will do the same about us. Although humans and chimpanzees can be profoundly similar in their spontaneous, everyday behavioral interactions, they can still be radically different in their interpretation of such behavior. Bering and Povinelli argue for a profound divide between human and chimpanzee cognition, a gap based on the unique human ability to form concepts about purely abstract things that cannot be directly observed. They describe them as concepts about causation in the "hidden" world—the world of forces and causes that lie behind the surface appearance of things, such as others' emotions, perceptions, and beliefs, or the forces impinging on inanimate objects, such as gravity, force, mass, and physical connection. Povinelli's (2003) experimental research on captive chimpanzees reveals that behaviors that appear to represent insight into causation are really quick studies, that is, the ability to link cause and effect without any insight into their actual relation.

Research on chimpanzee behavior in both the wild and captivity during the past 50 years provides ample evidence of commonalities between humans and chimpanzees in extractive foraging and hunting, social learning and intergenerational transmission of complex behaviors, social organization, behavioral patterns of social affiliation and conflict, and details of intelligence and cognition. The question remains as to whether there is evidence that these considerable commonalities in behavior have had the same impact on the life histories of the two species or on the configuration of the feeding niches they occupy, or whether they are even based on the same cognitive mechanisms.

LIFE HISTORIES OF WILD CHIMPANZEES AND HUMAN FORAGERS

Although both chimpanzees and humans are large-bodied, long-lived mammals, there are major differences in five critical parameters of their life history: survivorship to age of first reproduction, life expectancy at the beginning of the reproductive period, absolute and relative length of the postreproductive period, spacing between births of surviving offspring, and growth during the juvenile period (Kaplan, Hill, Lancaster, & Hurtado,

2000). Human and chimpanzee life-history parameters based on data from extant groups of hunter-gatherers and chimpanzees indicate that forager children experience higher survival to age 15 (60 vs. 35%) and higher growth rates during the first 5 years of life (2.6 vs. 1.6 kg/year). Chimpanzees, however, grow faster between ages 5 and 10, both in absolute and proportional weight gain. The early high weight gain in humans may be the result of the earlier weaning age (2.5 vs. 5 years), followed by provisioning of highly processed and nutritious foods.

The chimpanzee juvenile period is shorter than that for humans, with age at first birth of chimpanzee females about 5 years earlier than is true of forager women. This is followed by a dramatically shorter adult lifespan for chimpanzees. At age 15, chimpanzee life expectancy is an additional 15 years, whereas foragers can expect to live an additional 38 years, if they have survived to age 15. Importantly, women spend more than one-third of adult life in a postreproductive phase, whereas few chimpanzee females spend any postreproductive time. The overall survival probabilities and lifespan of the two species are striking: Less than 10% of chimpanzees born survive to age 40, but more than 15% of foragers survive to age 70!

Finally, despite the facts that human juvenile and adolescent periods last longer and human infants are larger than infant chimpanzees at birth, forager women are characterized by higher fertility. The mean interbirth interval between offspring when the first one survives to the birth of the second one is 1.62 times longer among wild chimpanzees than among modern forager populations.

To summarize, human foragers show a juvenile period 1.4 times longer and a mean adult lifespan 2.5 times longer than that of chimpanzees. Humans also experience higher survival at all postweaning ages, but slower growth rates during midchildhood. And despite a long juvenile period, slower growth, and a long postreproductive lifespan, forager women achieve higher fertility than do chimpanzees.

CONSUMPTION AND PRODUCTIVITY
THROUGH THE LIFE COURSE

The diets of foraging societies and chimpanzee communities demonstrate overlap in component categories but wide differences in relative composition (Kaplan et al., 2000). For example, hunted meat makes up about 2% of the chimpanzee diet but almost 60% of the forager diet. Chimpanzees rely on collected foods for 94% of their nutrition, especially ripe fruits. Such foods are nutritious, but they are neither hard to acquire nor learning-intensive. Humans, in contrast, depend on extracted or hunted foods for 91% of their diet. The data suggest that humans specialize in rare but nutrient-dense resources (e.g., meat, roots, nuts), whereas chimpanzees specialize in ripe fruit and fibrous plant parts. These fundamental differences in diet are reflected in gut morphology and food passage times, in which chimpanzees experience rapid passage of bulky, fibrous meals processed in the large intestine, whereas humans process nutritionally dense, lower volume meals that are more amenable to slow digestion in the small intestine.

Figure 11.1 presents the survivorship and net food production through the life course of humans and chimpanzees (Kaplan et al., 2000). Humans consume more than they produce for the first one-third of their life course. In contrast, chimpanzees are self-supporting by the age of 5. Thus, human juveniles, unlike chimpanzee juveniles, have an evolutionary history of dependency on adults to provide their daily energy needs. Furthermore, over one-half of chimpanzees are already dead by the age of independent feeding, whereas humans do not reach the 50% loss mark until they are over 30. Even more striking is the steady increase in productivity over consumption among humans into their 30s and early 40s. Further data also indicates that forager women take much longer than men to reach peak productivity. For-

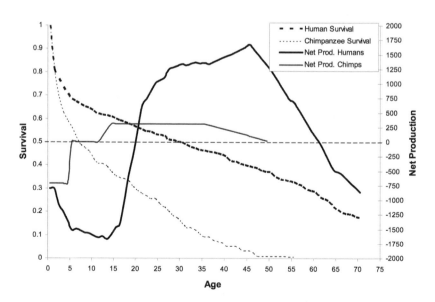

FIGURE 11.1. Net food production and survival: human foragers and chimpanzees. Based on Kaplan and Lancaster (2003).

ager males produce more than they consume in their late teens, but their peak productivity builds slowly from their early 20s and 30s, then is sustained for 20 or more years at a level of approximately 6,500 kcal per day. In contrast, forager women consume more than they produce until menopause. The provisioning of reproductive women and children has a powerful effect on the production of children by reducing the energy cost and health risk of lactation to the mother, and by lifting the burden of self-feeding from the juvenile. This permits a shortened interbirth interval without an increase in juvenile mortality.

The human adaptation is both broad and flexible in one sense, and narrow and specialized in another. It is broad in the sense that, as foragers, humans have existed successfully in virtually all of the world's major habitats. It is narrow and specialized in that it is based on a diet composed of nutrient-dense, difficult-to-acquire foods and a life history with a long, slow development, a strong commitment to learning and intelligence, and an age–profile of production shifted toward older ages. To achieve this diet, humans are very unproductive as children, have very costly brains, are extremely productive as adults, and engage in extensive food sharing, both within and between different ages and sexes.

CONCLUSION

Comparisons between humans and chimpanzees are productive when based on detailed scientific insight into the adaptations of the two species. Chimpanzees are not just close relatives. Their behavior and biology have also been researched during the past 100 years in numerous laboratories and field locations. Chimpanzees are probably the best-studied nonhuman species in the wild considering both the number of research sites and the extraordinary time–depth of extant data bases, some of which are approaching 50 years. The similarities between the two species are striking and evoke empathy in humans because of a common identity. However, careful scientific comparisons reveal a surprisingly vast gulf, suggesting that we may learn more about the two species and the niches they occupy by concentrating on their comparative differences. Life-history and dietary parameters reveal that the human line moved into a unique niche based on major changes in diet, with attendant shifts in reproduction, growth, length of life, survivorship, and social behavior. Furthermore, research into the actual cognitive mechanisms underlying behavioral parallels between the two species suggests that chimpanzees have little insight into their behavioral choices and are content with knowing what works, not why it does so. In contrast, the human mind focuses on the "unseen" world of causation, and beginning in the first year of life asks questions about why and how.

REFERENCES

Bering, J. M., & Povinelli, D. J. (2003). Comparing cognitive development. In D. Maestripieri (Ed.), *Primate psychology* (pp. 205–233). Cambridge, MA: Harvard University Press.

Boesch, C., Hohmann, G., & Marchant, L. F. (Eds.). (2002). *Behavioural diversity in chimpanzees and bonobos.* Cambridge, UK: Cambridge University Press.

Byrne, R. (1995). *The thinking ape: Evolutionary origins of intelligence.* Oxford, UK: Oxford University Press.

Chimpanzee Sequencing and Analysis Consortium. (2005). Initial sequence of the chimpanzee genome and comparison with the human genome. *Nature, 437,* 69–87.

Kaplan, H., Hill, K., Lancaster, J., & Hurtado, A. M. (2000). A theory of human life history evolution: Diet, intelligence, and longevity. *Evolutionary Anthropology, 9,* 156–185.

Kaplan, H. S., & Lancaster, J. B. (2003). An evolutionary and ecological analysis of human fertility, mating patterns, and parental investment. In K. W. Wachter & R. A. Bulato (Eds.), *Offspring: Human fertility behavior in biodemographic perspective* (pp. 170–223). Washington, DC: National Academies Press.

Lancaster, J. B., Kaplan, H., Hill, K., & Hurtado, A. M. (2000). The evolution of life history, intelligence, and diet among chimpanzees and human foragers. In F. Tonneau & N. S. Thompson (Eds.), *Perspectives in ethology: Evolution, culture and behavior* (Vol. 13, pp. 47–72). New York: Plenum Press.

Maestripieri, D. (Ed.). (2003). *Primate psychology.* Cambridge, MA: Harvard University Press.

McGrew, W. (2005). *The cultured chimpanzee: Reflections on cultural primatology.* Cambridge, UK: Cambridge University Press.

McGrew, W. C., Marchant, L. F., & Nishida, T. (Eds.). (1996). *Great ape societies.* Cambridge, UK: Cambridge University Press.

Povinelli, D. J. (2003). *Folk physics for apes: The chimpanzee's theory of how the world works.* Oxford, UK: Oxford University Press.

The Role of Examining the Costs and Benefits of Behaviors

✌ 12

Optimality Approaches and Evolutionary Psychology

A Call for Synthesis

HILLARD S. KAPLAN
STEVEN W. GANGESTAD

THE OPTIMALITY APPROACH

Through optimality approaches, evolutionary biologists attempt to model selection pressures. To do so, a theorist specifies a range of alternative "strategies" an agent can enact within a particular domain (e.g., differing amounts of effort to pursue matings, amounts of time to spend at particular food patches, number of sperm to inseminate, number of offspring to produce currently, amounts of allocation to immune function). The question asked is which of the possible strategies would be favored by natural selection (in the absence of genetic or developmental constraints). To answer it, the theorist must specify and then analyze the fitness costs and benefits of the possible strategies (see Parker & Maynard Smith, 1990). The strategy that maximizes the net benefits (fitness benefits minus costs) is the one that selection should favor.

This approach revolutionized theoretical biology in the 1960s and 1970s. Before then, biologists rarely thought systematically about selection in explicitly economic terms (maximization of benefits minus costs in the currency of fitness). Doing so led to an explosion of new theories, notably, many of the "middle-level evolutionary theories" (Buss, 1995) that evolutionary psychologists rely upon (e.g., parental investment theory, parent–offspring conflict, sex allocation theory, sperm competition theory, and optimal foraging theory). Today, cost–benefit modeling is a core approach within evolutionary biology and the dominant one in behavioral ecology.

As originally conceived, life-history theory (LHT) was just one of these theories—one that concerned optimal timing of life events (e.g., when to reproduce). Increasingly, however, biologists have found that the understanding of phenomena not traditionally thought of as "life-history" events in fact requires an explicit life-history approach. Decisions made at one point in time have effects on fitness that take place over the organism's life course from that point forward, and modeling those effects requires life-history thinking. Hence, LHT has increasingly subsumed cost–benefit analysis in many areas and has become a general analytical approach to understanding selection (see, e.g., Kaplan & Gangestad, 2005).

EVOLUTIONARY PSYCHOLOGY

Evolutionary psychology attempts to understand psychological adaptations. The mainstream approach has several core elements (e.g, Buss, 1995; Tooby & Cosmides, 1992):

1. Psychological adaptations are typically assumed to be domain-specific—information-processing specializations designed to accept specific input and act in particular ways on that input.

2. Each psychological adaptation is assumed to represent a solution to an ancestral adaptive problem (e.g., detection of cheaters in reciprocal exchange, cuckoldry avoidance, kin detection, avoidance of toxic foods). Psychological adaptations tend to be special-purpose and numerous, because each adaptive problem demands specific mappings of information to outcomes that cannot be handled proficiently by general purpose information-processing algorithms.

3. Typically, human psychological adaptations are universal. Just as (nearly) all individuals develop a liver, two legs, a spleen, and so on, so too do most individuals develop an array of species-typical psychological adaptations. Because individuals have different experiences, they exhibit different behavior, despite much species-typical psychological design.

Evolutionary psychology research programs generally seek to identify specific psychological adaptations (i.e., specify ways in which information is specially processed within specific problem domains). In general, research strategies either begin with a specific adaptive problem and ask what sort of psychological adaptations would have solved it, or begin with a psychological phenomenon and ask how it might reflect a solution to an adaptive problem. The approach has yielded many successes (e.g., Buss, 2005).

DEBATES BETWEEN HUMAN BEHAVIORAL ECOLOGISTS AND EVOLUTIONARY PSYCHOLOGISTS: ADAPTATION EXECUTERS VERSUS FITNESS MAXIMIZERS

Optimization Should Not Be Taken to Mean "Rational Fitness Maximization"

In the early 1990s, human behavioral ecologists and evolutionary psychologists debated the use of optimality approaches to understanding human behavior. Some human behavioral ecologists implied that optimality models could be used to directly understand the cognitive processes of human actors—that, in effect, people had evolved to calculate costs and benefits, as estimated in current, real time, to decide on a course of action that would maximize their fitness. Evolutionary psychologists observed that natural selection need not and, in many instances, could not lead to adaptations that could compute fitness benefits and costs, particularly in novel environments. Rather, selection would have resulted in adaptations that operated on useful, recurrent information structure in ancestral environments, which need not be adaptive in novel environments. For example, selection may have led to avoidance of sex with individuals with whom one had coresided during childhood, because such a strategy would have prevented incest. One need not assume that human actors avoid incest based on real-time, current calculations of the fitness benefits and costs of having sex with individuals who have particular degrees of relatedness to the actor. People are "adaptation executers," not "fitness maximizers" (at least in the specific sense discussed here). These caveats are important and obviate simplistic optimality explanations of proximate mechanisms, as if humans are literally "rational fitness maximizers."

Psychological Adaptations and the Lessons from Cost–Benefit Modeling: Solutions to Adaptive Problems Will Not Be Perfect

The assumptions underlying the standard paradigm in evolutionary psychology also require modification. The evolutionary-psychological approach often frames questions of selection in terms of "adaptive problems" in response to which organisms evolve "solutions." Though researchers may informally take into account costs of solutions, this approach does not explicitly frame questions of selection in terms of costs. The optimality approach, by contrast, does. Indeed, the optimality approach gains its leverage precisely because costs are explicitly taken into account. All features or activities require allocation of resources: energy, time, neural resources, and so on. Were it otherwise and individuals could expend unlimited energy at no cost, in principle, they could evolve to grow and develop so rapidly that they could begin reproducing immediately after birth, massively produce offspring, and preserve themselves such that they never age. In biological reality, however, individuals must live within finite energy "budgets" (themselves earned through energy and time expenditures), never spending more than they have available. Allocation of a finite budget entails trade-offs hence forces decisions about the relative value of possible ways to spend. Acquiring one expensive item means giving up others; consumption today may entail having less tomorrow.

As an outcome, individuals should not have evolved *perfect* solutions to adaptive problems. Take, for example, the "adaptive problem" of maintaining somatic tissue. Repair of soma in the face of factors that damage it (e.g., free radicals) is clearly an adaptive problem. And individuals have evolved specialized adaptations to repair soma. In principle, individuals could possibly repair tissue perfectly. Under the constraints of trade-offs, however, selection never favors perfect repair. The reason is that an optimal allocation of resources implies that the marginal gains of all possible allocations are equal. Were they not, an individual could do better by shifting resources from one allocation (where they are getting small marginal gains) to another (where they are getting more). To maintain soma perfectly, individuals would have to allocate resources to somatic repair that, as they approached perfection, would have very tiny marginal gains (indeed, at perfection, the marginal gains would be zero). Selection does not favor this solution. According to the disposable soma theory of aging, organisms deteriorate and senesce for precisely this reason (for discussion, see Kaplan & Gangestad, 2005).

This is but one example of many that could be used to illustrate the same point. Selection should not have favored perfect solutions to adaptive problems of finding a mate, inseminating females with sufficient numbers of sperm, preventing cuckoldry, navigating through space, perceiving intrinsic color, and so on. It should not have favored perfect solutions to these adaptive problems for the same reason it does not favor organisms that do not senesce: As effort invested in a solution nears perfection, the marginal gains from that effort become tiny and generally could be more profitably allocated to a different adaptation.

A PROPOSAL FOR UNIFYING EVOLUTIONARY PSYCHOLOGY AND OPTIMALITY MODELING

Optimality modeling can play an integral role in evolutionary psychology. Indeed, the core elements of evolutionary psychology are perfectly compatible with cost–benefit modeling within a life-history framework. Although not providing models of psychological processes, cost–benefit modeling does offer understanding of the ancestral selection processes that shaped adaptations. Furthermore, explicit cost–benefit thinking can lead to insights that are missed by alternative ways of thinking about selection.

This perspective need not imply that the structures of information-processing algorithms themselves are compromised (though they may be). In some realms, an algorithm that performs extremely well takes no more effort to build than a flawed one. All actual information *processing*, however, requires allocation of time and effort from limited shared resources (energy, attention, etc.). A life-history perspective implies that trade-offs in the allocation of these resources to the *utilization and operation* of specialized psychological adaptations compromise solutions in domains of adaptive problems.

Consider one example in further detail. Sexual jealousy is purportedly a specialized, evolved response to threats to a romantic relationship (e.g., Buss, 2000). In both sexes, a partner that is suspected of having sex with another person (or suspected of being interested in sex with another person) may signal that the mate may abandon the relationship for another partner (or divert resources into another relationship). In men, a partner's infidelity may also threaten cuckoldry, because men could potentially invest in offspring not their own. In men, then, sexual jealousy may be a particularly powerful motive designed to prevent cuckoldry (see Buss, 2000).

The theoretical argument that male sexual jealousy is at least partly a solution to an ancestral adaptive problems of cuckoldry is reasonable. From an optimality perspective, however, we should not expect men to prevent cuckoldry *at all costs*. Cuckoldry prevention requires allocation of time and energy to monitor mates and potential rivals. Furthermore, deserting a mate because cuckoldry may have occurred imposes costs of needing to find a new mate. Just as optimal allocation of effort cannot possibly prevent aging despite the tremendous benefits of survival, optimal allocation cannot possibly perfectly solve the problem of cuckoldry.

IMPLICATIONS OF IMPERFECT
SOLUTIONS TO ADAPTIVE PROBLEMS

The fact that selection should not favor perfect solutions to adaptive problems has a number of important implications for how psychological adaptations are conceptualized and investigated.

Conditional Allocation to Solutions

Ancestrally, conditions probably affected optimal allocation of effort into particular adaptive domains (by affecting the marginal gains of effort in different domains), leading selection to favor adjustments in allocations based on these conditions. To the extent that, within or across populations, or at different points across the lifespan, individuals are exposed to different conditions, they may differentially allocate resources to solving adaptive problems. This is not to deny the universal nature of design; rather, it is to emphasize the conditional nature of (potentially universal) allocation rules. Conditional allocation should not be a rare exception when it comes to allocating resources; optimality modeling suggests that it should be highly widespread.

For example, how much men invest in anticuckoldry tactics should depend on cues of their marginal benefits and costs. Hence, lower status men in some cultures may tolerate their wives bearing other men's children early in marriage (and even care for those children), because such a strategy appears to offer their best chance to reproduce (e.g., Marlowe, 2000).

Interconnectedness of Resource Allocation across Domains

Although information-processing specializations themselves may be modular, allocation of resources into their development and/or utilization cannot be independent. Rather, trade-offs mean that decisions about allocation of effort into particular domains have implications for allocation of effort into other domains. How much men allocate effort to avoiding cuckoldry should depend on the costs and benefits of not only cuckoldry avoidance but also competing activities.

Optimality Modeling Forces One to Think about
Intertemporal Implications of Allocations of Effort

The fitness effects of allocation decisions depend on how they aggregate throughout the life course, from the time the decisions are made until death. Individuals are expected to allocate effort to those adaptations that would most benefit (through time) them (in ancestral conditions).

For example, Mauck, Marschall, and Parker (1999) modeled the effect of mortality rate on male willingness to invest in an offspring not one's own. Deserting a mate entails costs to reproduction, particularly if one need find and attract a new mate following desertion. As the mortality rate increases, search time for mates is particularly costly, because it represents current allocation of effort for future benefits, which become more uncertain as the mortality rate increases. Hence, the model predicts that mortality rate decreases the net benefits of deserting a mate when paternity is uncertain, rendering investment in other males' offspring more likely.

Optimality Approaches Expect Coevolved Allocation Strategies

An optimality approach expects that allocations of effort to various tasks will have coevolved with one another such that, for instance, mating and parenting strategies consist of coadapted bundles of characteristics. As individual men see increased opportunities to have multiple mates, they may invest in offspring less (e.g., Gangestad & Simpson, 2000). Less investment in offspring may entail lower benefits from mate guarding and cuckoldry prevention. Conversely, if men pay high costs to ensure paternity (e.g., because mate guarding severely interferes with production activities—such as long-term hunting forays—in light of the ecology), they may also invest less in offspring.

Variations May Hold Important Keys to Understanding Adaptive Design

Evolutionary psychologists tend to assume the universality of adaptations. If many important universal adaptations may give rise to conditional allocation and, hence, individual differences in allocation and performance in different domains, the *variations* across and within populations that results may hold keys to understanding adaptations. They may reveal how individuals are designed to make trade-offs (see Schaller, Chapter 40, this volume).

Thinking about Trade-Offs Leads One to Think about Design Features That Lead Organisms to Make Adaptive Trade-Offs

How do organisms execute decisions to trade-off bundles of coadapted allocations, particularly given a modular design? Cost–benefit thinking leads one to ask and seek answers to these questions, which can yield fundamental insights into design. Endocrine hormones are messengers in distributed communication systems that can coordinate adaptive changes in whole suites of such modular features. Many endocrine systems may function to execute trade-offs. Conceptually, for instance, testosterone might be thought of as a hormone that facilitates male mating effort (e.g., Ellison, 2001) at the cost of lower parental effort or somatic maintenance. In theory, selection has shaped the testosterone system—the mechanisms that regulate its release and metabolism, as well as the precise distribution of testosterone receptors in structures—such that, based on inputs to the system, it leads to optimal allocations of effort to mating, parenting, and so on, in ancestral environments.

SUMMARY

In some past debates, optimality modeling advocated by some behavioral ecologists was contrasted with the evolutionary psychology approach, which focused on understanding psychological adaptations. These approaches are not mutually exclusive. Indeed, they are complementary and their synthesis is necessary. Evolutionary psychology focuses on understanding proximate adaptations in terms of ancestral function. Cost–benefit modeling provides a precise way of understanding ancestral selection. Furthermore, the cost–benefit approach yields insight into the nature of psychological design that alternative approaches lack. Evolutionary psychology can yield an understanding of how trade-offs are executed.

REFERENCES

Buss, D. M. (1995). Evolutionary psychology: A new paradigm for psychological science. *Psychological Inquiry, 6,* 1–30.

Buss, D. M. (2000). *Dangerous passions.* New York: Free Press.

Buss, D. M. (Ed.). (2005). *Handbook of evolutionary psychology.* New York: Wiley.

Ellison, P. T. (2001). *On fertile ground: A natural history of reproduction.* Cambridge, MA: Harvard University Press.

Gangestad, S. W., & Simpson, J. A. (2000). The evolution of human mating: The role of trade-offs and strategic pluralism. *Behavioral and Brain Sciences, 23,* 675–687.

Kaplan, H. S., & Gangestad, S. W. (2005). Life history theory and evolutionary psychology. In D. M. Buss (Ed.), *Handbook of evolutionary psychology* (pp. 68–95). New York: Wiley.

Marlowe, F. (2000). Good genes and paternal care in human evolution. *Behavioral and Brain Sciences, 23*, 611–612.

Mauck, R. A., Marschall, E. A., & Parker, P. G. (1999). Adult survival and imperfect assessment of parentage: Effects on male parenting decisions. *American Naturalist, 154*, 99–109.

Parker, G. A., & Maynard Smith, J. (1991). Optimality theory in evolutionary biology. *Nature, 348*, 27–33.

Tooby, J., & Cosmides, L. (1992). The psychological foundations of culture. In J. H. Barkow, L. Cosmides, & J. Tooby (Eds.), *The adapted mind: Evolutionary psychology and the generation of culture* (pp. 19–136). New York: Oxford University Press.

❧ 13

The Games People Play

PETER DESCIOLI
ROBERT KURZBAN

In the preface of *Evolution and the Theory of Games*, Maynard Smith (1982) observed that "game theory is more readily applied to evolutionary biology than to the field of economic behavior for which it was originally designed" (p. vii). This is largely because an important underlying assumption of game theory is that the agents it models are rational, making decisions based exclusively on the costs and benefits of available options. By the time Maynard Smith published his book, the fact that humans frequently departed from rationality in their decision making had been amply demonstrated, (e.g., Kahneman, Slovic, & Tversky, 1982), and research supporting this conclusion continues to accumulate.

As Maynard Smith (1982) pointed out, this criticism does not apply to genes. Genes can be considered to be agents that embody strategies that over the course of evolution are tested against alternative strategies. By the process of natural selection, genes (strategies) that lead to the best (fitness) outcomes with respect to others spread in a population. In this way, superior strategies emerge by virtue of the decision rules they employ. The fact that natural selection is sensitive only to fitness outcomes makes genes rational agents *par excellence*. Strategies are "chosen" by natural selection based solely on the reproductive outcomes of those strategies.

Some genes have been selected by virtue of their role in building cognitive mechanisms that compute responses to recurrent adaptive problems. When the adaptive problem involves strategic interaction, these mechanisms might function in a way that approximates game theoretic solutions. Crucially, this does not imply that these mechanisms will be well designed to solve game theoretic problems in the abstract, but only specific strategic problems. Thus, computational mechanisms designed for strategic interaction might or might not embody the principles of "rationality" that underpin neoclassical economics; they simply execute the computations that increased the fitness of genes relative to alternatives.

This idea, the intermediate role of cognitive mechanisms, justifies the preceding Maynard Smith quotation; humans should not be expected to be "rational" in the traditional sense of the term. However, the strategies embodied by human cognition can be informed by a consideration of the adaptive problems they were designed to solve. Considering these adaptive problems, especially interpersonal strategic interaction, can inform hypotheses about the mechanisms underlying the solution to these problems. Applying classical rational choice theory directly to human behavior embodies the same mistake as applying fitness maximization (Symons, 1992): It misses the crucial mediating role of cognition. Cognitive mechanisms were subjected to the rigors of natural selection, and this analysis should be used in theory construction (Cosmides & Tooby, 1994).

EXECUTING OR ALTERING EQUILIBRIUM STRATEGIES

A recurrent game theoretic structure can broadly select for two kinds of adaptations: (1) adaptations designed to execute equilibrium strategies, and (2) adaptations designed to alter the structure of the game to shift the equilibrium. The latter idea is the same concept that underlies contract theory in economics. When parties have an incentive to defect on a mutually agreed upon arrangement, binding contracts can change incentives such that the contractually compliant move is more advantageous than defection, because of the penalties for noncompliance. Contracts change payoffs and, hence, change the game structure.

The fact that adaptations can alter the game itself suggests that it is a mistake to examine games such as the prisoner's dilemma (PD) in isolation

from neighboring[1] games. Trivers (1971) "solved" the PD by adding probabilistic repetition; when the probability of continuation is great enough, the
interaction takes on the form of a stag hunt game, that is, it has two equilibria, one of which is mutual cooperation. Adaptations associated with reciprocal altruism, such as individual recognition and memory of interactions,
might have been favored by natural selection, because they changed PD iterations into stag hunt game interactions. Because adaptations can change
the game structure of interactions, it is crucially important to understand
the relations among different games.

These considerations suggest that researchers interested in strategic interaction should first identify the game that best models the adaptive problem of interest. Then, game theoretic analysis can be employed to formulate
hypotheses regarding cognitive solutions to the problem. Furthermore, researchers should carefully consider whether the "initial game conditions"
can select for adaptations that act to change the game itself.

TOWARD A TAXONOMY OF GAMES

An important step in using game theory more effectively in psychology is to
develop a taxonomy of games suited to that purpose. A good taxonomy
should help identify the game that best models a given adaptive problem,
and should clarify relations among games.

We start here by developing a basic taxonomy of the simplest type of
strategic interaction: two organisms, each with two options. Previous tax-
onomies of 2 × 2 games have been developed (e.g., Rapoport, Guyer, &
Gordon, 1976) but served a different, more exhaustive function. Even in
the simplest of these, considering only ordinal payoffs (outcomes ranked
1–4), there are 78 "basic" strategically distinct games. Although useful to
game theorists, this is a cumbersome guide to psychologists looking for the
right game to model an adaptive problem.

Our approach requires a few basic concepts: dominance, equilibrium,
and Pareto efficiency.[2] Briefly, one option (strictly) *dominates* another when

---

[1] By "neighboring" games, we refer to "neighborhood" in the mathematical sense. For example, a 2 × 2 game can be represented as an eight-element ordered set (the matrix payoffs), that
is, an eight-tuple point, x, that belongs to the space R^8. A neighborhood of x, $N_\varepsilon(x)$, is the set
of points (games) inside an eight-ball, B^8, with center x and radius $\varepsilon > 0$.

[2] For brevity, these concepts are simplified and applied only to 2 × 2 games. Regarding equilibrium, for this initial analysis, we ignore mixed strategy equilibria and consider only pure strategy equilibria.

the payoff of that option is better than the alternative, regardless of the other player's decision. An *equilibrium* is the case in which neither player can obtain a better outcome by changing strategy, assuming that the other player does not change strategy. Finally, *Pareto efficiency* (with two players) refers to an outcome such that there is no other outcome that makes at least one player better off while simultaneously making the other player no worse off.

Our analysis greatly reduces the number of simplest possible games. An ordinal 2×2 game can be reduced to a set of four strict preference relations ($\succ$) while retaining sufficient information to identify equilibria (see also Maynard Smith, 1982). One can think of this as ranking outcomes not only ordinally per se, but ordinally *conditional on the action of the other player*. For example, in the Pure Dominance game in Figure 13.1, if Player 2 chooses strategy $A2$, Player 1 prefers strategy $A1$ to $B1$; if Player 2 chooses strategy $B2$, Player 1 prefers $A1$ to $B1$. In symbols, for Player 1, $A1 \succ B1|A2$, and $A1 \succ B1|B2$. In this case, Player 1 has a *dominant strategy*, because $A1 \succ B1$ for both possible actions of Player 2. In contrast, in the Coordination game, Player 1's strategies exhibit no dominance. More generally, when preferences converge on a strategy, it is dominant, and when they differ depending on the action of the other player, strategies exhibit no dominance.

There are four possible configurations of two strict preference relations for each player, yielding 16 possible game matrices. Like Rapoport and colleagues (1976), we regard games with rows and/or columns and/or

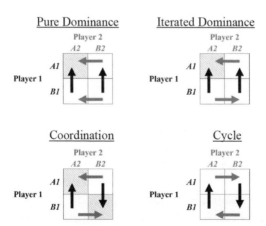

FIGURE 13.1. **Four most basic games.** Preference relations are represented as arrows pointing to more preferred outcome. Shaded outcomes are equilibria.

players interchanged as strategically equivalent. Thus, our analysis yields *four* strategically distinct games (see Figure 13.1).

A good taxonomy should distinguish among these four most basic games. Below we examine properties of each of these game types, including a partial set of subtypes, restricting discussion to those we believe to be the most relevant for evolutionary analysis.

The first game is a Pure Dominance game. Both players have strictly dominant strategies, resulting in a unique equilibrium. Two types of games can be distinguished by examining the Pareto efficiency of the equilibrium. When the equilibrium is Pareto deficient, the game is the familiar prisoner's dilemma. The adaptive significance of the PD is that the inefficiency generates a selection pressure for adaptations designed to alter equilibrium play: Adaptations associated with taking advantage of repeated PD games, discussed earlier, are examples. When the equilibrium is Pareto optimal, players benefit one another as a byproduct of doing what is best for themselves, essentially byproduct mutualism. The adaptive significance of the byproduct mutualism game is that it creates selection pressures favoring designs that are increasingly synergistic.

The second game is an Iterated Dominance game. Player 1 has a strictly dominant strategy. Player 2 does not have a dominant strategy, but does have a best response to Player 1's dominant strategy, yielding a unique equilibrium. Under these circumstances, the predictable behavior of Player 1 acts as a selection pressure on Player 2, favoring a design that makes use of Player 1's stable behavior. When the equilibrium $(A1, A2)$ is better for Player 1 than $(A1, B2)$, this will lead to selection for adaptations in Player 2 that complement Player 1's design, a process akin to mutualism. In contrast, when the equilibrium is a worse outcome than $(A1, B2)$, Player 2 is selected for a kind of parasitism of Player 1.

The third game is a Coordination game. Neither player has a dominant strategy in this game, and there are two equilibria. Three subcategories of this game can be identified by comparing the equilibria. When the equilibria are identical, the game is a Pure Matching game. This situation should lead to adaptations designed to coordinate on one or the other equilibrium, possibly through signaling, again leading to mutualism. An important application of this game is Gil-White's (2001) analysis of cultural norms as solutions to coordination games.

When one equilibrium Pareto dominates the other, the game is a stag hunt (or assurance) game. This should similarly lead to adaptations designed to achieve the superior equilibrium, though organisms can get "stuck" in the inferior equilibrium due to path dependencies, design constraints, and so forth. When players have differing preferences with respect to the two equilibria, the game is a battle of the sexes (chicken, hawk–dove) game, where the mix of strategies will depend on the payoffs at each equilibrium.

The fourth game is a Cycle game. Neither player has a dominant strategy in this game, and there is no equilibrium. Two types of this game can be identified by examining the Pareto ordering of the outcomes. First, a cycle game in which no outcome Pareto dominates any other outcome amounts to a game of pure opposition, as is often characteristic of predator–prey interactions. This can lead to selection for adaptations designed to conceal likely future actions or randomize behavior (Miller, 1997).

Second, if at least one outcome is Pareto dominant to one other outcome, the game is an interesting mixed-motive game that can favor counterintuitive adaptations. Consider an organism that evolves to emit a costly signal that decreases its own payoffs to one strategy more than another. This can change the organism's preferences and, when communicated to the other player, can lead to reciprocal adaptations that allow a Pareto superior outcome to be obtained (see Figure 13.2; Zahavi & Zahavi, 1997). These weakness-is-strength adaptations are puzzling absent game theoretic analysis.

CONCLUSION

Game theory provides a set of useful tools for thinking about adaptations designed to negotiate recurrent strategic problems. Here we have provided

FIGURE 13.2. Prey signaling. Some predator–prey interactions exhibit Pareto ordering of outcomes, because both prefer no chase to a chase that results in escape, as in the Initial Game above. This Cycle game has a mixed strategy equilibrium at roughly [(.6 Vigilant, .4 Eat), (.3 Ignore, .7 Chase)] with expected payoffs of (−2.1, −1.2). Suppose that a signal (e.g., calling to predators) has a small cost to *Vigilant* Prey (who will be likely to escape if detected), but is very costly to *Eating* Prey (who will be less likely to escape if detected). The signal induces an Iterated Dominance game with Pareto superior payoffs (−1, 0); thus, design for both signaling and reception would be favored by selection. Calling to predators is one of a number of counterintuitive examples of predator–prey communication described by Zahavi and Zahavi (1997).

a simple taxonomy of strategic situations in the hope that this proves useful for developing hypotheses about design features associated with various domains of social interaction. By identifying the appropriate game, and by specifying relations with neighboring games, generating predictions about the adaptations designed to play the game in question should be possible. In summary, we hope this analysis facilitates a crucial task: characterizing as clearly and closely as possible the games people play.

REFERENCES

Cosmides, L., & Tooby, J. (1994). Better than rational: Evolutionary psychology and the invisible hand. *American Economic Review, 84,* 327–332.

Gil-White, F. (2001). Are ethnic groups biological "species" to the human brain? *Current Anthropology, 42,* 515–554.

Kahneman, D., Slovic, P., & Tversky, A. (Eds.). (1982). *Judgment under uncertainty: Heuristics and biases.* New York: Cambridge University Press.

Maynard Smith, J. (1982). *Evolution and the theory of games.* Cambridge, UK: Cambridge University Press.

Miller, G. F. (1997). Protean primates: The evolution of adaptive unpredictability in competition and courtship. In A. Whiten & R. W. Byrne (Eds.), *Machiavellian Intelligence II: Extensions and evaluations* (pp. 312–340). Cambridge, UK: Cambridge University Press.

Rapoport, A., Guyer, M. J., & Gordon, D. G. (1976). *The 2 × 2 game.* Ann Arbor: University of Michigan Press.

Symons, D. (1992). On the use and misuse of Darwinism in the study of human behavior. In J. Barkow, L. Cosmides, & J. Tooby (Eds.), *The adapted mind: Evolutionary psychology and the generation of culture* (pp. 137–159). New York: Oxford University Press.

Trivers, R. L. (1971). The evolution of reciprocal altruism. *Quarterly Review of Biology, 46,* 35–57.

Zahavi, A., & Zahavi, A. (1997). *The handicap principle: A missing piece of Darwin's puzzle.* Oxford, UK: Oxford University Press.

🎔 14

Dynamical Evolutionary Psychology and Mathematical Modeling

Quantifying the Implications
of Qualitative Biases

DOUGLAS T. KENRICK
JILL M. SUNDIE

Although the topic of mathematical modeling draws a blank stare from many evolutionary psychologists, most of us are actually big fans, once we think about it. Trivers's classic arguments about reciprocal altruism, for example, or Haldane's kin selection quip about giving his life for two brothers or eight cousins, are simple models with which most of us are familiar. Mathematical modeling is merely a tool to extend logical reasoning, adding some numbers to increase precision.

Consider the classic prisoner's dilemma in Figure 14.1. In the standard setup on the left, each thief must decide whether to cooperate with his partner in crime (C), or defect on his partner by turning state's evidence (D). If B defects while A cooperates, B gets the best outcome (payoff of 7), and A the worst (payoff of 2). Though mutual cooperation yields the best group-level outcome, traditional economic models predict that each person will defect in the one-shot game.

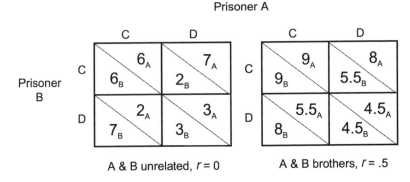

FIGURE 14.1. A set of payoffs that normally produces a prisoner's dilemma (left) may change if one's model considers different degrees of genetic relatedness between the prisoners.

One might not agree with the cold, hard logic underlying the simple prisoner's dilemma, but the beauty of formal models is that even disagreements can be quantified, and the implications of the new assumptions can be explicitly worked out. We can, for example, modify the traditional model to take account of evolutionarily relevant variables, such as inclusive fitness. If the thieves are brothers, one might reasonably factor in an r of .5, and assume that each prisoner's payoff includes his own plus half of his brother's payoff. As shown on the right in Figure 14.1, cooperation would then be the dominant strategy. Like all models, this is an extreme abstraction from the complexities of social life, but it nevertheless represents a straightforward way to quantify logical implications of inclusive fitness for strategic decision making.

As one adds additional factors (e.g., considering decisions by multiple interdependent players related in varying ways), simple models can quickly move beyond the limits of cognitive processing. When models get more complex, various computational aids (equations, computers) become essential for crunching out the quantitative implications of new logical assumptions.

Sometimes empirical researchers get suspicious when models get too far ahead of logic, producing outcomes that confuse more than they clarify. On the other side, sometimes models involve a lot of quasi-magical manipulations of mysterious equations only to produce outcomes that are exactly what you expected without all the malarkey. Like experiments, theories, statistics, and other scientific tools, models are not always helpful or insightful. But like all those other tools, they can help reveal patterns not visible to the naked eye. As Latané pointed out: "Computer simulation can be used as a 'derivation' machine,' a way of finding out what theories predict" (1996, p. 18).

Behavioral ecologists have frequently used modeling to clarify processes such as predator–prey ratios, or to determine which one of a set of plausible strategies is most resistant to invasion by other strategies. Psychologists are familiar with these but tend not to use modeling. In fact, not every researcher needs modeling in the same way that he or she needs statistics. Nevertheless, there are benefits of modeling of which psychologists could avail themselves. Reciprocally, ecologists, economists, and others who already use mathematical models could profit from empirical findings of evolutionary psychology (Kenrick & Sundie, 2006). Such findings can be useful in establishing the range of decision constraints used by people (and other animals).

BACKGROUND OF OUR DYNAMICAL EVOLUTIONARY APPROACH

The members of our research team have used computer simulations to explore questions at the interface of evolutionary psychology and dynamical systems theory (Kenrick, Li, & Butner, 2003; Kenrick et al., 2002). Our model incorporates four assumptions following directly from work in cognitive/evolutionary psychology:

1. Human psychological mechanisms can be conceived as a set of adaptive decision-rules.
2. Those decision rules embody conditional strategies designed to serve fundamental motivations associated with key problems regularly confronted by our ancestors.
3. Qualitatively different decision rules are associated with different problem domains.
4. As a function of random variations in local trade-offs, genetic variations, and other factors, individuals differ in the decision rules they use in any given domain.

Two additional assumptions incorporate insights from dynamical systems theory:

5. Decision mechanisms within any given individual unfold in dynamic interplay with the decision mechanisms of others in his or her social network.

6. Decision mechanisms in different problem domains have different dynamical implications, leading to very different sociospatial geometries (e.g., status hierarchies vs. romantic pair bonds vs. friendship networks).

EXPLORING THE IMPLICATIONS OF EVOLVED DECISION BIASES FOR DYNAMICAL SOCIAL NETWORKS

One series of simulations, depicted in Figure 14.2, explored the emergence of local norms of conflict versus cooperation between contiguous neighbors. The model began with a simple presumption that individuals would generally be motivated to match the strategies of the majority of their neighbors (cooperativeness when all your neighbors are hostile could result in exploitation; hostility toward peaceful neighbors forfeits the benefits of cooperation and elicits retribution). We explored how individual differences in thresholds for acting aggressively might change group-level outcomes, and how the effects of individual differences on those outcomes might vary depending on the numbers of individuals initially acting hostile or peaceful.

As illustrated in Figure 14.2, dynamical networks move toward self-organization under a very wide range of assumptions about the decision rules people use in any given system. Realizing the prevalence of self-organization helps us understand how stable yet variable social norms can emerge out of random fluctuations in individual motivation and behavior (see Kenrick et al., 2003, for additional discussion of this point). Another striking outcome is that individual differences in aggressive behavior thresholds matter much more in some circumstances than others. When the system is teetering near what dynamical researchers call a bifurcation point (i.e., wavering between two or more qualitatively distinct states), small, individual-level differences in reactivity to neighbors' behavior and/or minor differences in the spatial arrangement of aggressive and passive individuals can radically alter outcomes for the entire group. For example, a small number of aggressive individuals with a "short fuse" can draw the neighborhood into either uniform aggressiveness or peacefulness, depending on where those individuals are located. Under many circumstances, however, a group is inclined to develop a norm that biases in one direction or another, independent of individual variations among group members.

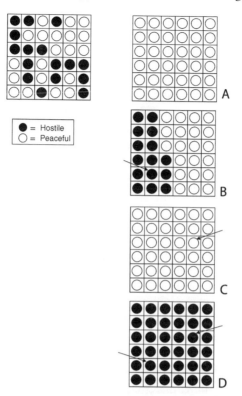

FIGURE 14.2. The left side depicts Day 1 in a neighborhood in which each person acts either cooperatively (open circles) or aggressively (black circles). If each person's behavior is updated daily to reflect the behavior of the majority of immediate neighbors, after several days the neighborhood will settle into total cooperativeness (as depicted in A). B through D depict outcomes when particular individuals in the neighborhood (shown by arrows) have very low thresholds for aggression (i.e., they will act aggressively if any of their neighbors were aggressive the previous day). In this neighborhood, the aggressive individual in B would dramatically change group-level outcomes, and the individual in C would have no effect. But the two together would completely change the group-level outcome, resulting in total aggressiveness instead of cooperativeness (as shown in D).

ROLE OF MODELING IN SCIENTIFIC INQUIRY

Like all methods, simulations have both limitations and strengths. Simulations share one key limitation with laboratory experiments—limited ecological validity. If the variables manipulated in an experiment, or programmed into a computer, are invalid, the outcomes will not reflect complex processes in the real world. To study what actually occurs in natural settings, descriptive methods such as naturalistic observation are best. However, descriptive methods yield intrinsically noisy data, often poorly suited to isolating causal processes. Artificial laboratory experiments, on the other hand, are uninformative about what actually occurs in natural settings, but quite informative about what could occur if certain conditions were met. Similarly, dynamical simulations have a special role in scientific discovery. Like experiments, simulations provide an opportunity to observe particular processes in isolation, by removing sources of extraneous influence that operate in the greater complexity of the real-world system (such as a real social group in which bidirectional influence between the members is continuously taking place). But simulations are different from experiments in that they bypass the human analogues altogether, reducing the isolated processes to clean mathematical or logical rules (Holland, 1998). The two versions of the prisoner's dilemma mentioned earlier are a simple illustration.

Simulations are most useful as one component of a multimethod research program. Cialdini (1995) recommended that laboratory experimenters cycle back and forth between observations of complex natural phenomena and the simpler and more controllable, but artificial, world of the laboratory. Computer simulations add an additional step between theory construction and empirical data collection, allowing the computer to play out a set of assumptions too complex for normal logical limitations. In a sense, such simulations allow us to see a few feet farther into the implications of our premises.

In simulating interactions between people in a social group, one begins with initial values based on logical analysis, theory, or existing empirical data that might be relevant. Simulations can inform us about whether our initial estimates are logically implausible (resulting in outcomes inconsistent with known conditions in natural systems), or they can suggest the range of values within which one's initial assumptions might hold. In another series of simulations, we used empirical data from real people to develop different decision rules by which individual men and women in simulated groups switched from restricted to unrestricted mating strategies, or vice versa (Gangestad & Simpson, 2000). Women estimated that the members of their sex would have a relatively higher threshold for changing from restricted to unrestricted behavior, whereas men estimated that the members of their sex would generally lean slightly in the opposite direction. Also, following previous empirical results, the initial numbers of unrestricted females were presumed to be slightly fewer than the numbers of unrestricted males. These simulations, based on real people's decision rules, indicated that the female bias toward restrictedness generally won out, with the majority of individuals in most simulated groups adopting a restricted strategy. As in the real world, such simulated groups often included smaller, self-maintaining pockets of unrestricted individuals that varied in size depending on random initial placements of individuals in neighborhoods (Kenrick et al., 2003).

Even though the initial differences between the sexes were small, the outcomes tended to be highly skewed. When we examined what would happen if both sexes adopted the male decision thresholds (analogous perhaps to what happens in homosexual male groups, cities with skewed sex ratios, or areas with randomly high concentrations of unrestricted women), groups became highly skewed toward *un*restrictedness over time. To know whether the results provided by such simulations reflect the realities of real social groups, however, a full-cycle approach is required, moving between the highly artificial but perfectly controlled simulation and the sloppier real world. Each of these steps is essential: Neither raw empiricism nor logical analysis without data is sufficient.

WHAT EVOLUTIONARY PSYCHOLOGY ADDS TO DYNAMICAL MODELING

Dynamical approaches have been fruitfully applied to a number of domains of social behavior in recent years (Latané, 1996; Nowak & Vallacher, 1998; Nowak, Vallacher, Tesser, & Borkowski, 2000). Explicitly incorporating evolutionary psychological concepts extends the previous work in at least two important ways. First, an evolutionary approach focuses attention on the particulars of individual differences. As we noted, individual differences can have profound consequences for network dynamics. Second, an evolutionary approach focuses attention on the key role of differential content. Research on dynamical systems has tended to focus on general processes such as self-organization—a process found in systems at all levels of complexity, from molecules to ecosystems (Kaufmann, 1995). Understanding these general processes represents an important advance in our understanding of the natural world. However, researchers studying living organisms are concerned with the particular forms of self-organization emerging from specific decision rules instantiated in particular types of organisms.

Humans are the product of a particular evolutionary history, and live in societies created and maintained by other members of this particular species. Therefore, when we develop models, it is important to consider particular decision constraints related to particular problem domains that recur within human social groups. We have elsewhere identified status seeking, coalition formation, self-protection, mate selection, mate retention, and parental care as key human social domains. As discussed earlier, very different decision biases operate in these different social domains. Furthermore, the decision rules associated with these domains are likely to have different implications for the sociospatial geometry of human networks and, consequently, different dynamic outcomes. Evolutionarily informed models of adaptive decision making can provide useful clues about the specifics of those differences, and dynamical systems models can help elucidate the fascinating variety of social norms that emerges from this shared set of human genetic predispositions.

REFERENCES

Cialdini, R. B. (1995). A full-cycle approach to social psychology. In G.C. Brannigan & M.R. Merrens (Eds.), *The social psychologists: Research adventures* (pp. 52–73). New York: McGraw-Hill.

Gangestad, S. W., & Simpson, J. A. (2000). The evolution of human mating: Trade-offs and strategic pluralism. *Behavioral and Brain Sciences, 23,* 573–587.

Holland, J. H. (1998). *Emergence: From chaos to order.* Reading, MA: Addison-Wesley.

Kaufmann, S. (1995). *At home in the universe: The search for the laws of self-organization and complexity.* New York: Oxford University Press.

Kenrick, D. T., Maner, J. K., Butner, J., Li, N. P., Becker, D. V., & Schaller, M. (2002). Dynamic evolutionary psychology: Mapping the domains of the new interactionist paradigm. *Personality and Social Psychology Review, 6,* 347–356.

Kenrick, D. T., Li, N. P., & Butner, J. (2003). Dynamical evolutionary psychology: Individual decision rules and emergent social norms. *Psychological Review, 110,* 3–28.

Kenrick, D. T., & Sundie, J. M. (2006). Dynamical evolutionary psychology: How social norms emerge from individual decision rules. In P. A. M. Van Lange & A. Kruglanski (Eds.), *Bridging social psychology: The benefits of transdisciplinary approaches* (pp. 285–292). Hillsdale, NJ: Erlbaum.

Latané, B. (1996). Dynamic social impact: The creation of culture by communication. *Journal of Communication, 46,* 13–25.

Nowak, A., Vallacher, R. R., Tesser, A., & Borkowski, W. (2000). Society of self: The emergence of collective properties in self-structure. *Psychological Review, 107,* 39–61.

Nowak, A., & Vallacher, R. R. (1998). *Dynamical social psychology.* New York: Guilford Press.

PART II

Fundamental
Metatheoretical Issues

Editors' Introduction

Evolutionary psychologists typically view the mind as a collection of multiple, varied, and specialized psychological adaptations, each shaped by selection to solve a specific adaptive problem. This perspective has been termed the "massive modularity" thesis. Several neurobiologists, developmental neuropsychologists, and philosophers have questioned its tenability. In essence, they claim that this view requires that brain maturation be precisely programmed by genetic information. Advances in developmental neurobiology, however, indicate that this is untenable. Instead, the way in which humans process information is constructed through prolonged interactions with the physical and social world, not via precise "prewired" programming (see Quartz & Sejnowski, 2002). Relatedly, developmental systems theorists argue that evolutionary psychology implies misleading views of how development actually occurs. Development transpires through interactions between elements that comprise a "developmental system," the outcomes of which depend on all of the elements rather than a privileged few. According to this perspective, genes do not function as "blueprints" that orchestrate development and result in "prespecified" outcomes. Rather, developmental processes are much more fluid, dynamic, and epigenetic; the introduction of new environmental influences may at times generate outcomes that are totally unexpected and cannot be anticipated from the selective history of an organism. A complete understanding of how a given outcome evolved, therefore, requires more sophisticated developmental science that many evolutionary psychologists seem to ignore.

Evolutionary psychologists have responded to these criticisms. They have argued, for example, that an adaptation does not imply that development is programmed directly by genes. Reliable information in the world guides development down adaptive trajectories. Genes affect developmental outcomes by leading individuals to be sensitive to certain information in the world, thereby exerting their effects through epigenetic developmental processes. The fact that neural development is not precisely programmed and occurs over long periods of time does not necessarily invalidate claims about adaptations made by many evolutionary psychologists. The existence of human psychological universals is itself evidence that development often does produce specific, reliable outcomes via some set of developmental processes.

This debate is cast by two key questions.

MODULARITY OF MIND
(MULTIPLICITY OF MENTAL FUNCTION)

One foundation of evolutionary psychology is that the mind should be "modular." Rather than being governed by a single, general problem-solving capacity, thinking may be the product of many different, specialized programs or algorithms, each of which solved a specific, recurrent problem associated with survival or reproduction during our ancestral past. According to this view, the mind is not one "organ"; it is better thought of as many interconnected organs.

"Is the mind modular? If so, how should various modules in the mind be conceptualized?"

We received two responses to this question. Elsa Ermer, Leda Cosmides, and John Tooby are evolutionary psychologists who defend the notion that psychological adaptations are specialized. H. Clark Barrett, a cognitively oriented anthropologist, has developed ways of thinking about modularity or functional specialization in the brain that fit well with what is known about how the brain works. He claims that specialized processes in which enzymes transform biochemical products may provide a useful metaphor for how neural structures could produce specialized, adaptive outcomes.

DEVELOPMENT AS THE TARGET OF EVOLUTION

Developmental systems theorists have argued that some evolutionary approaches make erroneous assumptions about psychological adaptations. Selection, they argue, operates on entire developmental systems. Those systems involve the interaction of genes and environments, which unfold across time and are contingent on the state of the organism at certain points during development. Psychological adaptations, therefore, emerge through development. According to this view, some evolutionary psychologists incorrectly assume that through the operation of historical selection on genes, psychological adaptations are the inevitable outcome of these systems.

"What are the most important implications of a developmental systems perspective for understanding psychological adaptations in humans?"

We solicited five responses to this question. Hunter Honeycutt and Robert Lickliter are developmental systems theorists who have criticized how evolutionary psychologists conceptualize development. Kim Sterelny, a philosopher of science with expertise in biology and cognitive science, has written extensively on developmental systems theory and its implications for understanding selection and evolution. H. Clark Barrett and Debra Lieberman are evolutionary psychologists who, in separate essays, defend evolutionary psychology metatheory against criticisms leveled by developmental systems theorists. Randy Thornhill, an evolutionary biologist, argues that both the adaptation-minded evolutionary psychologist and the developmental scientist offer important lessons from which the other can learn.

THE ROLE OF GROUP SELECTION

We posed a third metatheoretical question relevant to a different debate. Ever since Williams's (1966) blistering critique of early group selectionist theories (e.g., Wynne-Edwards, 1962), a variety of new group selectionist ideas have been proposed and elaborated. Multilevel selection—acknowledgment that selection can occur at the level of the gene, the individual, the group, and the clade—is now a well-accepted phenomenon. Even Williams (1992) has emphasized the importance of clade-level selection in explaining the spread of certain traits, such as sexual reproduction. Different theorists do not agree about the importance of group-level selection in hominid evolution, however. As discussed in our introductory chapter, group selection may also be common in cultural evolutionary processes. Thus, we posed the question of how important group selection may have been in the evolution of humans.

Most evolutionary biologists consider the individual to be the primary level at which phenotypic selection has occurred. In recent years, however,

5

some scholars have proposed that selection on the phenotypic features of groups might also have played a significant role in human evolutionary history.

"What has been the role of group selection in human psychological evolution? What are the implications, if any, of group selection for expanding our understanding human evolution?"

We obtained three responses to this question. David Sloan Wilson has been a champion of multilevel selection for many years and, indeed, much of the recent attention that group selection has received is due to his work. Extending their seminal line of thinking on dual inheritance theory, Robert Boyd and Peter J. Richerson explain how and why group selection could have operated via cultural evolution in humans. Finally, Robert Kurzban and C. Athena Aptikis clarify the nature of multilevel selection and suggest what kind of evidence is needed to marshal compelling support for the premise that group selection assumed an important role in human evolution.

REFERENCES

Quartz, S. R., & Sejnowski, T. J. (2002). *Liars, lovers, and heroes: What the new brain science reveals about how we become who we are.* New York: HarperCollins.

Williams, G. C. (1966). *Adaptation and natural selection: A critique of some current evolutionary thought.* Princeton, NJ: Princeton University Press.

Williams, G. C. (1992). *Natural selection: Domains, levels, and challenges.* New York: Oxford University Press.

Wynne-Edwards, V. C. (1962). *Animal dispersion in relation to social behavior.* Edinburgh, UK: Oliver & Boyd.

The Modularity of Mind

15

Functional Specialization and the Adaptationist Program

Elsa Ermer
Leda Cosmides
John Tooby

The term "module" means different things to different research communities. It first arose in artificial intelligence (AI) to refer to an absurdly simple concept: a mechanism or program that is organized to perform a particular function. By interconnecting these functionally specialized mechanisms, programmers found they could assemble highly intelligent computational systems.

A great deal of confusion over the term "module" was sown by Fodor (1983), who abandoned this original and simple meaning in favor of an eccentric set of criteria that ignores adaptive function and privileges "information encapsulation" (see Barrett, 2005). But Fodor's (1983) concept of a module is neither useful nor important for evolutionary psychologists. For evolutionary psychologists, the original sense of module—a program organized to perform a particular function—is the correct one, but with an evolutionary twist on the concept of function.

Evolutionary biology places restrictions on the concept of function (Williams, 1966). In evolved systems, the function of a mechanism refers to the problem it solved—the consequences it had—that caused the propagation of its genetic basis relative to that of alternative mechanisms. Because the architecture of the human mind acquired its functional organization through the evolutionary process, theories of adaptive function are the logical foundation on which to build theories of the design of cognitive mechanisms. Evolutionarily rigorous theories of adaptive function specify what problems our cognitive mechanisms were designed by evolution to solve, thereby supplying critical information about what their design features are likely to be— information that can guide researchers to discover previously unknown mechanisms in the mind. That is the essence of the adaptationist program.

Understanding these problems in detail leads one to expect the mind to be packed with functionally specialized mechanisms—modules in the older, better sense—that interact with one another to produce adaptive behavioral responses to the kinds of problems our hunter-gatherer ancestors had to solve, generation after generation, to survive and reproduce. The design of these mechanisms should be tailored to specific adaptive problems, such as predator avoidance, cheater detection, sexual attraction, mate choice, foraging, navigation, hunting, and coalitional cooperation. This adaptive tailoring often takes the form of content-rich, domain-specialized procedures that are useful in making inferences and decisions about one problem domain, but would be useless (or even harmful) if applied to a different problem domain.

For example, the "theory of mind" system is a set of domain-specialized programs designed to infer that the behavior of people is caused by invisible mental states—beliefs and desires (Baron-Cohen, 1995). This system is activated in response to people (and certain other agents), because it has a psychophysical front end: It is activated by cues, such as contingent reactivity and self-propelled motion, which were ecologically valid predictors of the presence of an agent in ancestral environments (Johnson, Slaughter, & Carey, 1998). The theory of mind system is not typically activated by rocks, buildings, and other things that lack these cues. And this is a good thing: Inferring mental states is useful for predicting the behavior of people, but useless for predicting the behavior of a rockslide. For nonagents, we have a functionally distinct set of domain-specialized programs, an object mechanics system (Leslie, 1994).

DOMAIN-GENERAL, DOMAIN-SPECIFIC: WHAT IS AT STAKE?

During most of the 20th century, research in psychology and the social sciences was dominated by the assumptions of what we have elsewhere called the standard social science model (Tooby & Cosmides, 1992). This model's fundamental premise is that the evolved architecture of the human mind is composed mainly of cognitive processes that are content-free, few in number and general purpose. These general purpose mechanisms fly under names such as "learning," "induction," "imitation," "reasoning," and "the capacity for culture," and are thought to explain nearly every human phenomenon. Their structure is rarely specified by more than a wave of the hand. In this view, the same mechanisms are thought to govern how one acquires a language and a gender identity, an aversion to incest and an appreciation for vistas, a desire for friends and a fear of spiders—indeed, nearly every thought and feeling of which humans are capable. By definition, these empiricist mechanisms have no inherent content built into their procedures, they are not designed to construct certain mental contents more readily than others, and they have no features specialized for processing particular kinds of content over others. In other words, they are assumed to operate uniformly, regardless of the content, subject matter, or domain of life experience on which they are operating. (For this reason, such procedures are described as *content-independent, domain-general*, or *content-free*). The premise that these mechanisms have no content to impart—that the mind is a "blank slate"—is what leads to a doctrine that was central to the behavioral and social sciences: that all of our particular mental content originated in the social and physical world, and entered through perception. As Aquinas put this empiricist tenet a millennium ago, "There is nothing in the intellect that was not first in the senses."

As we discuss, this view of central processes is difficult to reconcile with modern evolutionary biology. There are essential adaptive problems that humans must have been able to solve in order to have propagated, that cannot be solved by a small number of domain-general mechanisms. Indeed, there is a very large number of such problems, including kin-directed helping, nutritional regulation, foraging, navigation, incest avoidance, sexual jealousy, predator avoidance, social exchange, avoiding free riders—at a minimum, any kind of information-processing problem that involves motivation, and many others as well.

THE WEAKNESS OF
CONTENT-INDEPENDENT ARCHITECTURES

To some it may seem as if an evolutionary perspective supports the case that our cognitive architecture consists primarily of powerful, general purpose problem solvers: inference engines that embody the content-free normative theories of mathematics and logic. After all, wouldn't an organism be better equipped and better adapted if it could solve a more general class of problems over a narrower class?

This empiricist view is difficult to reconcile with evolutionary principles for a simple reason: Content-free, general purpose problem-solving mechanisms are extraordinarily weak—or even inert—compared to specialized ones. We have developed this argument in detail elsewhere (especially Cosmides & Tooby, 1987, 1994; Tooby & Cosmides, 1992), so we won't belabor it here. Instead, we simply summarize a few of the relevant points.

1. *Functional incompatibility: The "Stoppit" problem.* There is a Gary Larson cartoon about an "all-purpose" product called "Stoppit." When sprayed from an aerosol can, Stoppit solves lots of problems: It stops faucet drips, taxis, cigarette smoking, crying babies, and charging elephants. An "all-purpose" cognitive program is no more feasible for an analogous reason: What counts as adaptive behavior differs markedly from one problem domain to the next. An architecture equipped only with content-independent mechanisms must succeed at survival and reproduction by applying the same procedures to every adaptive problem. But there is no domain-general criterion of success or failure that correlates with fitness (e.g., what counts as a "good" mate has little in common with a "good" lunch or a "good" brother). Because what counts as the wrong thing to do differs from one class of problems to the next, there must be as many domain-specific subsystems as there are domains in which the definitions of successful behavioral outcomes are incommensurate (Tooby, Cosmides, & Barrett, 2005).

2. *Combinatorial explosion.* Combinatorial explosion paralyzes even moderately domain-general systems when encountering real-world complexity. As generality is increased by adding new dimensions to a problem space or new branch points to a decision tree, the computational load increases with catastrophic rapidity. A content-independent, specialization-free architecture contains no rules of relevance, domain-specialized procedural knowledge, or content-rich privileged hypotheses to restrict its search of a problem space, and so could not solve any biological problem of routine complexity in the amount of time an organism has to solve it. The question is not "How much specialization does a general purpose system require?" but rather "How many degrees of freedom can a system tolerate—even a specialized, highly targeted one—and still compute decisions in useful, real-world time?" Combinatorics guarantees that real systems can only

tolerate a small number. (Hence this problem cannot be solved by placing a few "constraints" on a general system.)

3. *Clueless environments.* Content-free architectures are limited to knowing what can be validly derived by general processes from perceptual information available during an individual's lifetime. This sharply limits the range of problems they can solve: When the environment is clueless, the mechanism will be too. Domain-specific mechanisms are not limited in this way. They can be constructed to embody clues that fill in the blanks when perceptual evidence is lacking or difficult to obtain.

Consider the following adaptive problem. Toxin-producing bacteria often colonize butchered meat, and plants foods contain an array of toxins to defend themselves against predators. Toxins the adult liver metabolizes with ease sometimes harm a developing embryo. This subtle statistical relationship among the environment, eating behavior, and fitness is ontogenetically "invisible": It cannot be observed or induced via general purpose processes on the basis of perceptual evidence. Women ingest thousands of compounds (including toxins) every day; embryos self-abort for many reasons; early-term abortions are often undetectable; the best trade-off between calories consumed and risk of teratogenesis is obscure. Even if a baby is born with defects, anything could, in principle, have been the cause: sex with a sibling, an injury she sustained, nutritious food she ate, seeing a water buffalo, a curse someone put on her—indeed, anything the mother experienced prior to the birth. A truly "open" mind—that is, one endowed only with content-free inference procedures—would have to evaluate all of them.

But the relation between food toxins and embryonic health can be "observed" phylogenetically, by natural selection, because selection does not work by inference or simulation. Natural selection "counts up" the actual results of alternative designs (in this case, designs regulating food choice) operating in the real world, over millions of individuals, over thousands of generations, and weights these alternatives by the statistical distribution of their consequences: Those design features that statistically lead to the best available outcome are retained. In this sense, it is omniscient: It is not limited to what could be validly deduced by one individual, based on a short period of experience; it is not limited to what is locally perceivable, and it is not confused by spurious local correlations. As a result, it can build programs, such as those that regulate food choice during pregnancy, that embody content-rich privileged hypotheses that reflect and exploit these virtually unobservable relationships in the world. For example, the embryo–toxin problem is solved by a set of functionally specialized mechanisms that adjust the threshold on the mother's normal food aversion system, lowering it when the embryo is most at risk (thereby causing the food aversions, nausea, and vomiting of early pregnancy) and raising it when caloric intake becomes a priority (Flaxman & Sherman, 2000; Profet, 1992). As a result, the mother avoids ordinarily palatable foods when they would threaten the embryo: She responds adaptively to an ontogenetically invisible relationship.

In short, functionally specialized designs endowed with content-rich, domain-specialized procedures allow organisms to solve a broad range of adaptive problems that could not be solved by a few domain-general, content-free programs. The mind probably does contain a number of functionally specialized programs that are relatively content-free and domain-general (Duchaine, Cosmides, & Tooby, 2001), but these can regulate behavior adaptively only if they work in tandem with a bevy of content-rich, domain-specialized ones that solve the aforementioned problems (Brase, Cosmides, & Tooby, 1998; Cosmides & Tooby, 2001).

HOW MUCH FUNCTIONAL SPECIALIZATION?

Some researchers accept the conclusion that the human mind cannot consist solely of content-independent machinery, but nevertheless continue to believe that the mind needs very little content-specific organization to function. Moreover, they believe that the correct null hypothesis—the parsimonious, prudent scientific stance—is to posit as few functionally specialized mechanisms as possible.

This stance ignores what is now known about the nature of the evolutionary process and the types of functional organization that it produces. Natural selection is a relentlessly hill-climbing process that tends to replace relatively less efficient designs with ones that perform better. Hence, in deciding which of two alternative designs is more likely to have evolved, their comparative performance on ancestral adaptive problems is the appropriate standard to use. AI researchers created modules because, by restricting a program's scope of operation, they did not need to engineer a trade-off between competing task demands: They realized that a jack-of-all-trades is a master of none. The same is true for naturally engineered systems. By restricting the scope of a mechanism, natural selection can produce an elegant solution to a *specific* adaptive problem, such as avoiding potentially teratogenic toxins during the first trimester of pregnancy. The solution produced—an adjustment on a food aversion system (which itself has elegant design features, eliciting disgust to smells, sights, and tastes that were ancestrally valid predictors of toxins)—is elegant. But no elegant solution is possible if the same mechanism must cause pregnancy sickness and mate choice. Or pregnancy sickness and mate choice and social exchange and . . .

Evolutionary biologists, human behavioral ecologists, paleoanthropologists, and game theorists have produced a battery of very specific analyses of many adaptive problems our ancestors faced. Take one of these problems and develop a task analysis for it. By carefully examining what, specifically, a mechanism capable of solving that problem would have to be able to do, one gets a sense of just how much functional specialization that mechanism will require to produce an elegant, good solution. For most adaptive problems we are aware of, the answer is: a lot.

REFERENCES

Baron-Cohen, S. (1995). *Mindblindness: An essay on autism and theory of mind.* Cambridge, MA: MIT Press.

Barrett, H. C. (2005). Enzymatic computation and cognitive modularity. *Mind and Language, 20,* 259–287.

Brase, G., Cosmides, L., & Tooby, J. (1998). Individuation, counting, and statistical inference: The role of frequency and whole object representations in judgment under uncertainty. *Journal of Experimental Psychology: General, 127,* 1–19.

Cosmides, L., & Tooby, J. (1987). From evolution to behavior: Evolutionary psychology as the missing link. In J. Dupre (Ed.), *The latest on the best: Essays on evolution and optimality* (pp. 277–306). Cambridge, MA: MIT Press.

Cosmides, L., & Tooby, J. (1994). Beyond intuition and instinct blindness: The case for an evolutionarily rigorous cognitive science. *Cognition, 50,* 41–77.

Cosmides, L., & Tooby, J. (2001). Unraveling the enigma of human intelligence: Evolutionary psychology and the multimodular mind. In R. J. Sternberg & J. C. Kaufman (Eds.), *The evolution of intelligence* (pp. 145–198). Hillsdale, NJ: Erlbaum.

Duchaine, B., Cosmides, L., & Tooby, J. (2001). Evolutionary psychology and the brain. *Current Opinion in Neurobiology, 11*(2), 225–230.

Flaxman, S. M., & Sherman, P. W. (2000). Morning sickness: A mechanism for protecting mother and embryo. *Quarterly Review of Biology, 75,* 1–36.

Fodor, J. (1983). *The modularity of mind.* Cambridge, MA: MIT Press.

Johnson, S. C., Slaughter, V., & Carey, S. (1998). Whose gaze will infants follow?: Features that elicit gaze-following in 12-month-olds. *Developmental Science, 1*(2), 233–238.

Leslie, A. (1994). ToMM, ToBy, and Agency: Core architecture and domain specificity. In L. Hirschfeld & S. Gelman (Eds.), *Mapping the mind: Domain specificity in cognition and culture* (pp. 119–148). New York: Cambridge University Press.

Profet, M. (1992). Pregnancy sickness as adaptation: A deterrent to maternal ingestion of teratogens. In J. Barkow, L. Cosmides, & J. Tooby (Eds.), *The adapted mind: Evolutionary psychology and the generation of culture* (pp. 327–365). New York: Oxford University Press.

Tooby, J., & Cosmides, L. (1992). The psychological foundations of culture. In J. H. Barkow, L. Cosmides, & J. Tooby (Eds.), *The adapted mind: Evolutionary psychology and the generation of culture* (pp. 19–136). New York: Oxford University Press.

Tooby, J., Cosmides, L., & Barrett, H. C. (2005). Resolving the debate on innate ideas: Learnability constraints and the evolved interpenetration of motivational and conceptual functions. In P. Carruthers, S. Laurence, & S. Stich (Eds.), *The innate mind: Structure and content* (pp. 305–337). New York: Oxford University Press.

Williams, G. C. (1966). *Adaptation and natural selection: A critique of some current evolutionary thought.* Princeton, NJ: Princeton University Press.

❧ 16

Modules in the Flesh

H. Clark Barrett

Is the mind modular? Any answer to this question must have at least two components: a definition and data. Because there is not yet wide-spread agreement about what we want "modularity" to mean, a satisfying answer to the modularity question is still out of reach. Most current debates about modularity are largely about semantics. People interested in facts are inclined not to get involved. Moreover, because of the narrow definition of modularity offered by Fodor (1983), most cognitive scientists, including Fodor himself, are inclined to believe that little in the mind is modular (Fodor, 2000). Modularity, according to this view, might be a useful con-cept for some little pieces of mental structure here and there, but not for *most* of psychology.

This view is mistaken. Most cognitive scientists associate modularity with specific features, such as isolation from other brain systems, whole-cloth innateness, and automaticity. This leads them to overlook what should, in fact, be regarded as the central feature of the modularity: *func-tional specificity* (Barrett & Kurzban, 2006; Tooby & Cosmides, 1992). This is the part of the modularity concept that the psychological sciences cannot afford to throw out. Among other things, it is a critical foundation for the testability of psychological theories. At present, the language of modularity, broadly construed (as opposed to Fodor's [1983] specific feature list), is the best language we have for talking about the functional specialization of mental processes. We might ultimately choose to not use the term "module" to refer to specialized information-processing structures, but we cannot discard the concept itself.

Different people mean different things by "modularity." Evolutionary psychologists have been particularly vocal in stressing that the prevalent view of modularity in the cognitive sciences, which is the view promulgated by Fodor (1983), is too narrow. This narrowness derives, in part, from the use of strict analogies with computational systems as instantiated in digital computers. Because the mind is obviously not literally a digital computer, it is not surprising to find that little or nothing in the mind has properties identical to those of computer hardware. Here I argue that if the modularity concept is to have any value as a source of insight about functional specificity, we must realize that digital computers are just the source domain of a metaphor, and that *real* modules, in *real* brains, should be expected to do things differently. We must look for modules "in the flesh," not modules in the abstract, as defined in computer science, mathematics, or philosophy.

DEFINITIONAL PROBLEMS

Much of the divisiveness of the modularity debate has stemmed from people taking the modularity question as a yes–no question, to be settled using a set of criteria established by Fodor (1983). It is now recognized, however, that substantial problems with Fodor's criteria may make them inappropriate for mental modularity in general (Barrett, 2005; Barrett & Kurzban, 2006; Hagen, 2005; Pinker, 2005; Sperber, 1996, 2005). In particular, Fodor's criteria, because they were proposed for only one kind of system (input/peripheral/perceptual systems), may not be appropriate for all brain systems.

Fodor reasoned that the problem faced by perceptual systems is to make correct inferences about the structure of the outside world from perceptual inputs. Based on this analysis, he proposed that input systems should operate automatically and should not be influenced by "beliefs" or inputs from other systems. He characterized modules as rigid, innately specified, hardwired pipelines bringing information to central systems (Barrett, 2005; Fodor, 1983).

Although these criteria could be useful for some low-level perceptual systems, they might apply rarely, if at all. Take, for example, Fodor's (1983) criterion of dissociation or "characteristic breakdown patterns." In real life, brain damage almost never produces clean breaks between systems (Shallice,

1988). The sloppiness of the breaks, even when they are directional, is often taken as evidence against distinct systems (Uttal, 2001). Another key property, "encapsulation," refers to the inaccessibility to other systems of computational processes that occur within modules (Fodor, 1983). This property might also be far from absolute in specialized brain systems, whose processes might be designed to interface and interact with other systems in principled ways. Empirically, we know that brain systems are densely interconnected rather than isolated (Van Essen, Anderson, & Felleman, 1992), so few systems are likely to be "informationally isolated" in the way that most cognitive scientists think about modules. However, this does not mean that they are not functionally specialized.

THINKING LIKE A BIOLOGIST

When a biologist looks at living things, he or she sees modularity everywhere: "Modular organization, like plasticity, is a universal property of phenotypes, the result of the universally branching nature of development" (West-Eberhard, 2003, p. 56). The modularity concept in biology shares something with Fodor's (1983) notion. Discreteness or chunking of the phenotype and underlying developmental processes is an important aspect of the concept, but it is also recognized that the concept must tolerate the fact that "everything is connected," and that features such as plasticity are *aspects* of modules, not at odds with them (West-Eberhard, 2003). West-Eberhard (2003) points to the bones of the vertebrate skull as an example: They are modular, and homologies between bones in different taxa can be established, yet the positions of sutures can vary across individuals within a species, and how they appear in the phenotype depends on complex interactions between the modules during development. One can imagine further analogies. For example, even though not all breaks are cleanly between modular bone components, the patterns, although noisy, might tell us something about the underlying modular structure.

It is possible, of course, that the human brain is not modular in any useful sense, or that it is only crudely modular, with large sections, such as the cortex, being essentially unstructured. Fodor (1983) has suggested that only peripheral or "input" systems are modular, and that the structures responsible for "higher" cognition—those parts of the mind responsible for reasoning, judgment, and decision making—are decidely unmodular. Fodor's definition of "modularity" is such that this becomes true virtually by definition. For example, one of his criteria for modularity is that stimuli are processed "automatically," and processing cannot be interfered with by contextual factors in stimulus presentation. By this criterion, "higher" cognitive processes, which are notoriously prone to context effects, are ruled out: For example, framing effects in judgment and decision making (Tversky & Kahneman, 1981) could not be the result of modular systems. But does this mean that the systems involved in judgment and decision making are not functionally specialized? This seems an odd conclusion to make, at least on the grounds of framing effects alone.

Here, again, it is useful to look to biology. Biologists do not endorse a single checklist of properties that is associated with functional specialization in all contexts. Instead, biologists argue that the core of specialization in biological systems is the fit between *form* and *function* (e.g., Allen, Bekoff, & Lauder, 1998). If the function of judgment and decision-making systems is to guide behavior flexibly in diverse contexts, we might expect these systems *not* to be structured such that they inflexibly and automatically produce the same outcome in all situations, regardless of context. To take another example, isolation of brain systems from each other might make sense for perceptual systems whose function is to produce rapid interpretations of stimuli with a minimum of information, but the form–function match of such a design would be poor for systems such as those responsible for mate choice, which would be expected to integrate information from many sources, over a longer timescale.

MODULES MADE OF MEAT

The use of metaphors from computer science and computational theory has led to enormous progress in the cognitive sciences. In particular, the equation of neural processes with algorithms allows us to bring to bear the formal apparatus of computation theory in logic and mathematics, with its enormous generative power (Fodor, 2000; Marr, 1982). However, metaphors can have costs. In particular, it is true of all metaphors that only some mappings between source and target domains are valid. The computational metaphor invoked by Fodor and others makes assumptions that are appropriate for silicon-based computers, but that might not be appropriate for all neural computational systems. For example, although the modules in computer software and hardware are often truly "encapsulated" in Fodor's sense (i.e., interfaced with only via their inputs and outputs), they are also sometimes (and partly as a consequence of this) truly dissociable, in that they can be cleanly removed, or snapped in or out, without causing a system crash or noticeably impacting the operation of other systems. Often these features exist because of the explicit intentions of a programmer (e.g., to buffer against system failure, or to allow code to be easily modified).

There are many places where this metaphor fails when applied to brains. For example, constraints on human programmers are not necessarily constraints on evolution. A new mutation may have a large number of complicated nonlinear effects, but their fitness impacts are not contingent upon "understanding" them by any agent. Unlike software or hardware, brains are not designed in a top-down fashion, but rather evolve through accretion of small changes. If brain processes contain subroutines, they probably differ from "snap-in" software modules in many ways.

Unlike silicon-based computers, minds are, as Minsky put it, "computers made of meat" (or, more accurately, neural tissue) (cited in Gardner, 2002). Turing's (1936) demonstration of the formal equivalence of computational systems is often used to dismiss the importance of this fact. However, features such as encapsulation may sneak in constraints from the Turing model—such as the serial nature of operations and the need for systems to "take turns" in accessing information—that are not constraints on neural systems and, therefore, make a difference relative to how brains actually do things.

TAKING THE ORGAN METAPHOR SERIOUSLY

Chomsky (1988) famously compared modular brain systems to organs. According to this metaphor, the brain is not a single organ but many organs. Often, the more biological side of the metaphor—what it might imply about development, plasticity, and even computational properties—is disregarded in favor of focusing on "innateness." But given that the brain really *is* a biological organ, what if we took the organ metaphor seriously?

Developmentally, organs arise much differently than do computer programs. For example, the fact that modules "emerge" through dynamic processes during development is not, as some have claimed, an alternative to an evolutionary view (e.g., Smith & Thelen, 2003). Similarly, the way in which modules might be "coded for" in the genome is not literally equivalent to the way that software modules are "coded for" in programming languages (Marcus, 2004). Any notion of modularity that is to survive as a scientific concept must be biologically realistic.

In terms of information processing, the architecture of modular brain systems is likely to differ substantially from that of computers. For example, conventional computers route information through a central processing unit (CPU), whereas information processing in brains is massively parallel and decentralized, yet still produces functional outcomes. Therefore, we must look to models in which processing can occur locally, in the absence of central control, but in which local elements can also interact in a functionally effective manner. In a recent paper, I explored one such model based on an analogy to enzymes (Barrett, 2005; see also Sperber, 1996).

THE ENZYME MODEL

Enzymatic systems have several features that may offer a useful model of how modular processing of information could occur in an open, decentralized system. In the enzyme model of cognition, the matching of inputs to procedures is done via a recognition process on analogy to substrate binding, which involves fuzzy parallel feature recognition, as in neural network categorization systems. The computation itself is a mapping of substrates to products, which are then made available to other systems.

Two features of enzymatic computation systems that may have important parallels to real brain systems are massive parallelism and self-selection. In Fodorean modular systems, information is routed to proprietary systems only, as if via pipes. In a "bulletin board" style enzymatic system, products are publicly broadcast, and selective processing is handled by the lock-and-key nature of substrate recognition. Self-selection may be an important feature of specialized processing at all levels of brain organization, because it obviates the need for a supervisor or prewired pipelines. Increasingly, the advantages of systems in which many "demons" or subroutines operate in parallel, interacting dynamically (competitively or cooperatively) to create emergent global organization, are being recognized (Holland, 1995; Minksy, 1987; Selfridge & Neisser, 1960). Other features of the enzyme model, such as tagging or modification of representations for consumption by other systems, modulation of activity between systems, by-product processing (as in metaphor), adjustment of processing via top-down feedback, and competition for processing based on goodness of fit, may also have analogies in real brain systems.

LOOKING FOR ANSWERS IN THE BRAIN ITSELF

It is clear that we cannot answer questions about modularity without deciding how we would know a module when we see it. Fodor's criteria are problematic, because they may match nothing in the brain when pushed to the limit, and because they were derived from design considerations based on problems faced only by some parts of the brain. Applying design criteria from one kind of system to another can be a major mistake. "Central" systems for planning, inference, and decision making face quite different problems than do perceptual systems, and so might have very different design features, such as integrating rather than excluding information, but may nevertheless be modular.

As elsewhere in biology, we must be prepared to be flexible in our use of the modularity concept, and most importantly, to know *why* we are invoking the concept. If we are looking for functionally specialized structures, we must be prepared to take the idea of structure–function correspondence seriously. The blind search for properties such as encapsulation or insensitivity to developmental environment makes no sense from this perspective. We should be prepared to let the brain inform us about how it solves problems, rather than deciding in advance.

REFERENCES

Allen, C., Bekoff, M., & Lauder, G. V. (Eds). (1998). *Nature's purposes: Analyses of function and design in biology.* Cambridge, MA: MIT Press.

Barrett, H. C. (2005). Enzymatic computation and cognitive modularity. *Mind and Language, 20,* 259–287.

Barrett, H. C., & Kurzban, R. (2006). Modularity in cognition: Framing the debate. *Psychological Review, 113,* 628–647.

Chomsky, N. (1988). *Language and problems of knowledge.* Cambridge, MA: MIT Press.

Fodor, J. (1983). *The modularity of mind.* Cambridge, MA: MIT Press.

Fodor, J. (2000). *The mind doesn't work that way.* Cambridge, MA: MIT Press.

Gardner, M. (2002). Foreword to Penrose, R. *The Emperor's New Mind.* Oxford, UK: Oxford University Press.

Hagen, E. H. (2005). Controversial issues in evolutionary psychology. In D. M. Buss (Ed.), *The handbook of evolutionary psychology* (pp. 145–175). New York: Wiley.

Holland, J. H. (1995). *Hidden order: How adaptation builds complexity.* Reading, MA: Addison-Wesley.

Marcus, G. (2004). *The birth of the mind.* New York: Basic Books.

Marr, D. (1982). *Vision: A computational investigation into the human representation and processing of visual information.* San Francisco: Freeman.

Minsky, M. (1987). *The society of mind.* New York: Simon & Schuster.

Pinker, S. (2005). So how does the mind work? *Mind and Language, 20,* 1–24.

Selfridge, O. G., & Neisser, U. (1960). Pattern recognition by machine. *Scientific American, 203,* 60–68.

Shallice, T. (1988). *From neuropsychology to mental structure.* Cambridge, UK: Cambridge University Press.

Smith, L. B., & Thelen, E. (2003). Development as a dynamic system. *Trends in Cognitive Sciences, 7,* 343–348.

Sperber, D. (1996). *Explaining culture: A naturalistic approach.* Oxford, UK: Blackwell.

Sperber, D. (2005). Modularity and relevance: How can a massively modular mind be flexible and context-sensitive? In P. Carruthers, S. Laurence, & S. Stich (Eds.), *The innate mind: Structure and content* (pp. 53–68). Oxford, UK: Oxford University Press.

Tooby, J., & Cosmides, L. (1992). The psychological foundations of culture. In J. H. Barkow, L. Cosmides, & J. Tooby (Eds.), *The adapted mind: Evolutionary psychology and the generation of culture* (pp. 19–136). New York: Oxford University Press.

Turing, A. M. (1936). On computable numbers, with an application to the Entscheidungsproblem. *Proceeds of the London Mathematical Society, Series 2, 42,* 230–265.

Tversky, A., & Kahneman, D. (1981). The framing of decisions and the psychology of choice. *Science, 211,* 453–458.

Uttal, W. R. (2001). *The new phrenology: The limits of localizing cognitive processes in the brain.* Cambridge, MA: MIT Press.

Van Essen, D. C., Anderson, C. H., & Felleman, D. J. (1992). Information processing in the primate visual system: An integrated system perspective. *Science, 255,* 419–423.

West-Eberhard, M.-J. (2003). *Developmental plasticity and evolution.* New York: Oxford University Press.

Development as the Target of Evolution

❧ 17

The Developmental Dynamics of Adaptation

HUNTER HONEYCUTT
ROBERT LICKLITER

Proponents of the neo-Darwinian synthesis of the last century effectively sidestepped the issue of development by treating it as a predominantly predetermined affair. Genetic factors were thought to determine both the physical and behavioral characteristics of an organism (the phenotype), and these internal factors were believed to be buffered from any experiential effects occurring during individual ontogeny. As a result, developmental processes became synonymous with the decoding of genetic programs for many biologists and psychologists working in the 1950s and beyond. Because neither this decoding process nor the activities and experiences of the organism were thought to influence the nature of germ-line genetic programs, the impact of development on evolution was thought to be of little significance. Consequently, many evolutionary biologists (e.g., Mayr, 1988) championed a view of phenotypic development that partitioned an individual's characteristics into those that were (1) evolved through selection and inherited (i.e., nature-based, genetically determined), and (2) those acquired during, and limited to, an individual's life cycle (nurture-based, environmentally determined).

However, partitioning elements of the phenotype into those specified by the genes and those specified by the environment is not really possible.

Evidence from modern research in genomics, developmental biology, and other developmental sciences supports a more dynamic, contextually contingent view of how organisms and their life cycles develop and evolve (Oyama, 2000; Robert, 2004; Rose, 1998). We now know that the development of any individual organism results from a complex web of spatially and temporally dependent interactions involving factors both internal and external to the organism. At each ontogenetic stage, new structural and functional relationships emerge from previous ones and are organized in relation to (and alter) the surrounding context. The impact of any single factor or set of factors (e.g., genes, hormones, diet, parents) is contingent upon the organization of the surrounding developmental system, so that the causes of development are always relational and distributed. As a result, no single factor can be said to unilaterally cause or control a particular developmental outcome. Genes are certainly an important factor for all development, but they carry no more privilege than any other reliably recurring developmental resource (e.g., zygotic constituents, cellular interactions, or conspecifics). Rather than being controlled by some inferred vital force, development is now understood to be a thoroughly epigenetic process.

Recently, we have shown how this dynamic and contingent view of individual development has yet to be adequately incorporated into modern evolutionary psychology (EP), in which development and behavior continue to be discussed in outdated and biologically implausible terms (see Lickliter & Honeycutt, 2003). Here we extend our critique of EP by focusing on its use of the term "adaptation." Our focus is not on the numerous problems associated with the strategy of "adaptationism." Instead, we point out how what counts as an adaptation and the processes responsible for the origins or maintenance of any adaptation must be updated in light of our current knowledge of individual development. Doing so will require substantial changes in the assumptive bases of EP.

PROBLEMS WITH THE RECEIVED
VIEW OF ADAPTATION

Although EP attempts to identify so-called "psychological adaptations" that guide and constrain human behavior, what constitutes an "adaptation" has always been a slippery issue in evolutionary biology. Nearly 40 years ago, Pittendrigh (1967) highlighted this difficulty by identifying several ways that the term "adaptation" is commonly used in evolutionary discourse. First, adaptation$_1$ can be used to describe a relation or correspondence be-

tween organism and environment, in that "organism A is fit for environment B" (and vice versa). Alternatively, adaptation$_2$ is used to refer to some
features or properties of the organism that serve a proximate end. For
example, it can be said that "features X of organism A are adaptations for
achieving some proximate function in environment Y." According to
Pittendrigh, this latter usage is the most favored because of what he perceived as a fundamental asymmetry between features of the organism and
features of its environment. This perceived asymmetry was based on the belief that only the genome of the organism can accumulate and retain developmental information over generations.

Pittendrigh (1967) went on to distinguish between two processes that
could bring about adaptation$_2$. One process involves the reorganization of
the organism in response to new environmental situations. This so-called
"somatic adaptation" can occur during the lifetime of the individual and
takes place without altering genomic content. Implied within this definition is the idea that because somatic adaptation does not alter genotypes, it
cannot help us explain evolutionary phenomena. A second process refers to
the transgenerational historical processes that generate adaptation$_2$ (properties or features of organisms) by altering genotypes. It is this sense of
adaptation that Pittendrigh promoted, and he (like most) treats natural selection as the historical process that brings about adaptation$_2$.

Few would argue with Pittendrigh's (1967) analysis of the various
meanings of the term "adaptation," and it is this understanding of adaptation$_2$
via natural selection that has been embraced and promoted within modern
EP (see, e.g., Buss, Haselton, Shackleford, Bleski, & Wakefield, 1998).
However, both Pittendrigh's and EP's gene-based understanding of adaptation reflects several erroneous assumptions regarding individual development. First, Pittendrigh preferred to explain adaptation$_2$ through the historical process of natural selection rather than the ontogenetic process of
somatic adaptation, primarily because the latter was not thought to alter genotypes (thus, it could not influence subsequent generations or evolution).
This rejection of somatic adaptation makes sense only if genes unilaterally
determine development, and only if genes alone provide transgenerational
information. Thus, Pittendrigh treats genotypes as a "phylogenetic memory
store" (p. 397) or inherited message that "specifies the constructional steps
that comprise development" (p. 395), wherein novelty is gained by "mutation and recombination" (p. 397). We now know, however, that a host of
temporally dependent resources, some internal and some external to the organism, are required for species-typical development. Genes cannot be
characterized as occupying a privileged position in the development of an

organism, because they are themselves regulated participants in the developmental process. For example, patterns of gene expression in brain areas associated with maternal behaviors in rats depend on pup-derived sensory stimulation (Fleming, Suh, Korsmit, & Rusak, 1994). Moreover, it is well known that gene expression depends on a host of epigenetic factors that persist across generations (i.e., cytoplasmic chemical gradients, DNA methylation patterns), so that changes in either genetic or extragenetic influences can lead to enduring transgenerational change in the phenotype (Jablonka & Lamb, 1995). EP has not addressed these types of findings in large part because its proponents continue to hold that genes are encapsulated units of heredity, insensitive to outside influence, and provide prespecified programs for developmental outcomes.

A second assumption of EP that we question involves the role of natural selection in the origins of adaptations. Explaining ontogenetic outcomes by appealing to the creative or designing role of natural selection is inherently misleading, because natural selection is not a creative force capable of producing phenotypes. Natural selection speaks only to the persistence or maintenance of adaptations in populations, not their origins in individuals. After all, as Gottlieb (2002) recently put it, to select for a given trait requires that the particular trait has *already* emerged in the development of individuals. Contrary to neo-Darwinian philosophy, evolutionary change at the levels of behavioral and morphological development can occur *prior to* changes in gene frequencies (Gottlieb, 2002). Shifts in behavior brought about by both changes in the environment and the resulting changes in the activity of the organism can lead to new relationships between elements of the developmental system within and across generations, which ultimately can lead to variations in anatomy, morphology, or physiology, independent of enduring changes in gene frequencies. Replacing the notion of genetic determination of adaptations with an appreciation of developmental dynamics widens our sense of developmental and evolutionary resources, and highlights the fact that the origins and maintenance of adaptations (i.e., the mutual fit or correspondence between an organism and its environment) must be credited to the probabilistic dynamics of developmental systems.

THE DIVIDENDS OF A DEVELOPMENTAL
VIEW OF ADAPTATION

Over the last century, evolutionists became less interested in understanding how whole, integrated organisms develop and turned their attention instead to the evolution of isolated characters or traits and the internal factors thought to determine them. Analyzing traits (particularly behavior) in this fragmented way has been a mainstay of modern EP since its inception. Decomposing the organism into a collection of parts that are discussed without reference to the whole organism as an adapted *and* adapting unit that is situated in a specific developmental milieu is bound to fail, however, because it is whole organisms that survive and reproduce (Robert, 2004). Modern EP assumes that behavior not only can come prepackaged in discrete problem-solving units (e.g., a "cheater detection" module), but also that the behaviors themselves are divorced from the contexts in which they occur, thereby allowing behavioral *processes* to get reified into properties (cognitive modules) of individuals. This problem is exacerbated when these properties are then reduced to genetic units (Rose, 1998).

Using the genetically based definition of adaptation promoted by Pittendrigh (1967), evolutionary psychologists attempt to identify adaptations (i.e., psychological mechanisms shaped by natural selection) thought to control human behavior and cognition. According to some accounts of EP, each person enters the world with a battery (hundreds or perhaps even thousands) of these specialized psychological adaptations (or "cognitive modules"), which are thought to come equipped with innate knowledge and procedures to process specific information and generate adaptive (or what once were adaptive) responses. From this view, our current modular architecture was designed by natural selection as our distant ancestors faced specific environmental challenges during the Pleistocene. Because of their evolutionary history, modules are believed to come fully assembled without (and prior to) any direct experience in the problem domain for which the module is specialized.

However, development (and evolution) simply does not work this way. It is biologically implausible to assume that cognitive modules can emerge de novo, developing and operating independently of experiential input. As with any other phenotypic feature, cognitive modules must differentiate from earlier forms and then get reintegrated into the living organism–environment system as a whole. Both differentiation and reintegration of cognitive modularity depend on a particular person's previous and ongoing experiences in a structured ecology. Social factors, for example, are not mere "triggers" that initiate genetic programs or latent modularized routines, as had been argued by several evolutionary psychologists. Instead, stability and change in social relationships play a formative role in any modular development and function. The types and number of modularized cognitive components (if any) are a consequence of a particular individual developing in particular environments, which for humans includes extensive and continuous cooperation, coordination, and competition with other conspecifics throughout the life cycle. It is difficult to imagine how a "cheater detection" module, "incest avoidance" module, or any other module that involves social interaction can get assembled and operate without regard to the particular social experiences had by or denied to any given individual. We simply know too much about individual development and behavior to support this type of view. Organisms do not come into the world with ready-made response systems. Rather, behavior emerges and is maintained or transformed across individual development through the transactions of inner and outer events and conditions occurring over the course of the organism's activity and experience. EP would gain much from focusing on the processes (including transgenerational processes) involved in modularization in all its complexity, rather than assuming that each module is fully represented in advance of its own development. Simply put, all traits and characters of organisms are constructed during development, whether or not they have an evolutionary history. There is no difference in kind.

If one must hold on to a division between nature and nurture, nature can no longer be identified with reliably present internal structures, and nurture, with everything else that interacts with these stable structures. Instead, nature and nurture must be stated in the language of dynamic processes, wherein nature (an individual's form and behaviors at a given time) emerges out of the process of nurture that involves epigenetic interactions among internal and external developmental resources over the course of development (Oyama, 2000).

REFERENCES

Buss, D. M., Haselton, M. G., Shackleford, T. K., Bleski, A. L., & Wakefield, J. C. (1998). Adaptations, exaptations, and spandrels. *American Psychologist, 53,* 533–548.

Fleming, A. S., Suh, E. J., Korsmit, M., & Rusak, B. (1994). Activation of Fos-like immunoreactivity in the medial preoptic area and limbic structures by maternal and social interactions in rats. *Behavioral Neuroscience, 108,* 724–734.

Gottlieb, G. (2002). Developmental–behavioral initiation of evolutionary change. *Psychological Review, 109,* 211–218.

Jablonka, E., & Lamb, M. J. (1995). *Epigenetic inheritance and evolution.* New York: Oxford University Press.

Lickliter, R. L., & Honeycutt, H. (2003). Developmental dynamics: Toward a biologically plausible evolutionary psychology. *Psychological Bulletin, 129,* 819–835.

Mayr, E. (1988). *Toward a new philosophy of biology: Observations of an evolutionist.* Cambridge, MA: Harvard University Press.

Oyama, S. (2000). *Evolution's eye.* Durham, NC: Duke University Press.

Pittendrigh, C. S. (1967). Adaptation, natural selection, and behavior. In A. Roe & G. G. Simpson (Eds.), *Behavior and evolution.* New Haven, CT: Yale University Press.

Robert, J. S. (2004). *Embryology, epigenesis, and evolution: Taking development seriously.* Cambridge, UK: Cambridge University Press.

Rose, S. (1998). *Lifelines: Biology beyond determinism.* New York: Oxford University Press.

ఞ 18

An Alternative
Evolutionary Psychology?

KIM STERELNY

WHAT IS DEVELOPMENTAL SYSTEMS THEORY?

Developmental systems theory (DST) is an alternative view of evolution
and evolutionary theory. I begin with a brief introduction to the central
ideas of DST, then explore some of the consequences of these ideas for our
view of human cognitive evolution. Developmental systems theorists offer
an alternative to both the neo-Darwinian synthesis and the contemporary,
gene–selectionist alternative to that synthesis. In doing so, they developed a
package of ideas about development, evolution, and the interaction of those
processes. First is *inheritance*. One central element of DST is an extended
view of inheritance. The flow of genes from parent to offspring is by no
means the only or even the most fundamental cause of cross-generational
parent–offspring similarities. Organisms inherit a matrix of interacting resources that contribute to generation-by-generation similarity. This matrix
includes not only genes but also cellular structures that modulate and control their expression; scaffolded and protected developmental environments
(e.g., nests and burrows); sometimes symbiotic microorganisms; and/or
culturally transmitted information. This view is radically at odds with
much contemporary thought, which is often depicted by the Weismannian

diagram in Figure 18.1 (see, e.g., Maynard Smith, 1975/1993). Genes both generate the phenotype of one generation and flow to the next. There is no evolutionarily consequential causal influence of N generation phenotypes on generation N + 1.

Of course, parents have causal impacts on the phenotypes of their offspring. But according to received wisdom, those influences do not accumulate into evolutionary changes across the generations. They do not transmit or sustain heritable variation in similarity. However, defenders of DST point to a wide range of cross-generational causal influences that sustain intergenerational similarity (for a review, see Jablonka & Lamb, 2005).

A Master Molecule?

Developmental systems theorists decenter the role of genes in development, not just inheritance. They do not think of genes as orchestrating development. Rather, the genes an organism inherits are one element of the developmental matrix whose interaction over time produces an organism. Every view of development is moderately interactionist: Every theory recognizes that genetic and environmental contributions are necessary for the development of any trait. But DST is radically interactionist. Its defenders do not think phenotypic traits can be productively split into two kinds, namely, those whose development is under the control of internal resources, and those whose development is under the control of environmental factors (Gray, 2001; Griffiths & Gray, 2004).

Niche Construction

DST emphasizes the active role of the organism in organism–environment interactions. Selection is an important force in evolution, one that results in

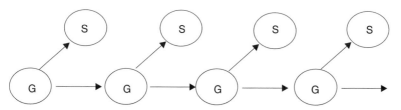

FIGURE 18.1. On the Weismannian view of inheritance, genetic information plays two roles: in constructing the phenotype (or soma[S]), and flowing to the next generation. In contrast, the phenotype of one generation has no selectable effect on the phenotype of the next generation.

lineages changing in important ways over time. But it is often wrong to think of lineages as passively accommodating to the demands of their environments. Evolving lineages often change their selective environment as they respond to selection. Termites, for example, do not merely *adapt to* their environment; they adapt their environment. Organisms, in part, construct their own niches (Lewontin, 1982; Odling-Smee, Laland, & Feldman, 2003).

Thus, developmental systems theorists think that (1) genes are just one element of inherited developmental resources; (2) they are but one critical element in the developmental matrix responsible for ontogeny; and (3) organisms in part construct their world, as well as adapt to it. That being said, a caution is in order. The defenders of DST are not a tightly integrated cadre, but rather a loose and evolving alliance from developmental psychology, developmental biology, evolutionary theory, and philosophy of biology—an alliance whose members only partially agree. Richard Lewontin, for example, would concur with (2) and (3), but perhaps not (1). DST is often dated from Lehrman's famous critique (1953) of Konrad Lorenz, which is radically interactionist, denying a principled distinction between internally driven and externally driven developmental sequences. The nearest thing the defenders of DST have to a manifesto is an edited collection, and even that contains plenty of disagreement (Oyama, Griffiths, & Gray, 2001).

DST AND HUMAN EVOLUTION

Arguably, DST is more plausible as a view of the evolutionary mechanisms that explain human evolution than as a general theory of evolutionary biology. Genetic inheritance is evolutionarily fundamental, even if it is not the only mechanism responsible for parent–offspring similarity. The gene centrism of standard evolutionary theory reflects a deep and important truth about evolution (Sterelny, 2004). But even the most enthusiastic gene centrist believes that cultural inheritance has been important in human evolution (Dawkins, 2003). Moreover, humans have surely changed their environments as much as they have accommodated to them. Think of the ways in which the invention of fire and cooking, shelters and clothes, tools and weapons, language, and agriculture and husbandry have modified the selective forces acting on human populations. Human evolutionary response is a response to a world we have partly created. Finally, the long and unproductive history of nature–nurture disputes suggests that there is something seriously wrong with the distinction between internally and environmentally dependent cognitive capacities (Bateson & Martin, 1999).

AGENT AND ENVIRONMENT

The evolutionary psychology of Barkow, Cosmides, and Tooby's celebrated collection (1992) is, as the title indicates, unashamedly adaptationist. Modular nativists expect the most central features of human cognitive organization to be adaptations, cognitive specializations built by natural selection for specific purposes (Barkow et al., 1992). But it is not just adaptationist. Their picture presupposes that selection shapes organisms to fit their niche. The relation between lineage and environment is *asymmetric*. This is a deeply implausible view of the relation between humans and our environments. We modify and reconstruct our world; each human generation inherits an environment that its predecessors have changed, and they often leave to their descendants a world that they have further changed. Sustained foraging, for example, depletes target species, leading to selection to extend the range of resources exploited and to harvest preferred prey species more efficiently. These foraging changes have social consequences for specialization and the division of labor. There are signals of such feedback loops in the paleoanthropological record (McBrearty & Brooks, 2000).

The active, world-transforming relation between humans and their environments has profound consequences for the types of adaptations we can expect to find in the human mind. The Cosmides–Pinker–Tooby picture presupposes that human selective environments have been stable. They have often written of the adaptation of our minds to an environment of Pleistocene foraging. Selection can build an innately structured module, wiring in much of the information an agent will need, only if environmental domains are stable. Even setting aside human influences on the environment, this assumption is questionable. Forager lifestyles vary enormously. The challenges facing Inuit seal hunters are very different from those of tribes in central Australia. Humans are geographically widespread, and have been so for a long time. Moreover, we evolved in a period of increasing climatic instability (Potts, 1996). Human niche construction increases both the instability and diversity of human environments. It leads to variation in physical, biological, and social environments. The social challenges in a hierarchical social world with stratification and a division of labor are very different from those in smaller, more egalitarian societies. Human minds are selected for adaptive responses to unpredictable, heterogeneous environments rather than the environments of a typical Pleistocene forager.

COGNITION, CULTURE, AND INHERITANCE

Language, culture, and cultural learning are central to the DST view of human cognitive evolution, for cultural transmission is an enormously important inheritance mechanism, one that accelerates both adaptation and diversification. It is less central to modular nativist evolutionary psychologists, especially those who accept an "evoked culture" model of the association between cognition and culture (Tooby & Cosmides, 1992, p. 116). For modular nativists, language is a template: It is a paradigm of a competence that is crucial, universal, and informationally demanding. Steven Pinker generalizes the case for a modular and nativist view of language to many other human competences. There is something correct about thinking of language as typical of human competences. Humans are "informavores." One achievement of cognitive psychology has been to show that ordinary human competences depend on our access to, and use of, significant amounts of information. How do we access the information we need? In stable environments, there is selection to build that information into our genome, avoiding the costs and risks of learning. Thus, there is something wrong with using language as a template for other competences, too. The fundamental structural features of language may be persistent enough for selection to have largely decoupled language acquisition from experience. I have just sketched the DST case for believing that, in this respect, language is atypical. In environments that change over a few generations, selection favors social learning. Parental information will not be out of date, so the costs of trial-and-error learning can be avoided. Many aspects of human environments do change at rates that should select for social learning, thus setting up a feedback loop, for accurate social learning has enabled humans to accumulate cognitive capital. The information and skill base of generation N is transmitted accurately enough to generation $N + 1$ for it to be available for further improvement and transmission. Ramping up the human skill base should also increase human capacities to change their environments. The effects of social learning select for enhanced social learning (Sterelny, 2003; Tomasello, 1999). It is no surprise, then, that members of generation $N + 1$ resemble members of generation N in part because of the culturally mediated flow of information from N to $N + 1$ (see Richerson & Boyd, 2005; Shennan, 2002).

NATIVISM

Defenders of DST are profoundly sceptical of nativist views of the mind. In part, this scepticism is empirical. They think nativist views of mind and behavior exaggerate the extent to which development is buffered against variation in environmental inputs. They are fond of citing studies that show subtle and unexpected environmental effects (e.g., the effects of prenatal experience and practice; Gottlieb, 1997). But it is also theoretical. Defenders of DST argue that the very concept of innateness is confused. It lumps together species typicality, adaptation, and developmental canalization in various forms. It is reasonable to ask whether the acquisition of theory of mind competence depends on learning. But if it does not, it does not thereby follow that it is an adaptation, buffered against environmental variation, genetically caused, and species-typical. The extent to which these characteristics travel together is an open and important empirical question, a fact that is obscured by using one construct for all these characteristics (Mameli & Bateson, 2006). Moreover, nativism often generates the illusion of an explanation where none really exists. Suppose that we show that the development of a trait is robust; its developmental trajectory is insensitive to variation in experience. Suppose it turned out that our capacity to recognize and respond to the attentional focus of other agents was robust in this way. That discovery would not in itself *explain* the development of joint attention. Informational metaphors in developmental psychology obscure this fact. Talk of human genomes as programs that direct the development of mind-reading capacities, or as coding information about the minds of other agents, can make it seem that one has an explanation of the development of our mind-reading abilities. Without an account of the nature of information and how it is used, that appearance is an illusion. Yet there is no account of how genes carry semantic information, or how semantic information is used in development (Griffiths, 2001).

CONCLUSION

Humans evolved in a world that was variable within and across time. Our lives depended on cognitively demanding interactions with our social, physical, and biological environments. Moreover, many human tasks are *interface tasks*. Collaborative hunting, for example, involves action that is simultaneously sensitive to its social, physical, and biological circumstances. Thus, humans have been selected for adaptive plasticity. But adaptive plasticity is not enough: Evolutionary psychologists have been correct to point to the developmental robustness of central human competences. Adaptive plasticity is supported by niche construction. We have responded to the informational demands imposed by human lifeways by learning to modify our environments informationally, as well as physically. We are both informational and physical engineers. Human developmental environments are informationally engineered to make the transmission of situation-specific skills robust and accurate. We did not need to wait for gene technology to engineer our own inheritance systems; it is as ancient as teaching (Sterelny, 2003, in press).

REFERENCES

Barkow, J. H., Cosmides, L., & Tooby, J. (Eds.). (1992). *The adapted mind: Evolutionary psychology and the generation of culture.* Oxford UK: Oxford University Press.

Bateson, P. P. G., & Martin, P. (1999). *Design for a life: How behavior and personality develop.* London: Jonathan Cape.

Dawkins, R. (2003). *A devil's chaplain: Reflections on hope, lies, science, and love.* Boston: Houghton Mifflin.

Gottlieb, G. (1997). *Synthesizing nature–nurture: Prenatal roots of instinctive behavior.* Hillsdale, NJ: Erlbaum.

Gray, R. (2001). Selfish genes or developmental systems?: Evolution without replicators and vehicles. In R. Singh, K. Krimbas, D. Paul, & J. Beatty (Eds.), *Thinking about evolution: Historical, philosophical and political perspectives: Festschrift for Richard Lewontin* (pp. 184–207). Cambridge, UK: Cambridge University Press.

Griffiths, P. E. (2001). Genetic information: A metaphor in search of a theory. *Philosophy of Science, 68*(3), 394–412.

Griffiths, P. E., & Gray, R. D. (2004). The developmental systems perspective: Organism–environment systems as units of evolution. In M. Pigliucci & K. Preston. *The evolutionary biology of complex phenotypes* (419–431). Chicago, University of Chicago Press.

Jablonka, E., & Lamb, M. (2005). *Evolution in four dimensions.* Cambridge, MA: MIT Press.

Lehrman, D. S. (1953). Critique of Konrad Lorenz's theory of instinctive behaviour. *Quarterly Review of Biology, 28*(4), 337–363.

Lewontin, R. C. (1982). Organism and environment. In H. C. Plotkin (ED.), *Learning, development and culture* (pp. 151–170). New York: Wiley.

Mameli, M., & Bateson, P. (2006). Innateness and the sciences. *Biology and Philosophy, 21*(2), 155–188.

Maynard Smith, J. (1993). *The theory of evolution.* Cambridge, UK: Cambridge University Press. (Original work published 1975)

McBrearty, S., & Brooks, A. (2000). The revolution that wasn't: A new interpretation of the origin of modern human behavior. *Journal of Human Evolution*, *39*(5), 453–563.

Odling-Smee, F. J., Laland, K. N., & Feldman, M. W. (2003). *Niche construction: The neglected process in evolution*. Princeton, NJ: Princeton University Press.

Oyama, S., Griffiths, P. E., & Gray, R. D., (Eds.). (2001). *Cycles of contingency: Developmental systems and evolution*. Cambridge, MA: MIT Press.

Pinker, S. (1997). *How the mind works*. New York: Norton.

Potts, R. (1996). *Humanity's descent: The consequences of ecological instability*. New York: Avon.

Richerson, P. J., & Boyd, R. (2005). *Not by genes alone: How culture transformed human evolution*. Chicago: University of Chicago Press.

Shennan, S. (2002). *Genes, memes and human history: Darwinian archaeology and cultural evolution*. London: Thames & Hudson.

Sterelny, K. (2003). *Thought in a hostile world*. New York: Blackwell.

Sterelny, K. (2004). Symbiosis, evolvability and modularity. In G. Schlosser & G. Wagner (Eds.), *Modularity in development and evolution* (pp. 490–516). Chicago: University of Chicago Press.

Sterelny, K. (in press). Cognitive load and human decision, or, three ways of rolling the rock up hill. In S. Stich, S. Laurence, & P. Carruthers (Eds.), *The innate mind: Culture and cognition*. Cambridge, UK: Cambridge University Press.

Tomasello, M. (1999). The human adaptation for culture. *Annual Review of Anthropology*, *28*, 509–529.

Tooby, J., & Cosmides, L. (1992). The psychological foundations of culture. In J. H. Barkow, L. Cosmides, & J. Tooby (Eds.), *The adapted mind: Evolutionary psychology and the generation of culture* (pp. 19–136). New York: Oxford University Press.

❧ 19

Development as the Target of Evolution

A Computational Approach to Developmental Systems

H. CLARK BARRETT

In evolutionary psychology, it is possible to distinguish between laws, things that are true everywhere and at all times, and heuristics, principles that are useful in the generation of hypotheses but are not a priori true. An example of a heuristic is that natural selection tends to cause the spread of mutations that increase the lifetime reproductive success of individuals. This is usually true, but it can be violated, as Hamilton showed. An example of a law is that natural selection occurs if, and only if, Darwin's three postulates are met, and it occurs inevitably in that case.

In the case of individual development, it is a law that only aspects of organisms that are heritable, and that influence the phenotype in ways that impact fitness, can be acted upon by natural selection. Many notions about what the role of genes must be in shaping these aspects of organisms, however, have only the status of heuristics. Rigorous definitions of the prerequisites for natural selection contain no reference to genes; they are formulated entirely in terms of the heritability of phenotypes (Endler, 1992). Genes play an important role in the generation of phenotypes and are an important mechanism of inheritance, but they are not the only one. Metaphorically speaking, natural selection only "sees" phenotypic outcomes. The multitude of causal factors involved in generating these outcomes are all possible candidates for the feedback loop of selection, one step of which can be represented as follows: distribution of phenotypes$_{time1}$ → differential fitness → distribution of phenotypes$_{time2}$.

Developmental systems theorists, and others interested in extragenetic factors in development, have emphasized this fact (Griffiths & Gray, 2001; Oyama, 2000; West-Eberhard, 2003). It is true, as they have stressed, that the target of natural selection is entire developmental systems: the entire array of processes and causal factors, including but not restricted to genes, that give rise to phenotypes. This insight has led to progress in areas such as gene–culture coevolution (Boyd & Richerson, 1985), niche construction (Laland, Odling-Smee, & Feldman, 2000), and extragenetic inheritance (Haig, 2002; Jablonka & Lamb, 1995). This insight can also be carried too far, however, as in the assertion that genes cannot "specify" phenotypic outcomes (Lickliter & Honeycutt, 2003). It is trivially true that phenotypic outcomes are contingent on many events and are therefore not causally predetermined in every detail. But if it were the case that genes could not specify phenotypic outcomes—in the limit, that they were random—then genetic evolution by natural selection could not occur at all. Darwin's postulates, which qualify as a bona fide law, guarantee that phenotypic outcomes *must* be specifiable, at least in a statistical sense, if natural selection is to occur. Confusing this statistical sense of "determination" with the rigid Laplacean notion of "determinism," absolute certainty of outcome, has been the cause of much unnecessary debate.

It is illogical to use the insight that natural selection acts on entire developmental systems to downplay the role of selection in shaping the phenotypes of organisms. As evolutionary psychologists, the converse should be our goal: To use this insight to understand better *how* natural selection shapes the phenotypic design of organisms. In this endeavor, it may be useful to begin by considering how we can use evolutionary laws to derive heuristics regarding how we might expect developmental processes to look.

RELIABLE DEVELOPMENT

Because it is the phenotypic endpoints (as well as midpoints) of development that contribute causally to selection, changes in developmental systems that produce fitness-enhancing changes in phenotypic outcomes tend to spread in populations. This means that natural selection shapes developmental systems so as to produce *reliably developing* outcomes given the statistical regularities that the population has experienced over the course of its evolution (weighted by the mass of the population that has been exposed to these regularities, their frequency of occurrence in time, their recency, etc.; Tooby & Cosmides, 1992). Reliably developing aspects of the phenotype often have the appearance of "innateness" in some respects. They are produced whenever the developing individual's environment sufficiently matches the ancestral one along relevant dimensions. For example, developmental schedules of some skills, such as the ability to distinguish between animates and inanimates, are relatively invariant across very different cultures and environments, suggesting that development is not "dose-dependent" along dimensions that vary between these populations (Barrett & Behne, 2005). However, this does not tell us what factors in the environment might contribute causally to development of the competence. Innateness in the folk sense of lack of environmental input is not mandated.

PROPER DEVELOPMENTAL TARGETS

Sperber (1994) distinguished between the proper domain of a computational device or system, which is the set of inputs that the system was designed by natural selection to process, and its actual domain, which is the set of inputs the system actually does process given its input criteria and the nature of the current environment. Whatever is available in the current environment that satisfies these criteria will be processed, whether evolutionarily novel or not. By analogy, one can speak of the proper developmental target of a developmental system: the set of reliably developing phenotypic outcomes that the system was designed, by natural selection, to produce (see Cosmides & Tooby, 2000, for a related discussion on the organizational mode and organizational domain of adaptations). For example, it is likely that natural selection has created a variety of developmental processes designed to produce fear of dangerous animals in the local environment (Barrett, 2005). This system could use environmental cues, such as size, force, and predatory movement cues, to narrow the fear response to appropriate targets. Based on these targets, a child might develop a fear of lions that, although not "innate" (lions per se are not prespecified as a target), is well within the proper range of developmental outcomes for the system. On the other hand, the same system might cause a child to acquire a fear of loud construction equipment. This would be an actual outcome of the developmental process, but not a proper one.

TYPE OUTCOMES AND TOKEN OUTCOMES

Fear of lions is an example of a developmental outcome that is a token of a more general type, fear of dangerous animals. In virtually all cases, the proper developmental target of a developmental system is a type of outcome that is more abstract than the actual, observed tokens, which contain a level of phenotypic detail that is not "specified" by the type. Consider, for example, the development of animal concepts. It is likely that humans, and many other animals, have been selected to develop individual concepts of classes or taxa of animals in the local environment, including dangerous predators and edible prey (e.g., Cheney & Seyfarth, 1990, on predator concepts in vervet monkeys). The developmental system dedicated to this in humans might cause an Inuit child in the Arctic to develop the concept PO- LAR BEAR given the relevant conditions. This is a token outcome of a more general type. A Shuar child in the Amazon basin, on the other hand, might develop the concept JAGUAR but never develop the concept POLAR BEAR. In each case, the conceptual structure contains details that are not specified by the system in any way (POLAR BEAR: white fur, able to swim; JAGUAR: ring- like spots, climbs trees). The type is always more abstract and under- specified than the tokens. Indeed, the system can produce token concepts that are entirely evolutionarily novel for humans (e.g., TYRANNOSAURUS REX; presumably, there was never selection on humans by dinosaurs).

The fact that the system is capable of producing an evolutionarily novel token of a *type* that is nevertheless the product of natural selection may in fact be more the norm than the exception in evolved developmental systems. This could help explain apparently evolutionarily novel skills such as playing chess or driving. We do not yet know what evolved competen- cies underlie these skills, so we cannot rule out that driving and chess may have components that are tokens of more general types of problem for which there are evolved solutions (e.g., object tracking, collision avoid- ance, strategic reasoning). In a sense, *every* problem that humans face is novel in its details. Every predator encounter, for example, is novel in an infinite number of ways. The question is whether it has features that can be mapped onto past situation types for which there are adaptations.

A COMPUTATIONAL APPROACH
TO EVOLVED DEVELOPMENTAL SYSTEMS

Cognitive scientists have identified three questions that one may ask about the design of an information-processing system:

What inputs does the system accept?

What are the operations that this system performs on the inputs?

What is the computational relation, or mapping function, between inputs and outputs (Tooby & Cosmides, 1992)?

Although such analyses have traditionally been applied to brain systems that are the end products of development, such as the visual system, it is possible to regard developmental systems as computational systems when they have been selected to produce outcomes of a particular type, even if the type is quite abstract (i.e., it has many open parameters). An early attempt at such an approach was Waddington's (1956) notion of an "epigenetic landscape," which points to how a formal computational approach to developmental systems might look. It would describe mapping functions between developmental circumstances and phenotypic outcomes. Proposing explicit hypotheses about such mapping functions could help to resolve long-standing controversies in the field over the roles of culture, environment, and individual experience in development by making testable predictions even without detailed knowledge of the underlying genetic system.

IMPLICATIONS FOR CURRENT DEBATES

Viewing developmental systems as the targets of selection is consistent with the evolutionary-psychological view that natural selection shapes the phenotypic design of organisms. It simply adds that selection does this by shaping the mechanisms that generate this design anew each generation during development, what Tooby, Cosmides, and Barrett (2003) call "design reincarnation" (see also Barrett, in press). This perspective casts doubt on certain traditional dichotomies and oppositions that are often used to call into question evolutionary-psychological interpretations of phenotypes. For example, although phenotypic variation between individuals across cultures or environments is often taken as de facto evidence against evolution playing a role in shaping that aspect of the phenotype, such variation does not by itself count as evidence for or against an evolutionary hypothesis. Instead, both the evolutionary and alternative hypotheses must specify the nature of variation that is expected, if any. We are in a position in which traditional notions of parsimony are questionable, and null hypothesis testing on the basis of these parsimony assumptions is weak (e.g., assume "learned" unless present in infancy; assume "not evolved" if culturally variable). A computational or design stance approach to developmental systems, one that asks what developmental outcomes the system is designed to produce and how, may help us move beyond the facile view of evolved structures as hardwired and inflexible, and more importantly, help us to understand better how human psychology actually works.

REFERENCES

Barrett, H. C. (2005). Adaptations to predators and prey. In D. M. Buss (Ed.), *The handbook of evolutionary psychology*. New York: Wiley.

Barrett, H. C. (in press). Modularity and design reincarnation. In P. Carruthers, S. Laurence, & S. Stich (Eds.), *The innate mind: Culture and cognition*. Oxford, UK: Oxford University Press.

Barrett, H. C., & Behne, T. (2005). Children's understanding of death as the cessation of agency: A test using sleep versus death. *Cognition, 96*, 93–108.

Boyd, R., & Richerson, P. (1985). *Culture and the evolutionary process*. Chicago: University of Chicago Press.

Cheney, D., & Seyfarth, R. (1990). *How monkeys see the world*. Chicago: University of Chicago Press.

Cosmides, L., & Tooby, J. (2000). Consider the source: The evolution of mechanisms for decoupling and metarepresentation. In D. Sperber (Ed.), *Metarepresentation* (pp. 53–115). New York: Oxford University Press.

Endler, J. A. (1992). Natural selection: Current usages. In E. F. Keller & E. A. Lloyd (Eds.), *Keywords in evolutionary biology*. Cambridge, MA: Harvard University Press.

Griffiths, P. E., & Gray, R. D. (2001). Darwinism and developmental systems. In S. Oyama, P. E. Griffiths, & R. D. Gray (Eds.), *Cycles of contingency: Developmental systems and evolution*. Cambridge, MA: MIT Press.

Haig, D. (2002). *Genomic imprinting and kinship*. Newark, NJ: Rutgers University Press.

Jablonka, E., & Lamb, M. J. (1995). *Epigenetic inheritance and evolution*. New York: Oxford University Press.

Laland, K. N., Odling-Smee, F. J., & Feldman, M. W. (2000). Niche construction, biological evolution, and cultural change. *Behavioral and Brain Sciences, 23*, 131–175.

Lickliter, R., & Honeycutt, H. (2003). Developmental dynamics: Toward a biologically plausible evolutionary psychology. *Psychological Bulletin, 129*, 819–835.

Oyama, S. (2000). *Evolution's eye*. Durham, NC: Duke University Press.

Sperber, D. (1994). The modularity of thought and the epidemiology of representations. In L. A. Hirschfeld & S. A. Gelman (Eds.), *Mapping the mind: Domain specificity in cognition and culture*. Cambridge, UK: Cambridge University Press.

Tooby, J., & Cosmides, L. (1992). The psychological foundations of culture. In J. H. Barkow, L. Cosmides, & J. Tooby (Eds.), *The adapted mind: Evolutionary psychology and the generation of culture* (pp. 19–136). New York: Oxford University Press.

Tooby, J., Cosmides, L., & Barrett, H. C. (2003). The second law of thermodynamics is the first law of psychology: Evolutionary developmental psychology and the theory of tandem, coordinated inheritances: Comment on Lickliter and Honeycutt. *Psychological Bulletin, 129*, 858–865.

Waddington, C. H. (1956). *Principles of embryology.* New York: Macmillan.

West-Eberhard, M.-J. (2003). *Developmental plasticity and evolution.* New York: Oxford University Press.

❧ 20

Evolutionary Psychology and Developmental Systems Theory

Debra Lieberman

One of the aims of evolutionary psychology and related fields is to map the developmental trajectory of our species-typical cognitive adaptations. Tools that evolutionary psychologists use to generate testable hypotheses and models of cognitive adaptations include consideration of the enduring selection pressures that played a causal role in shaping our cognitive circuitry. Selection pressures are statistically recurring features of the social, ecological, biological, or physical world that affect the probability of survival and reproduction, however distally (Tooby & Cosmides, 1992). Some selection pressures may be external to the organism (e.g., predators, pathogens, and members of the opposite sex), whereas other selection pressures may derive from the changes the organism itself makes in its environment (e.g., for a specialist, depletion of a particular food source creates the adaptive problem of discovering new sources of energy). Regardless of the selection pressure's origin, consideration of ancestral conditions and the factors that significantly and repeatedly affected the probability of survival and reproduction can often greatly aid investigations of (1) the design of our evolved psychological adaptations, and (2) the manner in which these adaptations develop.

Recently, scientists who adopt a developmental systems perspective have taken aim at evolutionary psychology, suggesting that evolutionary psychologists ignore development and are ignorant about the multiple causal factors guiding the development of an organism's phenotype (e.g., Lickliter & Honeycutt, 2003). Nothing could be further from the truth. Evolutionary psychologists not only consider multiple causal factors in the *evolution* of particular traits (e.g., see Cosmides & Tooby, 1981, for a discussion of how multiple cellular factors produced two different sized gametes) but also the interaction of multiple factors in the *development* of an organism's phenotype (e.g., see Bugental, 2003, for a discussion of the multiple social factors that influence the life experiences of children born with medical and physical disorders). A misunderstanding of the theoretical framework employed by evolutionary psychologists has led to inaccurate portrayals of evolutionary approaches to understanding psychological processes (see Lickliter & Honeycutt, 2003; Oyama, Griffiths, & Gray, 2001). What follows is a brief discussion of developmental systems theory (DST), what it has to offer an evolutionary psychological approach to understanding the mind, misconceptions that some developmental systems theorists hold regarding evolutionary psychology, and an example of how an evolutionary psychological approach does indeed consider development based on my own work on the development of sexual aversions between close genetic relatives.

WHAT IS DST?

DST is an approach to understanding the evolution and development of organisms. The main platform of DST challenges all dichotomous accounts of development and human behavior that attempt to partition the causal factors governing the production of an organism's phenotype into specific contributions made by, for example, the organism's genes and, separately, the organism's environment. Perhaps most objectionable to DST is the notion that development can be viewed as an unfolding of genetic programs against a passive environmental backdrop. Rather, proponents of DST argue that development occurs through the interplay of multiple causal factors, both internal and external to the organism. According to Oyama and colleagues (2001), "DST views both development and evolution as processes of construction and reconstruction in which heterogeneous resources are contingently but more or less reliably reassembled for each life cycle" (p. 1).

Evolutionary psychologists, perhaps along with most scientists today, would agree that all features of an organism are joint products of the organism's genes and environment. Partitioning the phenotypic effects due to one's genes and those due to the environment is not a goal of evolutionary psychology; behavioral genetics is a field that tries to identify the heritability of particular traits, that is, the proportion of variance *between individuals* that can be attributed to genetic differences. Furthermore, evolutionary psychologists would agree with developmental systems theorists' statement that development results from the interaction of multiple causal factors. But this statement does no work; that is, it does not explain *why* the "heterogeneous resources" are assembled in the particular ways they are versus the infinite number of other possible constructions and reconstructions. Evolutionary psychology offers a framework for answering this question by considering specific causal factors and how they impacted an organism's probability of survival and reproduction.

In contrast, proponents of DST do not privilege any single causal factor (especially a genetic one) in the explanation of the evolution or development of an organism's phenotype. Rather, their goal is to restore the balance by considering multiple causal factors (i.e., the heterogeneous resources) as potentially *equal* contributors to an organism's phenotype: "Not only is most standard interactionism shot through with asymmetries, but the notions of causal *symmetry*, or *parity*, which do have a democratic ring, inform the very concept of a developmental system" (Oyama, 2001, p. 183; original emphasis). In other words, DST starts with the assumption that no single factor or selection pressure (e.g., nuclear DNA, mitochondrial DNA, pathogen, predator) can provide a causal account of an organism's phenotype. As holistic and harmonious as this may sound, equality of causal factors is not something to be assumed; it is something to be demonstrated empirically. It is more rigorous to start with scientific first principles and build a model from which hypotheses may be generated, rather than design a model around an ideology and ignore (or privilege) certain causal accounts.

WHAT DOES DST ADD TO THE INVESTIGATION OF PSYCHOLOGICAL ADAPTATIONS?

The main contribution of DST is an assumption already present in current evolutionary approaches to studying human behavior: Genes are but one of a host of heterogeneous causal factors governing the evolution and development of organisms. Indeed, in evolutionary psychology, this is the starting point from which *hypotheses are generated* regarding the kinds of psychological adaptations expected to exist given the recurring features of the different environments our species encountered over many generations: biological (e.g., pathogens, non-nuclear DNA), physical (e.g., gravity, temperature, light), ecological (e.g., food sources, predators), and social (e.g., mates, mate competitors). Unlike DST, however, evolutionary psychology has a coherent and rigorous model guiding the investigation of (1) the causal forces responsible for the evolution of the multiple domains of human psychology, (2) the kinds of cognitive programs expected to have evolved as a result of the repeated interactions with our ancestral environments, and (3) how our species-typical psychological adaptations develop over the course of the life cycle. Additionally, understanding the mind in terms of the functions it evolved to perform also lends insight into the manner in which psychological systems can become impaired and, potentially, repaired.

In contrast to an evolutionary psychological framework, aside from the noncontroversial viewpoint that genetic and nongenetic factors contribute to development and have important consequences for the evolutionary trajectory of a species, DST makes no specific predictions and, consequently, is of little use scientifically. This has even been acknowledged by a few of DST's main proponents: "What we have come to term *developmental systems theory* is not a theory in the sense of a specific model that produces predictions to be tested against rival models. Instead, it is a general theoretical perspective on development, heredity and evolution" (Oyama et al., 2001, pp. 1–2, original emphasis). Unlike other metatheoretical models (e.g., evolutionary psychology), DST makes few, if any, specific predictions regarding the kinds of phenotypes, or design features, expected to exist. A theoretical model that makes no predictions has little value in the scientific arena.

DST'S OBJECTIONS TO EVOLUTIONARY PSYCHOLOGY

Despite the lack of a rigorous theoretical model from which hypotheses may be generated or a clear understanding of the principles of evolutionary psychology, a number of researchers within DST have taken aim at the theoretical framework of evolutionary psychology and, in the process, exposed their misunderstandings of the field (e.g., Lickliter & Honeycutt, 2003). Here I discuss two assumptions that proponents of DST mistakenly attribute to evolutionary psychology: (1) phenotypic traits or characters can be prespecified in advance of individual ontogeny, and (2) genes contain the program or instructions for the prespecification of phenotypic traits, and the environment (or experience) simply provides the trigger for these pro-grams to be expressed (Lickliter & Honeycutt, 2003). Put simply, these are misattributions that, once clarified, will allow for a renewed co-investigation of how complex psychological adaptations develop.

Traits Can Be Prespecified

According to proponents of DST, evolutionary psychologists believe "that the bodily forms, physiological processes, and behavioral dispositions of organisms can be specified in advance of the individual organism's develop-ment" (Lickliter & Honeycutt, 2003, p. 820); that is, evolutionary psychol-ogists believe in preformationism. What is missing, claim DST proponents, is an appreciation of how nongenetic factors, including aspects of the phys-ical world (e.g., temperature, light, pH, the social environment), may influ-ence the development of an organism. Again, nothing could be further from the truth. Evolutionary psychology maintains there is a reliably developing, species-typical body plan (or two body plans, if one considers the sexes separately) that occurs within a range of parameters (e.g., physical, biologi-cal, and social). Changing any single parameter may change the trait. But within a certain range of parameters, it is not shocking to specify that a de-veloping human embryo is likely (not guaranteed, due to factors such as genetic mutations) to possess a head, two arms, two legs, a visual system, systems for storing and releasing glucose, a system for detecting faces, and systems for avoiding sexual relations with close genetic relatives. Surely neither DST proponents nor evolutionary psychologists believe that a child placed on Mars would develop as he or she would have on Earth.

So if evolutionary psychologists appreciate that nongenetic factors in-fluence the development of an organism, what is the fuss about? One possi-bility is that DST misinterprets discussions of "reliably developing features" within evolutionary psychology as being synonymous with predetermin-istic explanations. According to Tooby, Cosmides, and Barrett (2003), de-velopmental systems theorists

> seem confused by the profound difference between the true claim that nor-mal members of a species embody predictable programs promoting reliable development, and the very distinct and false claims that following such de-velopmental programs to a predetermined outcome is inevitable, unmodi-fiable, specified solely "in the genes" without regard to environment, or even that such developmental programs are necessarily hard to modify. (pp. 860–861)

Though this misinterpretation has been spelled out clearly, proponents of DST continue to mischaracterize the main tenets of evolutionary psychology.

Genes as Instructions; Environments as Triggers

Another caricature drawn by proponents of DST is that evolutionary psychologists view genes purely as instructions and environments purely as triggers. For example, Lewontin (2001) suggests that scientists adopting an adaptationist framework see ontogeny "as an *unfolding* of a form, already latent in the genes, requiring only an original triggering at fertilization and an environment adequate to allow 'normal' development to continue" (p. 60, original emphasis). The correct view, Lewontin maintains, is that "genes, organisms, and environments are in reciprocal interaction with each other in such a way that each is both cause and effect in a quite complex, although perfectly analyzable, way" (p. 61). Indeed, evolutionary psychology approaches the web of interactions, whereby forms fit functions and multiple factors impinge on the development and survival of an organism, and provides a method for investigating why those forms exist and how they affected survival and reproduction. This method assumes that organisms not only inherit genetic material from past generations but also inherit sensitivities to particular aspects of past environments. Evolutionary psychologists do *not* maintain that the environment is passive; rather, features of the environment influence and are influenced by existing organisms. Furthermore, evolutionary psychologists do not subscribe to preformationism and similarly disagree that forms are "latent in the genes." It would seem, then, that what started as a misattribution has revealed common ground shared by evolutionary psychology and DST.

AN EXAMPLE OF EVOLUTIONARY DEVELOPMENTAL PSYCHOLOGY: DEVELOPMENT OF A SEXUAL AVERSION TOWARD CLOSE GENETIC RELATIVES

Contrary to DST proponents' claims that evolutionary psychology ignores development, much work in the field of evolutionary psychology has centered on the development of cognitive abilities (e.g., see Barrett, 2005; Duchaine, Yovel, Butterworth, & Nakayama, 2006; German & Leslie, 2001). An entire issue of the *Journal of Experimental Child Psychology* (July 2003, Vol. 85) was dedicated to research programs aimed at uncovering the developmental trajectory of a diverse set of psychological abilities using an evolutionary perspective. Topics included aggression, morality, theory of mind, and kin detection and inbreeding avoidance.

The domain of inbreeding avoidance provides a good illustration of how one can investigate an aspect of human psychology from an evolutionary perspective. Starting with a consideration of the selection pressures that existed in ancestral environments and how they impacted an individual's probability of survival and reproduction, it is possible to generate testable hypotheses regarding the kinds of psychological adaptations (i.e., functionally specialized neural circuitry) that evolved to respond to that particular aspect of the environment in a way that led, on average, to an increase in reproductive success.

There are sound biological reasons why psychological mechanisms designed to avoid mating with a close genetic relative are expected to exist. Throughout our species' evolutionary history, the selection pressures posed by deleterious recessive mutations (e.g., Bittles & Neel, 1994) and short-generation pathogens (e.g., Tooby, 1982) would have severely and negatively impacted the health and viability of offspring of individuals who were close genetic relatives. As a result, individuals who avoided mating with close genetic relatives, and instead, mated with someone who did not share an immediate common ancestor, would have enjoyed greater reproductive success. Indeed, evidence from human and nonhuman populations has illustrated the deleterious consequences of inbreeding (e.g., Hepper, 1991).

Given the existence of this adaptive problem (i.e., the avoidance of sexual relations with close genetic relatives), psychological mechanisms for inbreeding avoidance are expected to exist in those species, such as humans, in which sexually mature individuals regularly encountered one another over the life cycle. But how during development do we learn who counts as a close genetic relative? What systems govern the development of sexual aversions toward those categorized as close kin? Whereas DST would suggest that such systems developed through the equal contribution of multiple factors, genetic and nongenetic alike (which does no work and takes us right back where we started), one of the tools evolutionary psychologists use to answer these kinds of questions is to adopt an engineering perspective; that is, what would a well-designed system whose function was to avoid inbreeding look like?

One model of an inbreeding avoidance system has been proposed by Lieberman, Tooby, and Cosmides (2003). Accordingly, two components are required: (1) systems that estimate the probability of relatedness (i.e., kin detection mechanisms), and (2) systems that use estimates of relatedness to regulate sexual attraction and avoidance accordingly. The detection of kin is hypothesized to rely on evolutionarily and ecologically valid cues, that is, features of the world that correlated with genetic relatedness in ancestral environments. To the extent that different cues signaled the presence of different kinds of kin (e.g., mother, father, offspring, and sibling), different detection systems are expected to exist. For example, cues signaling that an individual is a mother (e.g., the female who breast-fed me) are likely to differ from the cues signaling that someone is a sibling (e.g., the individual with whom I coresided from early childhood); different kinds of information may have been relevant throughout development for identifying different types of family members. In addition to social cues, information derived from the expression of various underlying gene complexes, such as the major histocompatibility complex, may also aid in the detection of kin (Weisfeld, Czilli, Phillips, Gall, & Lichtman, 2003).

It is possible to investigate empirically the nature of the cues the mind uses to detect kin by quantitatively matching individual variation in the developmental parameters hypothesized to serve as cues to kinship with individual variation in opposition to incest. The logic underlying this method is that the absence of a cue, or set of cues, will result in lower sexual aversions, whereas the presence of a cue, or cues, will result in heightened sexual aversions. Progress has been made in understanding human kin detection systems due to the generation of models such as the one described previously that consider the kinds of environments that existed ancestrally, and the regularities evolution could have zeroed in on to shape systems that decreased the probability an individual mated with a close genetic relative.

CONCLUSION

In closing, despite some misunderstandings, developmental systems theorists and evolutionary psychologists are aligned in their goal to uncover our species-typical architecture and how it develops over the lifespan. The difference is the framework employed to guide such investigations. Whereas DST starts with the assumption that behavioral dispositions and physical traits are an emerging interaction between everything with equal importance, evolutionary psychologists start with specific selection pressures and hypotheses regarding the probable functional design of organisms confronted with those selection pressures. DST would be strengthened by developing a more rigorous program of research capable of generating specific, testable models and hypotheses. Ultimately, this will allow for more meaningful scientific debate and foster scientific progress.

REFERENCES

Barrett, H. C. (2005). Adaptations to predators and prey. In D. M. Buss (Ed.), *The handbook of evolutionary psychology* (pp. 200–223). New York: Wiley.

Bittles, A. H., & Neel, J. V. (1994). The costs of human inbreeding and their implications for variation at the DNA level. *Nature Genetics, 8,* 117–121.

Bugental, D. B. (2003). *Thriving in the face of childhood adversity.* Hove, UK: Psychology Press.

Cosmides, L., & Tooby, J. (1981). Cytoplasmic inheritance and intragenomic conflict. *Journal of Theoretical Biology, 89,* 83–129.

Duchaine, B., Yovel, G., Butterworth, E. J., & Nakayama, K. (2006). Prosopagnosia as an impairment to face-specific recognition mechanisms: Elimination of the alternative hypotheses in a developmental case. *Cognitive Neuropsychology, 23,* 714–747.

German, T. P., & Leslie, A. M. (2001). Children's inferences from knowing to pretending and believing. *British Journal of Developmental Psychology, 19,* 59–83.

Hepper, P. G. (1991). *Kin recognition.* Cambridge, UK: Cambridge University Press.

Lewontin, R. C. (2001). Gene, organism, and environment. In S. Oyama, P. E. Griffiths, & R. D. Gray (Eds.), *Cycles of contingency: Developmental systems and evolution* (pp. 59–66). Cambridge, MA: MIT Press.

Lickliter, R., & Honeycutt, H. (2003). Developmental dynamics: Toward a biologically plausible evolutionary psychology. *Psychological Bulletin, 129,* 819–835.

Lieberman, D., Tooby, J., & Cosmides, L. (2003). Does morality have a biological basis?: An empirical test of the factors governing moral sentiments regarding incest. *Proceedings of the Royal Society of London B, 270,* 819–826.

Oyama, S. (2001). Terms and tension: What do you do when all the good words are taken? In S. Oyama, P. E. Griffiths, & R. D. Gray (Eds.), *Cycles of contingency: Developmental systems and evolution* (pp. 177–193). Cambridge, MA: MIT Press.

Oyama, S., Griffiths, P. E., & Gray, R. D. (2001). Introduction: What is developmental systems theory? In S. Oyama, P. E. Griffiths, & R. D. Gray (Eds.), *Cycles of contingency: Developmental systems and evolution* (pp. 1–11). Cambridge, MA: MIT Press.

Tooby, J. (1982). Pathogens, polymorphism, and the evolution of sex. *Journal of Theoretical Biology, 97,* 557–576.

Tooby, J., & Cosmides, L. (1992). The psychological foundations of culture. In J. H. Barkow, L. Cosmides, & J. Tooby (Eds.), *The adapted mind: Evolutionary psychology and the generation of culture* (pp. 19–136). New York: Oxford University Press.

Tooby, J., Cosmides, L., & Barrett, H. C. (2003). The second law of thermodynamics is
    the first law of psychology: Evolutionary developmental psychology and the the-
    ory of tandem, coordinated inheritances: Comment on Lickliter and Honeycutt
    (2003). *Psychological Bulletin, 129,* 858–865.
Weisfeld, G. E., Czilli, T., Phillips, K. A., Gall, J. A., & Lichtman, C.M. (2003). Possible
    olfaction-based mechanisms in human kin recognition and inbreeding avoid-
    ance. *Journal of Experimental Child Psychology, 85,* 279–295.

21

The Importance of Developmental Biology to Evolutionary Biology and Vice Versa

RANDY THORNHILL

I emphasize two topics in this essay. One is some findings of developmental biology that are salient for the study of the evolution of human behavior (and of living organisms in general) but are not applied by researchers as widely as they should be. The second is that ontogenies of organisms are designed by Darwinian selection, a reality that some investigators in two approaches that strive to synthesize developmental biology and evolutionary biology—developmental systems theory (DST) and evolutionary developmental biology (EDB or "evo-devo")—do not appreciate fully as being necessary for such synthesis.

Lickliter and Honeycutt (2003), West-Eberhard (2003), and others have emphasized that the erroneous belief of alternative genetic versus environmental causes responsible for a phenotype's ontogeny and inheritance is widespread in various forms in the current literature of evolutionary biology. Inheritance is the transmission of a phenotype between generations, which requires the phenotype's ontogeny. A useful discussion of biology's concept of inheritance is provided by Flinn and Alexander (1982) in their critique of dual inheritance models of human cultural behavior. According to dual inheritance, cultural traits are transmitted by social learning mechanisms such as teaching, imitation, and cosocialization, but biological traits are transmitted by genes. As Flinn and Alexander point out, dual inheritance is anchored in the empirically falsified notion that genes and environment are alternative causes in development and inheritance, and in the related empirically false view that genetic causes—some would say, environmental causes—are so primary and powerful that they do not need the other causal category to create phenotypes.

Modern biology is very clear on why this duality in causation is nonsense. First, phenotypic fidelity across generations, regardless of whether the phenotypic trait is influenced causally by social learning (e.g., language type, form of marriage rule, pattern of nepotism, incest avoidance) or not (e.g., five-fingered hands) requires both the relevant, trait-specific genetic and environmental developmental causes repeating between generations. Second, because trait inheritance involves trait ontogeny, the two causal types are necessarily equally important. DST, then, is on target in criticizing the claim made by some researchers in EDB that genes have a privileged causal role in inheritance, or even that genes are the exclusive units of inheritance (see critique by Jablonka & Lamb, 2002, of Robert, Hall, & Olson, 2001).

Environmental ontogenetic causes are all the developmental causes other than the genes per se (i.e., other than the genome). Hence, ontogenetic environmental causes involve maternal effects, including those of the egg, which is the primary between-generation "bridging phenotype," to use West-Eberhard's (2003) term; paternal effects; effects of conspecifics other than parents; physiology and structure within cells and outside cells within the organism; physical features, such as climate; and heterospecifics. The relevance and timing of each of the environmental ontogenetic causes mentioned depend on the particular trait.

The terms "genetic" and "biological" are synonymous in the dual inheritance view criticized by Flinn and Alexander (1982). Actually, the study of genetic causes is merely one subfield of biology—genetics—not all that is biological. There is no scientific justification for using alternative causal terms such as "biological" or "genetic" versus "cultural" or "environmental" in discussions of ontogeny and inheritance. Similarly, there is no justification in giving genes or environment more power in ontogeny or inheritance, nor in claiming that one environmental cause or one genetic cause is more important in a phenotype's ontogeny and inheritance than another in the same or in the other general causal category. For example, in the ontogeny of a cultural behavior, conspecifics are a part of the causal environment but are of no more importance than any of the many other environmental and genetic causes involved. I believe that the continuing confusions about inheritance and ontogeny stem primarily from inadequate appreciation of the concept of causation in biology (see below).

Development frequently is characterized as resulting simply from an interaction of genetic and environmental causes. Ontogeny, however, is not this kind of interaction, because genetic and environmental causes do not interact in isolation. Their action always depends on a pre-existing phenotype, which itself is an ontogenetic product and player (West-Eberhard, 2003).

Each of the environmental and genetic causes of a trait is specific in its role in ontogeny as a result of a history of Darwinian selection favoring functional developmental traits, thereby producing developmental adaptations. Evolutionary biologists are correct in criticizing DST for not paying enough attention to the functional design of ontogeny (see Tooby, Cosmides, & Barrett, 2003). The same criticism can be directed at EDB, a diverse field, but one in which identifying deep genetic homologies in the Tree of Life is a major effort (Raff, 2000; Robert et al., 2001). The phylogenetic persistence of the genes that play a causal role in development is an important area of research. When a genetic homology is known fully, however, one must still ask why the associated phenotype persisted phylogenetically, a question that can be answered only by adaptationism (see my essay on reconstructing evolutionary history, Chapter 1, this volume).

In biology, heritability is a concept different from inheritance. Heritability is about *differences* among individuals within a population and identifies the degree to which genetic variation accounts for these differences. The empirical finding that some trait (e.g., eye color) has a significant heritability in humans means that differences in eye color among individuals reflect their genetic differences in part. Such a finding does not mean that an individual's eye color is not environmentally caused. This is an impossibility, because the individual's eye color, and every one of its other traits, is a product of ontogeny.

Lickliter and Honeycutt (2003) from the position of DST, and West-Eberhard (2003) from that of evolutionary biology, correctly point out that the component of evolutionary theory concerned with the generation of phenotypic variation, the raw material for evolution, is biased inaccurately in favor of genetic causation. Biologists often say that the evolution of a new character begins with the rise of a mutation that encodes it. This not only privileges genetic causation but also errs in its claim that a trait is encoded in the genes, a preformationist view. Actually, development creates all new phenotypic variants, including ones that provide a fitness advantage over pre-existing traits. Genetic variation may or may not initially underlie the relevant phenotypic variation. If not, frequently, genetic variation will soon accommodate the natural selection process, and evolution (change in allele frequencies) can occur (see West-Eberhard, 2003, for a discussion of genetic accommodation).

Lickliter and Honeycutt (2003), West-Eberhard (2003), and others have stressed that Darwinian selection acts on phenotypes and not, as many have claimed, on genes. The reason selection cannot act on genes is because genes alone give nothing to act upon: Genes per se cannot make a phenotype. The confused view that selection acts on genes perhaps arises from the error of equating selection and evolution. "Selection" is differential reproductive success of individuals due to their phenotypic trait differences, and its occurrence does not depend on heritability in the trait variation affecting fitness. Evolution involves changes in allele frequencies in a population, which can be caused by selection but is not selection itself. "Evolution" is defined typically by biologists as changes in trait frequencies and their associated allele frequencies. DST adds that the traits changing in frequency in evolution are developmental systems, phenotypes that show intergenerational fidelity due to inheritance. This is consistent with the broad view of evolution held by most biologists.

There is "causal democracy" in ontogenesis, to borrow the term Oyama (2000) used to emphasize the equal causal power between genetic and environmental causes. There is also causal democracy *within* each of these two causal types. This view is straightforward from the concept of causation in science.

DST's conception of causation is that of complex, nonadditive, dynamic interactions that are diffuse throughout the developmental system. This view is supported by the vast evidence for epigenesis but should not be taken to mean that a new concept of causation is necessary for the study of ontogeny. Lickliter and Honeycutt (2003) have proposed that a "relational conception of causation" may be required for ontogeny. Their notion is that development is so complicated that causation is elusive, even incomprehensible; hence, a new model is needed. However, although the ontogeny of each feature of a phenotype does indeed reside in relations among many components, each component is an appropriate target for causal investigation.

In practice across all sciences, "cause" means that without which an effect or phenomenon will not occur. In biology, a cause is always only a partial explanation; one that is necessary but not sufficient to create the trait or other phenomenon. To identify a cause of human language (e.g., a specific type of social learning, or the *FOXP2* gene) is to identify a causal necessity for language, but only one of many necessities. Any such identification does not say that any one cause is more important than any other cause; this would be a misunderstanding of causation. Gene knock-out studies that target specific genes and can lead to an absence of some phenotypic trait demonstrate the nature of genetic causation of the trait. Because the targeted gene is a partial cause, such studies actually knock out the whole epigenetic causal system that accounts for the phenotypic trait. This encompassing effect, however, in no way implies that the targeted gene is not causal in the ontogeny of the trait. That causes are partial allows the reductionistic scientific method to succeed in their discovery. The only scientifically justified holistic approach is not an alternative to the reductionism used in biology. Instead, appropriate reductionism/holism pursues many partial causes, both proximate and ultimate, of a feature of life.

The rejection of the distinction between proximate and ultimate causation is "a key basis for [DST] arguments against . . . most evolutionary psychologists" (Lickliter & Honeycutt, 2003, p. 969). Evolutionary psychologists, however, have emphasized that DST's failure to recognize this distinction and to understand that development is a proximate cause seriously brings into question the validity of DST (e.g., Buss & Reeve, 2003; Tooby et al., 2003). This disagreement between DST and evolutionary psychology is unfounded. The distinction between "proximate" and "ultimate" is useful because it is a meaningful carving of causal categories, which is important in reductionist analysis of phenotypes. "Proximate" refers to causes that act across the individual's lifetime, from conception to death, to produce its phenotypic features. Of course, all these causes are ontogenetic, but their discovery is promoted by carving them into categories: genetic, molecular, biochemical, physiological, hormonal, social learning, and so on. "Ultimate" refers to the two categories of causes that bring about their effects in evolutionary history: the phylogenetic origin of a phenotype by ontogenetic processes, and the phenotype's evolutionary maintenance after its origin. Thus, contrary to many discussions, development is a proximate *and* an ultimate cause of phenotypes; which one applies depends on one's timescale of reference.

Genetic causes of phenotypes also are both proximate and ultimate in the same way. The genetic mutations that causally contributed to the ontogeny of the first estrogen receptors (proteins) occurred about 450 million years ago (Thornton, Need, & Crews, 2003). These mutations were part of the evolutionary origin, hence an ultimate cause, of modern vertebrate estrogen receptors. The subsequent retention by natural selection of the receptors and their associated genes is an ultimate cause, too. When modern genes act in the ontogeny of the receptors of an extant vertebrate, their causation is proximate.

The term "ultimate" refers to causation that accounts for the existence of proximate causes. It does not mean causation that is more important than proximate causation. A complete understanding of any biological feature entails knowing all its proximate and ultimate causes, and each of its two ultimate causes, phylogenetic origin and evolutionary maintenance, are of equal importance for completely understanding its evolutionary history. Some DST and EDB researchers have not appreciated fully that to understand comprehensively the evolution of ontogenies requires adaptationism, with its focus on ultimate causes of trait maintenance in the Tree of Life. The adaptationist research program can separate developmental adaptations from developmental by-products, as well as discover the functional design of developmental adaptations and, hence, the ultimate selection causes of ontogenies (see my essay on reconstructing evolutionary history, Chapter 1, this volume).

ACKNOWLEDGMENT

Steve Gangestad and Jeff Simpson provided useful comments on the manuscript.

REFERENCES

Buss, D. M., & Reeve, H. K. (2003). Evolution psychology and developmental dynamics: Comment on Lickliter and Honeycutt (2003). *Psychological Bulletin, 129,* 848–853.

Flinn, M. V., & Alexander, R. D. (1982). Culture theory: The developing synthesis from biology. *Human Ecology, 10,* 382–400.

Jablonka, E., & Lamb, M. (2002). Creating bridges or rifts?: Developmental systems theory and evolutionary developmental biology. *BioEssays, 24,* 290–291.

Lickliter, R., & Honeycutt, H. (2003). Developmental dynamics and contemporary evolutionary psychology: Status quo or irreconcilable views?: Reply to Bjorklund (2003), Krebs (2003), Buss and Reeve (2003), Crawford (2003), and Tooby et al. (2003). *Psychological Bulletin, 129,* 866–972.

Oyama, S. (2000). Causal democracy and causal contributions in developmental systems theory. *Philosophy of Science, 67,* S332–S347.

Raff, R. A. (2000). Evo-devo: The evolution of a new discipline. *Nature Reviews: Genetics, 1,* 74–79.

Robert, J. S., Hall, B. K., & Olson, W. M. (2001). Bridging the gap between developmental systems theory and evolutionary developmental biology. *BioEssays, 23,* 954–962.

Thornton, J. W., Need, E., & Crews, D. (2003). Resurrecting the ancestral steroid receptor: Ancient origin of estrogen signaling. *Science, 301,* 1714–1717.

Tooby, J., Cosmides, L., & Barrett, H. C. (2003). The Second Law of Thermodynamics is the first law of psychology: Evolutionary developmental psychology and the theory of tandem, coordinated inheritance: Comment on Lickliter and Honeycutt (2003). *Psychological Bulletin, 129,* 858–865.

West-Eberhard, M. J. (2003). *Developmental plasticity and evolution.* New York: Oxford University Press.

The Role of Group Selection

❦ 22

The Role of Group Selection in Human Psychological Evolution

DAVID SLOAN WILSON

It is impossible to evaluate the role of group selection in human psychological evolution without taking the turbulent history of the subject into account. The theory of group selection begins with Darwin (1871), who realized that altruistic behaviors are selectively disadvantageous within groups and require a process of selection among groups to evolve. In the following famous passage from *The Descent of Man and Selection in Relation to Sex,* Darwin used group selection to explain the evolution of behaviors associated with human morality: "It must not be forgotten that although a high standard of morality gives but a slight or no advantage to each individual man and his children over other men of the same tribe, yet that an increase in the number of well-endowed men and advancement in the standard of morality will certainly give an immense advantage to one tribe over another" (p. 166).

Darwin's insight was shared by the first architects of population genetics theory, including Ronald Fisher, Sewall Wright, and J. B. S. Haldane (Sober & Wilson, 1998). Unfortunately, many other biologists naively assumed that adaptations can evolve "for the good of the group" without requiring special conditions. This position was widely criticized in the 1960s, especially by Williams in his book *Adaptation and Natural Selection*

(1966). Williams accepted multilevel selection as a theoretical framework, agreeing with Darwin, Fisher, Wright, and Haldane that group-level adaptations can evolve only by a process of group-level selection and are often opposed by selection among individuals within groups. Williams then made an additional claim that group selection can be ignored, because it is almost invariably weak compared to within-group selection. This additional claim turned multilevel selection into what became known as the *theory of individual selection.*

Williams and other critics were so successful that group selection became a heretical concept, as anyone who lived through the period can attest. All of the theories that became the foundation for the study of social behavior, including inclusive fitness theory, reciprocal altruism, game theory, and selfish gene theory, were developed as alternatives to group selection. It became almost mandatory for the authors of books and articles to assure their readers that group selection was not being invoked.

The rejection of group selection was especially problematic for the study of human evolution. Anyone who studies humans must acknowledge that we are a highly cooperative species, and that our cooperation extends beyond genetic relatives and narrow reciprocators. It is also inescapably true that human evolution has been influenced by interactions among groups, in addition to interactions within groups. How can these facts be reconciled with the claim that groups are not important units of selection?

The current literature is in complete disarray on this issue. Some authors still warn their readers about group selection, as if nothing has changed since the 1960s. Other authors regard group selection as an important force in human evolution, especially when it comes to cultural evolution. Still others avoid mentioning the term "group selection," as if it never existed in the history of evolutionary biology. There is a resolution to this lack of consensus, but it requires a "back to basics" approach that the field as a whole has been reluctant to undertake. The rest of this essay will show how Darwin's original insight was correct, and how more recent advances in knowledge can be better understood within the context of multilevel selection theory than as an alternative.

HOW TO DETERMINE LEVELS OF SELECTION

Multilevel selection theory is a stepwise procedure for calculating evolutionary change in a population that is subdivided into groups. The first step is to identify the groups of locally interacting individuals and other aspects of the population structure, such as how the groups are formed, dispersal among groups, and so on. The second step is to determine the direction and intensity of natural selection within single groups. In Darwin's passage about human morality, he conjectured that moral traits do not increase in frequency within single groups and might well decrease in frequency compared to the traits associated with immorality. The third step is to determine the direction and intensity of natural selection among groups in the total population. If some groups persist longer and produce more dispersers than other groups, then this will alter the frequency of alternative traits in the total population, as surely as evolutionary change within single groups. Darwin conjectured that groups of moral individuals contribute more to the total population than do groups of immoral individuals. The final outcome of evolution depends upon the relative strength of within- and between-group selection, similar to a final vector made up of two component vectors. Darwin conjectured that group selection was sufficiently strong to favor the traits associated with human morality, despite their selective neutrality or disadvantage within single groups. Subsequent theories of multilevel selection might seem complicated, because they are stated in mathematical form, but they all preserve the very simple logic of Darwin's passage, which is easy for anyone to understand.

WHY GROUP SELECTION WAS REJECTED IN THE 1960s

The rejection of group selection was based upon three arguments, like the legs of a stool. First, theoretical models available at the time made between-group selection appear weak compared to within-group selection. Second, there was no compelling empirical evidence in favor of group selection. Third, other theoretical frameworks, such as inclusive fitness theory, game theory, and selfish gene theory, seemed to offer more robust explanations of cooperation and altruism, without invoking group selection. These arguments appeared invincible at the time, but all three began to be questioned, even as early as the 1970s. When we examine their status in the 21st century, it becomes obvious that *the original consensus was in error,* however difficult it might be to acknowledge the fact in sociological terms.

THE THEORETICAL PLAUSIBILITY
OF GROUP SELECTION

I often encounter the skeptical attitude that theoretical models count for little in the absence of good, hard evidence, but a careful reading of the lit-

erature reveals that the 1960s consensus was based almost entirely on theoretical plausibility arguments. The selective advantage of selfishness within
groups just seemed more robust than the group-level advantages of altruism. It therefore meant something when group selection became more plausible on the basis of subsequent theoretical models. For example, all of the
early models assumed that altruistic and selfish behaviors are coded directly by altruistic and selfish genes, which causes phenotypic variation
within and among groups to become tightly coupled with genetic variation.
Evolutionary psychologists might verbally reject simplistic assumptions
about genetic determinism, but those very assumptions are built into the
theoretical models. As soon as we make the genotype–phenotype relationship
more complicated, via mechanisms such as individual phenotypic plasticity,
social norms reinforced by punishment, and social transmission processes,
between-group selection becomes a force to be reckoned with, even in large
groups of unrelated individuals (Richerson & Boyd, 2004; Wilson, 2004).
In general, group selection can no longer be rejected on the basis of its theoretical implausibility, especially in the case of human evolution.

THE EMPIRICAL EVIDENCE FOR GROUP SELECTION

The empirical evidence in favor of group selection might have been slim in
the 1960s, but the evidence against group selection was also slim. Williams
(1966) used the theoretical implausibility of group selection to argue that any
hypothesis framed in terms of individual selection—no matter how speculative—is more parsimonious and should therefore be preferred to a hypothesis
based on group selection. Arguments based on parsimony are weak at best
and become completely invalid when alternative hypotheses are equally plausible. Would any ecologist argue on the basis of parsimony that competition is
more important than predation? Both are plausible, and their relative importance must be determined empirically on a case-by-case basis. In just the same
way, the direction and strength of within- and between-group selection must be
determined on a case-by-case basis, if both are theoretically plausible.

The closest that Williams (1966) came to a rigorous empirical test was
for sex ratios, leading him to predict that female-biased sex ratios would
provide evidence for group selection. The subsequent discovery of many
examples of female-biased sex ratios led Williams (1992, p. 49) to accept
the evidence for group selection, stating that "I think it desirable . . . to realize that selection in female-biased Mendelian populations favors males,
and that it is only the selection among such groups that can favor the fe-

male bias." Williams also acknowledged the importance of group selection in disease evolution as part of his more general interest in Darwinian medicine (Williams & Nesse, 1991, p. 8), stating, "The evolutionary outcome will depend on the relative strengths of within-host and between-host competition in pathogen evolution." See Sober and Wilson (1998, Chapters 1–3) for other empirical examples of group selection and more detailed discussions of these examples.

Some of the best recent evidence for group selection comes from microbial organisms, in part because they are such elegant systems for ecological and evolutionary research spanning many generations. There is no doubt whatsoever that the problems of altruism and selfishness that Darwin addressed in his passage on human morality, and which have traditionally been studied in insects and social vertebrates, also exist in microbial organisms. Moreover, microbial evolution is undeniably influenced by between-group selection, in addition to within-group selection (e.g., Velicer, 2003). The claim that group selection is invariably weak is just plain false on the basis of empirical evidence, which requires an evaluation on a case-by-case basis.

ARE THE ALTERNATIVE THEORIES REALLY ALTERNATIVES?

No matter what they are called, all evolutionary models of social behavior share a certain number of core assumptions. All assume that social interactions take place within multiple groups, because this is a biological reality that cannot be ignored. All converge on the same definition of groups for any particular trait (e.g., sentinel behavior or resource utilization), or else the calculation of fitness will simply be incorrect. If social interactions take place in groups of $N = 10$, two-person game theory won't do. Once the existence of multiple groups is acknowledged and details of the population structure are determined on the basis of the biology of the situation, the basic logic of multilevel selection theory can be applied, no matter what the model is called. In virtually all cases, the traits regarded as altruistic or cooperative are selectively disadvantageous within groups and require between-group selection to evolve, exactly as Darwin conjectured in his passage about human morality. The main exception to this rule concerns models that result in multiple local equilibria, all of which are internally stable by definition. In this case, group selection is required to favor local equilibria that function best at the group level, which is sometimes called *equilibrium selection*.

The fact that all evolutionary models of social behavior are multigroup models that obey the simple logic of multilevel selection does not detract from their significance. The insights that we attribute to inclusive fitness theory, game theory, and other theoretical frameworks remain as important as ever but can be understood in terms of the parameters of multilevel selection theory (e.g., the balance between levels of selection), without requiring additional parameters. In addition, a single, unified conceptual framework reveals new possibilities, such as complex interactions leading to substantial phenotypic variation among large, randomly formed groups (Wilson, 2004).

MAJOR TRANSITIONS IN EVOLUTION

A major event in evolutionary theory occurred with the discovery that individual organisms are the social groups of past ages. Evolution proceeds not only by small mutational change but also by groups and symbiotic communities becoming so integrated that they become higher-level organisms in their own right. Despite multilevel selection theory's turbulent history, it is the accepted theoretical framework for studying major transitions. There is agreement that selection occurs within and among groups, that the balance between levels of selection can itself evolve, and that a major transition occurs when selection within groups is suppressed, enabling selection among groups to dominate the final vector of evolutionary change. Genetic and developmental phenomena such as chromosomes, the rules of meiosis, a single-cell stage of the life cycle, the early sequestration of the germ line, and programmed death of cell lineages are interpreted as mechanisms for stabilizing the organism and preventing it from becoming a mere group of evolving elements. The evolution of social insect colonies also falls within the paradigm, with genetic relatedness only one of several factors that can be understood in terms of multilevel selection without requiring additional parameters. As Wilson and Holldobler (2005, p. 13367) put it in a recent review: "Group selection is the strong binding force in eusocial evolution."

HUMAN EVOLUTION AS A MAJOR TRANSITION

The paradigm of major transitions did not emerge until the 1970s and didn't become generalized until the 1990s, with books such as *The Major Transitions of Evolution* (Maynard Smith & Szathmary, 1995). Even though these developments are very recent, it is becoming clear that human evolution falls within the paradigm. Human moral systems can be regarded as mechanisms that suppress selection within groups, enabling between-group selection to become the primarily evolutionary force, just like chromosomes and the rules of meiosis (Boehm, 1999). Our capacities for social transmission, language, and other forms of symbolic thought are fundamentally communal activities that required a shift in the balance between levels of selection before they could evolve. The human major transition was a rare event, but once established, it enabled our species to achieve worldwide ecological dominance. Wilson and Holldobler (2005, p. 13371) stress the parallels with social insect evolution as follows: "Rarity of occurrence and unusual pre-adaptations characterized the early species of *Homo* and were followed in a similar manner during the advancements of the ants and termites by the spectacular ecological success and preemptive exclusion of competing forms by *Homo sapiens.*"

One reason that group selection is an important force in human evolution is because cultural processes have a way of increasing phenotypic variation among groups and decreasing it within groups. If a new behavior arises by a genetic mutation, it remains at a low frequency within its group in the absence of clustering mechanisms such as associations among kin. If a new behavior arises by a cultural mutation, it can quickly become the most common behavior within the group. Evolutionary biologists who study cultural evolution are nearly unanimous about the importance of cultural group selection in human evolution (e.g., Richerson & Boyd, 2004).

ON THE NEED FOR A NEW CONSENSUS

Making a decision typically involves encouraging diversity at the beginning to evaluate alternatives, but then discouraging diversity toward the end to achieve closure and to act upon the final decision. It can be very difficult to revisit an important decision that has been made and acted upon, but that is precisely what needs to be done in the case of the 1960s consensus about group selection (Wilson, 2006). It might seem amazing that multilevel selection can be revived and even become the unifying theoretical framework for sociobiology, until we realize that Williams and others always accepted its basic logic. The passages I quoted earlier show how easily Williams himself reverted back to multilevel selection thinking, once he decided that group selection is a significant evolutionary force for specific traits such as sex ratio and disease virulence. Evolutionary psychologists need to make the same decision for the traits that they study. Darwin was essentially right, and multilevel selection provides a way to understand our groupish nature at face value.

REFERENCES

Boehm, C. (1999). *Hierarchy in the forest: Egalitarianism and the evolution of human altruism.* Cambridge, MA: Harvard University Press.

Darwin, C. (1871). *The descent of man and selection in relation to sex.* New York: Appleton.

Maynard Smith, J., & Szathmary, E. (1995). *The major transitions of evolution.* New York: Freeman.

Richerson, P. J., & Boyd, R. (2004). *Not by genes alone: How culture transformed human evolution.* Chicago: University of Chicago Press.

Sober, E., & Wilson, D. S. (1998). *Unto others: The evolution and psychology of unselfish behavior.* Cambridge, MA: Harvard University Press.

Velicer, G. J. (2003). Social strife in the microbial world. *Trends in Microbiology, 11,* 330–337.

Williams, G. C. (1966). *Adaptation and natural selection: A critique of some current evolutionary thought.* Princeton, NJ: Princeton University Press.

Williams, G. C., & Nesse, R. M. (1991). The dawn of Darwinian medicine. *Quarterly Review of Biology, 66,* 1–22.

Wilson, D. S. (2004). What is wrong with absolute individual fitness? *Trends in Ecology and Evolution, 19,* 245–248.

Wilson, D. S. (2006). Human groups as adaptive units: Toward a permanent concensus. In P. Carruthers, S. Laurence, & S. Stich (Eds.), *The innate mind: Culture and cognition.* Oxford, UK: Oxford University Press.

Wilson, E. O., & Holldobler, B. (2005). Eusociality: Origin and consequences. *Proceedings of the National Academy of Sciences of the United States of America, 102,* 13367–13371.

🖧 23

Group Selection:
A Tale of Two Controversies

ROBERT BOYD
PETER J. RICHERSON

During the question-and-answer session after a conference talk or department colloquium, someone often asks us about our position on group selection. Unlike most questions, this one often has the same tone that you hear in discussions of polarized political topics such as free trade, school vouchers, or intelligent design. It is as if the questioner supposes that group selection is something you must be for or against: Either you think that group selection leads to the evolution of altruistic behaviors that benefit whole populations, or you think only individual selection matters. Well, for better or worse, we don't think either of these things. In this essay, we argue that group selection does not usually lead to the evolution of traits that are good for populations or species if they are also costly to individuals. Nonetheless, group selection played an important role in the evolution of human psychology leading to the evolution of prosocial motives.

It is important be clear about what we mean by "group selection." The controversy began in the early 1960s, when V. C. Wynne-Edwards proposed that a number of interesting behaviors evolved in birds because they promoted group survival. Populations in which the behavior was common prospered, whereas those in which it was rare perished. Although casual group functionalism was common in those days, Wynne-Edwards was much clearer than his contemporaries that it was selection among groups that gave rise to such group-level adaptations. Wynne-Edwards's book generated a storm of controversy, and luminaries such as George Williams and John Maynard Smith penned critiques explaining why this mechanism, then called "group selection," could not work. The result was the beginning of an ongoing and highly successful revolution in our understanding of the evolution of animal behavior, a revolution that is rooted in careful thinking about the individual and nepotistic function of behaviors.

So far, so good. In the early 1970s, however, things got muddled when George Price outlined a powerful new mathematical formalism that describes natural selection operating in a series of nested levels: among genes within an individual, among individuals within groups, and among groups. While Price's multilevel selection approach and the older gene-centered approaches are mathematically equivalent, the multilevel approach has proven to be very useful for understanding many evolutionary problems. However, it has also led to confusion about what kinds of evolutionary processes should be *called* "group selection." Some people use "group selection" to mean the process that Wynne-Edwards originally envisioned—selection between large groups made up of mostly geneologically distantly related individuals. Others use "group selection" to refer to selection involving any kind of group in a multilevel selection analysis, even pairs of individuals interacting in something as simple as the hawk–dove game.

The real scientific question is: Can selection among large groups of distantly related individuals, sometimes labeled "interdemic group selection," lead to the evolution of group beneficial traits when it is opposed by individual selection? The answer to this question is fairly clear: Only when groups are very small or there is little gene flow between them. To see why, it is useful to introduce Price's formalism. In a population structured into groups, the change in frequency of a gene undergoing selection, Δp, is given by

$$\Delta p \; \alpha \; \underbrace{V_G \beta_G}_{\text{between groups}} \; + \; \underbrace{\overline{V_W \beta_W}}_{\text{within groups}}.$$

The first term gives the change due to selection between groups, and the second gives the change in frequency due to selection within groups. The β's reflect the effect of the behavior on the fitness of groups (β_G) and individuals (β_W). A behavior is beneficial to the group when it increases group fitness, or $\beta_G > 0$. If it is costly to the individual, $\beta_W < 0$. The V's are the variance in gene frequency between groups (V_G) and within groups (V_W). Population genetics theory tells us that when groups are large, and if there is even a modest amount of migration among groups, the variance between individuals will be much larger than the variance between groups (Rogers, 1990). Thus, unless selection within groups is much weaker than selection among groups ($\beta_G \gg \beta_W$), group selection cannot overcome opposing individual selection. Most people believe this means that group selection is never important in evolution.

However, they are wrong. Group selection can play a very important role in determining evolutionary outcomes when there are multiple, stable equilibria. Interestingly, this idea predates Wynne-Edwards and his critics. Beginning in the 1930s, the great population geneticist Sewall Wright outlined his "shifting balance" theory of evolution. Wright knew from his empirical work that interactions between genes often lead to evolutionary systems with multiple equilibria. The simplest case is underdominance at a single locus. Suppose that there are two alleles, A and B, and that the fitnesses of the three genotypes are $W_{AA} = 1$, $W_{AB} = 1 - s$, and $W_{BB} = 1 + t$. It is easy to see that populations in which either allele is common can resist invasion by the alternative allele. For example, if A is common, most of the A alleles are in AA homozygotes and thus have average fitness of 1, whereas most B alleles are in heterozygotes and have fitness $1 - s$. The same goes for a population in which B common. This means that if A is initially common, individual selection will never lead to the spread of the B allele, even though it leads to higher fitness.

However, group selection *can* lead to the spread of the B allele. Suppose that a large population is subdivided into a number of partially isolated groups linked by low rates of gene flow. In some demes, A is common; in others, B is common. Now, let us apply the Price equation to this population. Because one of the two alleles is common, V_W is small in all subpopulations. Because selection in different subpopulations pulls in opposite directions, the average value of β_W over all subpopulations also tends to be small. Thus, the within-group component of the Price equation is close to zero—selection within groups has little effect on the frequency of the two alleles.

Now consider the between-group term. As long as selection is strong compared to migration, there will be lots of variation among groups, because within-group selection is maintaining these differences. Thus, if the fact that the B allele has higher average fitness translates into between-group selection, this process will lead to the spread of that allele. This can happen in at least two different ways. Higher average fitness could lead to greater migration, and this in turn could lead to the spread of the B allele through differential proliferation, the basis of the third phase of Wright's shifting balance model (Boyd & Richerson, 2002; Gavrilets, 1995). Alternatively, B will spread if groups with higher average fitness have lower extinction rates and new groups are formed by the fissioning of existing ones (Boyd & Richerson, 1990).

We believe an analogous group selection process has played a crucial role in the evolution of human cooperation. Humans, even human foragers, cooperate to create group benefits. Warfare provides a good example. Historically, known hunter-gatherers organized raiding parties numbering 50 or 100 individuals (e.g., Kroeber, 1976). In these raiding parties, each individual risked life and limb for the benefit of the entire enterprise. Evolutionary thinkers typically explain such behavior as resulting from the "three R's": reputation, reciprocation, and retribution. If cowards and deserters are despised by others in their group and, as a consequence, suffer social costs—lose status, mating opportunities, the benefits of mutual aid when ill or injured—they may be motivated to fight, even if prosocial motivations are entirely absent from their psychology. However, this explanation is incomplete. The three R's can stabilize *any* behavior. If everybody agrees that individuals must do X and punish those who don't do X, then X will be evolutionarily stable as long as the costs of being punished exceed the costs of doing X. Reputation, reciprocity, and retribution are an essential part of the story, because they explain why cooperative behavior can persist. They are not the whole story, because they do not, by themselves, explain why cooperative behavior should be more common than any other behavior.

As far as we can see, the only answer on the table explaining why the three R's lead to cooperation in large groups is cultural group selection. As pointed out by Axelrod and Hamilton (1980), cooperation in very small groups can readily be explained by the combination of kin selection and reciprocal altruism, but all of the analyses done so far suggest that this is not true of larger groups (see Boyd & Richerson, 1988, 1992; Gardner & West, 2004; Panchanathan & Boyd, 2004). Within-group processes driven by the cultural analogue of genetic drift (see Young, 1998) do not systematically lead to group-beneficial behavior. By contrast, once cultural adaptation arises and is sufficiently powerful to maintain cultural differences between neighboring social groups, intergroup competition will lead to the spread of cultural norms that increase group success in such competition. These social norms will then be enforced by the three R's.

This argument suggests that the evolution of cooperative systems of norms is a side effect of rapid, cumulative cultural adaptation. Adaptation by cultural evolution brought humans big benefits, especially in the climatic chaos of the later Pleistocene. However, it also generated lots of variation between groups, and this in turn caused group selection to be a much more important force in human cultural evolution than it was in genetic evolution. The best evidence from archaeology suggests that humans first began to rely on cumulative cultural adaptations roughly a half a million years ago. If this inference is correct, it means that humans have been living in social environments shaped by cultural group selection for a long time. In such social environments, natural selection on genes and culture at the individual and kin-group levels should favor psychological mechanisms such as empathy, guilt, and shame, which make it more likely that individuals will behave prosocially and thereby avoid sanctions that result from violating group social norms. The coevolutionary response of our innate social instincts to the selection pressures of living in rule-bound, prosocial, tribal-scale communities substantially reshaped our social psychology (Richerson & Boyd, 2005).

REFERENCES

Axelrod, R., & Hamilton, W. D. (1980). The evolution of cooperation. *Science, 211,* 1390–1396.

Boyd, R., & Richerson, P. J. (1988). The evolution of reciprocity in sizable groups. *Journal of Theoretical Biology, 132,* 337–356.

Boyd, R., & Richerson, P. J. (1990). Group selection among alternative evolutionarily stable strategies. *Journal of Theoretical Biology, 145,* 331342.

Boyd, R., & Richerson, P. J. (1992). Punishment allows the evolution of cooperation (or anything else) in sizable groups. *Ethology and Sociobiology, 13,* 171–195.

Boyd, R., & Richerson, P. J. (2002). Group beneficial norms spread rapidly in a structured population. *Journal of Theoretical Biology, 215,* 287–296.

Gardner, A., & West, S. (2004) Cooperation and punishment, especially in humans. *American Naturalist, 164,* 753–764.

Gavrilets, S. (1995). On phase three of the shifting balance theory. *Evolution, 50,* 1034–1041.

Kroeber, A. L. (1976). *Handbook of the Indians of California.* New York: Dover.

Panchanathan, K., & Boyd, R. (2004). Indirect reciprocity can stabilize cooperation without the second-order free rider problem. *Nature, 432,* 499–502.

Rogers, A. R. (1990). Group selection by selective emigration: The effects of migration and kin structure, *American Naturalist, 135,* 398–413.

Richerson, P. J., & Boyd, R. (2005). *Not by genes alone: How culture transformed human evolution.* Chicago: University of Chicago Press.

Young, P. (1998). *Individual strategy and social structure.* Princeton, NJ: Princeton University Press.

🙿 24

On Detecting the Footprints
of Multilevel Selection in Humans

ROBERT KURZBAN
C. ATHENA AKTIPIS

ON THE EXISTENCE OF MULTILEVEL SELECTION

Everything else being equal, genes that cause a larger number of copies of themselves to come into existence relative to alternative genes on the same locus tend to be the ones that persist. This uncontroversial position lies at the heart of all coherent theories of evolution by natural selection, including theories of group selection or, as we refer to it here, multilevel selection (MLS). A common misconception in this debate is that MLS and individual or genic-level selection are rival theories (see Wilson, 1983). This could not be further from the truth. All sensible varieties of MLS consider the causal effect that a particular strand of DNA has on its own rate of replication, through either processes such as sexual reproduction, or processes by which the generation of copies of the gene is facilitated.

The logic behind MLS is identical to the logic surrounding kin selection theory and is based on the same mathematical foundations (Price, 1970). According to kin selection theory (Hamilton, 1964), genes can be selected (i.e., increase in frequency) if they have the effect of causing copies of themselves to replicate more successfully relative to an alternative gene at that locus. Similarly, MLS theory posits that genes can be selected (increase in frequency) if they cause copies of themselves to replicate more successfully than the relevant alternative genes (e.g., Sober & Wilson, 1998).

MULTILEVEL SELECTION
AND POPULATION STRUCTURE

This is not to say that MLS occurs under all conditions. For selection to act at the level of the group, certain conditions must be fulfilled, just as is the case with kin selection. Kin selection requires interactions among individuals in which there are sufficient opportunities for the delivery of benefits to those related by descent at a relatively low cost to the organism delivering the benefits (where costs and benefits are related in the way expressed by Hamilton's rule, $C < rB$). Hamilton's rule is derived from the likelihood that the gene coding for the benefit-delivering trait will be present in the relative (by descent) who is receiving the benefit. Similarly, MLS is, at its core, based on the likelihood that a gene coding for a benefit-delivering trait will be present in the individuals who are receiving that benefit, regardless of the relatedness of those individuals. This can occur when a population is subdivided into several groups, when there are sufficient between-group genetic differences, and when there are subsequent differences in survival and growth/reproduction of these groups. There must also be a moderate amount of migration, regrouping, or budding, so that the subgroups do not remain isolated (see Sober & Wilson, 1998).

As an example of such a population structure, consider the case of highly social and cooperative spiders, which have a highly skewed sex ratio (10:1 female to male). Large, inbreeding subpopulations of spiders send out colonies that go extinct with appreciable frequency. A gene that caused a spider in such a colony to produce male rather than female offspring would almost certainly be at a within-colony advantage. The persistence of the skewed sex ratio strongly implies countervailing selective forces that prevent this gene from spreading. As Avilés (1993, p. 340) puts it: "Social spiders are perhaps unusual in having attained a degree of population subdivision that, according to even the most conservative group selection models, would make their characterization in a group selection example hardly controversial."

THE FOOTPRINTS OF MULTILEVEL SELECTION

The process of MLS leaves footprints because the process works by virtue of the effects that genes have on the replication of other genes in the same group. This means that adaptations sculpted by MLS will have particular properties, allowing inferences to be drawn about their selective history. In similar fashion, sexual selection can be identified because it also leaves marks of its passing. As Miller (2000) has pointed out, sexually selected adaptations can be identified because they tend to be extreme or exaggerated, have no function outside their role in attracting mates, have high heritability, and tend to be unique as opposed to shared cross-specifically. Because sexually selected adaptations have this collection of properties, the peacock's tail, for example, is identifiable as having been sexually selected.

Similar arguments can be applied to distinguishing the level at which there has been a history of selection because of predictable features suggesting that selection operated at a particular level. In particular, traits selected at a given level (gene, organism, or group of organisms) should have features that are designed to be functional at that level.

This has implications for making inferences about the history of selection based on observed design features. Specifically, different levels of selection lead to adaptations designed to produce benefits at different levels of organization, so it is often possible to backwards induce the level(s) at which selection was acting by examining the features of a given adaptation. Adaptations clearly designed to deliver benefits to the group in the environment in which the adaptation evolved indicate that selection acted at the group level (e.g., skewed sex ratios). Adaptations clearly designed to deliver benefits to the individual imply that selection most likely acted at the level of the individual.

However, care must be exercised in drawing these inferences, because *a history of selection at one level does not preclude the possibility that selection simultaneously acted at another level.* Adaptations designed to provide benefits at one level in the environment in which that adaptation was selected might also be designed to provide benefits at another level. In similar fashion, *evidence that an adaptation was sculpted by selection at the individual level is not evidence that selection did not act on that adaptation at a higher level of organization as well.*

MULTILEVEL SELECTION AND COGNITION

As psychologists, we believe that the proper place to look for the footprints that distinguish the level at which selection has acted on behavioral adaptations is the level of evolved cognitive architecture. Indeed, the argument about whether MLS ever operates is unproductive (Wilson, 1983). Instead, the crucial research goal should be to describe carefully the design features of cognitive mechanisms in such a way that inferences about the selective history are possible.

If the structure and function of a cognitive mechanism appears to be designed to provide benefits at the level of the group in the environment where humans evolved (the EEA, or the environment of evolutionary adaptedness; Bowlby, 1969), then this suggests that selection acted at the group level to select that trait. Similarly, when the mechanism appears to be designed to provide individual benefits (in the EEA), this suggests that selection acted at the individual level. However, *it is always possible that selection acted to favor the trait at both the individual and group levels.* Distinguishing the level at which selection acted requires a careful scrutiny of the design of the cognitive system to determine the benefits the mechanism was designed to deliver in ancestral environments. By examining the benefits and costs at each level, we can distinguish between these possibilities (see Table 24.1). Relying on only the current costs and benefits generated by cognitive systems is insufficient to address this issue. Several recent examples are illustrative.

Certain behaviors seen in modern environments appear to benefit the group at a cost to the individual, such as donations to charities, contributions to collective goods, and self-sacrifice in intergroup conflict. However, before we conclude that these behaviors were selected only at the level of the group, it is necessary to consider the possible selection pressures that sculpted the cognitive systems that gave rise to these behaviors, and the cost–benefit structure associated with these acts. For example, if we presume that the possibility for anonymous altruism was rare in the EEA, these systems might have been shaped by individual-level selection driven

TABLE 24.1. Inferring the Level at Which Selection Acted

		Group	
		EEA cost	EEA benefit
Individual	EEA cost	N/A	Group selection, not individual selection
	EEA benefit	Individual selection, not group selection	Individual and group selection

Note. By examining the benefits a cognitive mechanism was designed to deliver in ancestral environments, as well as the concurrent costs, the level, or levels, at which adaptations were selected can be inferred. For example, mechanisms designed to provide benefits to the individual that entail a cost to the group are likely to have been selected at the individual level but not at the group level.

by the benefits through reputational gains from such altruistic acts (Miller, 2000). In this case, we should expect cognitive design features that cause individuals to be more altruistic when being observed, a result that is consistent with numerous experimental findings (e.g., Hoffman, McCabe, & Smith, 1996). If, however, selection for the relevant cognitive mechanisms acted at *only* the group level, we would not expect individuals to behave differently when being observed. In short, finding that altruistic behavior is sensitive to cues that one is being observed implies a role for individual selection but does not rule out the possibility of a role for MLS. What it does tell us, however, is that there are mechanisms designed to provide benefits at the individual level (by behaving more altruistically when it might affect one's reputation), so selection probably acted at the individual level to produce that adaptation.

CONCLUSION

The inherent uncertainty about the details of ancestral human populations, in terms of both the payoffs for their behaviors and the nature of the population structure, makes the role that MLS played in human evolution necessarily speculative. It is plausible that MLS forces were at play over the course of human evolution. The details of these conditions are beyond the scope of this essay, but a number of people have pointed out evidence that suggests humans lived in groups with relatively frequent social interactions, that there was an intermediate level of migration among groups, and that there was the possibility of assortment. Even though there is substantial skepticism that ancestral human population structures would have led to substantial amounts of MLS, some researchers have suggested that processes associated with the acquisition of information through socially transmitted representations would potentially have yielded fertile ground for MLS at the cultural level (Boyd & Richerson, 1985).

Similarly, it is possible that certain mechanisms that generated behaviors leading to greater assortment were selected because they increased the strength of group-level selection. In other words, traits that caused cooperative individuals to group together probably increased the likelihood of selection at the group level. These traits then could have been selected with the cooperative group-beneficial traits, increasing the frequency of both the group-beneficial traits and the traits that increase assortment (thereby increasing the likelihood of selection at the group level). For example, a strategy as simple as always cooperating and moving away from uncooperative partners or groups might constitute a group-beneficial trait that increases the strength of selection at the group level. Simulations have shown that this strategy can both be selected for and enable overall increases in cooperation (Aktipis, 2004).

Considerable debate remains regarding the evolution of cooperation in groups. The lack of consensus makes our central point even more important. In the absence of agreement about the evolutionary origin of cooperation in groups, an important guide will be the features of the computational system underlying cooperative decision making. If there were consensus on the correct theory for the evolution of cooperation in groups, or even if there were simply a small number of competing models that made unambiguously contrasting predictions, proper experimentation would be considerably easier. In the absence of this convenient state of affairs, carefully designed experiments that allow inferences about the level at which selection acted are urgently needed. These experiments, and their interpretation, should focus on the costs and benefits to the individual and group that the cognitive mechanisms involved were designed to deliver in ancestral environments, rather than an exclusive focus on the costs and benefits that they generate in modern environments. There are, we hope, many kinds of design features that will help us to detect the footprints of individual and multilevel selection.

ACKNOWLEDGMENTS

This material is based on work supported under a National Science Foundation Graduate Research Fellowship.

REFERENCES

Aktipis, C. A. (2004). Know when to walk away: Contingent movement and the evolution of cooperation in groups. *Journal of Theoretical Biology, 231,* 249–260.

Avilés, L. (1993). Interdemic selection and the sex ratio: A social spider perspective. *American Naturalist, 142,* 320–345.

Bowlby, J. (1969). *Attachment and loss: Vol. 1. Attachment.* New York: Basic Books.

Boyd, R., & Richerson, P. J. (1985). *Culture and the evolutionary process.* Chicago: University of Chicago Press.

Hamilton, W. D. (1964). The genetical evolution of social behaviour. *Journal of Theoretical Biology, 7,* 1–16.

Hoffman, E., McCabe, K., & Smith, V. L. (1996). Social distance and other-regarding behavior in dictator games. *American Economic Review, 86,* 653–656.

Miller, G. (2000). *The mating mind: How sexual choice shaped the evolution of human nature.* New York: Doubleday.

Price, G. (1970). Selection and covariance. *Nature, 227,* 520–521.

Sober, E., & Wilson, D. S. (1998). *Unto others: The evolution and psychology of unselfish behavior.* Cambridge, MA: Harvard University Press.

Wilson, D. S. (1983). The group selection controversy: History and current status. *Annual Review of Ecology and Systematics, 14,* 159–187.

PART III

Debates Concerning Important Human Evolutionary Outcomes

Editors' Introduction

The fundamental controversies covered in the two previous sections revolved around how human evolutionary behavioral science ought to be conducted: What should evolutionary explanations of human behavior look like? What standards of evidence should be used to test these explanations? And, more broadly, what sources of evidence can evolutionary behavioral scientists draw upon to generate or test specific evolutionary hypotheses? The controversies featured in the final section of the book stem from debates over specific claims about important evolutionary outcomes that make humans such a unique species. We canvassed five controversies:

KEY CHANGES IN THE EVOLUTION
OF HUMAN PSYCHOLOGY

Although sharing many characteristics with our closest ancestors, humans have certain unique psychological features. These novel features presumably arose in response to selection imposed by environmental pressures in the ecological niches that our ancestors occupied during the course of evolutionary history.

"*What evolutionary changes in hominid evolution are most central to understanding human psychology? What ecological niches led to the selection of these features?*"

We solicited three responses to this question. H. Clark Barrett, Leda Cosmides, and John Tooby expand upon the argument that human entry into "the cognitive niche" fueled many evolutionary events in the hominid line. Mark Flinn and Richard Alexander argue that human "ecological dominance" elevated social selection to the rank of the most important evolutionary force operating on humans, with dramatic results. Steven Mithen, an archeologist, suggests that the most important evolutionary changes in human cognition flowed from theory of mind capacities, specialized intelligences needed to interact effectively with the social, natural, and technological world; holistic communication, language, music, and cognitive fluidity; and the "extended mind."

BRAIN EVOLUTION

Brain size expanded tremendously during the evolution of hominids. Many argue that brain size expansion is vital to understanding the evolution of humans and modern psychological adaptations.

"What caused the massive brain expansion in the hominid line? What are the implications of these evolutionary changes for understanding of modern humans?"

The forces that led to human brain evolution have long been of central concern to human biologists. Traditionally, two views have dominated: (1) that large brains were selected to foster food acquisition in intellectually challenging foraging niches, and (2) that large brains were selected to foster effective social competition for resources. In recent years, a third view has emerged: (3) The large human brain evolved as a sexually attractive "ornament"—the human equivalent of a peacock's tail—through sexual selection and competition for mates. Most recently, it has been argued that the brain's architecture may be strongly constrained by conserved developmental processes, such that (4) selection for the larger size of one brain feature may "carry along" with it increases in other brain areas. We have responses that articulate and defend all four views. Hillard S. Kaplan, Michael Gurven, and Jane B. Lancaster address ecological foraging theory (though expanded here to incorporate social outcomes of the "human adaptive complex"), Robin Dunbar writes on the "social brain" theory, Geoffrey Miller argues for the sexual selection hypothesis, and Barbara L. Finlay discusses the implications of conserved neurodevelopmental processes for understanding human brain evolution.

GENERAL INTELLECTUAL ABILITY

Humans have a remarkable capacity to engage in abstract thinking, which is partly rooted in their ability to manipulate arbitrary symbols. Some psychologists view this abstractive ability as the hallmark of human intelligence and mental adaptation, the ability that has allowed humans to attain ecological dominance and successfully populate all corners of the globe. This could be the key element to understanding human cognitive evolution.

"What is the significance of general abstractive ability in understanding the evolution of humans?"

We solicited three essays on this topic. David C. Geary situates the ability to generate and manipulate symbols within a wider set of affective, cognitive, and modular systems, highlighting how these systems are then tied to general intelligence. Satoshi Kanazawa proposes that abstract intelligence is simply a specialized adaptation for dealing with a particular domain of problems—problems with novel elements. By contrast, Steven Mithen suggests that the hallmark of human abstract intelligence is the ability to generalize adaptations specialized for particular domains to other content domains.

CULTURE AND EVOLUTION

Humans create culture in all societies; that is, they establish sets of beliefs and norms that regulate social interactions and practices, and that shape specific understandings of the world. Across different human groups, however, the nature and content of culture varies fairly widely.

"How can culture be understood from an evolutionary perspective? What does the emergence of culture tell us about key aspects of human evolution? How does culture interface with human adaptations?"

Because this set of issues has attracted a great deal of attention from scholars in different sectors of evolutionary science, six sets of authors addressed this topic. Expanding on ideas from dual inheritance thinking, Robert Boyd and Peter J. Richerson explain how group selection could have acted on cultural practices to facilitate the spread of adaptive—and occasionally maladaptive—beliefs and values. Pascal Boyer outlines a new way of conducting social science and accounting for culture, which he terms "integrative science." This approach ignores traditional divisions between different levels of reality, and melds tools and findings from evolutionary biology, game theory, economics, cultural anthropology, cognitive psychology, and neuroscience. Mark Flinn and Kathryn Coe tackle the many paradoxes of the human brain, ranging from its costs to the speed with which it evolved, to its capacity to alter behavior rapidly, to its ability to generate novel solutions to assorted problems. To explain these anomalies, they discuss possible "red queen" processes involving human social evolution and arms races among coalitions and human cultural evolution and information arms races. Adopting a behavioral ecologist's stance, Kim Hill critiques evolutionary psychology's core assumptions of extreme cognitive modularity, as well as their purported ties to adaptive behavior. He then discusses how culture—especially socially transmitted information and enforced rules—often dictates "optimal" behavior. Robert Kurzban attempts to reconcile seeming disparate assumptions about the gullibility versus skepticism of social learners. In doing so, he advances an integrative, domain-specific cultural epidemiology model. Finally, Mark Schaller suggests that it is time for evolutionary psychologists to embrace cultural variability the same way it heralds human universals. He proposes how certain cross-cultural differences might be exploited to test evolutionary hypotheses, how such differences could be used to generate deeper evolutionary theorizing, and how the exploration of our evolutionary origins may explain certain cross-cultural diversities.

THE EVOLUTION OF MATING BETWEEN THE SEXES

Human mating and relations between men and women appear to differ substantially from those of our nearest primate relatives.

"What are the most important features of hominid mating systems? How do the typical relations and interactions between the sexes add to our understanding of specific mating adaptations? How might an understanding of the evolution of human mating systems deepen our understanding of modern humans and relations between women and men?"

We solicited three responses to this question. Based on his theorizing and empirical research on mating in humans, David M. Buss discusses how ideas flowing from parental investment theory can be applied to understand the enactment of different mating strategies, the conditions under which the sexes ought to experience conflict and cooperation, and how the evolution of love might be understood. Offering an alternative viewpoint, Wendy Wood and Alice H. Eagly discuss their biosocial model of human mating. They propose that the key to understanding human mating systems is to understand why some features of mating are variable across different societies and others are universal. Finally, Randy Thornhill reviews recent theory and empirical evidence that casts new light on the evolution of estrus, extended sexuality, concealed ovulation, and "dual sexuality" in human females.

Key Changes in the Evolution of Human Psychology

໒ 25

The Hominid Entry into the Cognitive Niche

H. CLARK BARRETT
LEDA COSMIDES
JOHN TOOBY

W hy is the human mind designed in the way it is, and why does it seem to differ profoundly from that of even our closest living relatives? Traditionally, scholars have attempted identify *the* factor that they believe encapsulates human uniqueness: Big brains, intelligence, language, symbol manipulation, the capacity to imitate and to acquire culture, tool use, expanded working memory, sociality, understanding intentions, and self-awareness have all been proposed as candidates. Scholars have often been tempted to link their candidate difference to a single evolutionary selection pressure or event: East African drought, the ice ages, hunting, warfare, large social groups, and so on. In our opinion, the search for a single breakthrough capacity or a single cause of the unique features of human design distorts a balanced effort (1) to map correctly the mechanisms comprising our evolved, species-typical psychological architecture, and (2) to understand the numerous and distinct selection pressures that built them. A natural science of humans is not like physics—with a few underlying general laws waiting to be discovered in intellectual quantum leaps. It is more like inventorying and tracing out detailed circuit diagrams for each subsystem

in a newly encountered and highly complex engineered system, such as an
aircraft; that is, our psychological architecture appears be a heterogeneous
collection of computational devices or programs, each shaped by different
subcomponents of natural selection to serve distinct evolved functions. Because some of these programs can benefit from particular types of information produced by others, innovations in some devices will have far-reaching
but specific consequences on a subset of the other mechanisms, while still
maintaining many of their core similarities to homologous systems in other
species. For example, the human ability to cooperate, read intentions, and
represent dispositions—functional in their own right—have presumably reshaped some aspects of our mating psychology, contributing to the emergence of durable, quasi-exclusive mateships. Hence, it is better to make
sense of our architecture's subcomponents—unique or not—in terms of
their functions and coadapted functional interrelationships than to section
off artificially those facets that are unique, and consider them in isolation.
Accepting that many of our psychological mechanisms will have been modified over evolutionary time for diverse reasons, it is nevertheless possible
to identify a loose theme that underlies some of the more radical features of
human design. What appears most singular about human psychological
evolution is the assembly or retooling of various adaptations to support our
entry into what has been called *the cognitive niche* (Cosmides & Tooby,
2000, 2001; Tooby & DeVore, 1987). These species-transformative modifications are primarily related to the acquisition, manipulation, and application of information. A distinctly human niche was based on developing an
unprecedented new subsistence economics of information and knowledge
use, involving, for example, the greater use of lower quality information,
the greater use of novel interrelationships among information, and breakthroughs in lowering the cost of acquiring and maintaining large bodies of
information. Here we sketch some components of what we believe a full account will eventually include.

WHAT IS TO BE EXPLAINED?

Humans have vastly increased the number of pathways by which they reach
diverse instrumental ends. What explains this dramatic broadening of successful action?

1. *Improvisational intelligence.* The systems that cause celestial navigation in birds, dead-reckoning in desert ants, and food aversion learning in

rats, humans, and other omnivores are the expressions of various dedicated intelligences. A "dedicated intelligence" is a computational system that evolved to solve a predefined, target set of problems, usually achieved through domain-specialized procedures that are designed to expect and to exploit evolutionarily enduring regularities in a given problem domain (e.g., the invariant mechanics of rigid objects in three-dimensional space). Dedicated intelligences evolve their solutions over evolutionary time in response to these regularities. "Improvisational intelligence," in contrast, refers to a (hypothetical) computational ability to improvise solutions in developmental time to evolutionarily novel problems. Humans seem to have this ability to an unparalleled degree. Although all organisms would benefit by having this capacity, only one does, implying that its computational implementation must have huge costs associated with it, or the pre-conditions for evolving it are low probability (i.e., its evolution was sensitively path-dependent), or both.

Its benefits are obvious. Most species are locked in coevolutionary, antagonistic relationships with prey, rivals, parasites, and predators, in which move and countermove take place slowly, over evolutionary time. Improvisation puts humans at a great advantage; instead of being constrained to innovate only in phylogenetic time, humans engage in ontogenetic ambushes against their antagonists, with innovations that are too rapid with respect to evolutionary time for their antagonists to evolve defenses by natural selection. Armed with this advantage, hominids have rapidly expanded into new habitats, developed an amazing diversity of subsistence and resource extraction methods, caused the extinctions of innumerable prey species in whatever environments they have penetrated, and generated an array of social systems, artifacts, and representational systems immensely greater than that found in any other single species. As a knowledge-using species, we occupy the *cognitive niche*, using improvisational intelligence to solve problems that other species might approach solely with highly specialized, rapidly deployed but somewhat inflexible computational and physical specializations (Tooby & DeVore, 1987).

2. *Improvisational intelligence depends on access to local, transient, and contingent information.* Contrast, for example, the food acquisition practices of a bison with that of a !Kung San hunter. The bison's foraging decisions are (presumably) made for it by dedicated intelligences designed for grass and forage identification and evaluation. These adaptations are (relatively) universal to the species, and operate with relative uniformity across the species range. In contrast, the !Kung San hunter uses, among many other non-species-typical means and methods, arrows tipped with a poison found

on only one local species of chrysomelid beetle, and toxic only during the larval stage (Lee, 1993). This method of food acquisition is not a species-typical adaptation: Not all humans use arrows, poison their arrows, have access to a beetle species from which poison can be derived, or even hunt. Nor are any of the component relationships—between beetle larva and poison, between arrows and poison, or even between arrows and hunting—stable from a phylogenetic perspective. Each relationship on which this practice is based is a transient and local condition, and these contingent facts are being combined to improvise a behavioral routine that achieves an adaptive outcome: obtaining meat. Whatever the neural adaptations that underlie this behavior, they were not designed specifically for beetles and arrows, but they exploit these local, contingent facts as part of a computational structure that treats them as instances of a more general class (e.g., living things, tools, projectiles, prey). To yield novel implications for action, elements in these bodies of information are also densely inferentially cross-linked across conceptual boundaries that are computationally impermeable for other species (Barrett, 2005b; Cosmides & Tooby, 2000, 2001).

3. *Getting information from others, as well as from one's own experience, via culture, dramatically lowers the cost of acquiring large enough bodies of local, contingent information, making improvisional intelligence cost-effective.* Cognitive mechanisms underlying cultural transmission coevolved with improvisional intelligence, distributing the costs of the acquisition of nonrivalrous information over a much greater number of individuals, and allowing its cost to be amortized over a much greater number of advantageous events and generations (Tooby & DeVore, 1987). Unlike other species, cultural transmission in humans results in the ratchet-like accumulation of knowledge (Richerson & Boyd, 2004).

4. *Language dramatically lowers the cost of socially sharing information.* Language is a human-specific set of cognitive adaptations (Pinker, 1994). It acquires special significance when considered as a central element in the hominid entry into the cognitive niche, because of its effects on the economics of information acquisition and use. Utterances are a low-cost way of sharing information about the habitat and social world: They solve coordination problems necessary for coalitional cooperation to occur; expand the number of minds that can jointly cooperate to improvise a tool, hunting method, or other novel solution to a problem; and allow these improvised solutions to be communicated to and thereby benefit kin and cooperative partners.

5. *Theory of mind mechanisms lower the cost of social inference, and hence of socially shared information.* The ability to make inferences about representations in the minds of others (Baron-Cohen, 1995; Leslie, 1987) dramatically facilitates language (Sperber & Wilson, 1995) and the social transmission of knowledge.

6. *Scope syntax: The successful harnessing of local, transient, and contingent information requires the emergence of a suite of cognitive adaptations that police the ever-shifting boundaries of applicability of sets of contingently true representations.* The problem with representing contingently true relationships is that—outside a narrow envelope of conditions where they are applicable—they are false and misleading. The substance taken from the larva for arrow making is toxic during one season, but not another, or in another area, or when taken from another species or life stage. This whole new universe of information could not have been exploited by humans without the coevolution of cognitive machinery for tracking and inferring the circumstances under which contingent information can be treated as true or must be quarantined off. The human mind contains a rich set of cognitive adaptations—a scope syntax (Cosmides & Tooby, 2000; Leslie & Frith, 1990)—for regulating the scope of applicability of representations about contingent information. These include conditional, suppositional, and counterfactual reasoning; the ability to decouple representations and bind them into separate, noninteracting sets; the ability to store representations with various tags of truth, falsehood, and degrees of belief; metarepresentations; and the ability to perform mental simulations offline, with inferential products decoupled from the behavioral consequences they would ordinarily trigger (Cosmides & Tooby, 2000, 2001; Leslie, 1987; Tooby & Cosmides, 2001). Even human oddities, such as fiction, become intelligible: Fiction is a set of contingent representations, useful for deriving generalizations, but in which the scope of direct applicability has shrunk to zero.

7. *Improvisational intelligence rests on a foundation of dedicated intelligences.* Unguided improvisational intelligence would suffer disastrously from combinatorial explosion, so it must instead include the participation of a large set of domain-specialized, inference systems that manifest dedicated intelligence (Cosmides & Tooby, 2001), including ones for object mechanics (Leslie, 1994), tool use (Defeyter & German, 2003; German & Barrett, 2005), intuitive biology (Barrett, 2005a; Medin & Atran, 1999), social inference (Baron-Cohen, 1995), social exchange (Cosmides & Tooby, 2005), and numerous others. These supply improvisational intelligence with many forms of useful inference to link representations together use-

fully, guiding thought away from vast spaces of barren and useless concatenation.

VIRTUOUS CIRCLES AND SELECTED RAMIFICATIONS

These adaptations both depend on, and make possible, scores of other modifications in human design. Here are two examples:

1. *Humans cooperate to an unprecedented extent.* Social exchange and reciprocation allow individuals to exploit transient differences in their momentary needs and values to achieve gains in trade. The human mind includes cognitive specializations for engaging in social exchange (Cosmides & Tooby, 2005), including n-party exchange (Tooby, Cosmides, & Price, 2005). Improvisational intelligence vastly expands the potential for mutually beneficial trade, but gains in trade from improvised solutions can only be achieved if potential cooperators can infer what others want, believe, and plan to do. Consequently, the theory of mind system (Baron-Cohen, 1995; Leslie, 1987) greatly facilitates cooperation. Humans also exhibit the zoologically rare ability to cooperate in large groups composed of unrelated individuals, greatly increasing the potential productivity of human labor, including, unfortunately, collective aggression.

2. *Male provisioning of women and children.* Although common in birds, male provisioning of females and offspring is rare among mammals, especially Old World primates. The increase in the improvisational ability to acquire previously unattainable high-quality foods, such as meat, shifted the cost-effectiveness for males of provisioning mates and offspring. Consequently, human males evolved motivational adaptations that make possible durable, high-investment mateships and extended relationships of paternal care. In turn, the expanded provision of meat and other high-quality nutrients provided the fuel necessary to support a developing brain made expensive by the addition of all the adaptations necessary to sustain improvisational intelligence, language, and cooperation (Kaplan & Robson, 2002; Wrangham & Conklin-Brittain, 2003).

In short, the ecological niche that humans entered is a novel one, involving the harnessing and exploitation of a kind of information that other species found too costly to acquire and too mercurial to trust: local, transient, contingent information.

REFERENCES

Baron-Cohen, S. (1995). *Mindblindness: An essay on autism and theory of mind.* Cambridge, MA: MIT Press.

Barrett, H. C. (2005a). Adaptations to predators and prey. In D. M. Buss (Ed.), *The handbook of evolutionary Psychology* (pp. 200–223). New York: Wiley.

Barrett, H. C. (2005b). Enzymatic computation and cognitive modularity. *Mind and Language, 20,* 259–287.

Cosmides, L., & Tooby, J. (2000). Consider the source: The evolution of adaptations for decoupling and metarepresentation. In D. Sperber (Ed.), *Metarepresentations: A multidisciplinary perspective* (pp. 53–115). New York: Oxford University Press.

Cosmides, L., & Tooby, J. (2001). Unraveling the enigma of human intelligence: Evolutionary psychology and the multimodular mind. In R. J. Sternberg & J. C. Kaufman (Eds.), *The evolution of intelligence* (pp. 145–198). Hillsdale, NJ: Erlbaum.

Cosmides, L., & Tooby, J. (2005). Neurocognitive adaptations designed for social exchange. In D. M. Buss (Ed.), *The handbook of evolutionary psychology* (pp. 584–627). Hoboken, NJ: Wiley.

Defeyter, M. A., & German, T. P. (2003). Acquiring an understanding of design: Evidence from children's insight problem solving. *Cognition, 89,* 133–155.

German, T. P., & Barrett, H. C. (2005). Functional fixedness in a technologically sparse culture. *Psychological Science, 16,* 1–5.

Kaplan, H. S., & Robson, A. (2002). The co-evolution of intelligence and longevity and the emergence of humans. *Proceedings of the National Academy of Sciences of the United States of America, 99,* 10221–10226.

Lee, R. B. (1993). *The Dobe Ju/'Hoansi* (2nd ed.). New York: Holt, Reinhart and Winston.

Leslie, A. (1987). Pretense and representation: The origins of "theory of mind." *Psychological Review, 94,* 412–426.

Leslie, A. (1994). ToMM, ToBy, and Agency: Core architecture and domain specificity. In L. Hirschfeld & S. Gelman (Eds.), *Mapping the mind: Domain specificity in cognition and culture* (pp. 119–148). New York: Cambridge University Press.

Leslie, A., & Frith, U. (1990). Prospects for a cognitive neuropsychology of autism: Hobson's choice. *Psychological Review, 97,* 122–131.

Medin, D., & Atran, S. (Eds.). (1999). *Folkbiology.* Cambridge, MA: MIT Press.

Pinker, S. (1994). *The language instinct: How the mind creates language.* New York: HarperCollins.

Richerson, P., & Boyd, R. (2004). *Not by genes alone: How culture transformed human evolution.* Chicago: University of Chicago Press.

Sperber, D., & Wilson, D. (1995). *Relevance: communication and cognition* (2nd ed.). Oxford, UK: Blackwell.

Tooby, J., & Cosmides, L. (2001). Does beauty build adapted minds?: Toward an evolutionary theory of aesthetics, fiction and the arts. *SubStance, 30*(1), 6–27.

Tooby J., & DeVore, I. (1987). The reconstruction of hominid behavioral evolution through strategic modeling. In W. Kinzey (Ed.), *Primate models of hominid behavior* (pp. 183–237). New York: State University of New York Press.

Tooby, J., Cosmides, L., & Price, M. (2006). Cognitive adaptations for *n*-person exchange: The evolutionary roots of organizational behavior. *Managerial and Decision Economics, 27,* 103–129.

Wrangham, R., & Conklin-Brittain, N. (2003). Cooking as a biological trait. *Comparative Biochemistry and Physiology A, 136,* 35–46.

26

Runaway Social Selection in Human Evolution

MARK FLINN
RICHARD ALEXANDER

Darwin (1871) recognized that there could be important differences between selection occurring as a consequence of (1) interaction with ecological factors, such as predators, climate, and food; and (2) interactions among conspecifics (i.e., members of the same species competing with each other over resources such as nest sites, food, and mates). The former is termed "natural selection" and the latter, "social selection," of which sexual selection may be considered a special subtype (see Glossary for definitions of key terms). The pace and direction of evolutionary changes in behavior and morphology produced by these two types of selection—natural and social—can be significantly different (Alexander, 1974, 2005; Fisher, 1930; West-Eberhard, 1983, 2003).

Here we examine the process of "runaway social selection" and its importance for explaining the extraordinary sociality of humans and associated adaptations, including linguistic and sociocognitive skills such as language, theory of mind (ToM), creativity and imagination, self-awareness, foresight, and consciousness. We suggest that as our hominin ancestors became increasingly "ecologically dominant," a within-species arms race involving complex coalitions based on extensive networks of reciprocity, including so-called "indirect reciprocity" (Alexander, 1987, 2006) emerged, facilitated by the use of socially transmitted information.

SOCIAL SELECTION

Organisms face many obstacles that potentially diminish survival and reproduction. Some of these challenges involve competitive social interactions among conspecifics for essential resources, such as nest sites, preferred locations at feeding sites and water holes, and mates. Social competition has produced a wide variety of adaptations. For example, weapons such as horns, teeth, and spurs are used in competition for mates across a wide range of taxa (Andersson, 1994). Males and females influence copulatory behavior of mates with a variety of behavioral, morphological, and physiological tools (e.g., Eberhard, 2004; Patricelli, Uy, & Borgia, 2003). Distress calls help recruit relatives to assist in social conflicts. Strategic positioning within aggregations facilitates the use of conspecifics as cover via the "geometry of the selfish herd." Complex, coordinated social behaviors appear necessary for successful coalitionary actions such as border patrols (Watts & Mitani, 2001) and displacement of dominant individuals (Conner & Whitehead, 2005).

Darwin (1871, p. 256) proposed sexual selection as a process that involved "the advantage which certain individuals have over other individuals of the same sex and species, in exclusive relation to reproduction." Separating selective pressures involved with competition for mates from other aspects of social competition is difficult, in part because, as Williams (1966, p. 59) observed, "all adaptation must relate to reproduction." In effect, "reproduction is everything, and survival is nothing, except insofar as it contributes to reproductive success" (Ghiselin, 1997, p. 292). And from the other direction, mate choice can be based on assessment of social abilities, as well as survival components from natural selection, such as parasite resistance. Some aspects of reproductive competition, moreover, do not involve social interaction at the level of the individual vehicles, for example, gamete competition. Disentangling the components of social selection is not an easy task; perhaps this is partly why Darwin and subsequent evolutionary thinkers have not provided a widely accepted description. Another reason might be the relatively few species for which nonsexual social selection is a dominant evolutionary force.

Of particular interest here are information-processing capacities associated with social competition. We posit that runaway social selection was the primary pressure shaping several key human brain adaptations. Other social species, such as chimpanzees, dolphins, orcas, crows, and elephants, are less extreme examples.

RUNAWAY SOCIAL SELECTION:
CONSPECIFIC RED QUEENS

Selection that occurs as a consequence of interactions between species can be intense and unending—for example, with parasite–host Red Queen evolution (Hamilton, Axelrod, & Tanese, 1990) and other biotic arms races (van Valen, 1973). Intraspecific social competition may generate selective pressures that cause even more rapid and dramatic evolutionary changes. Relative to natural selection, social selection has the following characteristics (West-Eberhard, 1983):

1. Because competition among conspecifics can have especially strong effects on differential reproduction relative to other ecological pressures, the intensity of social selection (and consequent genetic changes) can be very high.

2. Because the salient selective pressures involve competition among members of the same species, the normal ecological constraints are often relaxed for social selection. Hence, traits can evolve in seemingly extreme and bizarre directions before counterbalancing natural selection slows the process. If traits favored by social selection also provide benefits in regard to natural selection, as, for example, in the human brain's ability to design useful tools for contending with Darwin's traditional hostile forces of nature, then such constraints would be even further relaxed.

3. Because social competition involves *relative* superiority among conspecifics, the bar can be constantly raised in a consistent direction generation after generation, in an unending arms race.

4. Because social competition can involve multiple iterations of linked strategy and counterstrategy among interacting individuals, the process of social selection can become autocatalytic, with its pace and directions partly determined from within, generating what might be termed "secondary Red Queens." For example, reoccurrence of social competition over lifetimes and generations can favor flexible phenotypic responses, such as

social learning, that enable constantly changing strategies. Phenotypic flexibility of learned behavior to contend with a dynamic target may benefit from enhanced information-processing capacities, especially in regard to foresight and scenario building (Suddendorf & Corballis, 1997).

The conditions we have listed for social selection have been most extensively considered for mate competition. Fisher (1930) rekindled interest in Darwin's concept of sexual selection, identifying several key aspects of a directional runaway process that could result in seemingly bizarre or arbitrary traits such as elaborate visual (e.g., peacock tails) or auditory (e.g., warbler songs) displays. Such traits would have no evolutionary function in solitary species that were selected in regard to their abilities to contend with strictly ecological factors. But species in which reproduction was determined in part by social competition are a different evolutionary story (e.g., Iwasa & Pomiankowski, 1995). Social competition over mates may be indirect, as in the case of a gray tree frog choosing males on the basis of their call characteristics (Gerhardt, 2005). Mate choice preferences for the relative extremes of a trait (e.g., the longest tail) can drive a runaway process of sexual selection (Andersson, 1994; Eberhard, 2004; Fisher, 1930). The links between social selection from mate choice and natural selection have been difficult to determine. Mate choice for traits such as resistance to pathogens could have important advantages, although assessment of honest advertisement of heritable true fitness is problematic (Hamilton, 1999). The intensity of selection for pathogen resistance could be enhanced by social selection involving mate choice (e.g., Borgia, Egeth, Uy, & Patricelli, 2004). Increased predation risk and other ecological factors, however, may constrain such displays (e.g., Endler, 1988).

CONCLUDING REMARKS

Within-species Red Queen dynamics can generate especially strong social selection. Decreasing constraints from natural selection, combined with increasing social competition, generate a potent runaway process. Human evolution appears to be characterized by such circumstances (Flinn, Geary, & Ward, 2005). Humans, more so than any other species, appear to have become their own most potent selective pressure, via social competition involving coalitions (Alexander, 2005; Geary & Flinn, 2002; Wrangham, 1999) on the one hand, and dominance of their ecologies involving niche construction (Laland, Odling-Smee, & Feldman, 2000) on the other. The primary functions of the most extraordinary human mental abilities—language, imagination, self-awareness, ToM, foresight, scenario building, and consciousness—involve the negotiation of social relationships (Allman, 1999; Flinn, Ward, & Noone, 2005). The multiple-party reciprocity and shifting nested subcoalitions characteristic of human sociality may generate especially difficult information-processing demands for these cognitive facilities that underlie social competency.

GLOSSARY: DEFINITIONS OF KEY CONCEPTS

Ecological dominance: The relative lack of selection from extrinsic causes compared with the relative importance of selection from interactions with conspecifics. From this perspective, the term does more than indicate a species' success in contending directly with Darwin's hostile forces of climate, predation, and resource scarcity. Although rhinoviruses, kudzu, and many species of beetles are highly successful in their respective ecologies, they are not ecologically dominant in this sense. Their phenotypes have been, and continue to be, primarily designed by selection involving extrinsic forces, rather than by interactions with members of their own species.

Taking another example, although part of ecological dominance involves relative lack of selection from biotic interactions including predation, this is not sufficient. The top guild predators themselves, such as eagles, bears, lions, tigers, and orcas, and large animals with effective protection, such as elephants and sperm whales, are relatively free from predation. But resource scarcity (e.g., getting food) and pathogens may still be significant selective pressures relative to contending with conspecifics, particularly in regard to evolution of the brain. The critical factor in ecological dominance is the extent to which a species has become its own selective pressure, its own principal hostile force of nature.

Natural selection: Selection occurring as a consequence of forces "in nature." Adaptations are produced as a consequence of success or failure in dealing with aspects of the abiotic and heterospecific biotic environments. Examples include Darwin's hostile forces of food shortages, predators, pathogens, and harsh climate.

Runaway social selection: Sir Ronald Fisher (1930) identified the potential for positive feedback loops in sexual selection involving mate choice for the relative extreme of a trait. Females benefit from heritable choice biases because their sons (and grandsons) are more likely to be chosen. Richard Alexander (2005) extended this concept, recognizing that choice of social partners for reciprocity can also involve a directional, runaway process. We suggest a further generalization to all aspects of social selection in which competition favors a relative extreme in a positive feedback loop. In this vein, one might identify a process of runaway cultural selection for relative extremes (e.g., faster cars, better weapons).

Selection: Differential success of phenotypic variants that result in differential success of organic germ-line replicators (heritable genetic units; for reviews, see Dawkins, 1982; West-Eberhard, 2003; Williams, 1966).

Social selection: Selection occurring as a consequence of interaction among individuals of the same species. It is useful to distinguish sexual and nonsexual social selection (for reviews, see Alexander, 1974, 2005; West-Eberhard, 2003). Adaptations are produced as a consequence of success or failure in dealing with the social environment. Examples include competition among conspecifics for food or nest sites (nonsexual), or mates (sexual selection) (Darwin, 1871).

REFERENCES

Alexander, R. D. (1974). The evolution of social behavior. *Annual Review of Ecology and Systematics, 5,* 325–383.

Alexander, R. D. (1987). *The biology of moral systems.* Hawthorne, NY: Aldine de Gruyter.

Alexander, R. D. (2005). Evolutionary selection and the nature of humanity. In V. Hosle & C. Illies (Eds.), *Darwinism and philosophy* (pp. 301–348). South Bend, IN: University of Notre Dame Press.

Alexander, R. D. (2006). *The challenge of human social behavior. Evolutionary Psychology, 4,* 1–32.

Allman, J. (1999). *Evolving brains.* New York: Scientific American Library.

Andersson, M. (1994). *Sexual selection.* Princeton, NJ: Princeton University Press.

Borgia, G., Egeth, M., Uy, J. A. C., & Patricelli, G. L. (2004). Juvenile infection and male display: Testing the bright male hypothesis across individual life histories. *Behavioral Ecology, 15*(5), 722–728.

Conner, R. C., & Whitehead, H. (2005). Alliances II. Rates of encounter during the resource utilization: A general model of intrasexual alliance formation. *Animal Behavior, 69,* 127–132.

Darwin, C. R. (1871). *The descent of man and selection in relation to sex.* London: Murray.

Dawkins, R. (1982). *The extended phenotype.* San Francisco: Freeman.

Eberhard, W. G. (2004). Rapid divergent evolution of sexual morphology: Comparative tests of antagonistic coevolution and traditional female choice. *Evolution, 58*(9), 1947–1970.

Endler, J.A. (1988). Sexual selection and predation risk in guppies. *Nature, 332,* 593–594.

Fisher, R. A. (1930). *The genetical theory of natural selection.* Oxford, UK: Clarendon.

Flinn, M. V., Geary, D. C., & Ward, C. V. (2005). Ecological dominance, social competition, and coalitionary arms races: Why humans evolved extraordinary intelligence. *Evolution and Human Behavior, 26*(1), 10–46.

Flinn, M. V., Ward, C. V., & Noone, R. (2005). Hormones and the human family. In D. Buss (Ed.), *Handbook of evolutionary psychology* (pp. 552–580). Hoboken, NJ: Wiley.

Geary, D. C., & Flinn, M. V. (2002). Sex differences in behavioral and hormonal response to social threat. *Psychological Review, 109*(4), 745–750.

Gerhardt, H.C. (2005). Advertisement-call preferences in diploid–tetraploid treefrogs (*Hyla chrysoscelis* and *Hyla versicolor*): Implications for mate choice and the evolution of communication systems. *Evolution, 59*(2), 395–408.

Ghiselin, M. T. (1997). *Metaphysics and the origin of species.* Albany: State University of New York Press.

Hamilton, W. D. (1999). The three queens. In *Narrow roads of gene land* (Vol. 2, pp. 601–666). Oxford, UK: Oxford University Press.

Hamilton, W. D., Axelrod, R., & Tanese, R. (1990). Sexual reproduction as an adaptation to resist parasites (A review). *Proceedings of the National Academy of Sciences of the United States of America, 87,* 3566–3573.

Iwasa, Y., & Pomiankowski, A. (1995). Continual change in mate preferences. *Nature, 377,* 420–422.

Laland, K. N., Odling-Smee, J., & Feldman, M. W. (2000). Niche construction, biological evolution, and cultural change. *Behavioral and Brain Sciences, 23,* 131–175.

Patricelli, G. L., Uy, J. A. C., & Borgia, G. (2003). Multiple male traits interact: Attractive bower decorations facilitate attractive behavioural displays in satin bowerbirds. *Proceedings of the Royal Society of London B, 270,* 2389–2395.

Suddendorf, T., & Corballis, M. C. (1997). Mental time travel and the evolution of the human mind. *Genetic, Social, and General Psychology Monographs, 123*(2), 133–167.

Van Valen, L. (1973). A new evolutionary law. *Evolutionary Theory, 1,* 1–30.

Watts, D. P., & Mitani, J. C. (2001). Boundary patrols and intergroup encounters in wild chimpanzees. *Behaviour, 138,* 299–327.

West-Eberhard, M. J. (1983). Sexual selection, social competition, and speciation. *Quarterly Review of Biology, 58,* 155–183.

West-Eberhard, M. J. (2003). *Developmental plasticity and evolution.* Oxford, UK: Oxford University Press.

Williams, G. C. (1966). *Adaptation and natural selection.* Princeton, NJ: Princeton University Press.

Wrangham, R. W. (1999). Evolution of coalitionary killing. *Yearbook of Physical Anthropology, 42,* 1–30.

℘ 27

Key Changes in the Evolution of Human Psychology

STEVEN MITHEN

The most important evolutionary changes in hominid cognition resulting in the unique psychological features of the human mind today are the following: theory of mind by 1.8 million years ago; specialized intelligences for interacting with the social, natural, and technological world by 0.5 million years ago; advanced holistic communication by 0.25 million years ago; language, music, and cognitive fluidity by 0.1 million years ago; and the extended mind by 0.05 million years ago. These evolutionary developments were cumulative and cannot be divorced from changes in human anatomy in general, especially those relating to bipedalism. I have discussed this evolutionary history at length in two books, *The Prehistory of the Mind* (1996) and *The Singing Neanderthals* (2005), with the latter focusing on the evolution of music and language. Readers should refer to these books for an elaboration of the arguments briefly summarized in this chapter.

THEORY OF MIND

A common assumption among paleoanthropologists is that the common ancestor we shared with the chimpanzee around 6 million years ago had a mind/brain similar to that of the chimpanzee today. Although this assumption fails to account for the evolutionary history of the chimpanzee mind/ brain during the last 6 million years, it is not unreasonable in light of what we know about the lifestyle, brain size, and anatomy of our earliest hominid ancestors. If we use this assumption to identify what aspects of human psychology have evolved in the *Homo* lineage since that common ancestor, we face the problem of characterizing the chimpanzee mind/brain to establish the "starting point" of this evolutionary history. Psychologists differ as to what cognitive abilities they attribute to chimpanzees today, especially with regard to whether chimpanzees possess a "theory of mind" or are just clever behaviorists (e.g., see Byrne & Whiten, 1988, 1992; Carruthers & Smith, 1996; Povinelli, 1993; Russon, Bard, & Parker, 1996; Tomasello, Call, & Hare, 2003).

My view is that the observational and experimental evidence indicates that chimpanzees either entirely lack a theory of mind or have a theory of mind in a very weak sense, and are perhaps able to infer the desires but not the beliefs of other individuals. The evolution of more advanced theory of mind abilities, perhaps a third or even fourth level of intentionality, is most likely one of the earliest developments in human cognitive evolution, probably relating to the increase in brain size that occurred between 2.0 and 1.5 million years ago (Dunbar, 2004; Ruff, Trinkhaus, & Holliday, 1997). The selective pressure for this aspect of cognitive evolution ultimately derives from the increasing aridity of East African landscapes after 3.5 million years ago. This resulted in hominids living in larger groups to reduce predator risk and to maximize foraging efficiency, most likely relating to the scavenging of carcasses (Dunbar, 1993). Reproductive success within relatively larger groups should have depended upon managing alliances and friendships with other members of the group; those individuals with theory of mind abilities should have been at a selective advantage at these tasks (Aiello & Dunbar, 1993; Mithen, 1996). Although such selective pressures most likely account for the enlargement of the brain at this period of human evolution, this was only possible due to a network of changes relating to diet, bipedalism, and technology. These enabled a higher quality diet, and a reduction in the size and energetic demands of the gut (Aiello & Wheeler, 1995).

MULTIPLE, SPECIALIZED INTELLIGENCES

By 1.8 million years ago, *Homo ergaster* appeared in Africa and rapidly dispersed into Asia and Europe (Straus & Bar-Yosef, 2001). For much of the

Middle Pleistocene, however, there were probably local extinctions and further dispersals from Africa by descendants of *H. eragster* rather than permanent settlements. It may not have been until 0.5 million years ago that this was established, at least in northern Europe. This period of human evolution saw the development of Acheulian technology involving the production of hand axes that have a deliberately imposed morphology, which often was highly symmetrical and technologically far more demanding than Oldowan choppers to manufacture (Pelegrin, 1993). Because the cognitive requirements for making such artifacts are quite different from those for social interaction, which, again, are quite different from those required for exploiting Pleistocene landscapes, Mithen (1996) argued that *H. eragster* and all hominid descendants other than *H. sapiens* had relatively specialized but isolated cognitive domains of technological, natural history, and social intelligences, with the latter encompassing theory of mind abilities. The principles of natural selection lead us to expect on an *a priori* basis that cognitive structures could evolve in this domain-specific or highly modular manner (Cosmides & Tooby, 1994).

The evolution of this domain-specific mentality is a critical step in human cognitive evolution, because it created hominids, which were in some ways very similar to modern humans, and in others, very different. It explains why big game hunting and manufacture of sophisticated stone tools were possible, whereas there are no traces of, say, art, ritual, architecture or complex tools made from animal bones. All of the latter require cross-modal thought, or what I term "cognitive fluidity," and only appear 100,000 years ago in association with *H. sapiens* (Mithen, 1996). In general terms, the marked absence of creativity and innovation by *H. ergaster, H. heidelbergensis, H. neanderthalensis,* and other large-brain hominids, except for *H. sapiens,* suggests a domain-specific mentality that enabled a narrow range of activities to be undertaken with high levels of expertise.

PROTOLANGUAGE: ADVANCED HOLISTIC COMMUNICATION

Between 0.6 and 0.25 million years ago, hominid brain size enlarged dramatically, reaching—and in some cases exceeding—the 1,200–1,500 cc volume, characteristic of H. sapiens today (Ruff et al., 1997). This encephalization is most likely explained by the evolution of advanced vocal and gestural communication systems that can be described as protolanguage. This was partly reliant on the existence of theory of mind abilities: Unless one appreciates that another individual has different knowledge than one's own, there is limited need for communication (Dunbar, 1998; Mithen, 1999).

Theories regarding the nature of protolanguage fall into two "camps": those who believe that protolanguage was "compositional" in character, and those who believe it was "holistic." The essence of compositional theories is that protolanguage consisted of words with limited, if any, grammar. Bickerton (1990, 1998, 2000), the main proponent of this view, argues that human ancestors, and relatives such as the Neanderthals, may have had a relatively large lexicon of words, each of which related to a mental concept such as "meat," "fire," "hunt," and so forth. They were able to string such words together but could only do so in a near arbitrary fashion. Jackendoff (1999) suggests that simple rules such as "agent first" might have reduced potential ambiguity. The transformation of such protolanguage into language required the evolution of grammar—rules that define the order in which a finite number of words can be strung together to create an infinite number of utterances, each with a specific meaning.

Alternative views regarding protolanguage have recently emerged that fall into the category of "holistic" theories (e.g., Arbib, 2002, 2003; Wray, 1998, 2000). By using the term "holistic," proponents of this approach mean that the precursor to language was a communication system composed of "messages" rather than words; each hominid utterance was uniquely associated with an arbitrary meaning. But the hominid multisyllable utterances would not have comprised smaller units of meaning (i.e., words) that could be combined together in either an arbitrary fashion or by using rules to produce emergent meanings.

I favor the holistic approach to protolanguage, because it provides a better account for the character of the archaeological record. The marked cultural stasis in the Middle and early Late Pleistocene record is in accord with the notion that hominids had a relatively limited number of holistic phrases (Mithen, 2005; Wray, 1998). Nevertheless, these would have constituted a communication system considerably more complex than that of living primates today, and elsewhere I (Mithen, 2005) have characterized it as being holistic, manipulative, multimodal, musical, and mimetic ("Hmmmm").

Numerous selective pressures would have existed during the Pleistocene for the evolution of this communication system. Changing life-history patterns would have been important (Bogin, 2003), especially the phenomenon of secondary altriciality that arose from the opposing evolutionary forces of bipedalism (requiring a narrow pelvis) and encephalization (ideally requiring a wide pelvis). The evolutionary compromise was that hominids gave birth to effectively immature infants that would have required increased levels of maternal care and would have created selective pressures for enhanced mother–infant communication (Dissanayake, 2000; Falk, 2004). Male–female social relations would also have changed due to increase in body size (Key & Aiello, 1999) and the likely development of female kin networks, partly to provision for, support, and protect nursing mothers (Hawkes, O'Connell, & Blurton-Jones, 1997; O'Connell, Hawkes, & Blurton-Jones, 1999). Female choice of mating partners most likely increased, requiring enhanced levels of vocal, gestural, and cultural display by males—a possible explanation for the symmetry imposed on many hand axes (Kohn & Mithen, 1999). The colonization of new landscapes and big game hunting would also have created selective pressures for enhanced communication, most likely involving the mimicry of animal noises and movements (Donald, 1991; Mithen, 2005).

The evolution of protolanguage was facilitated by anatomical changes that arose from bipedalism and dietary change, notably, the descent of the larynx and reduced dentition to create a larger oral cavity (Aiello, 1996). Both of these would have increased the range and diversity of vocalizations, without having been specifically selected for enhanced communication. Further anatomical changes that are evident within *H. heidelbergensis* or *H. neanderthalensis* were most likely the result of such selection, notably, enlargement of the nerves from the brain to the tongue, as measured on fossil specimens by the size of the hypoglossal canal (Kay, Cartmill, & Balow, 1998) and, similarly, the nerves passing through the thoracic vertebrae that control the diaphragm and, hence, breathing (MacLarnon & Hewitt, 1999). The inner ear also evolved within this time period to enable levels of sound perception equivalent to our levels today (Martínez et al., 2004). That these evolutionary developments did not lead to language is evident from the continued cultural stasis and absence of symbolic artifacts within the archaeological record, especially noticeable among the Neanderthals of Europe (Mithen, 2005).

LANGUAGE AND COGNITIVE FLUIDITY

The fossil and archaeological records suggest that language is restricted to *H. sapiens* because only in this species do we see the appearance of symbolic objects and creative thought. The best guess from paleoanthropology is that the evolution of language is directly associated with the speciation of *H. sapiens* soon after 200,000 years ago in Africa (Ingman, Kaessmann, Paabo, & Gyllensten, 2000; McDougall, Brown, & Fleagle, 2005). This view is supported by the likely date for the most recent mutation in the *FOXP2* gene (Enard et al., 2002), which appears to be related to grammatical complexity (Bishop, 2002).

Language most likely arose from the "segmentation" (Wray, 1998) or "fractionation" (Arbib, 2002) of holistic utterances used by the immediate ancestor of *H. sapiens* in Africa, sometimes referred to as *H. helmei* (McBrearty & Brooks, 2000). This resulted in the creation of words that could then be recombined to create novel utterances. Although the possibility of segmentation has been questioned (e.g., Bickerton, 2003), its feasibility has been demonstrated by computational models (e.g., Kirby, 2000, 2002), and it is the process of language origins that is most compatible with the evidence from the paleoanthropological record. I (Mithen, 2005) argue that rather than the holistic communication system evolving directly into compositional language, it would have diverged into two specialist communication systems: one specializing in communicating information that we now call language, and the other, in expressing emotion that we call music.

Once language appeared, it would have had profound consequences for human cognition (Carruthers, 2002). Language changed the way we think by "collapsing" the domain-specific mentality that had provided the structure of the human mind since the time of *H. ergaster*. According to Carruthers, by using imagined sentences in our heads, the outputs of one type of cognitive domain could now be combined with those from others to create a new type of conscious thought. He terms this process "intermodular integration," whereas I use the term "cognitive fluidity."

This lies at the root of the cultural developments that first became apparent 70,000 years ago, with the discoveries of incised ochre pieces and pierced shell beads from Blombos Cave in South Africa that most likely carried symbolic meanings (Henshilwood et al., 2002, 2004). The seeming time lag between 200,000 and 70,000 years ago may reflect no more than the relative lack of knowledge about the African archaeological record of this period (McBrearty & Brooks, 2000), or that a critical population density threshold that was crossed soon after 100,000 years ago had consequences for cultural transmission (Shennan, 2000). *H. sapiens* initially dispersed into the Near East 100,000 years ago, where the first burials with unambiguous ritual activity are found. Later dispersals gave rise to the modern human populations in Europe 40,000 years ago (Mellars, 2004). The first painted caves and carved art objects, around 30,000 years ago, formed part of the Upper Palaeolithic culture that also involved major developments in technology. Modern humans also spread from Africa into

Australasia, and by 30,000 years ago had reached its southernmost extremities.

Many of the cultural developments of modern humans after 50,000 years ago illustrate the phenomenon of cognitive fluidity (Mithen, 1996). Perhaps the clearest example is the development of ideas about supernatural beings, as is evident from paintings and carvings of half-human/half-animal figures, such as the lion–man of Hohenstein-Stadel or the "sorcerer" of Trois Frères. To conceive of such entities, humans had to combine what they knew about people from their social intelligence with that about animals from their natural history intelligence to create the idea of a being that did not physically exist in the "real" world. Similarly, to make the hunting weapons of the Late Pleistocene, people had to combine what they knew about manufacturing tools (from technical intelligence) with what they knew about animals (from natural history intelligence) to design the specialized implements that replaced the general purpose hunting weapons, which had existed for much of human evolution. And when the Ice Age came to an end 10,000 years ago, people could have begun farming only if they were able to care for plants and animals in the same manner that they cared for their children—by applying their social intelligence to the realm of natural history. In general, cognitive fluidity provided humans with the capacity for metaphor and analogy, which, arguably, lies at the root of all art, science, and religion (Mithen, 1996).

THE EXTENDED MIND

Cognitive fluidity created both the need and the possibility for the final key step in the evolution of the human mind—the extension beyond the brain and into material culture. Today, we extend our capacity for memory by using spoken/sung/material mnemonics, and by storing information in books, CDs, and so forth. Similarly, we extend our computational abilities by using calculators and computers. We can trace the start of this process within the very earliest art, especially that depicting supernatural beings. Although cognitively fluid minds can come up with ideas of supernatural beings, such ideas are evolutionarily "unnatural." As a consequence, they are difficult to hold within our minds and transmit to others. Try, for instance, explaining to someone the concept of the "Holy Trinity," or try understanding this as someone describes it to you, or that of the Aboriginal "Dreamtime." As Day (2004) has explained, "One of the bedevilling problems about dealing with gods is that . . . they are never really *there*" (p. 116, original emphasis); hence, we have difficulty in knowing not only how to communicate with them but also how to think about them.

Modern humans compensate for this by the use of material symbols that provide "cognitive anchors" (Mithen, 1998a, 1998b). Whether supernatural beings are made tangible in representative manner, as we suppose the lion–man from Hohlensetin-Stadel is doing, or in abstract form as in the Christian Cross, such material symbols function to help conceptualize and to share the religious entities and ideas that one believes. In this regard, such objects constitute an extension of the human mind. The same principle applies with regard to scientific ideas: These are dependent upon externalizing the ideas in material form, whether as mathematical formulae, diagrams in three dimensions, or even virtual reality models.

The material extensions of the mind facilitate the communication and exchange of ideas. More significantly, they enable such ideas to be further manipulated within our own minds in a manner that the brain alone cannot achieve. And so, in contrast to all previous *Homo* species, modern humans have used material culture to become far more intelligent than nature ever intended. The process of extending the mind by the use of technology that began at least 70,000 years ago continues unabated today. Indeed, we are what Clarke (2003) has described as *Natural Born Cyborgs*: Cognitive evolution continues by cultural means.

REFERENCES

Aiello, L. C. (1996). Terrestriality, bipedalism and the origin of language. In W. G. Runciman, J. Maynard-Smith, & R. I. M. Dunbar (Eds.), *Evolution of social behaviour patterns in primates and man* (pp. 269–290). Oxford, UK: Oxford University Press.

Aiello, L. C., & Dunbar, R. I. M. (1993). Neocortex size, group size, and the evolution of language. *Current Anthropology, 34*, 184–193.

Aiello, L. C., & Wheeler, P. (1995). The expensive-tissue hypothesis. *Current Anthropology, 36*, 199–220.

Arbib, M. A. (2002). The mirror system, imitation and the evolution of language. In C. Nehaniv & K. Dautenhahn (Eds.), *Imitation in animals and artifacts* (pp. 229–280). Cambridge, MA: MIT Press.

Arbib, M. A. (2003). The evolving mirror system: A neural basis for language readiness. In M. H. Christiansen & S. Kirby (Eds.), *Language evolution* (pp. 182–200). Oxford, UK: Oxford University Press.

Bickerton, D. (1990). *Language and species*. Chicago: University of Chicago Press.

Bickerton, D. (1998). Catastrophic evolution: The case for a single step from protolanguage to full human language. In J. Hurford, M. Studdert-Kennedy, & C.

Knight (Eds.), *Approaches to the evolution of language: Social and cognitive biases* (pp. 341–358). Cambridge, UK: Cambridge University Press.

Bickerton, D. (2000). How protolanguage became language. In C. Knight, M. Studdert-Kennedy, & J. Hurford (Eds.), *The evolutionary emergence of language* (pp. 264–284). Cambridge, UK: Cambridge University Press.

Bickerton, D. (2003). Symbol and structure: A comprehensive framework for language evolution. In M. H. Christiansen & S. Kirby (Eds.), *Language evolution* (pp. 77–93). Oxford, UK: Oxford University Press.

Bishop, D. V. M. (2002). Putting language genes in perspective. *Trends in Genetics, 18*, 57–59.

Bogin, B. (2003). The human pattern of growth and development. J. L. Thompson, G. E. Krovitz, & A. J. Nelson (Eds.), In *Patterns of growth and development in the genus* Homo (pp. 14–44). Cambridge, UK: Cambridge University Press.

Byrne, R. W., & Whiten, A. (Eds). (1988). *Machiavellian intelligence: Social expertise and the evolution of intellect in monkeys, apes and humans.* Oxford, UK: Clarendon Press.

Byrne, R. W., & Whiten, A. (1992). Cognitive evolution in primates: Evidence from tactical deception. *Man, 27,* 609–627.

Carruthers, P. (2002). The cognitive functions of language. *Brain and Behavioral Sciences, 25,* 657–726.

Carruthers, P., & Smith, P. (Eds.). (1996). *Theories of theories of minds.* Cambridge, UK: Cambridge University Press.

Clark, A. (2003). *Natural born cyborgs: Minds, technologies and the future of human intelligence.* Oxford, UK: Oxford University Press.

Cosmides, L., & Tooby, J. (1994). Origins of domain specificity: The evolution of functional organization. In L. A. Hirschfield & S. A. Gelman (Eds.), *Mapping the mind: Domain specificity in cognition and culture* (pp. 85–116). Cambridge, UK: Cambridge University Press.

Day, M. (2004). Religion, off-line cognition and the extended mind. *Journal of Cognition and Culture, 4,* 101–121.

Dissanayake, E. (2000). Antecedents of the temporal arts in early mother–infant interaction. In N. L. Wallin, B. Merker, & S. Brown (Eds.), *The origins of music* (pp. 389–410). Cambridge, MA: MIT Press.

Donald, M. (1991). *Origins of the modern mind.* Cambridge, MA: Harvard University Press.

Dunbar, R. I. M. (1993). Coevolution of neocortical size on group size in primates. *Journal of Human Evolution, 20,* 469–493.

Dunbar, R. I. M. (1998). Theory of mind and the evolution of language. In J. R. Hurford, M. Studdert-Kennedy, & C. Knight (Eds.), *Approaches to the evolution of language* (pp. 92–110). Cambridge, UK: Cambridge University Press.

Dunbar, R. I. M. (2004). *The human story.* London: Faber & Faber.

Enard, W., Przeworski, M., Fisher, S. E., Lai, C. S., Wiebe, V., Kitano, T., et al. (2002). Molecular evolution of *FOXP2,* a gene involved in speech and language. *Nature, 418,* 869–872.

Falk, D. (2004). Prelinguistic evolution in early hominins: Whence motherese? *Behavioral and Brain Sciences, 27,* 491–503.

Hawkes, K., O'Connell, J. F., & Blurton-Jones, N. G. 1997. Hadza women's time allocation, offspring provisioning, and the evolution of long post-menopausal lifespans. *Current Anthropology, 38,* 551–578.

Henshilwood, C. S., d'Errico, F., Yates, R., Jacobs, Z., Tribolo, C., Duller, G. A. T., et al. (2002). Emergence of modern human behaviour: Middle Stone Age engravings from South Africa. *Science, 295,* 1278–1280.

Henshilwood, C. S., d'Errico, F., Vanhaeren, M., van Niekerk, K., & Jacobs, Z. (2004). Middle Stone Age shell beads from South Africa. *Science, 304,* 404.

Ingman, M., Kaessmann, H., Paabo, S., & Gyllensten, U. (2000). Mitochondrial genome variation and the origin of modern humans. *Nature, 408,* 708–713.

Jackendoff, R. (1999). Possible stages in the evolution of the language faculty. *Trends in Cognitive Sciences, 3,* 272–279.

Kay, R. F., Cartmill, M., & Balow, M. (1998). The hypoglossal canal and the origin of human vocal behaviour. *Proceedings of the National Academy of Sciences of the United States of America, 95,* 5417–5419.

Key, C. A., & Aiello, L. C. (1999). The evolution of social organization. In R. Dunbar, C. Knight, & C. Power (Eds.), *The evolution of culture* (pp. 15–33). Edinburgh, UK: Edinburgh University Press.

Kirby, S. (2000). Syntax without natural selection: How compositionality emerges from vocabulary in a population of learners. In C. Knight, M. Studdert-Kennedy, & J. R. Hurford (Eds.), *The evolutionary emergence of language: Social function and the origins of linguistic form* (pp. 303–323). Cambridge, UK: Cambridge University Press.

Kirby, S. (2002). Learning, bottlenecks and the evolution of recursive syntax. In E. Briscoe (Ed.), *Linguistic evolution through language acquisition: Formal and computational models* (pp. 173–204). Cambridge, UK: Cambridge University Press.

Kohn, M., & Mithen, S. J. (1999). Handaxes: Products of sexual selection? *Antiquity, 73,* 518–526.

MacLarnon, A., & Hewitt, G. P. (1999). The evolution of human speech: The role of enhanced breathing control. *American Journal of Physical Anthropology, 109,* 341–343.

Martínez, I., Rosa, M., Arsuaga, J.-L., Jarabo, P., Quam, R., Lorenzo, C., et al. (2004). Auditory capacities in Middle Pleistocene humans from the Sierra de Atapuerca in Spain. *Proceedings of the National Academy of Sciences of the United States of America, 101,* 9976–9981.

McBrearty, S., & Brooks, A. (2000). The revolution that wasn't: A new interpretation of the origin of modern human behavior. *Journal of Human Evolution, 38,* 453–563.

McDougall, I., Brown, F. H., & Fleagle, J. G. (2005). Stratigraphic placement and age of modern humans from Kibish, Ethiopia. *Nature, 433,* 733–776.

Mellars, P. (2004). Neanderthals and the modern human colonization of Europe. *Nature, 432,* 461–465.

Mithen, S. J. (1996). *The prehistory of the mind: A search for the origin of art, science and religion.* London: Thames & Hudson/Orion.

Mithen, S. J. (1998a). A creative explosion?: Theory of mind, language and the disembodied mind of the Upper Palaeolithic. In S. Mithen (Ed.), *Creativity in human evolution and prehistory* (pp. 165–192). London: Routledge.

Mithen, S. J. (1998b). The supernatural beings of prehistory and the external storage of religious ideas. In C. Renfrew & C. Scarre (Eds.), *Cognition and material culture: The archaeology of symbolic storage* (pp. 97–106). Cambridge, UK: McDonald Institute of Archaeological Research.

Mithen, S. J. (1999). Palaeoanthropological perspectives on the theory of mind. In S. Baron-Cohen, H. T. Flusberg, & D. Cohen (Eds.), *Understanding other minds: Perspectives from autism and cognitive neuroscience* (pp. 494–508). Oxford, UK: Oxford University Press.

Mithen, S. J. (2005). *The singing neanderthals: The origin of music, language, mind and body.* London: Weidenfeld & Nicolson.

O'Connell, J. F., Hawkes, K., & Blurton-Jones, N. G. (1999). Grandmothering and the evolution of Homo erectus. *Journal of Human Evolution, 36,* 461–485.

Pelegrin, J. (1993). A framework for analysing prehistoric stone tool manufacture and a tentative application to some early stone industries. In A. Berthelet & J. Chavaillon (Eds.), *The use of tools by human and non-human primates* (pp. 302–314). Oxford, UK: Clarendon Press.

Povinelli, D. J. (1993). Reconstructing the evolution of the mind. *American Psychologist, 48,* 493–509.

Ruff, C. B., Trinkaus, E. & Holliday, T. W. (1997). Body mass and encephalization in Pleistocene *Homo. Nature, 387,* 173–176.

Russon, A. E., Bard, K. A., & Parker, S. T. (1996). *Reaching into thought: The minds of the great apes.* Cambridge, UK: Cambridge University Press.

Shennan, S. J. (2000). Population, culture history and the dynamics of culture change. *Current Anthropology, 41,* 811–835.

Straus, L. G. & Bar-Yosef, O. (Eds.). (2001). Out of Africa in the Pleistocene. *Quaternary International, 75,* 1–3.

Tomasello. M., Call, J., & Hare, B. (2003). Chimpanzees understand psychological states—the question is which ones and to what extent. *Trends in Cognitive Sciences, 7,* 153–156.

Wray, A. (1998). Protolanguage as a holistic system for social interaction. *Language and Communication, 18,* 47–67.

Wray, A. (2000). Holistic utterances in protolanguage: The link from primates to humans. In C. Knight, M. Studdert-Kennedy, & J. R. Hurford (Eds.), *The evolutionary emergence of language: Social function and the origins of linguistic form* (pp. 285–302). Cambridge, UK: Cambridge University Press.

Brain Evolution

℘ 28

Brain Evolution and the Human Adaptive Complex

An Ecological and Social Theory

HILLARD S. KAPLAN
MICHAEL GURVEN
JANE B. LANCASTER

This essay considers human brain evolution in terms of a larger set of coevolved traits, which we refer to as *the human adaptive complex* (HAC). The *embodied capital theory of human life-history evolution* explains the evolution of human brain size, development, and function as components of a coadapted complex of traits, including (1) the life history of development, aging, and longevity; (2) diet and dietary physiology; (3) energetics of reproduction; (4) social relationships among men and women; (5) intergenerational resource transfers; and (6) cooperation among related and unrelated individuals (Gurven & Kaplan, 2006; Gurven, Kaplan, & Gutierrez, 2006; Gurven & Walker, 2006; Kaplan, 1997; Kaplan, Gangestad, Lancaster, Gurven, & Robson, in press; Kaplan & Gurven, 2005; Kaplan, Hill, Hurtado, & Lancaster, 2001; Kaplan, Hill, Lancaster, & Hurtado, 2000; Kaplan, Mueller, Gangestad, & Lancaster, 2003; Kaplan & Robson, 2002; Robson & Kaplan, 2003).

According to the theory, the HAC is a very specialized niche, character-ized by (1) the highest-quality, most nutrient-dense, and largest-package-size food resources; (2) learning-intensive, sometimes technology-intensive, and often cooperative food acquisition techniques; (3) a large brain to learn and store a great deal of context-dependent environmental information and to develop creative food acquisition techniques; (4) a long period of juve-nile dependence to support brain development and learning; (5) low juve-nile and even lower adult mortality rates, generating a long productive life-span and population age structure with a high ratio of adult producers to juvenile dependents; (6) a three-generational system of downward resource flowing from grandparents to parents to children; (7) biparental invest-ment, with men specializing in energetic support, and women combining energetic support with direct care of children; (8) marriage and long-term reproductive unions; and (9) cooperative arrangements among kin and un-related individuals to reduce variance in food availability through sharing, and to acquire resources in group pursuits more effectively.

In the publications cited earlier, we have shown that the majority of the foods consumed by contemporary hunter-gatherers worldwide are calorically dense hunted and extracted resources taken from a protected substrate (e.g., underground, in shells), accounting for 35–60% of calories. Extractive foraging and hunting proficiency generally does not peak until the mid-30s because they are learning- and technique-intensive. Hunting, in particular, demands great skills and knowledge that takes years to learn, with the amount of meat acquired per unit time more than doubling from age 20 to 40, even though strength peaks in the early 20s. This learning-intensive foraging niche generates large calorie deficits until age 20, fol-lowed by great calorie surpluses later in life. This life-history profile of hunter-gatherer productivity is only economically viable with a long adult lifespan. Among hunter-gatherers without access to Western medicine, peo-ple can expect to live about 40 more years if they survive age 15, and an additional two decades if they survive to age 45. Chimpanzees, our closest living relative, can expect to live only to age 27 if they survive to age 15. Parents and grandparents often finance the juvenile learning phase through food transfers.

These data, as well as cross-species analyses of primate brain size and life history (e.g., Kaplan et al., 2003, in press), provide substantial support for learning-based, dietary (ecological) theories of primate brain expansion and for the coevolution of age of first reproduction, longevity, and brain size. There are, however, alternative *social* models of brain ex-pansion. The social brain hypothesis (e.g., Byrne, 1995; Dunbar, 1998) is generally formulated as the evolution of *Machiavellian intelligence* in response to a social arms race of political maneuvering and information manipulation in large groups. Recently, in a proposed signaling version of the social hypothesis, selection for intelligence derives from its ability to signal mutational load in mating competition (Miller, Chapter 30, this volume).

In this chapter, we develop embodied capital theory to include social capital. In doing so, our goal is to incorporate both social and ecological forces in brain evolution in a unified theory of the HAC.

COOPERATION AND THE
HUMAN ADAPTIVE COMPLEX

Human food acquisition is inherently social in a number of ways. First, the mix of hunting and gathering in which people engage to maximize the rate of nutrient gain per unit effort results in a division of labor by sex (and, to some extent, by age). The human commitment to carrying, rather than caching, children and to providing high-quality child care (a trait shared throughout the primate order) is incompatible with hunting, because it involves long-distance walking and often dangerous pursuits. As a result, in all foraging groups, women allocate the majority of their time to gathering and child care, and men, to hunting (although the exact mix depends on ecology). Associated with this division of labor is the practice of marriage and family formation. All human groups recognize marriage as a bond that regulates sexual activity (especially of women), in which a man and a woman form a cooperative bond in raising children. This bond is generally characterized by intensive food sharing within the family and a division of labor in the organization of other household tasks and child care. Moreover, in foraging groups, the reproductive careers of men and women are highly linked. Although divorce is common in many foraging groups, most couples have the majority of their children together, and men often have their last child when their wives reach menopause. The relationship between men and women in foraging societies is arguably the most intense and multifaceted cooperative relationship in which they engage.

Second, social learning plays a critical role in the intergenerational transmission of knowledge and practices. Moreover, social learning probably increases the rate at which human children, adolescents, and adults learn how to hunt and gather efficiently (Blurton Jones & Marlowe, 2002). Forager children and adolescents have years of experience listening to others tell stories and anecdotes about different foraging activities, before ever engaging in these activities themselves. In nonhuman primates, the frequency of social transmission of information strongly predicts wide-ranging variation in primate brain size, and most of this information pertains to foraging (Reader & Laland, 2002).

A third characteristic is that human diets are inherently risky, and food sharing is a fundamental component of the HAC. At the individual level, foraging luck is often highly variable. Hunting, in particular, can produce highly variable returns, especially in the case of large game. Food sharing among families is practiced by foragers to even out the daily food supply and buffer against the risks associated with large, mobile packages of food. A social brain also becomes increasingly important in the context of strategic sharing of game (Stanford, 1999). For example, efficient sharing requires the monitoring of meat and other contributions made by other group members.

Fourth, human foraging, especially hunting, is often more effectively done in cooperative groups. Many species can be prevented from escaping predation by groups of cooperating hunters. In cooperative foraging activities, individual roles are often well specified, and the coordination is intentional and consciously understood by all members of the cooperative party.

When all of this is put together, the complexity and intensity of human cooperative relationships, especially among nonkin relationships such as spouses and friends, is unparalleled. Cooperation is risky and fragile given that the possibility of defection always looms in the background. As a result, choice of partners in contexts where cooperation can have profound effects on people's lives puts a large premium on intelligence.

SOCIAL CAPITAL AND THE COMPETITIVE
MARKET FOR COOPERATORS

We now introduce the concept of *social capital*, borrowed from sociology and economics, to evolutionary discourse as applied to HAC. Whereas social capital has been traditionally thought of as the web of connections that one attains through family and friends (Coleman, 1988; Putnam, 2000), Lin (1999) provides an individually based definition of "social capital" as investment in social relations with expected returns. We offer a modified definition: "Social capital" is *information or perceptions embodied in other individuals with expected fitness returns through its effects on social interactions.*

In the case of nonhuman primates, social capital is mainly in the form of information about dominance relations and sexual/reproductive states or qualities. For example, the social capital for dominant individuals is information stored in the brains of subordinates, based on a history of previous interactions. Dominants can expect a return on this capital to the extent that this information affects the behavior of subordinates. As a result, dominants can often obtain priority access to a feeding site or sexual partner with a simple facial or bodily gesture.

The Human Case: Social Capital and Access to Resources

We propose that in traditional human groups, social capital investment is very significant and cognitively demanding, exerting considerable selective force on human psychology and intelligence. Social capital, however, plays a different role in people's lives than in those of nonhuman primates, given the special features of the HAC described earlier.

There is increasing evidence that food is not shared equally with all band members in most hunting and gathering societies, except under specific circumstances (Gurven, 2004). People have preferred partners with whom reciprocal exchange is greatest. The most common social arrangement appears to be one of variably sized food distribution networks, depending on the food resource and its means of obtainment. In many groups, there is significant producer control over sharing and limited scope of partners. For example, among Hiwi foragers, hunters tend to exercise control over how much and with whom they share meat, restricting those who receive shares to some 15–20% of potential recipients in large groups (Gurven, Hill, Kaplan, Hurtado, & Lyles, 2000). Thus, there is a potential market for cooperative partners. The ability to engage in profitable partnerships may require a great deal of social intelligence, particularly the ability to understand how one's actions will affect future access to food and food exchange.

This logic may explain why humans commonly cooperate in experimental games and punish defectors (Henrich et al., 2001). The tendency to cooperate on the first move allows people to experience greater gains from cooperation and to demonstrate their quality as potential cooperators in future interactions. People have a moral approach to these problems, because a more Machiavellian approach, which would take advantage of all opportunities for defection in one-shot games, is outcompeted by a moral psychology when there is uncertainty about the possibility of being detected as a defector and the costs of being labeled as a cheater have great long-term consequences. Runaway selection on the ability to detect signs of a Machiavellian strategy in the context of a food acquisition strategy that depends on cooperation and sharing may have been of great importance in the evolution of social intelligence and moral reasoning.

Human psychological traits and social norms of sharing are likely to reflect the relative strengths of two opposing forces: gains from cooperation and possibilities for free-riding (Tooby, Cosmides, & Price, 2006). These opposing forces may have led to the evolution of general moral sentiments, supported by both the emotional–motivational psychology of individuals and common cultural norms. This reasoning predicts that natural selection has shaped our psychology to possess the following traits: (1) perceptual sensitivity to potential gains from cooperation; (2) motivation to take advantage of those gains; (3) perceptual sensitivity to opportunities for free-riding; (4) motivation to avoid being free-ridden; (5) motivation to take advantage of opportunities for free-riding; (6) perceptual sensitivity to the short- and long-term personal costs and benefits of social norms regarding cooperative behavior (from the perspectives of both self and others); (7) motivation to negotiate social norms, so that personal benefits from cooperation and free-riding are maximized; and (8) motivation to obey and enforce social norms, so that punishment is avoided and those who disobey norms or fail to enforce them are punished.

Social Capital, Mating, and Marriage

Human marriage is probably the most complex cooperative relationship in which we engage. It involves the production and processing of resources for familial consumption, the distribution of those resources, the provision of child care, the production and maintenance of belongings and residential amenities, and sexual rights and responsibilities. The ability to coordinate the allocation and execution of those responsibilities (i.e., the ability to "get along") is fundamental to successful marriage, and it appears to play a role in mate choice. In traditional societies, it is common to hear remarks about success and failure in coordinating and getting along as reasons for why marriages succeed or fail.

One problem that people face in mate choice is that long-term dependency and multiple dependency make mate switching more costly for humans. Once one has reproduced with a given partner, a change in partners can entail reduced investment in those previous children. Moreover, most mate choice occurs before economic abilities are proven. For example, at marriage age (around 20), Aché and Tsimane men are only 25 and 50% proficient as hunters (respectively) as they will be at their peak in their mid-to-late 30s.

Thus, from the perspective of both men and women, there are great gains from choosing a good partner, and there are also great risks of economic and sexual defection. For the most part, it is a long-term choice with direct consequences for fitness. It is further complicated by the fact that partners contribute to fitness not only through behavior but also through genetic inputs, which can lead to either further complementarities or to conflicts of interest. Marriages redirect social interaction and cooperation not only within the pair bond but also across members of respective extended families.

Social capital is likely to play an important role in mate choice. Capital affecting perceptions about fairness, industriousness, loyalty, promiscuity, and economic abilities is likely to influence mate choice decisions by both men and women. Some of the same factors affecting the choice of production and sharing partners may also affect the choice of marriage partners.

Such considerations leave ample room for display behavior. Whereas over the long run the primary motivation for economic production may be the raising of a family, symbolic forms of production and sharing may be important investments in social capital. Some proportion of food-sharing behavior is likely to be symbolic investments in social capital affecting future cooperative interactions. Importantly, as emphasized by others (Bird, 1999; Hawkes, 1990; Smith, 2004), displays of hunting competence and generosity may play an important role in mating success. In fact, many foraging and forager–horticulturalist societies, such as the !Kung and the Tsimane, practice bride service, in which young men hunt to feed their future father-in-law's family before having full marital rights.

Moreover, because intelligence and cognitive ability are likely to be important in food production, social access to shared food, and efficient child care, we might expect young men and women to invest in social capital through displays of social and ecological intelligence. We might also expect people to be very discriminating in their appreciation of those displays. In addition, as discussed by Miller (Chapter 30, this volume), to the extent that such displays are honest advertisements of genetic fitness and mutational load, there would be another incentive to engage in and discriminate among displays.

CONCLUSION

Our proposal is that ecological and social intelligence, coupled with specific psychological characteristics, are fundamental components of the

HAC. This psychology, the complex analytical brain, and the extended life history coevolved in the hominid line, all because of the dietary shift toward large, high-quality food packages and division of labor in food production and child care. It is this feeding adaptation that generates gains from cooperation. In this sense, both social and foraging intelligence are ecologically determined.

Cooperative strategies, however, also entail gains from, and risks of, defections. This places a premium on decisions about when and with whom to cooperate. Behaviors that facilitate being selected as a cooperative partner may have played a great role in individual and family food consumption patterns. Given that marriage is a fragile and complex human social relationship, it may have played an important role in shaping both our intelligence and our psychological characteristics.

In addition, some of the cognitive substrates for solving economic and social problems are probably shared. For example, inferences about animal behavior, such as likely escape strategies if the hunter's presence is detected, are critical for hunting success. Animal "mind-reading" and human mind-reading may involve similar cognitive abilities, including the ability to discriminate among types of minds (deer, child, adult friend, adult enemy, etc.). To the extent that such substrates are shared, selection would act on the total effects of increased abilities, summed over all routes through which those abilities affect fitness. In a recent review of the comparative anatomy of primate brains, Rilling (2006) notes that natural selection uniquely modified the human brain to deviate from the rules of brain design that obtain among other primates. He points to a unique evolutionary modification in the prefrontal cortex associated with symbolic thinking, knowledge of appropriate social behavior, decision making, planning, cognitive control, and working memory. Bering and Povenilli (2003; Povenilli, 2003) propose that the critical divide between the minds of apes and humans is not just the difference of 1000 cc of volume in order to do the same things much better, but an entirely unique feature of cognition, an ability to think about things that cannot be directly observed by the senses. Humans can think about the hidden world of causation—the world of forces and causes that lie beneath the surface appearance of things such as emotions and thoughts of others or perceptions and beliefs about forces impinging on inanimate objects such as gravity, force, mass, and physical connection. This is the world of *why* and *how*. We can take for an example the classic behavior of chimpanzee termite fishing. The naive chimpanzee sees the association of a probe and the acquisition of termites and can quickly emulate what he sees but without any attention to the qualities of a successful tool in terms of flexibility, length, and diameter. The association of probe and outcome can be learned rapidly but the critical intervening variables must be learned through trial and error. Similarly, the simplest level of a theory of the mind might be tested through the interpretation of gaze. A chimpanzee clearly makes use of information about whether an individual faces or has the back turned toward him but cannot discriminate between a blindfolded or gagged demonstrator in terms of what the person might see and hence know.

In contrast to the chimpanzee's unquestioned skill at extracting statistical regularities about what objects do and how they behave, the world of why and how is one that humans never stop thinking about, whether the issue is what others are thinking, how a tool works, or why people get sick (Bering & Povenilli, 2003). Humans crave insight and are so committed to knowing causation that they will confabulate if necessary or attribute minds and emotions to trees and weather. This desire to command the unseen world of causation links social and foraging intelligence as well as all other human endeavors through a single process of insight and understanding, a shared cognitive substrate for the unique performances of the human mind.

In this sense, embodied capital in the form of social and foraging skills are inevitably linked and probably coevolved since they utilize the same brain mechanisms. The abilities to scenario-build in solving both foraging and social problems, to engage in high-level abstract logical reasoning, and to think insightfully about the hidden world of causation appear to have evolved in one lineage only. Perhaps our species is an outlier, precisely because the human adaptive complex demands both *ecological* and *social* intelligence.

REFERENCES

Bering, J. M., & Povenilli, D. J. (2003). Comparing cognitive development. In D. Maestripieri (Ed.), *Primate psychology* (pp. 205–233). Cambridge, MA: Harvard University Press.

Bird, R. (1999). Cooperation and conflict: The behavioral ecology of the sexual division of labor. *Evolutionary Anthropology, 8*, 65–75.

Blurton Jones, N. G., & Marlowe F. W. (2002). Selection for delayed maturity: Does it take 20 years to learn to hunt and gather? *Human Nature, 13*, 199–238.

Byrne, R. W. (1995). *The thinking ape: The evolutionary origins of intelligence.* Oxford, UK: Oxford University Press.

Coleman, J. (1988). Social capital in the creation of human capital. *American Journal of Sociology, 94*, S95–S120.

Dunbar, R. I. M. (1998). The social brain hypothesis. *Evolutionary Anthropology, 6,* 178–190.

Gurven, M. (2004). To give or to give not: An evolutionary ecology of human food transfers. *Behavioral and Brain Sciences, 27,* 543–583.

Gurven, M., Hill, K., Kaplan, H., Hurtado, M., & Lyles, B. (2000). Food transfers among Hiwi foragers of Venezuela: tests of reciprocity. *Human Ecology, 28,* 171–218.

Gurven, M., & Kaplan, H. (2006). Determinants of time allocation to production across the lifespan among the Machiguenga and Piro Indians of Peru. *Human Nature, 17*(1), 1–49.

Gurven, M., Kaplan, H., & Gutierrez, M. (2006). How long does it take to become a proficient hunter?: Implications for the evolution of extended development and long life span. *Journal of Human Evolution, 51,* 454–470.

Gurven, M., & Walker, R. (2006). Energetic demand of multiple dependents and the evolution of slow human growth. *Proceedings of the Royal Society of London, Series B: Biological Sciences, 273,* 835–841.

Hawkes, K. (1990). Why do men hunt? Benefits for risky choices. In E. Cashdan (Ed.), *Risk and uncertainty in tribal and peasant economies* (pp. 145–166). Boulder, CO: Westview Press.

Henrich, J., Boyd, R., Bowles, S., Camerer, C., Gintis, H., McElreath, R., et al. (2001). In search of *Homo Economicus*: Behavioral experiments in 15 small-scale societies. *American Economic Review, 91,* 73–79.

Kaplan, H. (1997). The evolution of the human life course: Between Zeus and Salmon. In K. Wachter & C. Finch (Eds.), *The biodemography of longevity* (pp. 175–211). Washington, DC: National Academy of Sciences.

Kaplan, H., & Bock, J. (2001). Fertility theory: The embodied capital theory of life history evolution. In N. J. Smelser & P. B. Baltes (Eds.-in-Chief), *The international encyclopedia of the social and behavioral sciences* (pp. 5561–5568). Amsterdam: Elsevier.

Kaplan, H., Gangestad, S., Lancaster, J., Gurven, M., & Robson, A. (in press). The evolution of diet, brain and life history among primates and humans. In W. Roebocks (Ed.), *Guts, brains, food and the social life of early hominids.* Amsterdam: University of Amsterdam Press.

Kaplan, H., & Gurven, M. (2005). The natural history of human food sharing and cooperation: a review and a new multi-individual approach to the negotiation of norms. In H. Gintis, S. Bowles, R Boyd, & E. Fehr (Eds), *Moral sentiments and material interests: The foundations of cooperation in economic life* (pp. 75–113). Cambridge, MA: MIT Press.

Kaplan, H. S., Hill, K., Hurtado, A. M., & Lancaster, J. B. (2001). The embodied capital theory of human evolution. In P. T. Ellison (Ed.), *Reproductive ecology and human evolution.* Hawthorne, NY: Aldine de Gruyter.

Kaplan, H. S., & Robson, A. J. (2002). The emergence of humans: The coevolution of intelligence and longevity with intergenerational transfers. *Proceedings of the National Academy of Sciences, 99,* 10221–10226.

Kaplan, H., Hill, K., Lancaster, J. B., & Hurtado, A. M. (2000). A theory of human life history evolution: Diet, intelligence, and longevity. *Evolutionary Anthropology, 9*, 156–185.

Kaplan, H., Mueller, T., Gangestad, S., & Lancaster, J. (2003). Neural capital and life-span evolution among primates and humans. In C. E. Finch, J. M. Robine, & Y. Christen (Eds.), *Brain and longevity* (pp. 69–98). New York: Springer-Verlag.

Leibenberg, L. (1990). *The art of tracking: The origin of science.* Cape Town: David Phillip.

Lin, N. (1999). Building a network theory of social capital. *Connections, 22,* 28–51.

Povenilli, D. J. (2003). *Folk physics for apes: A chimpanzee's theory of how the world works.* Oxford, UK: Oxford University Press.

Putnam, R. (2000). *Bowling alone: The collapse and revival of American community.* New York: Simon & Schuster.

Reader, S. M., & Laland, K. N. (2002). Social intelligence, innovation, and enhanced brain size in primates. *Proceedings of the National Academy of Science of the United States of America, 99,* 4436–4441.

Rilling, J. K. (2006). Human and nonhuman primate brains: Are they allometrically scaled versions of the same desing? *Evolutionary Anthropology, 15,* 65–77.

Robson, A., & Kaplan, H. (2003). The co-evolution of longevity and intelligence in hunter-gatherer economies. *American Economic Review, 93,* 150–169.

Smith, E. A. (2004). Why do good hunters have higher reproductive success? *Human Nature, 15,* 343–364.

Stanford, C. G. (1999). *The hunting apes: Meat eating and the origins of human behavior.* Princeton, NJ: Princeton University Press.

Tooby, J., Cosmides, L., & Price, M. (2006). Cognitive adaptations for *n*-person exchange: The evolutionary roots of organizational behavior. *Managerial and Decision Economics, 27,* 103–129.

🜂 29

Evolution of the Social Brain

ROBIN DUNBAR

The social brain hypothesis offers an explanation for primates' unusually large brains for their body size compared to all other vertebrate groups and, within that, the fact that human brains are particularly large even by primate standards. It proposes that the evolution of these large brains is a consequence of the social world being computationally more demanding than anything an animal does in the physical world (Barton & Dunbar, 1997; Byrne & Whiten, 1988; Dunbar, 1998).

One reason why this might be so is that the social world is a virtual world rather than a physical world of the kind with which one can engage directly. The social world requires an individual to imagine the future behavior of other organisms, and this in turn may require it to imagine the other organism's mental states. These aspects of the world cannot be observed or engaged with directly, but have to be constructed in the mind. The computational costs of doing so may be significantly increased if all the individuals concerned are not actually physically present, so that virtual individuals have to be factored into the relationships exhibited in a more direct sense by those individuals who are immediately present (Barrett, Henzi, & Dunbar, 2003).

In this chapter, I briefly review the evidence for the social brain hypothesis, then explore some of the more specific consequences for humans that follow from it.

THE SOCIAL BRAIN
IN EVOLUTIONARY PERSPECTIVE

Until Byrne and Whiten (1988) proposed the social brain hypothesis (initially known as the Machiavellian intelligence hypothesis), it had largely been assumed that brain evolution, broadly among the vertebrates, but specifically among the primates, reflected the demands of everyday survival, primarily food gathering. Conventional wisdom suggested that among primates, large brains were associated with large-range areas or frugivory (both of which were assumed to reflect the computational demands of large-scale mental maps), extractive foraging (in which food items embedded in some kind of matrix from which they need to be extracted made heavy demands on the animals' problem-solving abilities) or, in the case of humans, tool making. However, all of these hypotheses have ultimately been found wanting, either on empirical grounds or on grounds of parsimony.

First, it is important to appreciate that as it has enlarged, the primate brain has not done so as a homogenous entity; rather, it is a mosaic of components that have changed size at different rates. In particular, the neocortex has enlarged at a disproportionately faster rate (Finlay & Darlington, 1995). The neocortex is essentially a mammalian invention, and large neocortices are a primate speciality. The neocortex forms a thin sheet of just six layers of cells wrapped around the core vertebrate brain, yet its volume ranges between 50 and 80% of total brain volume in primates (compared to between 10 and 50% in nonprimate mammals). Consequently, when we ask why primate brain size has increased, we are really asking why primate neocortex size has increased. Any explanation in terms of specific cognitive abilities associated with specific components in the brain (e.g., mental mapping capacities associated with the hippocampus, or the mating system associated with particular neuronal bundles and neuroendocrines in voles) falls short of explaining why the whole neocortex should enlarge as much as it has.

Second, whereas there is *prima facie* evidence for correlations between total brain volume and degree of frugivory, range size, and day journey length, these correlations are much weaker or disappear altogether when neocortex size is used as a more appropriate index of change in brain size. More importantly, they disappear altogether when the influence of social group size is partialed out. This suggests that correlations with these eco-logical variables may be a consequence of group size correlating with (or determining) range size and day journey length and, hence, that they are consequences rather than causes of brain evolution. Similarly, despite its at-tractiveness as an explanation, the extractive foraging hypothesis has so far failed to yield convincing evidence in its favor (not least because it has been difficult to devise a quantitative metric of the extractiveness of foraging, and only a handful of species can readily be identified as extractive forag-ers: Dunbar, 1995).

Finally, when these various ecological hypotheses are put in direct contest with indexes of the social brain hypothesis, the latter receive the balance of support at the expense of the former (Dunbar, 1992). In this context, the core tests of the social brain hypothesis have used social group size as the principal index of social complexity. Despite the crudeness of this index, it has nonetheless yielded strong significant correlations with relative neocortex size in a number of mammalian taxa, including primates, carnivores, cetaceans, bats, and neurologically advanced—but not neuro-logically primitive—insectivores (Dunbar & Bever, 1998; Morino, 1998). More importantly, neocortex size in primates has been shown to correlate with a number of behavior indexes that reflect social complexity more di-rectly. These include grooming clique size (Kudo & Dunbar, 2001), male mating strategies (Pawlowski, Lowen, & Dunbar, 1998), social play (Lewis, 2001), frequency of tactical deception (Byrne & Corp, 2004), and length of the period of juvenile socialization (Joffe, 1997).

These latter findings emphasize the crucial role that social skills play in the evolution of the brain. Though it might be possible to argue that the evidence does not wholly disprove all the nonsocial (i.e., ecological) hy-potheses (Deaner, Nunn, & van Schaik, 2000), it would be difficult to ex-plain how any of the ecological hypotheses could result in such frequent correlations between neocortex volume and the various disparate indexes of social complexity. In this context, it is important to remind ourselves that the social hypothesis is itself, of course, ultimately an ecological expla-nation. The evolution of the social brain did not take place merely to make group living for the sake of group living possible; rather, it occurred to en-able animals to live in groups that were in turn designed to solve some problem of day-to-day survival or reproduction. The issue is whether these ecological problems are solved directly by individuals acting alone (i.e., us-ing their own powers of deduction and cause–effect learning) or socially by individuals collaborating to achieve a more effective solution. The social brain hypothesis explicitly argues for the second proposition.

THE SOCIAL BRAIN IN HUMAN EVOLUTION

Human societies are complex, and provide what would seem to be an un-promising case on which to test the social brain hypothesis, especially given the fact that the regression equation relating group size to neocortex volume in primates (and that for hominoids, in particular) predicts that humans should have a group size of only about 150. In fact, it turns out that humans do have a consistent grouping of exactly this size. A number of analyses of census data on human group sizes suggest that humans from many different economies and continents exhibit a consistent grouping level that encompasses about 150 individuals (Dunbar, 1993; Hill & Dunbar, 2003). Indeed, even though humans (similar to most other primates) live in hierarchically structured societies, where lower level groups are included in a higher-level grouping, these various groupings have a consistent numerical relation to each other at a scaling ratio of about three (Zhou, Sornette, Hill, & Dunbar, 2005). Because social subgroup size has also been shown to correlate with neocortex size in primates (Kudo & Dunbar, 2001), this suggests that the scaling of these groupings may itself be related to some aspect of the social brain.

COGNITION AND THE SOCIAL BRAIN

Although we have a relatively robust view of the relation between relative brain size and social group size, we have very limited knowledge about how this effect is mediated. The fact that neocortex volume correlates specifically with the length of the juvenile period and not with other life-history components (Joffe, 1997) clearly implies that socialization (and, hence, the learning of social kills) plays an important role. However, we have little knowledge about what the nature of these social cognitive skills might be. Two types of evidence give us some insight into what might be involved.

First, within the primates, a number of grade shifts can be identified in the relation between social group size and neocortex size. The most important of these is the separation into parallel groupings that, respectively, separate prosimians, simians, and hominoids. That apes lie to the right of the simians raises an obvious question: Why is it that apes need more neocortex volume (i.e., more computational power) to maintain groups of a given size than do monkeys? Aside from expensive and presumably functionless accidents of history, it is difficult to discern any obvious feature of the animals' biology that differentiates these two groups sufficiently to require additional computational demands, other than the fact that, compared to monkeys, apes typically live in communities that are more dispersed than those of monkeys. What is important in this context is that these societies commonly exhibit a fission–fusion form of organization; that is, the subgroups into which the community is divided constantly fuse and separate. One implication of this is that species living in fission–fusion social systems are forced to consider the interests and effects of individuals who are not, at any given moment, physically present.

Second, a very considerable literature now points to the importance of social cognition in human social relationships. The main emphasis in this literature has been on theory of mind (also known as mind reading or mentalizing) in young children. Theory of mind (ToM) is equivalent to second-order intentionality (the capacity to understand the contents of another individual's mind, or the ability to assert, "I believe you think that . . ."). Children acquire ToM at around 4 years of age (Astington, 1993), and much of the work in this area has focused on the processes involved. However, virtually no work has been done on the natural history of social cognition beyond this point, despite the fact that children continue to develop cognitively through several more orders of intentionality by the time they reach adulthood. In fact, normal adults achieve fifth-order intentionality ("I believe you think that I suppose that you want me to understand that . . . ") as a matter of course (Kinderman, Dunbar, & Bentall, 1998).

This performance level on the part of normal human adults contrasts with that seen in animals. There is general agreement that monkeys (and probably other mammals and birds) cannot aspire to more than first-order intentionality (i.e., the ability to believe something factual about the world). However, there is some evidence that chimpanzees (and perhaps all great apes) can aspire to second-order intentionality (Hare, Call, & Tomasello, 2001; O'Connell & Dunbar, 2003). If these values are taken as benchmarks, it turns out that the intentionality capacities of these three groups of taxa (humans, apes, and monkeys) have a very simple linear relation to absolute frontal lobe volume (Dunbar, 2003).

The implication of this rather surprising finding is that the computational demands of social cognition—and especially the advanced forms of social cognition represented by ToM—necessitate a proportionately heavy investment in neural wetware. Moreover, given that the occipital regions of the brain are already dedicated to essential sensory processing and related association areas, this additional neural matter has to come in the frontal regions. That should be no surprise considering that the brain develops and has evolved from back to front: Increases in brain volume primarily reflect additional volume in the frontal areas of the brain rather than a proportional increase in all regions of the cortex.

REFERENCES

Astington, J. W. (1993). *The child's discovery of the mind.* Cambridge, MA: Cambridge University Press.

Barrett, L., Henzi, S. P., & Dunbar, R. I. M. (2003). Primate cognition: From "What now?" to "What if?" *Trends in Cognitive Science, 7,* 494–497.

Barton, R. A., & Dunbar, R. I. M. (1997). Evolution of the social brain. In A.Whiten & R. Byrne (Eds.) *Machiavellian intelligence II* (pp. 240–263). Cambridge, UK: Cambridge University Press.

Byrne, R., & Corp, N. (2004). Neocortex size predicts deception rate in primates. *Proceedings of the Royal Society of London B, 271,* 1693–1699.

Byrne, R., & Whiten, A. (Eds.). (1988). *Machiavellian intelligence.* Oxford, UK: Oxford University Press.

Deaner, R. O., Nunn, C. L., & van Schaik, C. P. (2000). Comparative tests of primate cognition: different scaling methods produce different results. *Brain, Behavior and Evolution, 55,* 44–52.

Dunbar, R. I. M. (1992). Neocortex size as a constraint on group size in primates. *Journal of Human Evolution, 22,* 469–493.

Dunbar, R. I. M. (1993). Coevolution of neocortex size, group size and language in humans. *Behavioral and Brain Sciences, 16,* 681–735.

Dunbar, R. I. M. (1995). Neocortex size and group size in primates: A test of the hypothesis. *Journal of Human Evolution, 28,* 287–296.

Dunbar, R. I. M. (1998). The social brain hypothesis. *Evolutionary Anthropology, 6,* 178–190.

Dunbar, R. I. M. (2003). Why are apes so smart? In P. Kappeler & M. Pereira (Eds.), *Primate life histories and socioecology* (pp. 285–298). Chicago: Chicago University Press.

Dunbar, R. I. M., & Bever, J. (1998). Neocortex size predicts group size in carnivores and some insectivores. *Ethology, 104,* 695–708.

Finlay, B. L., & Darlington, R. B. (1995). Linked regularities in the development and evolution of mammalian brains. *Science, 268,* 1578–1584.

Hare, B., Call, J., & Tomasello, M. (2001). Do chimpanzees know what conspecifics know? *Animal Behavior, 61,* 139–151.

Hill, R. A., & Dunbar, R. I. M. (2003). Social network size in humans. *Human Nature, 14,* 53–72.

Joffe, T. H. (1997). Social pressures have selected for an extended juvenile period in primates. *Journal of Human Evolution, 32,* 593–605.

Kinderman, P., Dunbar, R. I. M., & Bentall, R. P. (1998). Theory-of-mind deficits and causal attributions. *British Journal of Psychology, 89,* 191–204.

Kudo, H., & Dunbar, R. I. M. (2001). Neocortex size and social network size in primates. *Animal Behavior, 62,* 711–722.

Lewis, K. (2001). A comparative study of primate play behaviour: Implications for the study of cognition. *Folia Primatologica, 71,* 417–421.

Morino, L. (1998). What dolphins can tell us about primate evolution. *Evolutionary Anthropology, 5,* 81–86.

O'Connell, S., & Dunbar, R. I. M. (2003). A test for comprehension of false belief in chimpanzees. *Evolution and Cognition, 9,* 131–139.

Pawlowski, B. P., Lowen, C. B., & Dunbar, R. I. M. (1998). Neocortex size, social skills and mating success in primates. *Behaviour, 135,* 357–368.

Zhou, W.-X., Sornette, D., Hill, R. A., & Dunbar, R. I. M. (2005). Discrete hierarchical organization of social group sizes. *Proceedings of the Royal Society of London B, 272,* 439–444.

❧ 30

Brain Evolution

GEOFFREY MILLER

The human brain is where human nature lives. So, for at least a century, most researchers have viewed brain size expansion as the central mystery of human evolution—far more important than the evolution of upright walking, round buttocks, opposable thumbs, hairless bodies, long head hair, thick penises, everted lips, male beards, female breasts, pointy chins, or skin color. Brain size in our lineage tripled in the last 2 million years, from a chimp-sized average of about 450 cc, around 2 million years ago. Brain size increased in several steps from those early australopithecines to *Homo erectus* to archaic *Homo sapiens* to anatomically modern humans, reaching its current size of about 1,250 cc by around 150,000 years ago (Pearson, 2004; Rightmire, 2004). Different brain areas scaled up fairly proportionally (Finlay, Darlington, & Nicastro, 2001), though there was some disproportionate expansion of neocortex (Oxnard, 2004), especially prefrontal white matter (Schoenemann, Sheehan, & Glotzer, 2005). This fairly rapid, prefrontal-biased brain size expansion suggests a functional expansion of behavioral capacities, driven by directional selection.

The question is, what selection pressures drove brain size upward in our ancestors? Selection pressures can be parsed in different ways. There are different modes of selection: natural versus sexual selection, ecological versus social selection, simple optimization versus coevolutionary arms races, and selection for practical adaptations versus selection for costly signals. There are different types of competition across species (with pathogens, parasites, predators, and ecological rivals) and within species (arms races between parents and offspring, males and females, and dominants and subordinates). And there are different levels of selection: gene, individual, group, species.

Every possible mode, type, and level of selection has been identified as a possible cause of human brain expansion by someone, somewhere. Stanford argues that big brains are for hunting big game (Stanford & Bunn, 2001). Dunbar (2005) argues that they are for managing complex social relationships in hunter-gatherer bands. Whiten and Byrne argue that they are for manipulating and deceiving band-mates (Byrne & Corp, 2004; Whiten & Byrne, 1997). Flinn argues that they are for attaining ecological dominance through social competition (Flinn, Geary, & Ward, 2005). Boyd and Richerson (2005) argue that they are for learning cultural innovations with group survival payoffs. I argue that they are for attracting sexual partners (Miller, 2000). How can we determine which selection pressures were probably most relevant? Whenever we have too many plausible theories, it helps to add some empirical constraints.

First, brains are so costly that they could not have grown bigger without directional selection favoring some behavioral capacities that required a size increase. The fitness benefits of bigger brains had to exceed the fitness costs of bigger brains. These costs include energy, obstetric problems, and psychopathology. The human brain is about 2% of body mass and .05% of body cell count but consumes about 20% of the body's calories (24 watts out of about 120 watts at rest) and 15% of its oxygen. Also, it is hard for human females to give birth to big-brained babies—birth complications are much more common than among other apes, and human infants must be born several months premature (compared to a normal ape development schedule) to fit through the birth canal. Finally, big human brains are prone to dramatic behavioral malfunctions at much higher rates than those observed in great apes, such as schizophrenia, depression, anxiety disorders, obsessive–compulsive disorders, autism, religiosity, and runaway consumerism. It is important to distinguish between adaptations that reduced the relative costs of big brains—such as higher paternal investment (Kaplan et al., 2000) or more meat-eating that allowed a smaller, cheaper gut (Aiello & Wells, 2002)—versus selection pressures that increased the benefits of big brains. Cost-minimizers may have been necessary but not sufficient for brain expansion.

Second, the human brain seems computationally excessive compared to what would be needed for any well-specified cognitive task. The 20 billion neurons in the human cerebral cortex can perform roughly 1 quadrillion (10^{15}) computational operations per second. Suppose that a chimp-sized brain can only perform one-third this many—say, 330 trillion, using perhaps 7 billion cortical neurons. The chimp-sized brain suffices for a highly adaptable, creative, social primate, capable of complex emotions, tool making, social intelligence, and moral intuition. The quandary is this: What evolutionary problems are too complex to be solved by the chimp brain's 300 trillion operations per second, but can be solved by the human brain's 1 quadrillion operations per second? Artificial neural network models rarely require more than a few thousand units (simulated neurons) to solve "complex" computational problems such as recognizing a few hundred distinct human faces, or a few thousand words from a speech stream. The human brain seems like computational overkill.

Third, it is not enough to identify some behavioral task that sounds computationally difficult but ancestrally useful, because almost all such tasks are already solved by many species of smaller-brained animals. Complex "extended phenotypes" (animal architecture and tools) are constructed by spiders, termites, weaverbirds, bowerbirds, beavers, and chimpanzees (Hansell, 2005). Complex social intelligence is shown by hyenas, wolves, elephants, dolphins, whales, baboons, and great apes (de Waal & Tyack, 2003). Complex social foraging for diverse, transient food sources is shown by many species, from pigeons to lions (Giraldeau & Caraco, 2000). Less well-known examples are even more puzzling. The common honeybee, *Apis mellifera*, does complex, socially coordinated foraging using a six-lobed brain totaling 0.139 mm^3 (Haddad et al., 2004). Our brains are about 9 million times larger, so even a typical 40,000-bee colony survives with one-200th the aggregate brain volume of a human. A worker bee weighs about 80 milligrams, so the colony's total bee weight is about 3.2 kilograms, or one-20th of a human. Why do we need 10 times as much brain per body mass as a bee colony?

Fourth, there is a peculiar disjunction between brain paleontology and brain genetics. Paleontology suggests that brain size approached its modern average with the evolution of anatomically modern humans about 150,000 years ago in Africa (Pearson, 2004). Since then, brain size has apparently been at a phenotypic equilibrium. However, brain size is not at a genetic equilibrium: It shows higher heritability (about .89) than almost any other human trait. Brain size also remains moderately correlated (about +.30 to +.40) with general intelligence (McDaniel, 2005; Miller & Penke, in press; Thoma et al., 2005), and the correlation is genetically mediated (Posthuma et al., 2002). Intelligence is also correlated with body symmetry, a standard index of developmental stability and low mutation load (Prokosch et al., 2005; Thoma et al., 2005). Moreover, some brain-size-increasing alleles seem to have evolved quite recently in genes such as *Microcephalin* around 37,000 years ago (Evans et al., 2005), *APSM* around 5,800 years ago (Mekel-Bobrov et al., 2005), and some sphingolipid-related genes within the last 1,000 years (Cochran, Hardy, & Harpending, 2006). These findings suggest that brain size is under mutation–selection balance, with directional selection continuing to favor larger brains and higher intelligence during recent evolutionary history, but recurrent harmful mutations continuing to erode brain size and intelligence.

Until a few years ago, it looked as if there was an equally strange disjunction between brain size expansion and technocultural evolution. Big human brains evolved by 150,000 years ago, yet the European archaeological record showed few behavioral innovations until the "Upper Paleolithic revolution" around 35,000 years ago (Mellars, 2005), when our ancestors invaded Europe and replaced Neanderthals. However, better African archaeology has now shown that distinctly human behavioral innovations (e.g., stone blades, microliths, bone tools, big-game hunting, fishing, long-distance trade, pigment use, and body ornamentation) were arising throughout the Middle Paleolithic in Africa (ca. 200,000 through 35,000 years ago; McBrearty & Brooks, 2000). Thus, there is now a more consistent time line between human paleontology and archaeology, but archaeology remains fairly agnostic about the fitness payoffs for higher brain size.

Fifth, there are sex differences in brain size and growth pattern. Modern human brain size averages 1,300 cc in males and 1,180 cc in females (Miller & Penke, in press). This 10% difference develops largely after birth, is not eliminated by correcting brain size for body size differences (Joffe et al., 2005; Nyborg, 2005), and actually underestimates the 16% difference in cortical neuron number (19 billion in females, 23 billion in males; Pakkenberg & Gundersen, 1997). Male brains also show more dramatic developmental changes during their later adolescence, with more gray-matter pruning and white-matter growth (De Bellis et al., 2001; Luders et al., 2005). Such sex differences in brain size and growth suggest that sex-blind theories of human brain expansion are unlikely to be viable.

Together, these five empirical constraints—high costs, computational excess, cross-species comparisons, persistent heritability, and sex differences—render some brain evolution models more likely than others. Models focused on hunting, foraging, ecological dominance, and paternal investment (e.g., Aiello & Wells, 2002; Flinn et al., 2005; Kaplan, Lancaster, & Hurtado, 2000; Stanford & Bunn, 2001) seem best-suited to explain how we afforded the costs of big brains. They seem less compelling at explaining the fitness payoffs of big brains given that many smaller-brained species are carnivorous, omnivorous, or paternal.

To explain rapid expansion in a costly organ such as the brain, an evolutionary positive-feedback loop seems most appropriate. This is a common feature of all three major contenders—the social intelligence model (Byrne & Corp, 2004; Dunbar, 2005; Whiten & Byrne, 1997), the sexual selection model (Miller, 2000a), and the cultural group selection model (Boyd & Richerson, 2005). Each posits a runaway cognitive arms race—whether between individuals, sexes, or groups—that can nicely explain the high costs, apparent computational excess, and phylogentic uniqueness of the human brain. Also, each model allows some scope for costly signaling effects (Miller, 2000b) to amplify the fitness-dependency of brain size and function, possibly explaining the persistent heritability of brain size and its correlations with general intelligence, body symmetry, and mental health (Prokosch et al., 2005; Shaner, Miller, & Mintz, 2004; Thoma et al., 2005). Finally, insofar as hominid males always show higher reproductive variance than females, each model would also predict somewhat higher male payoffs for successful cognitive competition, and could thus explain the slightly larger male brain size and later brain maturation schedule. Thus, each of the three brain-expansion models remains empirically plausible and awaits further research.

REFERENCES

Aiello, L. C., & Wells, J. C. K. (2002). Energetics and the evolution of the genus *Homo*. *Annual Review of Anthropology, 31*, 323–338.

Boyd, R., & Richerson, P. J. (2005). *The origin and evolution of cultures.* Oxford, UK: Oxford University Press.

Byrne, R. W., & Corp, N. (2004). Neocortex size predicts deception rate in primates. *Proceedings of the Royal Society of London B, 271*, 1693–1699.

Cochran, G., Hardy, J., & Harpending, H. (2006). Natural history of Ashkenazi intelligence. *Journal of Biosocial Science, 38*(5), 659–693.

De Bellis, M. D., Keshavan, M. S., Beers, S. R., Hall, J., Frustaci, K., Masalehdan, A., et al. (2001). Sex differences in brain maturation during childhood and adolescence. *Cerebral Cortex, 11*(6), 552–557.

de Waal, F. B. M., & Tyack, P. L. (Eds.). (2003). *Animal social complexity: Intelligence, culture, and individualized societies.* Cambridge, MA: Harvard University Press.

Dunbar, R. (2005). *The human story: A new history of mankind's evolution.* London: Faber & Faber.

Evans, P. D., Gilbert, S. L., Mekel-Bobrov, N., Vallender, E. J., Anderson, J. R., Vaez-

Azizi, L. M., et al. (2005). *Microcephalin*, a gene regulating brain size, continues to evolve adaptively in humans. *Science, 309*, 1717–1720.

Finlay, B. L., Darlington, R. B., & Nicastro, N. (2001). Developmental structure in brain evolution. *Behavioral and Brain Sciences, 24*(2), 263–308.

Flinn, M. V., Geary, D. C., & Ward, C. V. (2005). Ecological dominance, social competition, and coalitionary arms races: Why humans evolved extraordinary intelligence. *Evolution and Human Behavior, 26*(1), 10–46.

Giraldeau, L. A., & Caraco, T. (2000). *Social foraging theory.* Princeton, NJ: Princeton University Press.

Haddad, D., Schaupp, F., Brantm, R., Manz, G., Menzel, R., & Haase, A. (2004). NMR imaging of the honeybee brain. *Journal of Insect Science, 4*, 7.

Hansell, M. (2005). *Animal architecture.* Oxford, UK: Oxford University Press.

Joffe, T. H., Tarantal, A. F., Rice, K., Leland, M., Oerke, A. K., Rodeck, C., et al. (2005). Fetal and infant head circumference sexual dimorphism in primates. *American Journal of Physical Anthropology, 126*(1), 97–110.

Kaplan, H., Hill, K., Lancaster, J., & Hurtado, A. M. (2000). A theory of human life history evolution: Diet, intelligence, and longevity. *Evolutionary Anthropology, 9*(4), 156–185.

Luders, E., Narr, K. L., Thompson, P. M., Woods, R. P., Rex, D. E., Jancke, L., et al. (2005). Mapping cortical gray matter in the young adult brain: Effects of gender. *NeuroImage, 26*(2), 493–501.

McBrearty, S., & Brooks, A. S. (2000). The revolution that wasn't: A new interpretation of the origin of modern human behavior. *Journal of Human Evolution, 39*(5), 453–563.

McDaniel, M. A. (2005). Big-brained people are smarter: A meta-analysis of the relationship between in vivo brain volume and intelligence. *Intelligence, 33*, 337–346.

Mekel-Bobrov, N., Gilbert, S. L., Evans, P. D., Vallender, E. J., Anderson, J. R., Hudson, R. R., et al. (2005). Ongoing adaptive evolution of *ASPM*, a brain size determinant in *Homo sapiens. Science, 309*, 1720–1722.

Mellars, P. (2005). The impossible coincidence: A single-species model for the origins of modern human behavior in Europe. *Evolutionary Anthropology, 14*(1), 12–27.

Miller, G. F. (2000a). *The mating mind: How sexual choice shaped the evolution of human nature.* New York: Doubleday.

Miller, G. F. (2000b). Mental traits as fitness indicators: Expanding evolutionary psychology's adaptationism. In D. LeCroy & P. Moller (Eds.), *Evolutionary perspectives on human reproductive behavior. Annals of the New York Academy of Sciences, 907*, 62–74.

Miller, G. F., & Penke, L. (in press). The evolution of human intelligence and the coefficient of additive genetic variance in human brain size. *Intelligence.*

Oxnard, C. E. (2004). Brain evolution: Mammals, primates, chimpanzees, and humans. *International Journal of Primatology, 25*(5), 1127–1158.

Nyborg, H. (2005). Sex-related differences in general intelligence g, brain size, and social status. *Personality and Individual Differences, 39*(3), 497–509.

Pakkenberg, B., & Gundersen, J. G. (1997). Neocortical neuron number in humans: Effects of sex and age. *Journal of Comparative Neurology, 384*, 312–320.

Pearson, O. M. (2004). Has the combination of genetic and fossil evidence solved the riddle of modern human origins? *Evolutionary Anthropology, 13*(4), 145–159.

Posthuma, D., De Geus, E.J. C., Baaré, W. F. C., Pol, H. E. H., Kahn, R. S., & Boomsma, D. I. (2002). The association between brain volume and intelligence is of genetic origin. *Nature Neuroscience, 5,* 83–84.

Prokosch, M., Yeo, R., & Miller, G. F. (2005). Intelligence tests with higher g-loadings show higher correlations with body symmetry: Evidence for a general fitness factor mediated by developmental stability. *Intelligence, 33,* 203–213.

Rightmire, G. P. (2004). Brain size and encephalization in early to mid-Pleistocene *Homo*. *American Journal of Physical Anthropology, 124*(2), 109–123.

Schoenemann, P. T., Sheehan, M. J., & Glotzer, L. D. (2005). Prefrontal white matter volume is disproportionately larger in humans than in other primates. *Nature Neuroscience, 8*(2), 242–252.

Shaner, A., Miller, G. F., & Mintz, J. (2004). Schizophrenia as one extreme of a sexually selected fitness indicator. *Schizophrenia Research, 70*(1), 101–109.

Stanford, C. R., & Bunn, H. T. (Eds.). (2001). *Meat-eating and human evolution.* Oxford, UK: Oxford University Press.

Thoma, R. J., Yeo, R. A., Gangestad, S. W., Halgren, E., Sanchez, N. M., & Lewine, J. D. (2005). Cortical volume and developmental instability are independent predictors of general intellectual ability. *Intelligence, 33*(1), 27–38.

Whiten, A., & Byrne, R. W. (Eds.). (1997). *Machiavellian intelligence II: Extensions and evaluations.* Cambridge, UK: Cambridge University Press.

฿ 31

E Pluribus Unum

Too Many Unique Human Capacities and Too Many Theories

BARBARA L. FINLAY

Plausible adaptive scenarios designed to account for the evolution of large brains in humans do not just successfully account for it, they do so many times over. We have no shortage of hypotheses. Indeed, we have too many, and all are probably correct, at least in part. The problem of accounting for human brain evolution is not choosing which one of the many ways our behavior differs from our nearest relatives is the essential one, but developing an explanatory scheme that encompasses all of them.

In this essay, I argue that the coordinated enlargement of the entire human brain gives the best account of the rapid emergence of our diverse capabilities. However, I first briefly review the range of proposals regarding the "first causes" of human brain enlargement.

SCENARIOS

Accounts of human evolution fall into various classes. Some appeal to particular behavioral adaptations, others to organizing principles particular to the human brain, and still others to a release from general constraints. Each explanation has been argued to be the critical factor, or the first factor, in the causal evolutionary chain. As critical human abilities are laid out, note how completely their functional domains encompass the surface of the cortex given our current understanding of structure–function relations within the cortex.

Behavioral Adaptations

The first domain is social living and various versions of the "social brain" hypothesis (Byrne & Whitten, 1988; Dunbar, 1998). The manifest benefits of coordinated group living for resource acquisition and sharing, protection from predation, and distribution of the demands of raising young are the basis of the power of these arguments, though theories vary widely concerning which aspects of perception or cognition are most central to the "social brain." Some researchers have drawn attention to the motor control aspects of facial control and oral mobility, which could have enabled concomitant perceptual changes leading to the appreciation of facial and verbal nuances (Stedman et al., 2004; Vargha-Khadem, Watkins, Alcock, Fletcher, & Passingham, 1995). The hierarchical structure of kin and group relationships, and the various operations required to understand embedded and transitive relationships, have also been likened to language structure. More recently, economics has come to the fore, examining the complex system of rules, mental accounting, and reward structures required to enable "cheater detection" and barter that underlies otherwise unaccountable human altruism (Tooby & Cosmides, 1992). This form of social accounting entails more than merely immediate accounting. It also entails a "theory of mind" to represent the intention of agents (Baron-Cohen, 1997), as well as a procedure for mapping events and outcomes onto their likely causal agents (Wegner, 2002). In another domain, an interesting coupling of sociality and longevity has emerged. The simple presence of another helper has been underscored by showing that grandmothers improve the reproductive success of their daughters and sons (Lahdenpera, Lummaa, Helle, Tremblay, & Russell, 2004). However, if offspring benefit as much by the knowledge of the elders as they do from their presence (which is likely but not yet demonstrated), additional brain space would be needed for 70 years of memories.

Another highlighted domain is finding (or making) food, including both hunting and foraging (Stanford, 1999). Hunts could have been made more profitable and less dangerous by symbolic representations that improved hunting strategies. Falk (2004), for example, has observed that the communicative, but not necessarily the symbolic aspect of language (e.g., mothers' speech to infants) might allow for better gathering, because females could have put babies down, while still retaining contact with them. Tools, from transitory textiles to enduring stone, are also central in various applications from food gathering, hunting, and food storage to preparation. Tool invention and construction underscore the importance of manual dexterity, spatial representations of objects and their transformations, learning, and planning (Ambrose, 2001).

A final domain of human behavioral expertise is long-term planning and modulating immediate motivations in the service of long-term goals. Aiello and Wheeler (1995), for example, point out in their "expensive tissue hypothesis" that the reciprocal relation of brain size and intestinal length probably required brainier primates to find fancier foods, that is, to remember the spatial and temporal layout of seasonally fruiting trees and other plants, which would have required both memory and planning. Many more analytical aspects of coordinating present wants with future needs have been discussed, particularly in the context of the special functions of the frontal lobe, working memory, and response inhibition.

Rubicons

A different kind of argument has also been made for human evolution, namely, that a single organizational change might underlie diverse abilities rather than a single catalyzing and altered behavioral domain of adaptive importance. The central candidate here is, of course, language. It has been argued that a feature of grammatical structure of language (recursion) is the critical difference that enabled the advent of language, and that language is in turn the critical vehicle for most major, subsequent cognitive changes (Hauser, Chomsky, & Fitch, 2002). This argument can be broadened (see Deacon, 1997) to posit that it is not language specifically, but symbolic ability in general that is the essential ingredient. Connectionist theorists have also proposed a version of the Rubicon model, in which a critical amount of processing power, working memory, or long-term memory might have produced a sudden acceleration in acquisition of language specifically, and cognition more generally (Elman et al., 1996).

Release from Constraints

"Constraints," defined as resource limitations, are fundamental to any evolutionary argument. Rather than the generalized form of "constraint," I use the term to mean independent changes in some feature of morphology or life history that indirectly permitted increases in brain size or behavioral complexity. Examples include Falk's "radiator hypothesis" (1990), which suggests that a change in brain circulation following upright posture allowed enough brain cooling to allow for rapid brain expansion. Similar arguments have been made that a change in jaw morphology might also have permitted cranial expansion.

HOW BRAINS CHANGE

Mammalian brains tend to change in a highly coordinated but not necessarily proportionate fashion. The cortex is probably as large as it should be in humans (as predicted from cortex size in other mammals), as are the subdivisions of the cortex. Which brain structures have enlarged at the fastest rate is strongly predicted by the order of neurogenesis, which is a measure of the rate at which precursor pools can proliferate before they become committed to their particular neuronal fate. This order is highly conserved across all mammalian radiations, such that a simple formula can be written to transform any mammal's developmental schedule to any other (Finlay, Darlington, & Nicastro, 2001). The duration of precursor genesis of each brain part can in turn be directly linked to the basic axes and segments of the embryonic brain. The structures that become disproportionately large when brains enlarge are those that lie on the most anterior and lateral parts of the original basal and alar axes, particularly in the forebrain. Which parts of the brain enlarge in response to evolutionary pressures can therefore be predicted by a structural variable that explains a vast majority of the variance, but not a functional one. The traditional view that strict structure–function links are the basis for selection (e.g., selection on auditory cortex size in an animal advantaged by speech) is not supported by the preponderance of data on brain change. No mammal has found it advantageous to enlarge any brain structure preferentially over the cortex.

The observation of predictable but disproportionate growth can be overinterpreted to infer that a late-generated, disproportionately enlarging structure such as the cortex might have no functional specializations and, hence, must be a general-purpose processing device in light of the fact that the cortex varies in evolution as a unit. The decoupling of tight structure–function links in the evolution of brain parts, however, merely requires that there be mechanisms for introducing functions into structures that have been made larger by rule, either in evolutionary time, developmental time, or "real" time. In the case of evolutionary time, variability that produced general brain enlargement could have been coupled with mutation or variability that directed new function into the space available through, say, a difference in connectivity or in the time constants of neurotransmitters. This would have resulted in a larger, functionally specialized region not necessarily different from the larger, functionally specialized area arising from the more traditionally conceived selection processes that have been proposed to be produced in a different sequence.

Introducing new functions into multimodal regions, such as the cortex in developmental or real time, however, implies an initial architecture that can be adapted to various functions. Innumerable examples of functional plasticity in most regions of the cortex indicate that this is true, one notable example being the activation of the visual cortex by Braille reading in the early and late blind (see Burton et al., 2002). In fact, an evolutionary history characterized by predictable–disproportionate structural proliferation would favor the survival of those animals possessing mechanisms to reallocate functions into quiescent regions of the brain. Any single one of the perceptual, cognitive, or motor modifications of human–primate behavior mentioned earlier could have provided the initial leverage to increase brain size. However, the possibility of dynamic reallocation of brain structure to function over every timescale now becomes even more important, particularly when one considers how behavior and/or culture transforms human niches.

PARTICULARS OF HISTORY
AND GENERALITIES OF MECHANISM

I am now prepared to argue that all of the theories listed at the outset of this chapter are probably true in part given that each one can be plausibly linked to greater fitness in our ancestors. The mechanism that might allow them all to be true is the coordinated enlargement of the brain. Certainly, there must have been some sequence in the accretion of cognitive abilities, but we are unlikely to be able to determine anything but the grossest outlines of any particular sequence. Arguments over what the exact first step was in hominid evolution are not of great interest, and they distract attention from the startling range of behavioral changes that have accumulated in short evolutionary time.

I conclude the chapter with a cautionary tale about an evolved feature in primates, about which we have learned a fair amount at all levels of analysis, and for which we have developed a plausible evolutionary history. This is trichromatic color vision (often erroneously called "color vision"). Trichromacy appears to have evolved at least three times, once in Old World monkeys (our direct ancestors) and twice in New World Monkeys (Jacobs, 1998). It does not appear in other mammals.

What permitted the profusion of this ability? Adequate selection pressure for the ability would appear always to have been available. Any animal evolving in visually complex, forested environments could take advantage of the obvious benefits of greater chromatic acuity in discriminating fruits and foliage, as well as more subtle and general benefits in scene segmentation. So far, there does not seem to be anything genetically different about the brains of trichromat primate species (especially considering that there are species of New World monkeys in which individuals can be dichromats or trichromats by chance, depending on which opsin photopigments are produced in their retinas). The difference in photopigments is very tiny, involving the substitution of one or two amino acids in critical spots that then change the best absorption of the opsin molecule. These changes are best understood in terms of the normal jitter seen in protein composition in genetic drift. What allows this genetic jitter to be useful to primates is the presence of a second visual system feature that only primates possess (see Finlay, Silveira, & Reichenbach, 2005; Mollon, 1989). This is the specialization for high-acuity central vision, the fovea, where the high density of cones and ganglion cells in central gaze has a one-to-one convergence ratio, unlike the several-to-one ratio in other mammals. The changed opsin absorption of a population of cones can thus find its way undiluted into the central nervous system, where general-purpose comparators allow its application to the diverse uses of color vision.

What, then, is the cautionary tale? We can certainly understand the evolution of trichromacy in general terms of multiple uses of color vision in complex environments, the ability of the visual cortex to extract difference signals of all sorts, and normal drift in gene transcription. The causal domains invoked include levels of analysis ranging from adaptive behavior to the genome. The causal forces of all these features are inadequate to account for the emergence of trichromacy, however, without the presence of a feature of visual organization, the fovea, which antedates trichromacy, is independent of it, and is adaptive even without it.

Trichromacy is trivial in complexity in comparison to understanding human cognition, and the evolutionary history of trichromacy could never have been deduced from the types of information typically used to speculate about human cognitive evolution. We will never know details of sequence, and we should stop arguing about it. What we can hope to know is how the multifunctional human cortex can be situated in a broader view of how brains change in evolutionary time.

REFERENCES

Aiello, L. C., & Wheeler, P. (1995). The expensive-tissue hypothesis: The brain and digestive system in human and primate evolution. *Current Anthropology, 36,* 199–221.

Ambrose, S. (2001). Paleolithic technology and human evolution. *Science, 29,* 1748–1750.

Baron-Cohen, S. (1997). *Mindblindness: An essay on autism and theory of mind.* Cambridge, MA: MIT Press.

Burton, H., Snyder, A. Z., Conturo, T. E., Akbudak, E., Ollinger, J. M., & Raichle, M. E. (2002). Adaptive changes in early and late blind: A fMRI study of Braille reading. *Journal of Neurophysiology, 87,* 589–607.

Byrne, R. W., & Whitten, A. (1988). *Machiavellian intelligence: Social expertise and the evolution of intellect in monkeys, apes and humans.* Oxford, UK: Clarendon Press.

Deacon, T. (1997). *The symbolic species.* New York: Norton.

Dunbar, R. (1998). The social brain hypothesis. *Evolutionary Anthropology, 6,* 178–190.

Elman, J. L., Bates, E. A., Johnson, M. H., Karmiloff-Smith, A., Parisi D., & Plunkett, K. (1996). *Rethinking innateness: A connectionist perspective on development.* Cambridge, MA: MIT Press.

Falk, D. (1990). Brain evolution in *Homo*: The "radiator theory." *Behavioural and Brain Sciences, 13,* 333–381.

Falk, D. (2004). Prelinguistic evolution in hominins: Whence motherese? *Behavioral and Brain Sciences, 27,* 491–503.

Finlay, B. L., Darlington, R. B., & Nicastro, N. (2001). Developmental structure in brain evolution. *Behavioural and Brain Sciences, 24,* 263–307.

Finlay, B. L., Silveira, L. C. L. , & Reichenbach, A. (2005). Comparative aspects of visual system development. In J. Kremers & L. C. L. Silveira (Eds.), *The visual system of primates* (pp. 37–72). New York: Wiley.

Jacobs, G. H. (1998). Photopigments and seeing: Lessons from natural experiments: The Proctor Lecture. *Investigative Ophthalmology and Visual Science, 39,* 2205–2216.

Hauser, M. D., Chomsky, N., & Fitch, W. T. (2002). The faculty of language: What is it, who has it, and how did it evolve? *Science, 298,* 1569–1579.

Lahdenpera, M., Lummaa, V., Helle, S., Tremblay, M., & Russell, A. F. (2004) Fitness benefits of prolonged post-reproductive lifespan in women. *Nature, 428,* 178–181.

Mollon, J. D. (1989). "Tho she kneeled at the place they grew": The uses and origins of primate color vision. In S. B. Laughlin (Ed.), *Principles of sensory coding and processing* (Vol. 146, pp. 21–38). Cambridge, UK: Company of Biologists.

Stanford, C.B. (1999). *The hunting apes.* Princeton, NJ: Princeton University Press.

Stedmann, H. H., Kozyaki, B. W., Nelson, A., Thesier, D. M., Sui, L. T., Lowi, D. W., et al. (2004). Myosin gene mutation correlates with anatomical changes in the human lineage. *Nature, 428,* 415 – 418.

Tooby, J., & Cosmides, L. (1992). The psychological foundations of culture. In J. H. Barkow, L. Cosmides, & J. Tooby (Eds.), *The adapted mind: Evolutionary psychology and the generation of culture* (pp. 19–136). New York: Oxford University Press.

Vargha-Khadem, F., Watkins, K., Alcock, K., Fletcher, P., & Passingham, R. (1995). Praxic and nonverbal cognitive deficits in a large family with a genetically transmitted speech and language disorder. *Proceedings of the National Academy of Sciences of the United States of America, 92,* 930–933.

Wegner, D. (2002). *The illusion of conscious will.* Cambridge, MA: MIT Press.

General Intellectual Ability

32

The Motivation to Control and the Evolution of General Intelligence

DAVID C. GEARY

The application of evolutionary principles to issues traditionally studied by psychological, cognitive, and brain scientists has the potential to expand substantively our understanding of these phenomena, as suggested by Darwin (1859). One of the most complex of these phenomena is general intelligence (g) and the accompanying ability to represent people, objects, or places symbolically, and to manipulate these symbols mentally. The ability to represent and to manipulate symbols mentally is a central human competency, but its evolutionary history is not fully understood. In the first section, I outline a model that places the ability to generate and to mentally manipulate symbols within a wider system of affective, conscious–psychological, cognitive, and modular systems that enable people to direct their behaviors toward attempts to achieve some degree of control over the resources that support life and that allow individuals to reproduce (Geary, 2005). In the second section, I highlight the basic cognitive and conscious–psychological systems that support the motivation to control. In the third section, I link these systems to g.

THE MOTIVATION TO CONTROL

Selection Pressures

Darwin and Wallace understood that natural selection is a harsh and unforgiving process and thus described it as a "struggle for existence" (1858, p. 54). Alexander (1989) argued that humans do not have to struggle quite as hard as other species, because of our extraordinary ability to modify and extract resources from the ecology, and to use these resources for survival and reproductive ends. Stated differently, humans are *ecologically dominant*, and once dominance was achieved, there was an important shift such that the competing interests of other individuals and coalitions of other people became the central pressure that influenced the evolution of brain and cognition in humans. Natural selection remained a "struggle for existence," but it became primarily a struggle with other people for control of ecological resources and social dynamics.

I am not arguing that individuals necessarily have a conscious, explicit motive to control other people (e.g., mates) or other species (e.g., prey species). Rather, the result of natural and sexual selection (e.g., competition for mates) should be the evolution of brain, cognitive, and affective systems that are sensitive to and process the types of information that covaried with survival and reproductive outcomes during human evolutionary history, and guided the expression of behaviors that brought about these outcomes. The achievement of absolute behavioral control would result in the creation of a "perfect world," that is, a world in which there are no predatory risks, other people behave in ways consistent with one's best interests; and biological (e.g., food) and physical (e.g., territory) resources are completely under one's control. In other words, selection pressures should have operated so that individuals with physical, cognitive, or behavioral traits that could achieve outcomes closest to this perfect world would have a survival or reproductive advantage. The primary obstacles to achieving these outcomes should have been the competing interests of other people and, when these were meshed with ecological dominance, the result would be a within-species evolutionary arms race (Alexander, 1989; Flinn, Geary, & Ward, 2005).

An arms race should also have resulted in the elaboration of folk psychological systems that supported social competition and cooperation, and an elaboration of the folk biological and physical (e.g., as related to tool use) systems that supported ecological dominance. A core feature of this arms race, however, is the advantage achieved by individuals who could compete in ways that differed from the routine. This variant or unpredictable behavior should have been important, because it might have rendered implicit folk knowledge, heuristics (i.e., automatically executed behaviors in response to specific conditions), and decision making less effective, thereby placing a premium on conscious, explicit, problem-solving mechanisms. The latter could have enabled the symbolic representation of past or future social conditions, and the mental rehearsal or simulation of social dynamics and various behavioral strategies that might then have been used to control these dynamics.

Organizing Model

My framework for organizing these control-related traits is shown in Figure 32.1. The foci of the behavioral biases and the supporting systems are the three general forms of resources that tend to covary with survival or reproductive prospects: social (e.g., mates), biological (e.g., food), and physical (e.g., territory). For humans, most of the corresponding competencies are captured by the domains of folk psychology, biology, and physics. These folk systems have evolved to process evolutionarily significant information

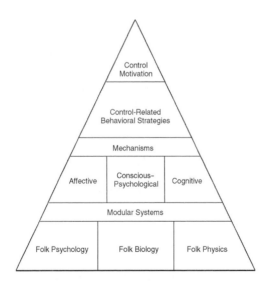

FIGURE 32.1. The apex and following section represent the focus of behavior on achieving control of the social, biological, and physical resources that covaried with survival and reproductive outcomes during human evolution. The midsection shows the supporting affective, conscious–psychological (e.g., self-awareness), and cognitive (e.g., working memory) mechanisms that support the motivation to control and operate on the modular and evolved folk systems shown at the base.

patterns that have been invariant across generations and within lifetimes, and that direct attention toward these patterns. Examples include the basic shape of a human face, biological motion of people or prey species, and so forth. However, the modular systems are plastic in that there are mechanisms within modularized domains that can accommodate individual differences, such as differences in the faces of two individuals (Geary, 2005).

The affective mechanisms guide behavioral strategies and are separated into emotions, which are observable behaviors (e.g., facial expressions), and feelings, which are nonobservable conscious representations of an emotional state (Damasio, 2003). Emotions provide social feedback and feelings provide feedback to the individual. Positive feelings provide reinforcement when behavioral strategies achieve significant goals, or at least a reduction in the difference between the current and desired state (i.e., the "perfect world"), and negative feelings prompt disengagement when behaviors do not result in this end.

CONSCIOUS–PSYCHOLOGICAL
AND COGNITIVE SYSTEMS

Whereas the function of folk systems is to process restricted and invariant forms of information (e.g., facial features), and guide heuristic-based decision making, the function of the conscious–psychological and cognitive systems is to process more macro, variant, and dynamic information patterns (e.g., social dynamics). The cognitive systems that support conscious–psychological representations include working memory, attentional control, and the ability to inhibit the execution of folk heuristics; the brain systems are described elsewhere (Geary, 2005). The result is the ability to form explicit and symbolic representations of situations that are centered on the self and on one's relationships with other people (Alexander, 1989; Tulving, 2002), or on one's access to biological and physical resources. The symbolic representations are of past, present, or potential future states and can be cast as visual images, in language, or as memories of personal experiences (i.e., episodic memories).

The evolved function of these conscious–psychological and cognitive mechanisms is to generate a mental simulation of the social, biological, or physical world and to inject a sense of self into these simulations. Self-awareness is potentially unique to humans and is coupled with the ability to project the self backward in time to recreate a social or other scenario, and to project the self into the future (Alexander, 1989; Tulving, 2002). As noted, humans are biased toward generating a fantasy representation of how the world "should" operate, that is, a representation of the world that would be most favorable to the individual's own reproductive and survival interests. This mental representation serves as a goal to be achieved and is compared against a mental representation of current circumstances. Working memory and attentional mechanisms serve as the platform for simulating social and other current circumstances, then using problem solving and reasoning to devise explicitly behavioral strategies that should reduce the difference between the current state and the fantasized ideal state. These problem-solving activities are ultimately directed toward the goal of attempting to achieve access to and control of social and other resources. Runaway selection may have contributed to the evolution of these cognitive and conscious–psychological systems given the advantages achieved by both the mental ability to project the self into the future and to generate and rehearse social strategies, and to anticipate and generate countermoves to others' social strategies. Other people, in turn, attempt to anticipate one's social strategies and devise their own countermoves.

GENERAL INTELLIGENCE

In 1904, Spearman published the first empirical evidence for the existence of a general mental ability. The basic finding is that above-average performance in one academic domain is associated with above-average performance in all other academic domains and with peer-ratings of intelligence and common sense. Spearman (1904, p. 285) concluded "that all branches of intellectual activity have in common one fundamental function (or group of functions)," which he termed general intelligence, or *g*. We now understand that *g* is better conceptualized as general fluid intelligence, or *g*F, and general crystallized intelligence, or *g*C (Cattell, 1963).

Recent research on *g*F has focused on identifying the cognitive and brain systems that define Spearman's (1904) function or functions (Kane & Engle, 2002). These processes include speed of processing basic pieces of information, consistency in the speed of processing the same information from one time to the next, speed and accuracy of identifying subtle variations in information, working memory capacity, and ability to focus attention. The bottom line is that intelligent individuals identify subtle variations in external information quickly and accurately. Once represented in the perceptual system (e.g., as a word), the information is processed quickly and is accurately represented in short-term memory. Through attentional focus, subsets of this information are explicitly and symbolically represented in working memory and made available to conscious awareness. In comparison to other people, intelligent individuals can hold more information in working memory and are better able to reason about and draw inferences from the associated symbolic patterns. The combination of a large working memory capacity and the ability to reason defines several of the core cognitive competencies that underlie gF.

My proposal is that research on gF has identified many of the core cognitive processes and brain systems that support the use of self-centered mental simulations and, thus, evolved as a result of runaway social competition and attendant selection pressures (see Geary, 2005). The ability to use these mental simulations is dependent on the core components of gF, that is, working memory and attentional control and, as Cattell (1963) proposed, function to deal with variation and novelty in social and ecological conditions. In other words, the 100 years of empirical research on g has isolated those features of self-centered mental models—the conscious–psychological and cognitive components of the motivation to control (see Figure 32.1)— that are not strongly influenced by content, and that enable explicit representations of symbolic information in working memory and an attentional-dependent ability to manipulate this information in the service of strategic problem solving. One important discrepancy involves self awareness, which is a core feature of self-aware mental models but not an aspect of gF. The reason for the discrepancy lies in the initial development and goal of intelligence tests, specifically, to predict academic performance, not social functioning or awareness of the self. Finally, gC can be decomposed into two general classes. The first includes knowledge learned during an individual's lifetime, as proposed by Cattell. The second includes inherent modular competencies and folk knowledge (Geary, 2005).

CONCLUSION

The behaviors, cognitions, brain systems, and other traits of all species, including humans, can be understood in terms of a motivation to control. Behavioral control is focused on the resources that covaried with survival and reproductive outcomes during human evolutionary history. The motivation to control is not explicit or conscious; rather, it reflects the function of evolved traits. The primary dynamic that has driven, and is currently driving, human evolution is competition with other people and groups of other people for resource control, including the control of the behavior of other people. These resources fall into three categories: social, biological, and physical. The brain, cognitive, affective, psychological, and behavioral biases that evolved to facilitate attempts to gain control of resources in these domains compose folk psychology, folk biology, and folk physics.

In addition to creating pressures for the elaboration of folk-psychological systems (e.g., theory of mind), social competition results in variation in social dynamics that cannot be accommodated by folk systems or decision-making heuristics. The result has been evolutionary pressures for the elaboration of brain and cognitive systems that can anticipate, mentally represent, and devise behavioral strategies to cope with these variant dynamics. The self-centered mental model is the conscious–psychological mechanism that evolved to cope with the variation created by complex social dynamics and to facilitate resource control under such conditions. The mental model enables the generation of a self-centered simulation of the "perfect world" and simulation of strategies to reduce the difference between this "perfect world" and current conditions; a "perfect world" is one in which other people behave in ways consistent with one's own best interests, and biological and physical resources remain under one's control. The cognitive systems that evolved to support the use of these self-centered mental models are known as general fluid intelligence, working memory, and attentional control.

REFERENCES

Alexander, R. D. (1989). Evolution of the human psyche. In P. Mellars & C. Stringer (Eds.), *The human revolution: Behavioural and biological perspectives on the origins of modern humans* (pp. 455–513). Princeton, NJ: Princeton University Press.

Cattell, R. B. (1963). Theory of fluid and crystallized intelligence: A critical experiment. *Journal of Educational Psychology, 54,* 1–22.

Damasio, A. (2003). *Looking for Spinoza: Joy, sorrow, and the feeling brain.* Orlando, FL: Harcourt.

Darwin, C. (1859). *The origin of species by means of natural selection.* London: Murray.

Darwin, C., & Wallace, A. (1858). On the tendency of species to form varieties, and on the perpetuation of varieties and species by natural means of selection. *Journal of the Linnean Society of London, Zoology, 3,* 45–62.

Flinn, M. V., Geary, D. C., & Ward, C. V. (2005). Ecological dominance, social competition, and coalitionary arms races: Why humans evolved extraordinary intelligence. *Evolution and Human Behavior, 26,* 10–46.

Geary, D. C. (2005). *The origin of mind: Evolution of brain, cognition, and general intelligence.* Washington, DC: American Psychological Association.

Kane, M. J., & Engle, R. W. (2002). The role of prefrontal cortex in working-memory capacity, executive attention, and general fluid intelligence: An individual-differences perspective. *Psychonomic Bulletin and Review, 9*, 637–671.

Spearman, C. (1904). General intelligence, objectively determined and measured. *American Journal of Psychology, 15*, 201–293.

Tulving, E. (2002). Episodic memory: From mind to brain. *Annual Review of Psychology, 53*, 1–25.

𝔯𝔞 33

The *g*-Culture Coevolution

SATOSHI KANAZAWA

WHAT IS THE ROLE OF GENERAL INTELLIGENCE IN THE COURSE OF HUMAN EVOLUTION?

In my view (Kanazawa, 2004a), general intelligence evolved as a domain-specific adaptation to deal with evolutionarily novel problems. In the long history of human evolution, a large number of psychological mechanisms evolved to solve recurrent adaptive problems of survival and reproduction. These psychological mechanisms in a sense "anticipate" the recurrent adaptive problems and provide solutions in the form of preferences, desires, emotions, and cognitions. In a sense, they do the thinking for us. Our ancestors, therefore, didn't really have to think in order to solve these adaptive problems; they only had to follow the dictates of their psychological mechanisms and do what they wanted to do or felt like doing. Our ancestors didn't have to think about what was good to eat; they simply ate what tasted good to them, and what tasted good to them provided sufficient calories and kept them healthy. Our ancestors didn't have to think about who would make ideal mates; they simply mated with those they found attractive, who then proved to be sufficiently good mates and invested sufficiently in their offspring.

Even in ancestral environments (e.g., the African savanna during the Pleistocene Epoch) in which most adaptive problems were recurrent, however, some problems were novel and nonrecurrent. If these non-recurrent, novel problems significantly hindered survival and reproduction of our ancestors, any psychological mechanism that allowed them to solve such problems would have been selected. Yet, because these problems were nonrecurrent, it was impossible for evolution by natural and sexual selection to "anticipate" their exact nature and design a module specifically for them. The adaptation would have to be able to solve a wide variety of unforeseen, evolutionarily novel problems. I believe that general intelligence—the ability to reason deductively or inductively, think abstractly, use analogies, synthesize information, and apply it to new domains—evolved as a domain-specific adaptation to solve evolutionarily novel problems.

In contrast to views held by other leading evolutionary psychologists (e.g., Cosmides & Tooby, 2002), I do not believe that general intelligence is domain-general *in its origin*. It evolved instead to solve problems in (originally) very narrow domains of life that presented evolutionarily novel problems. Much of life in the ancestral environments was stable, predictable, and recurrent, so general intelligence should not have been particularly important there.

My theory explains why general intelligence does not help us solve evolutionarily familiar problems, such as finding and keeping mates, parenting, socializing with friends and family, and finding our way home (Kanazawa, 2004a). General intelligence has become an important predictor of success in modern life (Gottfredson, 1997; Herrnstein & Murray, 1994) only because our environment has radically changed over the last 10,000 years and most problems that we encounter today are evolutionarily novel. In other words, the fact that general intelligence is so general today is the result of an accident of human evolutionary history.

I have elsewhere argued that the human brain, adapted as it is to the conditions of the ancestral environments, has difficulty comprehending and dealing with entities and situations that did not exist in the ancestral environment (Kanazawa, 2004b). For example, because realistic images of other humans, such as photographs, films, videos, and television, did not exist in the ancestral environment, our brain implicitly interprets all such images as real. As a result, people who watch certain types of television shows frequently are more satisfied with their friendships, as if they had more friends or socialized with them more regularly (Kanazawa, 2002). Our brain may assume that all realistic images of other humans we encounter repeatedly and who don't kill or hurt us, such as television characters, are friends.

If general intelligence evolved to solve evolutionarily novel problems (Kanazawa, 2004a), and if the human brain has difficulty dealing with evolutionarily novel entities and situations (Kanazawa, 2004b), then it follows that those who have greater general intelligence should possess a greater ability to comprehend such evolutionarily novel entities and situations than those who have less general intelligence. For example, more intelligent individuals should have less of a tendency to confuse their "TV friends" with real friends. Indeed, this appears to be the case. The effect of watching television on satisfaction with friendships, first discovered by Kanazawa (2002), is largely limited to those who have less than median intelligence. The frequency of watching television has no apparent effect on satisfaction with friendships among men and women above median intelligence (Kanazawa, 2006b).

As another example, it turns out that general intelligence *does* have an effect on the evolutionarily familiar problem of reproduction *if* it involves evolutionarily novel entities such as modern contraception. Less intelligent individuals have more children than more intelligent individuals, despite the fact that they do not want or desire to, because they have greater difficulty with the evolutionarily novel means of modern contraception. Reproduction is a more direct function of sexual activities among the less intelligent than among the more intelligent; in fact, the larger the number of sexual partners more intelligent individuals have had, the fewer children they have (Kanazawa, 2005).

The effect of general intelligence on the human ability to comprehend evolutionarily novel entities and situations can also explain why criminals on average have lower intelligence (Wilson & Herrnstein, 1985). Much of what counts as crime today, such as theft and interpersonal violence, may have been routine means of solving adaptive problems in the ancestral environments but is now proscribed by evolutionarily novel entities such as written laws, the police, and the judicial system. Perhaps those with lower intelligence unconsciously fail to comprehend these entities and resort to evolutionarily familiar (but now illegal) means to solve their adaptive problems.

HOW DID HUMANS COME TO POSSESS UNPARALLELED HEIGHTS OF INTELLIGENCE?

In the ancestral environments of the African savanna during the Pleistocene Epoch, general intelligence was singularly *un*important. It may have solved occasional novel problems, similar to how all evolved psychological mechanisms solve adaptive problems in their own domains. However, because the ancestral environments were relatively stable and unchanging, and the frequency of nonrecurrent, novel problems was by definition low, general intelligence should have been no more important for human survival and reproduction than any other evolved psychological mechanism in the ancestral environment.

Two exogenous shocks changed all of that. The first was the human exodus from Africa about 80,000 years ago, and the subsequent spread to the rest of the world (Oppenheimer, 2003). Given that our ancestors had spent all of their evolutionary history in Africa prior to the exodus, many features of any other environment were by definition evolutionarily novel, even though other features in the new environments may have been familiar. The second, even more consequential event was the advent of agriculture around 10,000 years ago. Given that our ancestors had spent their recent evolutionary history as hunter-gatherers, the advent of agriculture, and the sedentary life and permanently settled communities that it introduced, were also evolutionarily novel.

Now, both of these events might very well have been the *consequences* of human intelligence. It might have taken human intelligence to find the way out of Africa, in search of a new habitat, when the sea level decreased in response to the advance of ice caps in the northern hemisphere and the Gate of Grief at the mouth of the Red Sea became passable (Oppenheimer, 2003). And it might very well have taken the collective intelligence of some of our ancestors to invent agriculture as an entirely novel (yet more predictable) way of procuring food. For my purposes, however, I treat both events as exogenous to the evolution of human intelligence, as causes rather than consequences.

Once our ancestors found themselves permanently in evolutionarily novel environments, first as hunter-gatherers out of Africa, then as horticulturalists in permanent villages throughout the world, the selection pressure on general intelligence should have increased. Suddenly, more and more adaptive problems were evolutionarily novel and could not be solved with other domain-specific, evolved psychological mechanisms. Those who had greater general intelligence, who could solve such evolutionarily novel problems, attained greater reproductive success, and those who had less general intelligence and couldn't perished. The increasingly evolutionarily novel environments should have selected for greater general intelligence and accelerated its evolution. This way, the evolution of general intelligence depended on the environment and culture.

Not only can humans use their general intelligence to solve evolutionarily novel problems, but their solutions can also further alter the human environment and culture permanently. Intelligent humans could devise new tools, objects, institutions, and social arrangements, not only to solve adaptive problems, but also to prevent the recurrence of the same problems in the future. Our ancestors needed general intelligence to figure out how to escape with their lives when rivers overflowed following severe rainfalls. Once waters receded, they could use the same intelligence to build dikes to prevent future floods. Thus, towns and irrigation systems were built, followed by brick houses, horse carriages, organized armies, airplanes, and the Internet. Thus, the evolution of culture depended on general intelligence.

Every new element of culture (be it a monarchy or the computer) made our environment more and more evolutionarily novel, creating even greater selection pressure on general intelligence. And greater general intelligence in humans further altered human culture. General intelligence thus created ever more complex culture, and complex culture instigated ever higher levels of general intelligence.

Despite the countervailing, dysgenic forces today, in which people with lower intelligence have more surviving children than those with greater general intelligence, there are still strong selection pressures for intelligence. For example, many dangers to health and longevity today are evolutionarily novel (e.g., cigarettes, alcohol, junk food, automobiles, guns). More people die of lung cancer and diabetes than in interpersonal fights or attacks by wild animals. This may well be why more intelligent people, who can correctly recognize such evolutionarily novel dangers to health and avoid them, tend to be healthier and live longer (Gottfredson & Deary, 2004).

Epidemiologists and public health researchers have long believed that income inequality in society reduces the health and life expectancy of its population (Wilkinson, 1992). This first law of epidemiology, however, turns out to be false. Neither income inequality nor even economic development has any effect on health and life expectancy, *net of average intelligence*. People in more egalitarian or wealthier nations do *not* live longer, once intelligence is controlled. At the individual level, intelligence is as strong a predictor of health as income (Kanazawa, 2006a). General intelligence may thus evolve in true gene–culture coevolution.

REFERENCES

Cosmides, L., & Tooby, J. (2002). Unraveling the enigma of human intelligence: Evolutionary psychology and the multimodular mind. In R. J. Sternberg & J. C. Kaufman (Eds.), *The evolution of intelligence* (pp. 145–198). Mahwah, NJ: Erlbaum.

Gottfredson, L. S. (1997). Why *g* matters: The complexity of everyday life. *Intelligence*, 24, 79–132.

Gottfredson, L. S., & Deary, I. J. (2004). Intelligence predicts health and longevity, but why? *Current Directions in Psychological Science, 13,* 1–4.

Herrnstein, R. J., & Murray, C. (1994). *The bell curve: Intelligence and class structure in American life.* New York: Free Press.

Kanazawa, S. (2002). Bowling with our imaginary friends. *Evolution and Human Behavior, 23,* 167–171.

Kanazawa, S. (2004a). General intelligence as a domain-specific adaptation. *Psychological Review, 111,* 512–523.

Kanazawa, S. (2004b). The Savanna Principle. *Managerial and Decision Economics, 25,* 41–54.

Kanazawa, S. (2005). An empirical test of a possible solution to "the central theoretical problem of human sociobiology." *Journal of Cultural and Evolutionary Psychology, 3,* 249–260.

Kanazawa, S. (2006a). Mind the gap... in intelligence: Reexamining the relationship between inequality and health. *British Journal of Health Psychology, 11,* 623–642.

Kanazawa, S. (2006b). Why the less intelligent may enjoy television more than the more intelligent. *Journal of Cultural and Evolutionary Psychology, 4,* 27–36.

Oppenheimer, S. (2003). *Out of Eden: The peopling of the world.* London: Robinson.

Wilkinson, R. G. (1992). Income distribution and life expectancy. *British Medical Journal, 304,* 165–168.

Wilson, J. Q., & Herrnstein, R. J. (1985). *Crime and human nature: The definitive study of the causes of crime.* New York: Touchtone.

34

General Intellectual Ability

STEVEN MITHEN

"Humans have a remarkable ability to engage in abstract think-ing. . . ." This statement from the editors may initially appear straightfor-ward. To a paleoanthroplogist, however, it has a hugely problematic aspect: Which humans? I assume that the editors are thinking of *Homo sapiens*, the only type of human currently alive on the planet. But if by "human" they mean the genus *Homo*, we must acknowledge that there have been several species of human alive on the planet since our genus first appeared around 2 million years ago, and these species may have varied greatly with regard to their abilities at abstract thought.

The precise number of species known to have existed within the genus is ill defined, because different paleoanthropologists categorize the fossil record in different ways. There may have been as many as 10 species: *Homo habilis, rudolfensis, ergaster, erectus, antecessor, heidelbergensis, neanderthal-ensis, floresiensis, helmei,* and *sapiens.* We cannot discount the possibility of new discoveries: *Homo floresiensis* was discovered in 2003, to the astonish-ment of the academic world (Brown et al., 2004). Moreover, other than for the last 28,000 years, the date at which the last of the Neanderthals became extinct, several species of *Homo* were probably alive on the planet at the same time. Our lonely existence as the sole surviving member of our genus is a most peculiar state of affairs.

A "general intellectual ability" and "abstract thought" must have been characteristic of all of these *Homo* species, although not necessarily at the "remarkable" level to which the editors refer. Chimpanzees, our closest living relatives, have some "general intellectual ability," as is evident in their capacity at learning to manipulate symbols in "language" experiments. Because both chimpanzees and modern humans have a "general intellectual ability," this would most likely have also been present in their common ancestor 6 million years ago, and inherited by all members of the *Homo* genus. But chimpanzees are unquestionably constrained in their general intellectual abilities. They appear, for instance, to have a threshold of around 250 symbols, a limit that is rapidly surpassed by human children when they are acquiring language (Pinker, 1994). So the question is not whether members of the *Homo* genus had a general intellectual ability; rather, it is the level of development.

The editors phrase their question by characterizing human general intellectual ability as the "remarkable ability to engage in abstract thinking," which, they claim, is partly rooted in the ability to manipulate arbitrary symbols (a definition that could be challenged, but one that I will accept for the purposes of this chapter). The dilemma facing paleoanthropologists wishing to ask whether extinct members of our genus has this "remarkable capacity" is that abstract thought is, by definition, abstract—it need not leave material traces. Two million years ago, *H. habilis* may have had profound thoughts about the nature of the universe, morality, and truth; it may have believed in supernatural beings, undertaken mental mathematics, and composed poetry. Because such thoughts may have had no material correlates, paleoanthropologists are unable to infer with an absolute degree of confidence whether these thoughts actually existed.

To make such inferences, we are reliant on finding material correlates of abstract thinking in the form of artifacts that had symbolic meanings—artifacts that were either shaped or decorated, so that their meaning was arbitrary to their form. Pieces of art are obvious examples, especially those that are nonrepresentational. A problem that archaeologists face is that modern hunter-gatherers, indeed, modern humans in general, frequently attribute symbolic meanings to entirely unmodified found objects and to natural features of the landscape. We can never be sure that the extinct humans who otherwise left no material traces of symbolic thought did not do the same. But the absence of any objects that have been intentionally modified and lack a feasible utilitarian or other nonsymbolic interpretation suggests that we should err on the side of caution.

Objects that have symbolic meanings provide an invaluable aid to social interaction: We use them continually and are entirely surrounded by them. So it is unlikely that extinct humans would have had the capacity for symbolic thought but not express that capacity in material form, especially those humans that lived in the most challenging of environments and often on the very edge of survival. The absence of symbolic objects, therefore, most likely implies the absence of symbolic thought; hence, according to the editors' definition, those humans had no more than an unremarkable capacity to engage in abstract thinking.

Let us consider *H. neanderthalensis*, a type of human that lived in Europe between 250,000 and 28,000 years ago. We shared an ancestor with *H. neanderthalensis* no more than 500,000 years ago; physiologically, we are very similar, with equivalently sized brains. Moreover, Neanderthals made sophisticated stone artifacts, engaged in big game hunting, and survived through the extremely challenging environmental conditions of the last ice age. So if any type of human other than *H. sapiens* is likely to have had a remarkable capacity for abstract thought, it is the Neanderthals. Are there any material traces of such thought in the form of symbolic artifacts?

A few objects made by Neanderthals and their immediate ancestors have been claimed to have symbolic significance. But these are so rare, so varied in nature, and so unconvincing that they provide an insufficient basis for the inference of symbolic thought. There is, for instance, the so-called "Berekhat Ram" figurine, a piece of volcanic stone no more than 3 centimeters in size, found in a 250,000-year-old archaeological deposit at a site in Israel. Some claim that the stone was deliberately modified into a female form with head, bosoms, and arms (e.g., Marshack, 1997). Others—including myself—think that any similarity between the stone and a female form is entirely coincidental. It is equivalent to the faces we sometimes see in the clouds and the moon; it is in the eye of the beholder. A microscopic study of the stone has provided strong evidence that it was modified by a stone blade (D'Errico & Nowell, 1999). But this had most likely been for an entirely utilitarian purpose, perhaps to make a wedge to support an anvil. Alternatively, the incision might have been a by-product of blunting a razor-sharp flint flake, so that it could be used by children, or for a task that required a blunt edge, such as scraping fat off skin.

Another contentious artifact is the incised fragment of bone from Bilzingsleben, whose marks are believed by some to be part of a symbolic code (Mania & Mania, 1988). Although a member of *H. heidelbergensis* rather than a Neanderthal would have been responsible for this, verification of the Manias' interpretation would suggest that *H. neanderthalensis*, as a probable descendant of *H. heidelbergensis*, was also capable of making symbolic artifacts. A few lines, however, do not make a symbolic code, and the interpretation of artifacts such as the Bilzingsleben bone are dominated by subjective and highly biased evaluations (Mithen, 1996a). An alternative and more likely interpretation of the Bilzingsleben lines is that they derived from use of the bone as a support when cutting grass or meat, or perhaps even for beating out rhythms.

Those who cannot bear the idea that Neanderthals lacked symbolic thought claim that the Neanderthals lived such a long time ago that few, if any, symbolic artifacts would have survived (e.g. Bednarik, 1994). Time, however, is not the only determinant of preservation. Numerous, extremely well-preserved Neanderthal sites have provided many thousands of artifacts and bones, in addition to well-preserved burials. Yet all that can be found in such sites are a few pieces of scratched bone and stone (see Mellars, 1996).

A more challenging argument for the presence of symbolism comes from the possibility of Neanderthal body painting. Stone nodules containing the mineral manganese dioxide, which have been scraped with stone tools, have been found at several Neanderthal sites (D'Errico, personal communication, May 2005). Powdered manganese dioxide, which can be mixed with water or other liquids such as blood and tree sap to make black paint, was used by *H. sapiens* to paint cave walls after the species reached Europe 40,000 years ago. Numerous specimens of worked manganese dioxide nodules have come from the excavations at the Neanderthal occupied cave of Pech de l'Aze and are currently under analysis by D'Errico. He believes that the Neanderthals may have made substantial use of manganese dioxide pigment, with the evidence having been "missed" at many sites simply because the excavators did not expect to find it.

Given that the Neanderthals have left no traces of pigment on cave walls or artifacts, the most likely explanation is body painting. This need not imply the creation of symbolic images. We can guess that the Neanderthals were white-skinned, having evolved in high latitudes, and we know that they were big game hunters. It seems entirely plausible that the paint was simply used to camouflage their bodies. Alternatively, or perhaps in addition, it may have been used for cosmetic reasons—to emphasize an aspect of one's appearance as a means of sexual attraction.

Had Neanderthal pigment use been for symbolic purposes, I would expect to see a wider range of pigments represented at their sites, especially nodules of ochre to create red paint. This is the color that dominates the earliest symbolic activities of modern humans in Southern Africa, and it is a color that has far more evocative connotations than black: As Nicholas Humphrey (1984), the evolutionary psychologist, once described it, red is the "color currency of nature."

In addition to the absence of symbolic artifacts, there is a second major argument against the idea that Neanderthals had abstract thought—the immense stability of their culture. The tools they made and the way of life they adopted 250,000 years ago were effectively no different than those at the moment of their extinction, just under 30,000 years ago. Compare this to *H. sapiens*: It has been no more than 70,000 years since the first symbolic artifacts were manufactured (Henshilwood et al., 2002). In that 70,000 years, less than one-third of the whole duration of Neanderthal existence, our species has gone from living in small hunter-gatherer communities to the global-based, industralized society of today.

To claim that Neanderthal culture was stable neither dismisses an impressive degree of cultural diversity nor denies the complexity of their behavior. They also employed very high levels of knapping skill and made a variety of stone artifacts (Kuhn, 1995; Mellars, 1996), and we must assume that they also made tools from bone, wood, and other plant materials, even though these have not survived. Nonetheless, the absence of any new innovations throughout the time of Neanderthal existence is striking; they simply relied on selecting from a repertoire of tried and tested toolmaking methods.

The Neanderthals were teetering on the edge of survival. If ever a population of humans needed to invent bows and arrows, the means for storing food, needles and thread, and so forth, then it was the Neanderthals. But all of these only came with *H. sapiens*, which went on to invent farming, towns, civilization, empires, and industry.

There appears to be no case, therefore, to attribute the Neanderthals with a "remarkable ability to engage in abstract thinking." My own view is that their impressive cultural achievements were based on the possession of multiple, specialized intelligences—ways of thinking and stores of knowledge dedicated to the domains of sociality, natural history, and technology (Mithen, 1996b). In this regard, the statement of the editors can only be correct if "humans" is taken in the narrow sense to refer to *H. sapiens*. Even then, I would question its veracity, not in terms of whether the success of *H. sapiens* has been attained by a cognitive advantage over all species of *Homo*, but whether this is most productively characterized as the capacity for abstract thought. I would favor the capacity to create metaphor by what I term "cognitive fluidity"—the ability to integrate ways of thinking and stores of knowledge from different cognitive domains—and to extend the mind by the use of material culture (Mithen, 1996b, 1998).

REFERENCES

Bednarik, R. (1994). A taphonomy of palaeoart. *Antiquity, 68*, 68–74.

Brown, P., Sutikna, T., Morwood, M. J., Soejono, R. P., Jatmiko, Wayhu Saptomo, E., et al. (2004). A new small-bodied hominin from the Late Pleistocene of Flores, Indonesia. *Nature, 431,* 1055–1061.

D'Errico, F. & Nowell, A. (2000). A new look at the Berekhat Ram figurine: Implications for the origins of symbolism. *Cambridge Archaeological Journal, 10,* 123–167.

Henshilwood, C. S., d'Errico, F., Yates, R., Jacobs, Z., Tribolo, C., Duller, G. A. T., et al. (2002). Emergence of modern human behaviour: Middle Stone age engravings from South Africa. *Science, 295,* 1278–1280.

Humphrey, N. (1984). The colour currency of nature. In N. Humphrey, *Consciousness regained* (pp. 146–152). Oxford, UK: Oxford University Press.

Kuhn, S. (1995). *Mousterian Lithic technology.* Princeton, NJ: Princeton University Press.

Mania, D., & Mania, U. (1988). Deliberate engravings on bone artefacts of *Homo erectus. Rock Art Research, 5,* 91–107.

Marshack, A. (1997). The Berekhat Ram figurine: A late Acheulian carving from the Middle East. *Antiquity, 71,* 327–337.

Mellars, P. (1996). *The Neanderthal legacy.* Princeton, NJ: Princeton University Press.

Mithen, S. J. (1996a). On Early Palaeolithic "concept-mediated" marks, mental modularity and the origins of art. *Current Anthropology, 37,* 666–670.

Mithen, S. J. (1996b). *The prehistory of the mind: A search for the origin of art, science and religion.* London: Thames & Hudson/Orion.

Mithen, S. J. (1998). A creative explosion?: Theory of mind, language and the disembodied mind of the Upper Palaeolithic. In S. Mithen (Ed.), *Creativity in human evolution and prehistory* (pp. 165–192). London: Routledge.

Mithen, S. J. (2005). *The singing Neanderthals: The origins of music, language, mind and body.* London: Weidenfeld & Nicholson.

Pinker, S. (1994). *The language instinct.* New York: Morrow.

Culture and Evolution

35

Cultural Adaptation and Maladaptation: Of Kayaks and Commissars

ROBERT BOYD

Humans are an oddly contradictory species. On the one hand, we are spectacularly adaptable. Our species occupies a wider range of habitats, utilizes a much greater range of resources, and lives in a more diverse range of social systems than any other animal species. We constitute a veritable adaptive radiation, albeit one without any speciation. For better or worse, our ability to convert matter and energy into people in almost every terrestrial habitat has made us the earth's dominant species. At the same time, humans engage in spectacularly maladaptive behaviors. We take dangerous drugs, risk life and limb to reach mountain summits, restrict our fertility to attain economic and professional success, and march off to war to defend God or liberty or nation. How can it be that we are both so clever and so stupid?

In evolutionary psychology, the usual answer to the first part of the question is that we are talented adaptors, because we are so smart. Our brains are powered by an array of content-rich mental modules that enable us to respond adaptively to a much wider range of contingencies than any other species. The answer to the second part of the question is that we behave maladaptively because these modules are tuned to Pleistocene food-foraging environments and sometimes misfire in the very different environments of the present.

It is likely that people are smarter than the average bear (or primate), and that formerly adaptive predispositions sometimes cause us to do peculiar things. However, we do not think that these factors are the whole, or even the most important explanations, of either our success or our peculiarities. Instead, we think that culture is the key to our cleverness and our stupidities. Humans are much better at learning from others than any other animal. This ability is a powerful adaptive mechanism, because it allows populations of humans to gradually accumulate massive amounts of information about technology, ecology, and institutions over generations—much more than any individual human could invent on his or her own. However, it comes with a built-in trade-off: Culture provides a rich source of adaptive information, but to use it efficiently, individuals have to be "credulous," mainly adopting the beliefs of those around them. This credulity allows maladaptive beliefs to spread.

To convince yourself that human intelligence alone doesn't account for our ability to adapt, imagine that you and some friends are marooned on an arctic beach with a small cache of food. Help is *not* on the way; you're going to have to make it on your own. The Inuit survived here, so you might be able to survive too. There seem to be lots of seals in the sea, so maybe the first task is to build a kayak. You already know a lot—what a kayak looks like, roughly how big it is, and something about its construction. Nonetheless, you would likely fail. Suppose you make a passable kayak. To survive in the Arctic, you would still have to invent dozens of other tools—warm clothing, toggle harpoons, oil lamps, shelters built of skin and snow, goggles to prevent snow blindness, dog sleds, the tools to make these tools, and so on. And then you have to figure out how to use all of this stuff, where and when to hunt, where and when to gather, what is tasty, how to process food that you do manage to collect, and more. Then you must decide how to organize your society: how to regulate exchange of resources, organize marriage, resolve conflicts, and establish relationships with members of neighboring groups.

Individuals cannot learn to make complex, habitat-specific adaptations such as kayaks, oil lamps, and all the rest because, as Tooby and Cosmides (1992) have emphasized, widely applicable learning mechanisms are more imperfect and error prone than highly constrained, domain-specific ones. A kayak is a highly complex object with many different attributes. Designing a good one means finding one of the extremely rare

combination of attributes that produces a useful boat. The number of combinations of attributes grows geometrically as the number of dimensions increases, rapidly exploding into an immense number. The problem would be
much easier if we had a kayak module that constrained the problem, so we
would have fewer choices to evaluate. However, evolution cannot adopt
this solution, because environments change much too quickly and are far
too variable spatially for selection to shape the psychologies of arctic populations in this way. The same learning psychology that provides people with
all the other knowledge, institutions, and technologies necessary to survive
in the Arctic also has to do for birch bark canoes, reed rafts, dugout canoes,
rabbit drives, blow-guns, *hxaro* exchange, and the myriad marvelous, specialized, environment-specific technology, knowledge, and social institutions that human foragers have culturally evolved. Our general-purpose
learning and inference mechanisms simply aren't up to the task.

The Inuit could make kayaks, and do all the other things that they
needed to do to stay alive in the Arctic, because they could make use of a
vast pool of useful information available in the behavior and teachings of
other people in their population. The information contained in this pool is
adaptive, because even limited, imperfect learning mechanisms combined
with cultural transmission can lead to relatively rapid, cumulative adaptation. Even if most individuals imitate most of the time, some people will
attempt to improve on what they learned. Many of these attempts will be
unsuccessful, but occasionally innovators will succeed. Relatively small
improvements are easier to come by than large ones, so most successful innovations lead to small changes. These modest attempts at improvement
give behaviors a nudge in an adaptive direction on average. Cultural transmission preserves the advantageous nudges and exposes the modified traditions to another round of nudging. By the standards of ordinary evolution
by natural selection, many small nudges generate new adaptations very rapidly.

Cumulative cultural change is adaptive, because it generates complex,
habitat-specific adaptations using relatively domain-general cognitive mechanisms. The mind cannot be a blank slate: Cumulative cultural evolution
requires an evolved "guidance system." People must be able to evaluate
alternatives, to know that boats that don't sink and are easy to paddle are
better than leaky, awkward designs. They have to be able to judge whose
boats are best, and when and how to combine information from different
sources. The elaborate psychological machinery that allows children to
bootstrap general knowledge of the world is also clearly crucial. This guidance system is not "domain-general" in the sense that it allows people to

learn *anything*. It is highly specific to life on earth, in a regime of middle-sized objects, relatively moderate temperatures, living creatures, and small social groups. However, it *is* domain-general in the sense that nothing in our evolved psychology provides the crucial details about making kayaks. These crucial details were stored, preserved, and improved by the action of a population of evolved psychologies, using mechanisms that are equally useful for improving and preserving a vast range of knowledge.

This fact means that cultural adaptation comes with a built-in trade-off. The ability to learn from others gives humans access to extremely valuable information about how to adapt to the local environment on the cheap. But, like opening your nostrils to draw breath in a microbe-laden world, imitating others exposes the mind to maladaptive ideas. Selection cannot shape our psychology to protect us from this, because it cannot build a powerful, general-purpose learning device. A young Inuit cannot readily compute the optimal kayak design. He can try one or two modifications and see how they work, and he can compare the performance of the different designs he sees. But small samples, multiple dimensions of variability, and noisy data will severely limit his ability to choose the best design. If most of the people around him use an inferior design, so will he. And kayaks are an easy problem. Is witchcraft effective? What causes malaria? Are natural events affected by human pleas to their governing spirits? What sort of person should one marry? How many husbands are best? What mixture of devotion to work and family will result in the most happiness or the highest fitness? For hard questions such as these, it can be best mainly to imitate (for formal analyses, see Boyd & Richerson, 1985, 1995). When we imitate, we are vulnerable to adopting maladaptive ideas from the people around us.

Moreover, the fact that much culture is acquired from people other than parents means that, for some traits, there are lots of maladaptive behaviors to imitate. It is good that cultural variants are acquired from all kinds of people, not just parents, because sampling a wider range of models increases the chance of acquiring useful information. For most traits, this causes no problem—the fastest kayak is the fastest kayak, whether or not it belongs to Dad or to somebody else. But when parents are not the only source of information, maladaptive ideas in some domains are more likely to spread. For example, in the modern world, beliefs that increase the chance of becoming an educated professional can spread even if they limit reproductive success, because educated professionals have higher status and are more likely to be emulated. Professionals who are childless can succeed culturally as long as they have an important influence on the beliefs and goals of their students, employees, or subordinates. The spread of such maladaptive ideas is a *predictable* by-product of cultural transmission.

Group selection acting on culture also leads to the spread of genetically maladaptive beliefs and values. Different human groups have different norms and values, and the cultural transmission of these traits can cause such differences to persist for long periods of time. The norms and values that predominate in a group may affect the probability that the group survives, whether it is economically successful, whether it expands, and whether it is imitated by its neighbors. For example, suppose that groups with norms that promote patriotism are more likely to survive than groups lacking this sentiment. This creates a selective process that leads to the spread of patriotism. Of course, this process may be opposed by an evolved, innate psychology that makes us more prone to imitate, remember, and invent nepotistic beliefs than patriotic ones. The long-run evolutionary outcome would then depend on the balance of these two processes.

Much of an individual's behavior is a product of beliefs, skills, ethical norms, and social attitudes that are acquired from others with little modification. This does not mean that the evolved predispositions that underlie individual learning become unimportant. Without an evolved guidance system, cultural evolution would be uncoupled from genetic evolution. However, once cultural variation becomes heritable, it can respond to selection for behaviors that conflict with genetic fitness. Selection on genes that regulate the cultural system will balance the advantages of imitation against the risk of catching pathological superstitions. Our vulnerability to adopting dangerous beliefs may be the price we pay for the marvelous power of cumulative cultural adaptation. As the saying goes, "You get what you pay for."

REFERENCES

Boyd, R., & Richerson, P. J. (1985). *Culture and the evolutionary process*. Chicago: University of Chicago Press.

Boyd, R., & Richerson, P. J. (1995). Why does culture increase human adaptability? *Ethology and Sociobiology, 16*, 125–143.

Tooby, J., & Cosmides, L. (1992). The psychological foundations of culture. In J. H. Barkow, L. Cosmides, & J. Tooby (Eds.), *The adapted mind: Evolutionary psychology and the generation of culture* (pp. 19–136). New York: Oxford University Press.

36

The Envelope of Human
Cultures and the Promise
of Integrated Behavioral Sciences

PASCAL BOYER

THE QUESTIONS

Let me start with a list of difficult problems in the explanation of human
behavior, particularly of human culture. The point of this essay is to outline
and advocate a new way of doing social science and explaining culture,
which, for want of a better term, I call an *integrated* behavioral science that
ignores the (generally deceptive) divisions between "levels" or "domains"
of reality suggested by reified disciplinary boundaries. This approach would
combine tools and findings from evolutionary biology, game theory, economics, cultural anthropology, cognitive psychology, and neuroscience in
causal models of specific human behaviors.

For the sake of illustration, here is a far from exhaustive list of such
questions:

- What are the natural limits to family arrangements? Will they shift
  with new reproductive techniques and economic change?
- Can we have an intuitive understanding of large societies? Or are

our intuitive understandings of the social and political world limited to the small groups in which we evolved?

- Why are despised social categories essentialized? Why is it so easy to construct social stigma?
- What logic drives ethnic violence? Ethnic conflicts are more violent and seem less rational than traditional warfare. They sometimes involve whole populations as victims and perpetrators. What psychological processes fuel this violence?
- Why are there gender differences in politics? What explains women's exclusion from group decision making in most societies, and their reduced participation in other societies?
- How are moral concepts acquired? How do locally significant parameters affect general concepts of right and wrong?
- What drives people's economic intuitions? Does participation in market economies create an understanding of market processes?
- Are there cultural differences in low-level cognition? Or do we find very similar ways of categorizing and assigning causation, with variable explicit cultural theories?
- What explains individual religious attitudes? Why are some individuals more than others committed to the existence of supernatural agents?
- Why is there religious fundamentalism and extremism? Why should people want to oppress or kill others in the name of a supernatural agency?

THE TOOLS

Fortunately, in the last 30 years or so we have developed a series of tools that should allow an integrated answer to these questions. First, we have a much more precise knowledge of the *cognitive capacities* that support particular behaviors and of the neural underpinnings of these capacities. Second, we can take advantage of *economic models* of behavior, particularly game theoretical models that provide us with a precise way of describing any behavior in which considerations of costs and utility are relevant. Third, we can make better sense of human culture by placing it in its *evolutionary* context. Many human behaviors are the way they are because of natural selection, which occurred in ancestral social and natural contexts very different from modern or historical lifestyles.

The integrated approach to human culture requires that we acquire the good habit of combining these various tools *within the same models* rather than engage in abstract "cross-disciplinary" discussions that reinforce the very barriers they are supposed to overcome.

Also, we must lose some bad habits that hamper a proper integration of culture, cognition, and evolution. Here is one that does much damage in discussions of the evolved mind: the assumption that evolutionary considerations result in the formulation of universals and that, conversely, evolution is irrelevant to any behavior that displays any cultural variation. If this were the case, evolution would indeed be irrelevant to human culture in general (Boyer, 2000). I think this assumption is based on a profound but widespread misunderstanding of genes and behaviors.

A persistent misunderstanding in the social sciences is the notion that evolutionary models are only about "closed" behavioral programs, inflexibly developed regardless of the external circumstances. But evolution in humans and other species results in context-sensitive behaviors, in systems designed for appreciating when the conditions are optimal for this or that course of action (Boyd & Richerson, 1995). Female mice do not react to aggressive males in the same way when they have small infants compared to when they do not. Most primates know how to modify their behavior depending on their partner's social status. Such flexible decision making is all the more precious in humans, whose fitness depends on appreciating the value and consequences of extraordinarily numerous items of information about their social and natural world (Tooby & DeVore, 1987).

Consider, for instance, moral concepts. It is quite clear that they combine very similar intuitive notions of right and wrong with very different parameters in terms of what specific actions should count as good instances of either. Is robbing a stranger so bad? Is beating up people from another group inherently criminal? The notion that people's intuitions are just "cultural creations" leads nowhere. By contrast, such differences make much more sense once we realize that moral concepts and feelings may be adaptations for cooperation (Frank, 1988). As such, they are influenced by the local conditions in which trust and social exchange are established, and these vary for several economic and ecological reasons. The evolved capacity is not a fixed conception of right and wrong, but a disposition to frame exchange-relevant preferences in terms of these concepts, then associate them with these feelings.

Another related confusion concerns the role of rational choice and other economic models in understanding behavior. Ethnic conflicts, for instance, seem to be the epitome of irrational behavior—and so they are in the aggregate. But they persist because of motivations that make sense to individuals given the relational context in which they are trapped (Kuran, 1998). It may well be that extreme displays of violence are a form of signaling made necessary by the potential danger in being perceived as nonviolent. Signaling one's "toughness" may well be a human psychological adaptation for coalitional warfare. This is a promising model based on adaptive rationality.

EVOLUTION AND INNATENESS

Discussions of evolved mental structures often imply that one can draw a line between function that is specified at birth (supposedly the result of evolution) and function that emerges during development (supposedly the effect of external factors unrelated to evolution). Indeed, this seems to be the starting point of many discussions of "innateness" (Elman, Bates, Johnson, & Karmiloff-Smith, 1996) even though the assumption is biologically implausible. Genes influence development after birth. Conversely, fetuses receive a lot of external information before birth (which is why, for instance, they are prepared for the intonation contours of their mother's language).

Evolution results in not only a specific set of adult capacities but also a specific set of developmental pathways that lead to such capacities. This is manifest in the rather circuitous path to adult competence that children follow in many domains. For instance, young children do not build syntactic competence in a simple-to-complex manner, starting with short sentences and gradually adding elements. They start with a one-word stage, proceed to a two-word stage, then discard that structure to adopt their language's phrase grammar. Such phenomena are present in other domains too, as is discussed next.

Language acquisition requires people to interact with a child in a fairly normal way. Mechanical–physical intelligence requires a world furnished with some functionally specialized man-made objects. In this sense, inference systems are similar to teeth and stomachs, which need digestible foods rather than intravenous drips for normal development, or to the visual cortex which needs retinal input for proper development. What is "normal" about these normal features of the environment is not that they are inevitable or general (food from pills and intravenous drips may become common in the future, dangerous predators have vanished from the environments of most human beings), but that they were generally present in the environment of evolution. Children 100,000 years ago were born in an environment that included natural language speakers, man-made tools, gender roles, predators, gravity, chewable food, and other stable factors that made certain mental dispositions useful adaptations to those environmental features.

EVOLUTION AND THE BRAIN

Evolution does not create behaviors, but it does create brains with dispositions toward certain behaviors given certain conditions. The connection between evolutionary biology and cognitive science is, unfortunately, a very distant goal. This is mostly because a proper understanding of neural function seems to elude cognitive neuroscience despite its spectacular progress in the last 20 years; that is, we know little of the neural underpinnings of anything but the most basic, low-level cognitive functions.

Cognitive neuroscience brings as much puzzlement as illumination in terms of the implementation of evolved capacities and dispositions. The mainstream strategy in recent cognitive neuroscience has been to try and localize distributed networks specifically engaged in domain-neutral capacities, such as attention, categorization, or memory (Cabeza & Nyberg, 1997, 2000). This is proving to be an extremely difficult task, because each of these systems seems to require fine-tuned orchestration of multiple, lower-level networks.

To make things more complicated, the little we know may often be very misleading. For instance, some authors have taken the existence of some low-level "plasticity" in neural connections to imply that very few high-level structures could be genetically informed (e.g., Quartz & Sejnowski, 1997). Given that something as basic as the connectivity of sensory networks can be modified as a result of external environments (e.g., not only by lesions but also through normal environmental variation), how is it possible to imagine that much more complex neural structures (underpinning social exchange, hierarchy, mating decisions, etc.) are the outcome of genetic selection? Such limited evidence for low-level modifications is taken as a powerful argument against evolved, high-level cognitive structures.

A premise of this view is that the influence of genes should be much stronger on low-level than on high-level processes. That is to say, it is assumed that genes are mostly involved in building up sensory and perceptual systems, as well as some of the categorization systems that accompany them (e.g., simple object recognition or lexical identification). Their influence on forms of computation that are more distant from physical signal (e.g., reasoning about resources, feeling moral disgust) seems only indirect through the organization of lower-level structures. So, the argument goes, if we find plasticity in low-level connectivity, we should a fortiori find it in higher cognition.

This, however, may be largely misleading. There are both evolutionary and neuroscientific reasons to cast doubt on this common intuition. On strictly evolutionary grounds, one would predict precisely the opposite of this argument. Natural selection constrains a system inasmuch as it contributes to fitness. Inasmuch as phenotypic variations in one's sense of volume or length have no consequences on reproductive potential, we would expect natural selection to be blind to these differences. By contrast, a large difference in attractiveness criteria or social exchange capacities would certainly have immediate consequences for reproductive potential, so that we should imagine more evolutionary fine-tuning in such a domain. On neuroscientific grounds, it is difficult to claim, for instance, that plasticity in synaptic connectivity *entails* plasticity of high-level function given that we have no description of how synaptic connectivity or neural activity actually implement any high-level function.

So what makes this intuition so powerful when it comes to cognitive processes? Why do we tend to assume that if genes allow very different ways of perceiving distances, they cannot create very similar ways of understanding sexuality or social exchange? A plausible answer may be an a priori commitment to empiricist psychology. If we consider that complex cognitive processes (e.g., moral intuition, social exchange, romantic love) comprise combinations of simpler processes (e.g., pattern recognition, categorization, logical inference), then, of course, low-level plasticity may well result in high-level instability. This is (perhaps) a respectable philosophical commitment, but not an empirical statement of fact about brain processes.

WHY CULTURE?

All the questions listed earlier (as well as many similar ones an integrated behavioral science could address) are of social importance. Indeed, most people outside academia would assume that social scientists are working on these issues and getting closer to scientific answers. The reality is that a massive retreat from difficult questions in social sciences has been accompanied by the obsessive pursuit of obscure academic fads or fetishes. However, what matters here is not to complain about this, but to provide a way out of this predicament.

These questions are also of great theoretical interest, because they constitute a barely explored frontier of human knowledge, namely, explaining how a common set of dispositions creates social and historical diversity through dispositions to acquire certain kinds of cultural information (Sperber, 1996). In other words, what an evolutionarily-based, cognitively grounded anthropology should and could soon achieve is a description of the envelope of human cultures.

REFERENCES

Boyd, R., & Richerson, P. J. (1995). Why does culture increase adaptability? *Ethology and Sociobiology, 16*(2), 125–143.

Boyer, P. (2000). Cultural inheritance tracks and cognitive predispositions: The example of religious concepts. In H. Whitehouse (Ed.), *Mind, evolution and cultural transmission*. Oxford, UK: Berg.

Cabeza, R., & Nyberg, L. (1997). Imaging cognition: An empirical review of PET studies with normal subjects. *Journal of Cognitive Neuroscience, 9*(1), 1–26.

Cabeza, R., & Nyberg, L. (2000). Imaging cognition II: An empirical review of 275 PET and fMRI studies. *Journal of Cognitive Neuroscience, 12*(1), 1–47.

Elman, J. L., Bates, E. A., Johnson, M. H., & Karmiloff-Smith, A. (1996). *Rethinking innateness: A connectionist perspective on development*. Cambridge, MA: MIT Press.

Frank, R. (1988). *Passions within reason: The strategic role of the emotions*. New York: Norton.

Kuran, T. (1998). Ethnic norms and their transformation through reputational cascades. *Journal of Legal Studies, 27*(2), 623–659.

Quartz, S. R., & Sejnowski, T. J. (1997). The neural basis of cognitive development: A constructivist manifesto. *Behavioral and Brain Sciences, 20*, 537–596.

Sperber, D. (1996). *Explaining culture: A naturalistic approach*. Oxford, UK: Blackwell.

Tooby, J., & DeVore, I. (1987). The reconstruction of hominid behavioral evolution through strategic modeling. In W. Kinzey (Ed.), *Primate models of hominid behavior*. New York: State University of New York Press.

37

The Linked Red Queens of Human Cognition, Coalitions, and Culture

MARK FLINN
KATHRYN COE

Why are we all alone at the pinnacle of the particular direction
of rapid evolutionary change that led to the combination of traits
such as a huge brain, complex intellect, upright posture,
concealed ovulation, menopause, virtual hairlessness, a
physically helpless but mentally precocial baby, and above all our
tendency and ability to cooperate and compete in social groups
of millions?

—ALEXANDER (1990, p. 1)

RED QUEEN 1: HUMAN BRAIN EVOLUTION
AND THE COGNITIVE ARMS RACE

The human brain is an astonishing organ. Its cortex comprises 30 billion
neurons of 200 different types, each of which is interlinked by about a
thousand synapses, resulting in a million billion connections working at
rates of up to 10 billion interactions per second. The number of such events
occurring over a lifetime approaches a septillion. Quantifying the trans-
duction of these biophysical actions into specific cognitive activities (e.g.,

thoughts and emotions) is difficult, but it is likely that humans have more information-processing capacity than any other species (Roth & Dicke, 2005).

Our unusual cognitive abilities evolved at a rapid pace: Hominin cranial capacity tripled (450 → 1350 cc) in less than 3 million years, or roughly 100,000 neurons per generation. Structural changes such as increased convolutions, thickly myelinated cortical neurons, lateral asymmetries, von Economo neurons (spindle cells in the anterior cingulate cortex), and integration of the cerebellum also are highly significant (Allman, 1999). In comparison with the rates of change in other parts of the human genome, selection on genes involved with brain development was especially intense (Dorus et al., 2004; Gilbert, Dobyns, & Lahn, 2005).

The metabolic expense of building and running the large human brain is high: More than 50% of infant and 20% of adult energetic resources are used to support this neurological activity, which is more than an order of magnitude greater than that of a typical mammal. Perhaps even more costly in evolutionary terms is the extension of the juvenile period that delays reproduction for nearly a decade longer than the other hominoids, the apparent reason being that human minds need a very long time to master the information that is key to success as an adult (e.g., foraging skills, mating strategies, and social competencies).

In summary, the human brain is a big evolutionary paradox. It is very expensive, it evolved rapidly, it enables behavior to change quickly, and it generates unusual levels of novelty. Its primary functions include dealing with other human brains (Adolphs, 2003; Gallagher & Frith, 2003). The currency is not foot speed or antibody production, but the generation and processing of data in the social worlds of the human brain's own collective and historical information pools. Some of the standout features of the human brain that distinguish us from our closest relatives are asymmetrically localized in the prefrontal cortex, including especially the dorsolateral prefrontal cortex and frontal pole (Geary, 2005). These areas appear to be involved with "social scenario building" or the ability to "see ourselves as others see us so that we may cause competitive others to see us as we wish them to" (Alexander, 1990, p. 7), and are linked to specific social abilities such as understanding sarcasm (Shamay-Tsoory, Tomer, & Aharon-Peretz, 2005), moral reasoning (Moll, Zahn, de Oliveira-Souza, Krueger, & Grafman, 2005), and other sociocultural novelties (Baumeister, 2005; Deacon, 1997; Flinn, 1997, 2004), including learning the personalities, social biases, and so forth, of peers and adults in the local community and surrounding groups.

RED QUEEN 2: HUMAN SOCIAL EVOLUTION
AND THE ARMS RACE AMONG COALITIONS

Humans are an extraordinarily social species. As noted in Alexander's quotation at the beginning of this essay, we humans have the tendency and the ability to form group coalitions ranging from a few to many million individuals. We are the only species that resides in large coalitions with adult males who habitually provide extensive care for their offspring, families, and other kin. We are exceptionally cooperative—especially considering that our groups are composed of separately reproducing individuals, in contrast to other cooperative species such as the eusocial insects, with sterile workers whose reproductive avenues are inextricably bound to those of the queens—and we have developed elaborate systems of reciprocity. The primary function of our extensive within-group affiliation appears to involve competition with other groups of humans (Alexander, 2005; Wrangham, 1999). We cooperate in coalitions to compete, directly and indirectly, against other coalitions of humans. Our willingness to form coalitions at some individual cost appears based on the even greater costs of not being part of a coalition. If our group loses, then we almost invariably lose as individuals as well.

A few other species, such as chimpanzees and dolphins, are similarly characterized by the striking contrasts of within-group affiliation and between-group coalitionary aggression (Conner & Whitehead, 2005; Wrangham, 1999). What appears different about humans is the complexity and intensity of both within-group cooperation on the one hand, and between-group hostility on the other. As hominins became increasingly ecologically dominant, and as environmental and demographic factors diminished constraints on coalition size and structure, an arms race among increasingly effective coalitions emerged as a primary selective pressure (Flinn, Geary, & Ward, 2005). Many of the neurological changes in the evolving hominin brain reflect the increasing demands of negotiating complex coalitionary relationships (reviewed in Adolphs, 2003; Geary, 2005). Surprisingly, we know little about the neuroendocrine mechanisms that underlie the most unusual of human affiliative relationships, those among bonded males in a coalition.

RED QUEEN 3: HUMAN CULTURAL
EVOLUTION AND THE INFORMATION ARMS RACE

"Culture" may be viewed as a highly dynamic information pool that coevolved with the extensive information-processing abilities associated with our flexible communicative and sociocognitive competencies. With the increasing importance and power of information in hominin social interaction, culture and tradition may become an arena of social cooperation and competition (Baumeister, 2005; Flinn, 1997, 2004).

Keeping up in the hominin game required imitation. Getting ahead required creativity to produce new solutions to beat the current winning strategies. Random changes, however, are risky and ineffective—hence, the importance of cognitive abilities to hone choices among imagined innovations in ever more complex social scenarios. The theater of the mind that allows humans to "understand other persons as intentional agents" (Tomasello, 1999, p. 526) provides the basis for the evaluation and refinement of creative solutions to the never-ending novelty of the social arms race. We suggest that this process of filtering the riot of novel information generated by the creative mind favored the cognitive mechanisms for recursive pattern recognition in the "open" domains of both language and social dynamics (Geary, 2005; Suddendorf & Corballis, 1997). There appear to be similar conservative processes in the domain of culture. Another important function of traditions may be to demarcate coalitions and reinforce kin affiliation.

For many social scientists, *Homo sapiens* is the big-brained animal that has most magnificently elaborated cultural behavior. Whereas the "seeds of cultural capacity," Hoebel (1949, p. 43) wrote, "are in the great apes [who have] potentialities for learning, discovery and invention, only humans have so greatly elaborated culture and done so over a relatively short, some 100,000 years, period of time."

Culture, as it currently exists in the Westernized world, leads to the assumption that culture is characterized by rapid change and creativity, horizontal transmission, and identification with a group. Early anthropologists placed their focus on the human capacity for tool use and material culture, seeing them as the "shining ornaments . . . of man's solid mass of intellect" (Hazlitt, 1822, p. 204). This focus has led many scholars to argue that innovative technology is the most important characteristic of *H. sapiens*, and that creativity is a "human need" and "biological predisposition" (Dissanayake, 1992, p. 82). Culture enabled humans to be "built for speed" (Richerson & Boyd, 2000), the assumption being that subsistence technology for dealing with climatic change and other "natural" causes was the race. Another possibility is that social relationships were the more significant challenge with a moving target.

This focus on rapid change and creativity in the material world is understandable, because during the last 100,000 years, we have seen faster rates of behavioral change than in earlier periods in human evolution, a rate of change that has been rapidly accelerating during the last millennia, century, and decade. We suggest, however, that the relationship between culture and creativity is more complicated than this general temporal correlation might suggest. We propose that culture includes, to some degree, a restraining force on the creativity made possible by the evolution of the remarkable human brain. Before we assume that technological innovation always has been crucial in hominin evolutionary history, however, we might ask how creative *H. sapiens* has actually been, and in what domains. Creativity implies doing something new, in the sense of a change from what has been done before. *H. sapiens*, arguably, has seen more cultural persistence than it has change in some domains (Coe, 2003). "This lust for newness," Berenson (1948, p. 155) argued, is neither ancient nor universal. "Why," he asked, "has there been so little craving for novelty everywhere on earth?"

Spencer and Gillen (1927, p. 217) explained that "amongst all savage tribes, the Australian native is bound hand and foot by custom . . . What his fathers did before him that he must do." Not only has innovation and rapid change been rare, but, as Kroeber (1948, p. 257) explained, *H. sapiens* "is generally hidebound and unimaginative, and . . . its cultures are therefore inclined to be persistent. . . . On the whole the passive or receptive faculties of culture tend to be considerably stronger than its active or innovating faculties" (see discussion in Coe, 2003). Kroeber (1948, p. 256) continued, "Even in times of the most radical change and innovation there are probably several times as many items of culture being transmitted from the past as there are being newly devised."

Culture can be transmitted vertically from ancestors to descendents, from past to present, or horizontally among peers (Cavalli-Sforza, Feldman, Chen, & Dornbush, 1982; Fragaszy, 2003). Until quite recently, however, human culture was traditional, and the word "tradition" implies not only *persistence* from one generation to the next but also the method of transmission: Culture is passed from one generation of kin to the next, and this transmission requires intergenerational kinship cooperation (Kroeber, 1948). Tradition put a cap on unrestrained creativity, which, if promoted to the detriment of tested cultural knowledge, can result in breakdown of social relationships essential for human survival and reproduction. Although modern humans may be "built for speed," the ancestral encouragement, and even demand, that traditional behaviors be replicated has served for much of human evolution as a governor of cultural creativity in domains such as subsistence technology, religious beliefs and rituals, social manners, language, and even art.

Cultural transmission is not just information that simply diffuses among "groups"—it involves parents approving or disapproving of their children's behavior. Individuals sharing a common culture, or common traditions, will have inherited those traditions through their parents and other close kin from a common ancestor. Groups, to the extent they did exist, were defined by kinship and common ancestry, and referred to as clans and tribes.

A question that might be raised here, if we accept these premises, is why our ancestors had such little craving for novelty in certain domains of culture? This question raises another: Was our large, complex, and expensive brain selected for cultural innovation, with social relationships serving as a means to better material production, or was the selection for complex social behavior, with culture and innovation as handmaidens, or facilitators, of runaway social selection?

We all can probably accept that intragroup cooperation is essential to success in intergroup competition. We often assume, following Hobbes, that cooperative groups arose in response to external threats, and that some social creativity was involved in driving that cooperation. If social relationships existed prior to the arrival of that threat, then loyalty to one's group, which would have comprised individuals identified as kin and metaphorical kin, would produce a more effective fighting force (Coe, 2003). The same reactions that prepare mammals to fight or flee are aroused when higher primates perceive a threat to important social relationships (Flinn, 2006).

Whereas a Hobbesian vision of human cooperation would support the creation of "coalitions," commonly defined as groups that emerge to address a particular problem, coalitions, as we currently define them, tend to disappear when the problem is resolved (Coe, 2003). In clans and tribes, the cooperation has persisted for generations, and a child inherits the cooperative relationships of the parents. Enduring social relationships would not only facilitate cooperation to compete (Alexander, 2005) but also serve to promote the retention and transmission of knowledge from one generation to the next, thus avoiding costly trial-and-error learning, and they would have worked to protect the vulnerable, including fragile, vulnerable, and increasingly costly human offspring (e.g., Coe, 2003; Sperber & Hirschfeld, 2004). Traditions imply cooperation, in the sense that there must be cooperation between generations for the transmission of a tradition to occur. Pima girls cooperate with their mothers and grandmothers for over a decade to learn to weave a perfect basket. Traditions promote cooperation in that they identify the cooperating category of individuals—the clansmen—and are used to tell those clansmen how to cooperate with one another.

CONCLUDING REMARKS

We have attempted here to understand the three Red Queens of Brain, Society, and Culture, each running as fast as they might to keep up with the competition occurring in their realms. Their actions affect each other; indeed, they are linked in a complex coevolutionary venture. One can hardly move without the other, yet they drive each other down new paths. Their pace has been especially fast on the hominin game board, because of the unusual intensity of runaway social selection as our ancestors increasingly achieved ecological dominance. Unlike relatively static natural selection challenges, the hominin social environment became an increasingly auto-catalytic process, ratcheting up the importance of cognitive–social–cultural competencies and supporting brain systems. We humans are, in this sense, devices of our own creation.

GLOSSARY: DEFINITIONS OF KEY CONCEPTS

Culture: Information acquired and transmitted by social interactions (for discussion see Alexander, 1979; Flinn, 1997, 2004).

Indirect reciprocity: All reciprocity that is not direct. Exchanges of resources (material and information) via intermediaries with an undetermined time for return. Reputation is a key aspect of indirect reciprocity in human sociality (Alexander, 2006; Trivers, 1971).

Red Queen: A metaphor drawn by Leigh Van Valen (1973) from Lewis Carroll's *Through the Looking Glass* that captures the essence of evolutionary arms races. In the book, in response to Alice's complaint that they are not getting anywhere, the Queen says: "Now, here, you see, it takes all the running you can do to keep in the same place" (Carroll, 1871, chap. 2). The metaphor refers to the dynamic nature of adaptation when the competition is constantly changing and success is relative. The metaphor is further apt here because of the analogy with the "looking glass" as a mental space for imaginary social scenarios, possibly even involving "mirror neurons" (Rizzolati & Craighero, 2004) used to experience social chess mentally. See also Hamilton (1999).

Tradition: Behaviors and information that come from the past. In our usage, traditions are informational and behavioral components of phenotypes, transmitted from parent to child.

REFERENCES

Adolphs, R. (2003). Cognitive neuroscience of human social behavior. *Nature Reviews: Neuroscience, 4*(3), 165–178.

Alexander, R. D. (1979). *Darwinism and human affairs.* Seattle: University of Washington Press.

Alexander, R. D. (1990). *How did humans evolve?: Reflections on the uniquely unique species* (Museum of Zoology, Special Publication No. 1). Ann Arbor: University of Michigan Press.

Alexander, R. D. (2005). Evolutionary selection and the nature of humanity. In V. Hosle & C. Illies (Eds.), *Darwinism and philosophy* (pp. 301–348). South Bend, IN: University of Notre Dame Press.

Alexander, R.D. (2006). The challenge of human social behavior. *Evolutionary Psychology, 4*, 1–32.

Allman, J. M., (1999). *Evolving brains.* New York: Scientific American Library.

Baumeister, R. F. (2005). *The cultural animal: human nature, meaning, and social life.* New York: Oxford University Press.

Berenson, B. (1948). *Aesthetics and history in the visual arts.* New York: Pantheon.

Carroll, L. [Dodgson, C. L.]. (1871). *Through the looking-glass, and what Alice found there.* London: Macmillan.

Cavalli-Sforza, L. L., Feldman, M. W., Chen, K. H., & Dornbush, S. M. (1982). Theory and observation in cultural transmission. *Science, 218*, 19–27.

Coe, K. (2003). *The ancestress hypothesis: Visual art as adaptation.* New Brunswick, NJ: Rutgers University Press.

Conner, R. C., & Whitehead, H. (2005). Alliances II: Rates of encounter during resource utilization: a general model of intrasexual alliance formation. *Animal Behaviour, 69*, 127–132.

Deacon, T. W. (1997). *The symbolic species: The co-evolution of language and the brain.* New York: Norton.

Dissanayake, E. (1992). Homo aestheticus: *Where art comes from and why.* New York: Free Press.

Dorus, S., Vallender, E. J., Evans, P. D., Anderson, J. R., Gilbert, S. L., Mahowald, M., et al. (2004). Accelerated evolution of nervous system genes in the origin of *Homo sapiens. Cell, 119*, 1027–1040.

Flinn, M. V. (1997). Culture and the evolution of social learning. *Evolution and Human Behavior, 18*(1), 23–67.

Flinn, M. V. (2004). Culture and developmental plasticity: Evolution of the social brain. In K. MacDonald & R.L. Burgess (Eds.), *Evolutionary perspectives on child development* (pp. 73–98). Thousand Oaks, CA: Sage.

Flinn, M. V. (2006). Evolution and ontogeny of stress response to social challenge in the human child. *Developmental Review, 26*, 138–174.

Flinn, M. V., Geary, D. C., & Ward, C. V. (2005). Ecological dominance, social competition, and coalitionary arms races: Why humans evolved extraordinary intelligence. *Evolution and Human Behavior, 26*(1), 10–46.

Fragaszy, D. (2003). Making space for traditions. *Evolutionary Anthropology, 12*, 61–70.

Gallagher, H. L., & Frith, C. D. (2003). Functional imaging of "theory of mind." *Trends in Cognitive Sciences, 7,* 77–83.

Geary, D. C. (2005). *The origin of mind: Evolution of brain, cognition, and general intelligence.* Washington, DC: American Psychological Association.

Gilbert, S. L., Dobyns, W. B., & Lahn, B. T. (2005). Genetic links between brain development and brain evolution. *Nature Reviews: Genetics,* 581–590.

Hamilton, W. D. (1999). The three queens. In *Narrow roads of gene land* (Vol. 2, pp. 601–666). Oxford, UK: Oxford University Press.

Hazlitt, W. (1822). On the conduct of life; or, advice to a school boy. In *Essays of William Hazlitt: Selected and edited by Frank Carr.* London: Walter Scott.

Hoebel, E. A. (1949). *Man in the primitive world: An introduction to anthropology.* New York: McGraw-Hill.

Kroeber, A. L. (1948). *Anthropology: Race, language, culture, psychology, prehistory.* New York: Harcourt.

Moll, J., Zahn, R., de Oliveira-Souza, R., Krueger, F., & Grafman, J. (2005). The neural basis of human moral cognition. *Nature Reviews: Neuroscience, 6*(10), 799-809.

Richerson, P. J., & Boyd, R. (2000). The Pleistocene and the origins of human culture: Built for speed. *Perspectives in Ethology, 13,* 1–45.

Rizzolati, G., & Craighero, L. (2004). The mirror-neuron system. *Annual Reviews Neuroscience, 27,* 169–192.

Roth, G., & Dicke, U. (2005). Evolution of the brain and intelligence. *Trends in Cognitive Sciences, 9*(5), 250–257.

Shamay-Tsoory, S. G., Tomer, R., & Aharon-Peretz, J. (2005). The neuroanatomical basis of understanding sarcasm and its relationship to social cognition. *Neuropsychology, 19*(3), 288–300.

Spencer, B., & Gillen, F. J. (1927). *The Arunta: A study of a Stone Age people.* London: Macmillan.

Sperber, D., & Hirschfeld, L. (2004). The cognitive foundations of cultural stability and diversity. *Trends in Cognitive Sciences, 8*(1), 40–46.

Suddendorf, T., & Corballis, M. C. (1997). Mental time travel and the evolution of the human mind. *Genetic, Social, and General Psychology Monographs, 123*(2), 133–167.

Tomasello, M. (1999). *The cultural origins of human cognition.* Cambridge, MA: Harvard University Press.

Trivers, R. L. (1971). The evolution of reciprocal altruism. *Quarterly Review of Biology, 46,* 35–57.

Van Valen, L. (1973). A new evolutionary law. *Evolutionary Theory, 1,* 1–30.

Wrangham, R. W. (1999). Evolution of coalitionary killing. *Yearbook of Physical Anthropology, 42,* 1–30.

38

Evolutionary Biology, Cognitive Adaptations, and Human Culture

KIM HILL

An evolutionary understanding of human behavior and cognition has progressed considerably in the past 30 years. In the early years of "sociobiology," researchers, following behavioral biologists, proposed that human behaviors had evolved to maximize inclusive fitness (e.g., Alexander, 1979; Chagnon & Irons, 1979; Wilson, 1978), based on the assumption that behavioral mechanisms evolved in a way that generates fitness-maximizing behavior on average and in most contexts. Rarely did the early human sociobiologists contemplate the cognitive mechanisms that would be required to produce this outcome.

The sociobiological view (later subsumed into "behavioral/evolutionary ecology") was criticized by the founders of evolutionary psychology in the late 1980s (e.g., Barkow, Cosmides, & Tooby, 1992; Tooby & Cosmides, 1989). Specifically, evolutionary psychologists proposed that "fitness-maximizing" cognitive mechanisms were impossible to design (or evolve) and that, instead, the brain was organized into a series of domain-specific modules designed to solve particular adaptive problems efficiently and produce favorable outcomes only in the currency of the relevant proximate goal. This idea was illustrated with examples of a few likely domain-specific psychological mechanisms (ones for mate choice, extracting resources, detecting social cheaters, learning language, etc.) and rapidly expanded to include "mental modules" for almost every cognitive task that humans were observed to perform efficiently. The modular view was supported by persuasive logical arguments, but meanwhile, empirical studies of animal behavior increasingly demonstrated that specific goals in very different domains were regularly traded off to produce fitness maximizing outcomes (e.g., Lima & Dill, 1990).

TRADE-OFFS AND CONTEXT-SPECIFIC BEHAVIOR

Behavioral ecologists have continued to harbor reservations about the extreme modular view of cognition and the improbability of multiple disconnected domain-specific mechanisms producing anything remotely close to adaptive (i.e., fitness-maximizing) behavior. If animals such as fish and snails could evolve fitness-maximizing compromises between disparate goals such as foraging, mating, and predation avoidance, surely human cognition was designed in a similar fashion. Only with higher-level cognitive integration could domain-specific cognitive abilities truly be adaptive. And the closer that the weighting of proximate goals resulted in fitness-maximizing actions, the more likely that the trade-off cognitive mechanism would be favored by natural selection. The Swiss army knife analogy of the mind advocated by early evolutionary psychologists presents an obvious example of this problem. For the knife to be useful (i.e., adaptive), it must have an intelligent actor choosing which blade to employ and when to improvise when there is no appropriate blade for the job at hand (Smith, Borgerhoff Mulder, & Hill, 2001). The fitness-driven integrated view of cognition is supported by hundreds of studies in behavioral ecology showing trade-offs maximizing fitness at the foundation of all successful evolutionary theory about animal behavior (see Parker, 2006, for a review). Thus, even though evolutionary psychology has contributed a more sophisticated view of the way that cognition must be hierarchically organized, its emphasis on extreme domain specificity provides an incomplete understanding of adaptive cognitive organization. Not surprisingly, skepticism of extreme domain specificity theory is shared by other cognitive specialists as well (e.g., Fodor, 2001; Uttal, 2003).

A second weakness of early evolutionary psychology is rooted in the deduction that complex cognitive mechanisms underlying behavior should be universal in our species. Although undoubtedly true given the time necessary for the evolution of any complex mechanism, this fact has been misread to imply nearly invariant human behavioral patterns (i.e., universal behaviors rather than universal mechanisms) adapted to Pleistocene hunter-gatherer environments. Both the idea of invariant behavioral tendencies and the belief that they produce behaviors that make adaptive sense only in remote past environments are problematic. Although some proponents of evolutionary psychology were clearly aware that universal adaptations could produce substantial behavioral variation in different ecological–environmental contexts, early studies in evolutionary psychology almost always sought out universal behavioral patterns (poor treatment of stepchildren, male preference for younger mates, etc.). Evolutionary anthropologists, on the other hand, focused on explaining the variation in observed behavioral patterns (e.g., why treatment of stepchildren might be nearly identical to that of biological children in some circumstances, and why men might favor much younger mates in some societies but not in others). The anthropological interest in observed behavior rather than mechanisms led to a methodological emphasis on modeling of behavioral variation based on assumptions of phenotypic plasticity, contingency, and evolved reaction norms rather than invariant patterns.

Formal modeling leads behavioral scientists to focus on the relevant characteristics of the environment that elicit adaptive behavioral variation. And it is not obvious that the *relevant inputs* to the cognitive mechanisms that have evolved in the past are necessarily absent in modern environments. Whether the relevant characters of the environment have changed in ways that would lead to maladaptive behavior is an empirical question (Irons, 1998; Smith, 1998). Some of the most important breakthroughs in recent behavioral studies come from researchers who avoid assuming that all puzzling results are simply due to environmental mismatches with evolved psychological mechanisms (e.g., Fehr & Henrich, 2003). Finally, although cognitive mechanisms might be complex and evolve slowly, the tastes, preferences, and tendencies that determine the behaviors generated from such mechanisms can probably be altered by single genes; thus, they may be adapted to fairly recent conditions. For example, an increased tendency to cooperate with nonkin, to provide extensive paternal investment, to engage in negotiation rather than violence, or to prefer a particular body shape might have evolved during the time of Holocene farmers and city dwellers rather than that of remote Pleistocene Africa. There is no reason to assume that natural selection has stopped tweaking evolved preferences, and mutations that adjust behavioral tendencies should emerge at an increasingly more rapid rate through time, because of population growth, given that production of new mutations is a direct function of population size.

The emphasis on extreme domain specificity and the misinterpretation that complex mechanisms must result in universal behavioral patterns adapted to the Pleistocene have been reflected in methodology. Evolutionary psychologists have failed to develop explicit theoretical models of how cognitive mechanisms might handle trade-offs and result in adaptive behavior (optimality models), and to verify proposed evolutionary scenarios with rigorous data on the fitness outcomes associated with different behavioral patterns (Smith et al., 2001). Sociobiologists and behavioral ecologists, on the other hand, have been naive about the importance of cognitive design for understanding behaviors that do not always maximize fitness or are not appropriate for modern contexts. The shortcomings of both evolutionary fields have been partially corrected in the past few years, and I believe that the two fields will become increasingly indistinguishable as they incorporate each other's strengths.

Given the recent convergence of evolutionary psychology and human behavioral ecology–sociobiology, one might expect that the next generation of researchers will rapidly untangle all the major mysteries of human behavior and cognition. Unfortunately, I do not think that this will happen quickly. The main reason is that no branch of the evolutionary social sciences has an adequate understanding of human culture. Culture is a product of evolved cognitive mechanisms, but its existence may significantly alter behavioral patterns from those normally expected (from non-cultural organisms), and its emergence has probably uniquely shaped evolved human cognition and emotion. Because of culture, evolutionary researchers will need to develop some special theoretical models to predict adequately and understand human behavior.

CULTURE

For most animals, the factors that determine the payoffs to alternative behavioral options are straightforward—the physical characteristics of the environment, the behavior of predators, prey and competitor species, the location and behavior of potential mates, offspring survival with different levels of investment, and so forth. However, it is unclear how well unmodified models borrowed directly from behavioral ecology can predict human behavioral variation. Cross-cultural research suggests that to test ecological models on humans, cultural similarity must often be controlled (e.g., Borgerhoff Mulder, 2001). The fact that nearby populations belonging to the same ethnographic "culture" are often not considered independent data points in comparative studies even when they live in different habitats (e.g., grassland vs. woodland Selk Nam, coastal vs. inland Eskimos) illustrates the potential importance of culture in determining behavior. Ethnolinguistic affinity (implying shared cultural history) and geographic proximity (implying cultural diffusion) are contributing predictors of variation for a large number of behaviors that also respond to ecological payoffs, from economic patterns to mating arrangements, social structure, and even demographic trends. This is because socially transmitted information partially determines available options or alters their relative payoffs. Moreover, the punishments and rewards for adhering to specific social norms often override the cost–benefit rewards structure expected from noncultural constraints. In short, socially transmitted information and enforced rules often determine optimal behavior.

Few evolutionary researchers explicitly incorporate culture into an evolutionary perspective of human behavior (for notable exceptions, see Boyd & Richerson, 1985, 2005; Cronk, 1999; Richerson & Boyd, 2004). In the past 2 years, only 8% of the articles in the flagship journal *Evolution and Human Behavior* have considered the development or influence of culture on behavior as their main topic of study. Although anthropologists have grappled with the essence of culture and its effects for more than a century, they have produced a plethora of different definitions and a Panglossian view that culture explains all human behavior. Because most anthropological definitions include behaviors and material products as part of culture (see Cronk, 1999), they cannot provide a theoretical basis for modeling how culture influences behavior (given that behavior cannot determine itself). Evolutionary scientists working on culture have also failed to influence the social sciences to the extent that they should have, perhaps because evolutionary definitions of culture are too general, emphasizing socially transmitted information and not specifying the special types of information that humans transmit. Nearly every species transmits some information by social learning, but an overly broad evolutionary definition of "culture" (as socially transmitted information) had led many behavioral biologists to equate socially learned and locally variable traditions in a variety of nonhuman animals with human culture (Byrne et al., 2004). Indeed, some scholars now refer to animal groupings with different local traditions as "cultures." This view is probably misleading and undermines our ability to understand why *Homo sapiens* is a special species with special cognitive abilities. Instead, productive research will require evolutionary social scientists to recognize explicitly that human culture has several components that must be accounted for independently, that have independent properties, and that produce independent effects on behavior. Some of these components may be absent from other species (Hill, in press).

I propose that human culture consists of three types of socially transmitted information: (1) information about the world; (2) norms (i.e., rules of behavior) reinforced by punishments and rewards; and (3) signaling designed to perpetrate the rules and communicate adherence to a particular rule system. Other evolutionary theorists have discussed each of these components, but none have explicitly stated that their combination forms the essence of what we call "culture" in humans.

The first component of culture consists of socially learned information about techniques and technology, as well as facts of nature, and causal understandings of natural and supernatural phenomena. Because the information learned may be correct or incorrect, some scholars refer to such information as "beliefs." This component of culture is present in some primates and other nonhuman animals, but it does not appear to generate cumulative change, as it does in humans (Boyd & Richerson, 1996). The second component of culture defines the morality of a social group and can result in behaviors not predicted by acultural models of human behavior. Enforced rules are internalized to form values when individual actors deduce that a specific rule system serves their interests. The third component of culture consists of communication in the form of rituals (religious practices) and ethnic markers, which exist in conjunction with the rules component. It is unclear (and doubtful) whether any nonhuman species exhibit the second and third components of culture. Until this is established, I believe that it is inappropriate to talk about animal culture.

Research into the development and implications of culture should be a top priority for future studies in human cognition and behavior. The rules of any cultural group probably arise through a social bargaining process that often maximizes the mean utility of all participants in the negotiation process. At other times, norms are imposed to serve only the fitness interests of a small group. Social rules of behavior are often explicitly developed to solve potential intragroup conflicts in the most efficient way and to facilitate group-beneficial cooperation in the face of public goods problems. The most common cultural rules in hunter-gatherer societies, for example, are about dividing up "resources," such as potential mates (marriage rules), acquired food resources (sharing rules), access to food resources (territoriality), and regulating conflict (rules for ritual combat, warfare, settling disputes).

The ability to stabilize group norms may require language to negotiate what constitutes a breach of contract and to determine the appropriate penalties. Perhaps this is why humans uniquely develop enforced moral systems. Although we know that costly punishment of noncooperators is commonly expressed in humans (e.g., Fehr & Gachter, 2002), how this tendency evolved is still a fascinating problem (Boyd, Gintis, Bowles, & Richerson, 2003; O'Gorman, Wilson, & Miller, 2005). The same theoretical dilemma is confronted when we consider how rewarding those who diligently abide by the rules could evolve. Regardless of the explanation for evolved reinforcement of social rules, the production of beneficial social norms was probably favored by some type of cultural group selection, whereby groups that failed to develop norms were outcompeted and replaced by groups that did (Soltis, Boyd, & Richerson, 1995). Cultural group selection does not face the difficulties of genetic group selection, because inmigration of selfish variants is eliminated due to punishment of deviant types.

Once social norms are adopted, they must be transmitted to become stable. This often takes place during formal signaling sessions (rituals) that exist primarily to remind members of the social rules and to ensure that they are adopted by the next generation. These rituals are public, emotionally charged, and utilize nonverbal signals in a highly effective fashion to reinforce the status quo, often implying that norms are linked to supernatural rewards and punishments, as well as reinforcement by a large majority of peers. Because "rule abiders" generally prefer to interact with others who will "play by the same set of rules," ethnic marking in the form of adornments, dialects, and ritual participation emerges as a way to obtain social partners, allies, and mates (McElreath, Boyd, & Richerson, 2003). Importantly, this aspect of human culture is readily detectable in the archeological record and probably indicates when complex rule systems first emerged in hominin history.

Understanding culture is critical for future research in human cognitive evolution. Increasingly, evidence and theory suggest that the evolution of intelligence in humans and primates was mainly driven by social complexity (Dunbar, 2003; Kamil, 2004; Whiten & Byrne, 1997). However, social complexity in humans is unique. At some point in time, the main adaptive challenges that shaped human cognition came from utilizing socially learned information and competition–cooperation *in the context of making, breaking, modifying, and changing the enforced rules mentioned earlier.* Thus, human social competition consists of both direct interaction and political strategizing to influence the rule–enforcement system to one's advantage. This higher level of social complexity may explain unique human cognitive abilities. Likewise, unique social environments probably provided the context for the biological evolution of unique cognitive propensities found only in our species (e.g., Orbell, Morikawa, Hartwig, Hanley, & Allen, 2004; Tomasello, Carpenter, Call, Behne, & Moll, 2005). Because of culture, humans alone may have evolved the emotional underpinnings of anger, fairness, justice, and indignation that lead humans to judge those who violate norms in moral terms (jerks, sleazeballs, criminals) and react to certain behaviors as "disgusting," "revolting," "repulsive," and "deranged." In short, our unique humanity rests on the cultural components produced by and acting on the evolution of the human brain.

REFERENCES

Alexander, R. (1979). *Darwinism and human affairs.* Seattle: University of Washington Press.

Barkow J., Cosmides, L., & Tooby, J. (Eds.). (1992). *The adapted mind: Evolutionary psychology and the generation of culture.* New York: Oxford University Press.

Borgerhoff Mulder, M. (2001). Using phylogenetically controlled comparisons in anthropology: More questions than answers. *Evolutionary Anthropology, 10,* 99–111.

Boyd, R., & Richerson, P. J. (1985). *Culture and the evolutionary process.* Chicago: University of Chicago Press.

Boyd, R., & Richerson, P. J. (1996). Why culture is common, but cultural evolution is rare. *Proceedings of the British Academy, 88,* 77–93.

Boyd, R., & Richerson, P. J. (2005). *The origin and evolution of cultures.* Oxford, UK: Oxford University Press.

Boyd, R., Gintis, H., Bowles, S., & Richerson, P. (2003). The evolution of altruistic punishment. *Proceedings of the National Academy of Sciences of the United States of America, 100*(6), 3531–3535.

Byrne, R., Barnard, P. J., Davidson, I., Janik, V. M., McGrew, W. C., Miklosi, A., et al. (2004). Understanding culture across species. *Trends in Ecology and Evolution, 8,* 341–346.

Chagnon, N. A., & Irons, W. G. (Eds.). (1979). *Evolutionary biology and human social behavior: An anthropological perspective.* Boston: Duxbury Press.

Cronk, L. (1999). *That complex whole.* Boulder, CO: Westview Press.

Dunbar, R. (2003). The social brain: Mind, language and society in evolutionary perspective. *Annual Review of Anthropology, 32,* 163–181.

Fehr, E., & Gachter, S. (2002). Altruistic punishment in humans. *Nature, 415,* 137–140.

Fehr, E., & Henrich, J. (2003). Is strong reciprocity a maladaptation? In P. Hammerstein (Ed.), *Genetic and cultural evolution of cooperation* Cambridge, MA: MIT Press.

Fodor, J. (2001). *The mind doesn't work that way: The scope and limits of computational psychology*. Cambridge, MA: MIT Press.

Hill, K. (in press). Animal "culture"? In K. Laland & J. Galef (Eds.), *The question of animal culture*. New York: Academic Press.

Irons, W. G. (1998). Adaptively relevant environments versus the environment of evolutionary adaptedness. *Evolutionary Anthropology, 6*(6), 194–204.

Kamil, A. C. (2004). Sociality and the evolution of intelligence. *Trends in Cognitive Sciences, 8*, 195–197.

Lima, S. L., & Dill, L. M. (1990). Behavioural decisions made under the risk of predation: A review and prospectus. *Canadian Journal of Zoology, 68*, 619–640.

McElreath, R., Boyd, R., & Richerson, P. J. (2003). Shared norms and the evolution of ethnic markers. *Current Anthropology, 44*, 122–29.

O'Gorman, R., Wilson, D. S., & Miller, R. (2005). Altruistic punishing and helping differ in sensitivity to relatedness, friendship, and future interactions. *Evolution and Human Behavior, 26*, 375–387.

Orbell, J., Morikawa, T., Hartwig, J., Hanley, J., & Allen, N. (2004). "Machiavellian" intelligence as a basis for the evolution of cooperative dispositions. *American Political Science Review, 98*, 1–15.

Parker, G. (2006). Behavioral ecology: Natural history as a science. In J. R. Lucas & L. W. Simmons (Eds.), *Essays in animal behavior*. New York: Academic Press.

Richerson, P. J., & Boyd, R. (2004). *Not by genes alone: How culture transformed human evolution*. Chicago: University of Chicago Press.

Smith, E. A. (1998). Is Tibetan polyandry adaptive?: Methodological and metatheoretical analyses. *Human Nature, 9*(3), 225–261.

Smith, E. A., Borgerhoff Mulder, M., & Hill, K. (2001). Controversies in the evolutionary social sciences: A guide for the perplexed. *Trends in Ecology and Evolution, 16*, 128–135.

Soltis, J., Boyd, R., & Richerson, P. J. (1995). Can group-functional behaviors evolve by cultural group selection?: An empirical test. *Current Anthropology, 36*(3), 473–494.

Tomasello, M., Carpenter, M., Call, J., Behne, T., & Moll, H. (2005). Understanding and sharing intentions: The origins of cultural cognition. *Brain and Behavioral Sciences, 28*, 675–691.

Tooby, J., & Cosmides, L. (1989). Evolutionary psychology and the generation of culture: 1. Theoretical considerations. *Ethology and Sociobiology, 10*, 29–49.

Uttal, W. R. (2003). *The new phrenology: The limits of localizing cognitive processes in the brain*. Cambridge, MA: MIT Press.

Whiten, A., & Byrne, R. (Eds.). (1997). *Machiavellian intelligence II: Extensions and evaluations*. Cambridge, UK: Cambridge University Press.

Wilson, E. O. (1978). *On human nature*. Cambridge, MA: Harvard University Press.

✌ 39

Representational Epidemiology
Skepticism and Gullibility

ROBERT KURZBAN

At a recent conference,[1] Rob Boyd made the important point that the distinct human "trick" is the gradual accumulation of information by social transmission. Knowledge about the complex task of making kayaks, for example, is stored in people's heads and subsequently transmitted to other people's, enabling them to acquire the skills cheaply. This simultaneously eliminates the need for independent discovery and allows the accretion of new information (Boyd & Richerson, in press). A key aspect of this trick, he continued, is that social learners need to be *gullible*, willing to adopt the ideas and practices of others credulously. Requiring justification for representations inferred from social transmission can undermine the benefits conferred by social learning.

Interestingly, at the same conference, Martin Daly and Margo Wilson suggested that social learners need to be *skeptical*. Individuals' interests differ, and any number of people in the social world might for one reason or another wish others to adopt certain beliefs or practices that might *not* be in

---

[1] The Mind, Evolution, and Culture Conference, University of British Columbia, Vancouver, Canada, July 2004.

a learner's own interest. This includes even kin, as the principles that underpin parent–offspring conflict illustrate (Trivers, 1974). More generally, it has been argued that humans, as exceptionally social creatures, are embedded in complex strategic interactions that bring to the fore the possibility of various forms of deception (Byrne & Whiten, 1988).

These two views seem to imply that a crucial question is the extent to which the transmission of representations from one head to another is a process better characterized by gullibility or skepticism. It is possible that this framing of the question will help clarify the debate about culture and is relevant to understanding the epidemiology of representations, the core question surrounding "culture" (e.g., Sperber, 1996). According to this view, understanding cultural differences entails understanding how different representations come to inhabit the heads of their bearers, generally with the help of individuals in the social world.

By "gullible epidemiology," I mean that social learners replicate as nearly as they can representations in others' heads, without the requirement that these constructed representations be justified. By a "skeptical epidemiology," I mean that social learners do not represent as true the representations in others' heads without first scrutinizing the representation, adopting it in its original form only after additional processing. Sperber's (1996) concept of "half understood" information is useful in this context. Representations can be stored without being incorporated into one's set of "true" beliefs, but rather held in a metarepresentational buffer (Cosmides & Tooby, 2000), perhaps until additional information becomes available.

Neither system, gullible or skeptical, is obviously superior. Consider the well-known case of tortilla production. In some regions in the Americas, women boil corn with calcium oxide before subsequent processing into tortillas. This has beneficial nutritional consequences, but this is not why the practitioners say they engage in the practice—they do it because their mothers and grandmothers did so, and they (gullibly) accepted the practice. Of course, such a gullible system does not always lead to beneficial outcomes. There is also the well-known "cargo cult," in which native islanders in the Pacific replicated the form of Allied landing strips, waiting for the gods to send them booty-laden planes. Although this is obviously an unusual case, with vastly different technological representations abruptly sharing the same living space, it illustrates that gullible reproduction of others' cultural forms are not always useful and productive.

There are no doubt a large number of cultural institutions whose effects turn out to be beneficial (at the level of either the group or the individual), even absent the understanding or the intentions behind these ben-

efits. Examples of collectively beneficial outcomes without any single individual understanding the causal structure behind the benefits abound, and
their importance been appreciated by practitioners outside of anthropology
(e.g., Hayek, 1988). Skeptical epidemiology would impede the transmission of representations, undermining their accretion, the trick that, Boyd
argued, is responsible for human cultural adaptability in the face of the
many different niches that humans occupy.

Even the gullible adopter of cultural ideas must, of course, have *some*
criteria for replicating others' representations. This is why Boyd and others
have emphasized transmission rules such as *conformism* and *prestige-biased
transmission*, in which individuals replicate representations based on features other than the content of the representation, issues that have been
discussed at length elsewhere (e.g., Henrich & Gil-White, 2001).

DOMAIN-SPECIFIC CULTURAL EPIDEMIOLOGY

Of course, as Sperber and Wilson (1986), among others, have pointed out,
the transmission of information from one head to another is not a simple
and straightforward process. Information generated by one individual must
be subjected to substantial processing for the receiver of the information to
make the appropriate inferences. Social learning is an active process by
which learners generate inferences about the information content in the
mind of a teacher.

Given this inferential process, it is plausible, even likely, that different
procedures are applied to different contents. More specifically, it seems
likely that the inferential processes associated with different domains will
embody more or less gullibility on the part of the learner, depending on the
domain. The compromise between gullibility and skepticism that natural
selection had to strike was to preserve the benefits of social learning without coming to incorporate into one's beliefs ideas that would have fitness
disadvantages, particularly in the context of strategic social interaction.

Note that this domain-specific view does not diminish the importance
of transmission models developed by Boyd, Richerson, and others. The processes they describe—including transmission biases—might well be present in many different domains. The domain-specific approach might help
to explain why different biases are more or less important for different
kinds of contents.

Extreme cases are potentially illustrative. A great deal is known about
the rules by which word meanings are acquired, and children seem to come

equipped with inferential machinery that allows them to make very accurate guesses about the meanings of new lexical items, even though the problem of inducing this meaning is, from a strictly logical point of view, underdetermined. Given that there should be relatively little advantage that a teacher can gain at the expense of a learner from dissembling about the meaning of words, it seems sensible that selection should act to make this system gullible. A similar argument applies to syntax. Again, there is a convergence of interests in learners and teachers using the same syntactic rules to encode and decode sentences. Although the rules for acquiring syntax are obviously very different from the rules for acquiring lexical items, both embody a very profound gullibility (Pinker, 1994).

It is plausible that a similar argument applies to artifacts. Information about how to make a better kayak, tent, or axe might not be the sort of thing from which an individual will benefit by adopting a skeptical view. Indeed, neither skepticism nor gullibility is the crucial principle. As Boyd and Richerson (in press) put it, evaluating alternatives "*requires* an evolved 'guidance system' . . . " for determining "whose boats are best . . . " (p. 22, italics in the original). Very generally, because tools are a domain in which there is little conflict of interest and, therefore, little is to be gained by deception, the mechanisms for acquiring this knowledge from conspecifics might embody little skepticism; learning in the domain of tools might involve making the best inference about the underlying representation and trying to copy it as closely as possible.

This list of domains in which reconstructed representations, once inferred, are more or less accepted as true is, of course, a matter for empirical investigation. These domains might be several, and the importance of these domains probably depends on one's broader view of what constitutes the important elements of culture. Certainly, the accretion of tool knowledge has had, and continues to have, important consequences for the users of this type of information.

Other domains might be subject to greater skepticism and scrutiny, and the best examples of this are probably the domain of strategic social information, especially about social influence, intentions, power, norms, and, more broadly, obligations, mores, and the proper distribution of costs and benefits. Social learners need to be convinced and persuaded in social domains in a way that they do not in technological domains. Skeptical transmission should be predominant when individuals' costs and benefits are at stake.

This is not to say that people never adopt beliefs that work against their self-interest. Indeed, large numbers of people have adopted norms and beliefs that seem to work decidedly against their interests. The notion that social learning can be surprisingly gullible is both true and important. In the modern era, adoption of certain religious ideologies, for example, appear to motivate people to act in decidedly maladaptive ways.

There are, of course, intermediate cases. Many institutions that differ from one culture to the next might be very difficult to evaluate in terms of individuals' short- and long-term costs and benefits. The frequently cited example of the Nuer and the Dinka is a case in point. When differing norms require a substantial period of time before their costs–benefits to individuals and groups are clear, evolved computational mechanisms designed to apply more or less skeptical procedures for adopting a candidate belief might have little traction for evaluating them. It seems plausible that these intermediate cases provide grist for the mill of between-group epidemiological effects (Boyd & Richerson, 2005).

Finally, in some domains, the skepticism/gullibility with which representations are adopted seem to follow their own idiosyncratic rules. Boyer's (2001) work on the epidemiology of religious ideas is such a case. In this domain, the view that the most likely ideas to be generated and adopted are those that include one violation of an ontological type does not seem to have a function, but might rather be a by-product of mechanisms associated with directing attention.

CONCLUSION

Social learning, the causal process that underlies the epidemiology of representations, is unlikely to be globally skeptical or gullible because the mechanisms evolved to acquire and adopt ideas are likely to be specific to content domains. A mechanism that simply adopted beliefs from authority or prestige figures, independent of the domain in question, would be vulnerable to exploitation and quickly selected against. However, a mechanism that required a great deal of convergent evidence before accepting the semantics of a given lexical item, for example, would be at a selective disadvantage, requiring much longer to acquire words than other candidate systems.

Word learning, of course, does not entail the accretion of knowledge made possible by gullible acquisition of information about progressively more complex and functional artifacts. It seems likely that gullibility in some domains, such as tool use, does constitute an adaptive design for the underlying knowledge acquisition system. There is little doubt that this human trick has enormous consequences, including the breadth of habitats humans inhabit and the technological advancement the last several millennia have observed.

However, taken together, understanding culture, in the sense of representational epidemiology, might progress most productively by considering social learning as a phenomenon that is specific to particular content areas rather than being a general human capacity. Social learning is already relatively well understood in a number of areas, including word learning, food preferences, the acquisition of religious ideas, and so on. The rules that govern transmission in these domains are, of course, very different. The agenda for analyzing culture then is, unfortunately, a difficult one. The underlying rules of inference that allow for others' underlying representations to be inferred (Sperber & Wilson, 1986), as well as the subsequent rules for adopting (or not adopting) these representations, must be investigated on a domain-by-domain basis. This is an imposing and complex task. But it is difficult to imagine the agenda for understanding culture to be anything less.

REFERENCES

Boyd, R., & Richerson, P. J. (in press). Culture, adaptation, and innateness. In P. Carruthers, S. Laurence, & S. Stich (Eds.), *The innate mind: Volume 2. Culture and cognition.* Oxford, UK: Oxford University Press.

Boyer, P. (2001). *Religion explained: The evolutionary origins of religious thought.* New York: Basic Books.

Byrne, R. W., & Whiten, A. (1988). *Machiavellian intelligence: Social expertise and the evolution of intellect in monkeys, apes and humans.* Oxford, UK: Oxford University Press.

Cosmides, L., & Tooby, J. (2000). Consider the source: The evolution of adaptations for decoupling and metarepresentation. In D. Sperber (Ed.), *Metarepresentations: A multidisciplinary perspective* (pp. 53–115). New York: Oxford University Press.

Hayek, F. A. (1988). *The fatal conceit: The errors of socialism.* Chicago: University of Chicago Press.

Henrich, J., & Gil-White, F. (2001). The evolution of prestige: Freely conferred deference as a mechanism for enhancing the benefits of cultural transmission. *Evolution and Human Behavior, 22,* 1–32.

Pinker, S. (1994). *The language instinct: How the mind creates language.* New York: Morrow.

Sperber, D. (1996). *Explaining culture: A naturalistic approach.* Oxford, UK: Blackwell.

Sperber, D., & Wilson, D. (1986). *Relevance: Communication and cognition.* Oxford, UK: Blackwell.

Trivers, R. (1974). Parent–offspring conflict. *American Zoologist, 14,* 249–264.

🙰 40

Turning Garbage into Gold

*Evolutionary Universals
and Cross-Cultural Differences*

MARK SCHALLER

There's an old saying that one man's garbage is another man's gold. Scientists are fond of adapting this adage to their endeavors: "One person's noise is another person's signal," "One person's error variance is another's grant proposal"—that sort of thing. I'm reminded of this perspective when I hear evolutionary psychologists talk about cross-cultural differences. Evolutionary psychologists are professionally interested in human universals—cognitive mechanisms, and their cultural manifestations, that are common across all people in all places. Given this emphasis, cross-cultural differences are easily treated as a sort of garbage, as superficial noise masking the more fundamental panhuman mechanisms lurking within.

Cross-cultural differences are, of course, the focus of many productive programs of research conducted by cultural psychologists. Although some evolutionists might be tempted to view these documented differences as mere noise, plenty of empirical evidence reveals that it's a kind of noise that's worth listening to if we want to predict people's thoughts, feelings, and behavior.

To a large extent, any scholarly emphasis on human universals over cultural differences—or vice versa—is really just a matter of taste. And in matters of taste, there is a very human tendency to defend one's own preferences by denigrating the different preferences of others. Just as many cultural scholars are leery of evolutionary psychology, it is also common to find evolutionary psychologists who express some special distaste for the documentation of cross-cultural differences. That's too bad. Antipathy toward cross-cultural differences can blind evolutionary psychologists to some very promising and productive lines of inquiry.

The time has come, I think, for evolutionary psychologists to embrace cross-cultural variability with the same enthusiasm as we embrace human universals. This attitude has prevailed for years among many anthropologists (e.g., Boyd & Richerson, 2005), but it has yet to catch on much among evolutionary enthusiasts in psychology and the other cognitive sciences. What can we do about this? I have three suggestions—three wishes, perhaps—for lines of evolutionary psychological inquiry that grapple more fully with cross-cultural variability. If these wishes come true, the result should be a deeper appreciation for the many evolved mechanisms of the human mind, and their many implications within contemporary human environments.

WISH 1: EXPLOIT CROSS-CULTURAL DIFFERENCES TO TEST EVOLUTIONARY HYPOTHESES

Among the findings cited most commonly by evolutionary psychologists are those that document similarities across dozens of different cultures (e.g., Brown, 1991; Buss, 1989). There is no denying the rhetorical power of these findings. But there is also an unfortunate flip side to this rhetorical tool. When cross-cultural similarity is trumpeted as evidence for evolution, it is easy for skeptics to assume a sort of contrapositive corollary, and to argue that any evidence of cross-cultural variability must therefore undermine the evolutionary argument. This isn't so, of course. But the fact that many intelligent people think it is so suggests that evolutionary psychologists would be smart to tackle the implications of cross-cultural differences head-on.

In fact, for many evolutionary hypotheses, certain kinds of cross-cultural differences don't pose a problem so much as they pose an opportunity. Many evolutionary hypotheses logically imply specific differences between specific cultural populations, so existing cross-cultural variability provides a terrific—and often very convincing—test of those hypotheses.

Why is this? Because many evolved psychological mechanisms are functionally flexible and context-sensitive. These mechanisms operate as "decision rules" in which specific classes of stimuli trigger specific kinds of responses. Consider the psychology of fear. The capacity for fear evolved, surely, because the actual experience of fear can yield functional benefits in the presence of actual threats. But the experience of fear is not without costs either. For this reason, we don't go around being scared all the time; rather, fear is triggered by the perception of stimuli (e.g., sudden loud noises) that heuristically signal the actual presence of threat. It is this stimulus–response mechanism, and not merely the capacity for fear itself, that evolved. Similarly, just as the capacity for sexual desire evolved, so too did some set of stimulus–response mechanisms through which the actual experience of desire is stimulated by the perception of fitness-connoting cues (e.g., symmetry and other subjectively "attractive" physical features). Moreover, the operation of evolved stimulus–response mechanisms may be moderated by additional psychological inputs indicating further the functional utility of the response within some specific context. Thus, a fearful response to loud noises is particularly pronounced under conditions in which people feel especially vulnerable to harm—such as when they are in the dark (Grillon, Pellowski, Merikangas, & Davis, 1997). And men are likely to judge physically attractive women to be willing mates, especially under conditions in which they themselves are feeling especially romantically aroused (Maner et al., 2005).

Evolved stimulus–response mechanisms are moderated not only by moment-to-moment variations in context but also by chronic aspects of temperament and personality. The appearance of a coalitional outgroup triggers perceptions of danger more strongly in the dark and also among people who chronically perceive the world to be a dangerous place (Schaller, Park, & Faulkner, 2003). Similarly, just as men are especially likely to overestimate an attractive woman's sexual willingness when they are themselves temporarily aroused, they may also be more likely to do so if they chronically prefer a promiscuous approach to mating (Maner et al., 2005). It doesn't matter whether these chronic individual differences result from genetic variation or from differences in socialization practices; these differences can moderate the strength of the psychological response yielded by an evolved stimulus–response mechanism.

Cultural differences operate very much like other individual differences. Evolved stimulus–response mechanisms may be predictably moderated by any element of cultural knowledge that heuristically informs individuals about the functional utility of that stimulus–response mechanism. Just as the inescapable fact of personality differences provides an opportunity to test rigorously specified theories in evolutionary psychology, the inescapable fact of cultural differences also provides a terrific opportunity to test these theories—and potentially to provide compelling evidence in their support.

Here's an example: According to one evolutionary perspective on interpersonal attraction, subjective assessments of physical attractiveness are based on morphological features (e.g., symmetry) that are predictive of disease-resistance and long-term health outcomes. It is partially for this reason, presumably, that physical attractiveness plays such an important role in the process of mate selection. If so, it follows that individuals should be especially likely to use physical attractiveness as a mate-selection criterion under conditions in which the threat of disease is especially high. Gangestad and Buss (1993) cleverly capitalized on cross-cultural differences to test this evolutionary hypothesis. Consistent with the hypothesis, results revealed that individuals do place greater priority on a mate's physical attractiveness within cultures that historically have faced greater threats from parasitic diseases.

This is just one example, and it illustrates an empirical strategy that can be applied broadly to assist evolutionary inquiries into the workings of the human mind. When we employ this strategy, cross-cultural differences are no longer a conceptual nuisance; they're an empirical asset.

WISH 2: EMPLOY CROSS-CULTURAL DIFFERENCES TO INSPIRE DEEPER THEORIZING

The magnitude of the specific stimulus–response phenomenon might predictably differ across different cultural circumstances, but surely there should be universality in the existence of the basic stimulus–response phenomenon itself. It's tempting to think so. And if so, it may seem troubling to an evolutionary perspective when—as often happens—identical stimuli produce fundamentally different responses in different cultures. An obvious example occurs in the domain of food. The same food (e.g., durian, hamburger) may stimulate an appetitive response in one culture and inspire utter disgust in another.

Of course, this is not troubling at all; it is entirely compatible with an evolutionary perspective. The evolved stimulus–response mechanisms that generate affective responses to food aren't taking raw sensory information as their inputs. Nor are they taking immediate interpretations such as "durian" or "hamburger" as their inputs. Rather, their inputs—the stimuli that trigger the affective responses—are further interpretations in which the perceived information is appraised in some functionally meaningful way. What's universal here is not the link between some raw sensory stimulus and some specific psychological response, but the link between some functional appraisal ("edible food," "potential poison") and a specific psychological response.

This point has been made by many scholars, and has been applied particularly well to the study of emotions, within which the role of appraisal processes is fundamental (Mallon & Stich, 2000). This line of reasoning has implications for many other psychological phenomena as well. In some of my own evolutionarily informed research, I've explored the extent to which the perception of certain categories of people (e.g., coalitional outgroups, people with morphologically unusual physical features) automatically arouse cognitions connoting specific kinds of threat (e.g., threat of physical injury, threat of disease). But there is no single universal recipe for features that allow others to be appraised as members of a coalitional outgroup. Specific kinds of features—language, surname, skin color—may serve that purpose in some cultural contexts, but not others. Nor is there any single recipe for features that are morphologically unusual; subjective assessments of unusualness are dependent on the normative features in the local population. Consequently, even though evolved stimulus–response mechanisms may indeed be triggered when we encounter outgroup members or morphological oddities, the specific manifestation of these universal processes may look rather different depending on different cultural learning environments (Maner et al., 2005; Park, Faulkner, & Schaller, 2003).

It is one thing to acknowledge this point; it is quite another to figure out the details. To achieve that deeper scientific goal, it will be important to consider the relations between different kinds of mental modules implicated in the entire stream of psychological events through which sensory information eventually triggers some sort of consequential psychological response. At the very least, it will be necessary to consider relations between three kinds of modules:

1. The focal stimulus–response modules, through which functional inferences (e.g., "potential poison") trigger some specific psychological responses (e.g., disgust).

2. Appraisal modules, through which those functional inferences ("potential poison") are generated from raw sensory stimuli.
3. Learning modules, through which developing organisms learn the specific rules that help them efficiently appraise specific kinds of raw sensory stimuli in specifically functional ways.

It is easy to assert that all of these modules are adaptations (for a review of the evolution of learning modules, see Moore, 2004). And it is certainly useful to explore the operation of each kind of module on its own. Indeed, one by-product of the modular view of the human mind (which is certainly a popular view among evolutionary psychologists) is the implicit prescription to study each module in conceptual isolation. But the actual operations of these modules are not independent of each other. Information acquired through the operation of learning modules informs the operation of appraisal modules, and outputs of these appraisal modules serve as inputs into stimulus–response modules. The mind may indeed be a collection of functionally distinct modules, but to describe how the mind truly works—how it transforms simple sensory inputs into complicated cognitive outputs—it is necessary to articulate carefully the specific relations between these different modules.

So here is another reason why it will be worthwhile to take cross-cultural differences seriously: By confronting cross-cultural variability head-on, we force ourselves to think hard about learning and appraisal mechanisms, and the specific ways in which those mechanisms feed into the stimulus–response algorithms that are the primary focus of most evolutionary psychological inquiries. This sort of thinking should inspire more sophisticated theorizing. At the very least, it seems necessary if we want to offer more complete and coherent explanations for the complicated patterns of evidence that emerge when we observe different peoples in different environments.

I say this on the basis of personal experience. I'm not immune to the allure of explanatory parsimony, so in my research on evolved mechanisms of social cognition, I would really prefer not to observe cross-cultural differences. But empirical data don't always cooperate with my simplemindedness. Cultural variability keeps popping up. In attempting to confront this variability directly, and to tie it to a coherent evolutionary framework, my colleagues and I have had to consider not only the stimulus–response mechanisms of primary conceptual interest but also ancillary mechanisms pertaining to learning and appraisal (e.g., Maner et al., 2005; Park et al., 2003). The stories we ultimately must tell aren't nearly as simple as we might have hoped. But I'm convinced that we are getting closer to the truth about the way that evolved mental mechanisms actually operate.

WISH 3: EXPLORE THE EVOLUTIONARY ORIGINS OF CROSS-CULTURAL DIVERSITY

For those first two wishes to be fulfilled, evolutionary psychologists must be receptive to insights generated by our scholarly cousins who study culture and cultural differences. Happily, evolutionists can give just as well as we get. The tools of evolutionary psychology may help us address a fundamental question about culture that is often ignored by cultural psychologists themselves: How do these cultural differences arise in the first place?

This question is not addressed much by evolutionary psychologists. Sure, lots of evolutionists offer arguments about the adaptive value of culture, or about the ways evolved psychological mechanisms give rise to universal elements of culture (e.g., Atran & Norenzayan, 2004). There is also excellent work on evolved mechanisms that maintain different cultural practices after they have emerged (e.g., Henrich & Boyd, 1998). But the actual origins of cross-cultural diversity haven't received much serious attention. If there is a standard evolutionary explanation for cross-cultural differences, it's this: Because evolved psychological mechanisms are functionally flexible, they are responsive to differences in local ecologies—to the unique opportunities, threats, and constraints afforded by the physical and social world around them—and so different ecologies afford superficially different cultural solutions to the same underlying adaptive problems (Sperber & Hirschfeld, 2004; Tooby & Cosmides, 1992). This is entirely sensible. And because it's so sensible, it's tempting to think that there's not much to be gained by addressing the topic further.

On the contrary, there is plenty to be gained. It is easy to assert that cultural differences will emerge in response to different ecological circumstances, but our job isn't complete until we explain more fully just *how* this actually happens. How do specific ecological circumstances give rise to specific kinds of cultures? How do the particular thoughts and actions of individuals (which are highly variable within any population, even under identical ecological circumstances) coalesce into the coherent patterns of ritual and norm that define a culture?

This isn't easy stuff. The evolved psychological processes that shape patterns of cultural difference are responsive not only to obvious elements of the physical ecology but also to subtle and shifting aspects of the social ecology—such as the distribution of traits, attitudes, and behavioral tendencies within the population itself. We change our beliefs and behaviors in response to the inclinations of others in our ecological neighborhood; our neighbors consequently recalibrate their own beliefs and behaviors; and this affects us once more (see Kenrick & Sundie, Chapter 14, this volume). Over time, these dynamic interactions among neighbors can transform random variability across a social landscape into distinct clusters of different norms—the beginnings of coherent cultural differences (Harton & Bourgeois, 2004). How does evolutionary psychology fit in? Among other things, evolutionary considerations inform us about the kinds of information that are especially influential to others, about the specific kinds of social interactions that govern the direction and magnitude of social influence, and about the operation of individual decision rules that direct the propagation of information through these interactions. Preliminary work in this area of "dynamical evolutionary psychology" has begun to yield new insights about the origins of cultural differences in evolutionarily fundamental behavioral domains such as aggression, cooperation, and mating (Kenrick, Li, & Butner, 2003). This exciting new line of research implicates a whole new strategy through which the evolution of the human mind can be productively connected to the study of cross-cultural differences.

ENVOI

Evolutionists wax ecstatic about the diversity of life. Yet when we turn our attention to human nature, we tend to focus more on unity than on diversity. Evolutionary psychologists will surely continue to have a special affection for cross-cultural similarities. But that doesn't mean we can't love cross-cultural differences just as dearly. At the very least, we'll be wise to treat these differences as more than mere statistical noise. In articulating my three wishes, I've tried to identify a few research strategies through which cross-cultural differences can be transformed from subjective garbage into scientific gold. My hope is that scholars will put more effort into this kind of alchemy.

ACKNOWLEDGMENTS

This work was supported indirectly by research grants funded by the Social Sciences and Humanities Research Council of Canada, and by the U.S. National Institutes of

Health. I appreciate the support. I also thank Steve Heine for constructive comments on an earlier draft of this chapter.

REFERENCES

Atran, S., & Norenzayan, A. (2004). Religion's evolutionary landscape: Counterintuition, commitment, compassion, communion. *Behavioral and Brain Sciences, 27,* 713–770.
Boyd, R., & Richerson, P. J. (2005). *The origin and evolution of cultures.* New York: Oxford University Press.
Brown, D. E. (1991). *Human universals.* New York: McGraw-Hill.
Buss, D. M. (1989). Sex differences in human mate preferences: Evolutionary hypotheses tested in 37 cultures. *Behavioral and Brain Sciences, 12,* 1–49.
Gangestad, S. W., & Buss, D. M. (1993). Pathogen prevalence and human mate preferences. *Ethology and Sociobiology, 14,* 89–96.
Grillon, C., Pellowski, M., Merikangas, K. R., & Davis, M. (1997). Darkness facilitates acoustic startle reflex in humans. *Biological Psychiatry, 42,* 453–460.
Harton, H. C., & Bourgeois, M. J. (2004). Cultural elements emerge from dynamic social impact. In M. Schaller & C. S. Crandall (Eds.), *The psychological foundations of culture* (pp. 41–75). Mahwah, NJ: Erlbaum.
Henrich, J., & Boyd, R. (1998). The evolution of conformist transmission and the emergence of between-group differences. *Evolution and Human Behavior, 19,* 215–241.
Kenrick, D. T., Li, N. P., & Butner, J. (2003). Dynamical evolutionary psychology: Individual decision-rules and emergent social norms. *Psychological Review, 110,* 3–28.
Mallon, R., & Stich, S. (2000). The odd couple: The compatibility of social construction and evolutionary psychology, *Philosophy of Science, 67,* 133–154.
Maner, J. K., Kenrick, D. T., Becker, D. V., Robertson, T., Hofer, B., Neuberg, S. L., et al. (2005). Functional projection: How fundamental social motives can bias interpersonal perception. *Journal of Personality and Social Psychology, 88,* 63–78.
Moore, B. R. (2004). The evolution of learning. *Biological Review, 79,* 301–335.
Park, J. H., Faulkner, J., & Schaller, M. (2003). Evolved disease-avoidance processes and contemporary anti-social behavior: Prejudicial attitudes and avoidance of people with physical disabilities. *Journal of Nonverbal Behavior, 27,* 65–87.
Schaller, M., Park, J. H., & Faulkner, J. (2003). Prehistoric dangers and contemporary prejudices. *European Review of Social Psychology, 14,* 105–137.
Sperber, D., & Hirschfeld, L. A. (2004). The cognitive foundations of cultural stability and diversity. *Trends in Cognitive Sciences, 8,* 40–46.
Tooby, J., & Cosmides, L. (1992). The psychological foundations of culture. In J. H. Barkow, L. Cosmides, & J. Tooby (Eds.), *The adapted mind: Evolutionary psychology and the generation of culture* (pp. 19–136). New York: Oxford University Press.

The Evolution of Mating between the Sexes

﹩ 41

The Evolution of Human Mating Strategies

Consequences for Conflict and Cooperation

DAVID M. BUSS

Humans differ from chimpanzees, our closest primate relatives in many respects, but at least four of these are critical to mating. First, ovulation is relatively (although not entirely) concealed in the human female, in sharp contrast to the highly visible, bright red genital swellings that accompany ovulation in female chimpanzees. Second, human copulation occurs throughout the ovulatory cycle, whereas most chimpanzee copulation mostly occurs at or near the time of ovulation and genital swelling. Third, men and women form long-term mateships that can last years or decades; chimps do not. Fourth, men sometimes invest heavily in offspring, which includes providing resources, protection, and teaching skills, particularly if their certainty of paternity is relatively high. In contrast, chimpanzee males invest little in their progeny.

It requires taking a step back to realize how extraordinary these differences are. At some point in human evolutionary history, some women began to allocate their entire reproductive careers to a single male rather than to whomever was the reigning alpha male when they happened to be ovulating. Males began to guard their partners throughout the ovulation cycle, not merely when during ovulation, against rival males who might be tempted to lure their mates. Surplus resources that in many species went to the female as a specific inducement to copulation were channeled to the wife and children over the long term. Indeed, with these evolutionary changes, males now had added incentive to acquire surplus resources, mostly in the form of hunted meat. Long-term mating, in short, involved the allocation of reproductively relevant resources to a single mate (with some exceptions described below) over a primatologically unprecedented span of time.

THE MENU OF MATING STRATEGIES

Against this comparative species-typical backdrop, powerful evidence exists that both men and women have an evolved menu of mating strategies, not a single mating strategy. These strategies include long-term mating, short-term opportunistic mating, extrapair mating, serial mating, and possibly coercive or forced mating (Buss, 2003). Which strategy from this menu an individual woman or man pursues depends critically on a number of personal, social, environmental, and genetic variables, including personal mate value, operational sex ratio, prevailing social norms, ecological parasite prevalence, and heritable personality proclivities (Buss, 2003; Gangestad & Buss, 1993; Schmitt, 2005).

Men and women share many aspects of their mating psychology. Both sexes value kindness, intelligence, and health as long-term mate-selection criteria. Both sexes place a special premium on physical attractiveness when seeking short-term mates (Buss & Schmitt, 1993), and both tend to become extremely distressed when a long-term partner is discovered to be unfaithful. Both sexes sometimes attempt to poach mates who are in preexisting, committed relationships, either for short-term sexual liaisons or for longer-term committed matings (Schmitt, 2004; Schmitt & Buss, 2001). And both sexes engage in mate switching when the benefits outweigh the costs.

In contrast to these aspects of similarity between the sexes, women and men differ dramatically in some components of their mating psychology. Women more than men desire long-term mates who possess resources, a promising future resource trajectory (indicated by cues; e.g., ambition and social status), and slightly older age (which is correlated with provisioning ability). Men more than women desire long-term mates who are relatively young and physically attractive—both of which are signals of fertility and reproductive value (Buss, 1989b).

Men are more likely than women to fall in love at first sight, to desire and seek a variety of sex partners, to let less time elapse before seeking sexual intercourse, and to pursue extrapair copulations purely for sexual motivations. Women generally require more information about a man before falling in love, prefer a longer courtship period before engaging in sexual intercourse, and more often become emotionally involved with their affair partners.

CONFLICT BETWEEN THE SEXES

The basic mating strategies of men and women have profound implications for conflict and cooperation between the sexes. The mating strategies of individual men sometimes interfere with the preferred mating strategies of individual women, a phenomenon called *strategic interference* (Buss, 1989a). If a man is pursuing a short-term mating strategy and his preferred woman is pursuing a long-term mating strategy, the two will necessarily conflict. Empirical evidence suggests that men sometimes deceive women about the depth of their feelings and the intensity of their love to succeed in short-term mating (Buss, 2003; Haselton, Buss, Oubaid, & Anglietner, 2005). Women appear to have evolved both emotion circuits and behavioral strategies to prevent such deception. They devote more effort to assessing a man's long-term intentions, prefer a longer courtship process prior to consummation, and become emotionally upset when such male deception is discovered. According to strategic interference theory, emotional upset functions to alert individuals to the source of the interference, marks the interfering events for special encoding and memorial recall, and motivates action designed to prevent future episodes of strategic interference (Buss, 1989a).

The conflict runs both ways. Women pursuing a long-term mating strategy interfere with men pursuing a short-term mating strategy. Men, more than women, report emotional distress about a woman leading them to believe that sex is forthcoming, but saying no at the last minute (Haselton et al., 2005). Furthermore, women sometimes deceive men by appearing to offer "costless sex," then, over time, manage to transform the relationship into one that is longer-term, with more commitment (Buss, 2003). These conflicts have produced antagonistic coevolutionary arms races between the sexes (Buss, 2003; Gangestad, 2003).

Another key source of sexual conflict revolves around extrapair copulations (EPCs). Women who have EPCs jeopardize their regular mate's paternity probability. From the perspective of male reproductive interests, this produces potentially catastrophic costs in the form of his and his mate's investments being channeled to his rival's offspring rather than to his own. Men who have EPCs jeopardize their regular mate's access to his resources, portending the partial or total loss of his resources and commitment—both of which can get channeled to rival females.

Women and men appear to have evolved an array of adaptations to defend against these costs, including the emotion of jealousy and behavioral output of mate guarding, which ranges from vigilance to violence (Buss, 1988a; Buss & Shackelford, 1997). These adaptations have a number of sex-differentiated design features. Men, more than women, display greater distress about the sexual than about the emotional aspects of the infidelity, show greater memorial recall of cues to sexual rather than emotional infidelity, feel more threatened by intrasexual rivals who exceed them on economic resources of future resource prospects, are less likely to forgive a sexual than an emotional infidelity, and are more likely to terminate their relationship over a sexual than over an emotional infidelity (Buss & Haselton, 2005). Women, more than men show more distress about the emotional aspects of the infidelity, show greater memorial recall for cues to emotional infidelity, feel threatened by same-sex rivals who exceed them in facial or bodily attractiveness, are less likely to forgive an emotional than a sexual infidelity, and are more likely to terminate a relationship because of an emotional infidelity (Buss & Haselton, 2005).

As with the conflicts between the sexes around short-term versus long-term mating, conflicts surrounding infidelity are likely to have produced a profound sexually antagonistic coevolutionary arms race (Buss, 2000; Gangestad, 2003). If it has been reproductively advantageous for women to have EPCs under certain circumstances, yet detrimental to their cuckolded mates, an arms race will ensue. Men are likely to have evolved jealousy and mate-guarding mechanisms that are increasingly sensitive to subtle signals. These adaptations in turn impose selection pressures for adaptations in women that function to drive infidelity underground, increasingly concealing it to avoid the costs inflicted by jealous mates (and others) upon discovery (Buss, 2000). As women's affairs become increasingly surreptitious, men's jealousy adaptations in turn evolve to become even more sensitive to the muted signals.

Some of these adaptations likely evolved through logic described by error management theory (Haselton & Buss, 2000). Because the costs of failing to detect an infidelity that might occur, or has occurred, are likely to have been more severe than the costs of occasional false positives—suspecting an infidelity when none has occurred—selection has likely favored adaptations in men to err on the side of jealous paranoia (Buss, 2000).

In summary, the mating adaptations of each sex produce conflict with members of the opposite sex. At least in some domains, neither sex (at an individual level) can pursue its preferred mating strategy without interfering with the strategy preferred by some individual members of the other sex. Several perpetual cycles of sexually antagonistic coevolution have ensued, such as between deception and detection of deception, and between infidelity in each sex and adaptations in the other to guard against it.

It is important to bear in mind that "conflict between the sexes" does not refer to "men as a group" conflicting with "women as a group." Rather, each individual man is in strategic confluence with some individual women (e.g., a lover, a sister, a mother, a female friend) and in conflict with other individual women (e.g., those attempting to deceive them). Each individual woman is in strategic confluence with some individual men (e.g., a lover, a father, a brother, a male friend) and conflict with other individual men (e.g., those attempting to deceive him; Buss, 1996).

THE EVOLUTION OF LOVE

Although evolved mating strategies put individual men and individual women into conflict in certain domains, it is equally important to recognize the profound cooperation between the sexes. Men and women have always needed each other for both successful reproduction and the success of their progeny. The complex emotion called "love" may have evolved to promote the long-term cooperation between men and women in the service of producing reproductively successful offspring (Buss, 1988b, 2006; Fisher, 2004).

Contrary to widely held beliefs espoused by social scientists over the past century, there is now considerable evidence that love is not an emotion limited to Western culture. Rather, love appears to be a human universal, emerging widely in the ethonographic record (Jankowiak, 1995), as well as in contemporary cross-cultural studies (e.g., Buss, 1989b; Sprecher et al., 1994). The evidence in short suggests that the experience of love is universal in the sense that some individuals, in all cultures for which we have relevant data, experience love.

Love emerges primarily in the context of long-term mating and functions in part as a commitment device (Buss, 1988b). It is an emotion that signals the provisioning of key reproductively relevant resources, such as providing sexual access, portending sexual fidelity, promoting relationship exclusivity, promoting sexual actions that lead to successful conception, and providing signals of parental investment. Love, in short, represents a pinnacle of sorts in the evolution of long-term cooperation between the sexes. It typically occurs in three contexts in which the reproductive interests of a man and a woman maximally converge: when they are mated monogamously, when the odds of infidelity are low, and when they produce children who become the "shared vehicles" through which both sets of genes get transported into the future.

Nonetheless, love has a dark side. The loss of love, particularly when a woman permanently leaves a man who loves her, places women in peril of violence, stalking, and murder (Buss, 2005). These findings support the hypothesis that men's psychology of love contains design features that motivate them to keep a woman they love and go to desperate measures to prevent male rivals from possessing her.

CONCLUSIONS

Human mating strategies differ in pivotal ways from those of chimpanzees, our closest primate cousins. Relatively concealed ovulation, long-term mating, copulation throughout the ovulation cycle, and heavy male parental investment differentiate the two species. Both men and women have evolved a menu of mating strategies that range from long-term monogamous mating to short-term EPC mating.

Evolved mating strategies put individual men in conflict with individual women in certain contexts. Men who deceive women about their long-term intentions to gain short-term sexual access strategically interfere with women's long-term mating strategies. Women who deceive men about the probability of sex occurring, or about the costs associated with sex, interfere with men's short-term mating strategies. Men or women who pursue sex outside the bonds of a presumptively monogamous mateship inflict costs on their regular mates through reduction of paternity probability, the loss of reproductively relevant resources, or the risk of defection from the relationship entirely. Each sex has evolved adaptations with sex-differentiated design features to guard against costs inflicted by members of the opposite sex.

Despite the conflict that pervades human mating, men and women have always depended on each other for reproductive success. Profound cooperation, accompanied by cognitive–emotional love circuits, emerges primarily in the context of long-term mating. A deep understanding of human mating requires knowledge of the regions in which women and men get into conflict, as well as the regions in which their cooperation is profound.

REFERENCES

Buss, D. M. (1988a). From vigilance to violence: Tactics of mate retention. *Ethology and Sociobiology, 9,* 291–317.

Buss, D. M. (1988b). Love acts: The evolutionary biology of love. In R. Sternberg & M. Barnes (Eds.), *The psychology of love* (pp. 100–118). New Haven, CT: Yale University Press.

Buss, D. M. (1989a). Conflict between the sexes: Strategic interference and the evocation of anger and upset. *Journal of Personality and Social Psychology, 56,* 735–747.

Buss, D. M. (1989b). Sex differences in human mate preferences: Evolutionary hypotheses testing in 37 cultures. *Behavioral and Brain Sciences, 12,* 1–49.

Buss, D. M. (1996). Sexual conflict: Evolutionary insights into feminist and the "battle of the sexes." In D.M. Buss & N.M. Malamuth (Eds.), *Sex, power, conflict: Evolutionary and feminist perspectives* (pp. 296–318). New York: Oxford University Press.

Buss, D. M. (2000). *The dangerous passion: Why jealousy is as necessary as love and sex.* New York: Free Press.

Buss, D. M. (2003). *The evolution of desire: Strategies of human mating* (Rev. ed.). New York: Basic Books.

Buss, D. M. (2005). *The murderer next door: Why the mind is designed to kill.* New York: Penguin Press.

Buss, D. M. (2006). The evolution of love. In R. J. Sternberg & Karin Weis (Eds.), *The psychology of love* (pp. 65–86). New Haven, CT: Yale University Press.

Buss, D. M., & Haselton, M. G. (2005). The evolution of jealousy. *Trends in Cognitive Science, 9,* 506–507.

Buss, D. M., & Shackelford, T. K. (1997). From vigilance to violence: Mate retention tactics in married couples. *Journal of Personality and Social Psychology, 72,* 346–361.

Fisher, H. (2004). *Why we love: The nature and chemistry of romantic love.* New York: Holt.

Gangestad, S. W. (2003). Sexually antagonistic coevolution: Theory, evidence, and implications for human patterns of mating and fertility. In K. D. Wachter & R. Bulatao (Eds.), *Offspring: The biodeography of fertility-related behavior* (pp. 224–259). Washington, DC: National Academy of the Sciences.

Gangestad, S. W., & Buss, D. M. (1993). Pathogen prevalence and human mate preferences. *Ethology and Sociobiology, 14,* 89–96.

Haselton, M. G., & Buss, D. M. (2000). Error management theory: A new perspective on biases in cross-sex mind reading. *Journal of Personality and Social Psychology, 78,* 81–91.

382 IMPORTANT HUMAN EVOLUTIONARY OUTCOMES

Haselton, M., Buss, D. M., Oubaid, V., & Angleitner, A. (2005). Sex, lies, and strategic interference: The psychology of deception between the sexes. *Personality and Social Psychology Bulletin, 31,* 3–23.

Jankowiak, W. (Ed.). (1995). *Romantic passion: A universal experience?* New York: Columbia University Press.

Schmitt, D. P. (2005). Fundamentals of human mating strategies. In D. M. Buss (Ed.), *The handbook of evolutionary psychology.* New York: Wiley.

Schmitt, D. P. (2004). Patterns and universals of mate poaching across 53 nations: The effects of sex, culture, and personality on romantically attracting another person's partner. *Journal of Personality and Social Psychology, 86,* 560–584.

Schmitt, D. P., & Buss, D. M. (2001). Human mate poaching: Tactics and temptations for infiltrating existing mateships. *Journal of Personality and Social Psychology, 80,* 894–917.

Sprecher, S., Aron, A., Hatfield, E., Cortese, A., Potapova, E., & Levitskaya, A. (1994). Love: American style, Russian style, and Japanese style. *Personal Relationships, 1,* 349–369.

42

Social Structural Origins of Sex Differences in Human Mating

WENDY WOOD
ALICE H. EAGLY

The key to understanding hominid mating systems lies in an analysis of why some components of mating relationships are highly variable across societies and others are more universal. As we explain in this chapter, sex-typed physical attributes and related behaviors, especially women's childbearing and nursing, provide an organizing framework for human mating that is universal across societies. Within this framework, many sex-typed mating preferences vary across cultures, because men's and women's attributes and behaviors interact with local conditions to yield specific patterns of preferences.

BIOSOCIAL MODEL OF HOMINID MATING

Variability in human mating across cultures and ecologies reflects the species' sensitivity to local circumstances. Humans are endowed with this flexibility because they evolved in diverse environments with changeable conditions that impinged in differing ways on their reproductive outcomes. For example, especially in the late Pleistocene Epoch, climate appears to have been highly variable. Accommodating successfully to such ecological challenges required behavioral flexibility, enabled by an evolved capacity for social learning and the cumulation of culture (Richerson & Boyd, 2005). Comparative studies of primates have located humans' unique adaptation for cumulative culture in socially shared intentionality (Tomasello, Carpenter, Call, Behne, & Moll, 2005). These evolved capacities allow humans to produce novel solutions to the problems of reproduction and survival. Human innovation is evident in both tolerance for a wide range of different foods and diversity in mating arrangements.

Human flexibility does not imply that the mind is a blank slate. With respect to mating, evolutionary pressures shaped humans to favor healthy, fertile members of their own species who are of the sex complementary to their own. More specific mating preferences for partners with particular skills or personality traits emerge interactively from the evolved characteristics of the human species, individuals' developmental experiences, and their situated activity in society. These skills and traits gain meaning within the particular circumstances that people encounter in their culture and in their individual situations. This meaning takes the form of costs and benefits that are perceived to follow from choosing particular types of mates.

Beliefs about these costs and benefits are socially transmitted and shared within and between cultures. This learning is channeled largely through men's and women's social roles, because their lives are organized by these roles, which in turn create advantages for different types of mating relationships and partners (Eagly & Wood, 1999; Wood & Eagly, 2002). One way that social roles influence mating is through the formation of gender roles, by which people are expected to possess the characteristics that equip them for the activities that are typical of their sex. For example, to facilitate childrearing, women may be expected to be nurturing and kind. Gender roles, along with specific roles (e.g., occupation, marital status), then guide preferences for types of mates and relationships.

The influence of roles on behavior is mediated by various developmental and socialization processes as well as processes involved in social interaction and self-regulation. In addition, biological processes, such as hormonal changes, influence perceived costs and benefits by orienting men and women toward certain roles and facilitating certain behaviors. For example, hormonal influences on the perceived costs and benefits of mating could account for women's increased sexual interest during the portion of their monthly cycles when they are likely to be fertile.

Men's and women's social roles are themselves influenced by evolved physical attributes of the sexes and related behaviors, especially women's childbearing and nursing of infants and men's greater size, speed, and upper-body strength (Wood & Eagly, 2002). For a given society, the roles held by men and women are defined by the interaction between these evolved sex differences and the prevailing social, economic, technological, and ecological forces. The social roles that emerge from this interaction are characterized by a division of labor, because the physical endowments allow members of each sex to perform certain tasks efficiently, depending on a society's circumstances and culture. Specifically, childbearing and nursing of infants enable women to care efficiently for very young children and cause conflict with roles requiring extended absence from home and uninterrupted activity. Men's greater speed and upper-body strength facilitate their efficient performance of tasks that require intensive bursts of energy and strength. In short, sex-typed physical attributes and related behaviors are not a direct cause of mate preferences but instead exert their influence through biological, social, and psychological mechanisms. The attributes and related behaviors provide a universal framework that, in interaction with local conditions, yields sex-typed mate preferences that differ across cultures.

EVOLUTIONARY PSYCHOLOGY
ACCOUNTS OF HOMINID MATING

According to many evolutionary psychologists, human mating is organized by sexual selection pressures (see Buss, Chapter 41, and Thornhill, Chapter 43, this volume). In this view, male reproductive success depends on competition with other males, thus promoting evolved psychological attributes of aggressiveness and dominance and the physical attributes of larger size and greater strength. These characteristics emerge more strongly in species with polygynous mating systems, in which males engage in more intensive competition for mates and females favor mates who can provision and protect them and their offspring.

This sexual selection account of human mating patterns may seem consistent with the readily observed sex difference in human size. However, comparisons with other primate species show that the size difference in humans is relatively small, a finding inconsistent with the prominent role that evolutionary psychologists ascribe to male–male competition. Also, unlike highly dimorphic primate species, men and women have similarly sized canine teeth. Among primate species with low levels of dimorphism comparable to that of humans, considerable variability exists in mating systems and intensity of male–male competition (Plavcan & van Schaik, 1997). In addition, compared with other primate species, humans have a low operational sex ratio (i.e., the ratio of adult males to sexually available females; see

Wrangham, Jones, Laden, Pilbeam, & Conklin-Brittain, 1999), which is also compatible with low male–male competition instead of the higher levels inherent in polygynous mating systems. Finally, the modest sex difference in human size may well reflect selection pressures on females more than males, consistent with the increase in size of females relative to males as hominid evolution proceeded from *Australopithecus* to *Homo* species.

UNDERSTANDING HUMAN MATING SYSTEMS

Cross-Cultural, Cross-Temporal, and Individual Variation in Mate Preferences

Comparisons of mate preferences across cultures, time periods, and individuals within cultures provide support for our biosocial model of human mating preferences. These comparisons show that mating practices are flexibly emergent from the evolved physical attributes and related behaviors of men and women within social and ecological contexts (Eagly & Wood, 1999; Wood & Eagly, 2002). Furthermore, these effects are mediated by biological, social, and psychological processes. Our perspective rejects false dichotomies between the evolution of nature and culture but strives to understand the relation between them.

Cross-cultural variation in mate preferences of women and men reflects the divergent responsibilities and obligations inherent in their social roles. In societies with a strong division between male providers and female homemakers, women should seek a mate who is a good provider, and men should seek a mate who is a skilled homemaker and child caretaker. This good provider–domestic worker marital system should also generate sex-typed age preferences, given that older men are likely to have acquired resources, and younger women without resources are likely to value marriage and older partners with resources. In a test of these patterns, Eagly and Wood (1999) reanalyzed the data from Buss's (1989) study of the mate preferences of young adults from 37 diverse, primarily urbanized, cash-economy cultures. The characteristics that men and women desired in a mate were related to the extent to which the good provider–domestic worker division of labor was in place in each society. This division of labor in each culture was estimated with the Gender Empowerment Measure of the United Nations Development Programme, which represents the extent to which women participated equally with men in economic, political, and decision-making roles (see Eagly & Wood, 1999).

Consistent with the prediction that mate preferences reflect each sex's attempts to maximize outcomes within the societal structure, women's preferences for older mates and mates with resources and men's preferences for younger mates and mates with housekeeping and cooking skills were more pronounced in societies with a more traditional division of labor. Providing additional evidence that the preferences of men and women were a common response to a sex-typed division of labor, the sex differences in mate preferences tended to coexist within societies: In societies in which women expressed especially strong preferences for older mates with resources, men also expressed especially strong preferences for younger mates with domestic skills. Nonetheless, because a gender-equal division of labor had not been attained in any of the societies in the data set, the sex differences in mate preferences were present to some degree in all of the sampled societies.[1]

Also showing that mate preferences emerge flexibly from the division of labor, Sweeney (2002) documented cross-temporal changes within the U.S. population in the relation between economic prospects and marriage formation. The traditional tendency for higher earnings to increase the likelihood of marriage for men but not women has changed over time as earnings have become more important for women's marital prospects. As a result, the relations between earnings and marriage are now similar for men and women.

Our biosocial theory also has implications for individual differences in mate preferences within cultures. In general, persons who have a more traditional gender ideology prefer qualities in a mate that reflect a conventional homemaker–provider division of labor. That is, more traditional men have stronger preferences for younger mates with homemaker skills, and more traditional women have stronger preferences for older mates with breadwinning potential. This greater sex typing of mate preferences among individuals with traditional ideology has proven to be quite stable across a nine-nation sample (Eastwick, Eagly, Glick, Johannesen-Schmidt, Fiske, et al., in press).

The Importance of Patriarchy

Cross-cultural investigations have challenged aspects of evolutionary psychology accounts of human mating, especially the claim that men evolved a disposition to ensure paternity certainty by controlling women's sexuality. The sexual double standard, represented by greater control of female than

---

[1]The gender empowerment measure is calculated in part from the relative numerical representation of men and women in politics and management (see Eagly & Wood, 1999). Because women tend to be concentrated in roles with less power and status than men, gender equality on this index (i.e., a score of 1) cannot be interpreted as true equality of opportunity within a society. Thus, women's occupancy of 50% of managerial roles in contemporary societies would not mean that their power as managers would be comparable to that of men.

of male sexuality, is not a universal attribute of human mating systems. Whyte (1978) reported that in 75 nonindustrial societies selected to be geographically representative of world societies, only 43% had an extramarital double standard favoring greater promiscuity by men.

Instead of a universal phenomenon, sexual control of women is a historical development that emerged with societal complexity, much like other forms of patriarchy (e.g., male political power, property ownership by men). As societies developed in socioeconomic complexity, the tasks that became essential to economies required extensive training and skills development, high energy expenditure, and extended absences from home (Wood & Eagly, 2002). Women's reproductive activities limited their ability to engage in such tasks and to reap the social and economic capital inherent in them. The resulting male control of resources in more complex societies produced patriarchal social structures. In support of this analysis, anthropologists' assessments across ethnographic samples of world societies show that patriarchy is not a universal feature of human societies, and that approximately one-third of all pastoral and simple nomadic groups had egalitarian relations between the sexes (see Wood & Eagly, 2002).

Directly challenging the idea that sexual selection pressures produced a disposition for men to control women's sexuality, cross-cultural investigations have revealed that this control emerged with societal complexity; that is, the sexual double standard and the associated phenomenon of greater male than female sexual jealousy appear to have emerged with the development of socioeconomic structures within which sexual control of women acquired special utility. In Gaulin and Schlegel's (1980) review of nonindustrial societies, sexual control emerged with societal practices that imbued childbearing with economic implications in the form of property inheritance through male lines. Under these conditions, control over women's sexuality enabled men to ensure certainty of paternity and consequent economic advantage. Consistent with this argument, the sexual double standard was least prevalent in societies with simpler economies.

The patriarchal social structures that became prevalent as societies increased in socioeconomic complexity were associated with higher levels of male sexual jealousy, which also provided a mechanism for controlling women's sexuality. This interpretation is consistent with Reiss's (1986) finding in 80 nonindustrial societies that several indexes of patriarchy (e.g., patrilineal inheritance, patrilocal residence, importance of private property) predicted the tendency of husbands to manifest intensified sexual jealousy (see also Hupka & Ryan, 1990). The presence of this relationship does not, of course, mean that sexual jealousy is absent in men or women of any society given that sex is a valuable resource even in societies that legitimize extramarital relationships (see Wood & Eagly, 2002).

Additional challenge to the idea that men have evolved a disposition to experience sexual jealousy comes from Harris's (2005) failure to find supporting sex differences in five lines of evidence. For example, according to a meta-analytic investigation of jealousy-inspired homicides across 20 cultures that adjusted for base rates for murder, men were no more likely than women to commit murder out of jealousy. Also, European and U.S. college students' reports of their experiences of sexual jealousy revealed no consistent tendency for men to respond with greater jealousy than women to imagined or real sexual infidelity.

The lack of consistent evidence for patriarchy and sexual control of women, especially in simpler societies, raises questions about the plausibility of the evolutionary psychology assumptions about male sexual control. Simpler societies are presumably more similar than complex societies to the social contexts in which humans evolved as a species, thus favoring the display of evolved dispositions. Given the cross-cultural evidence that we have reviewed in this chapter, it seems that evolutionary psychologists have observed sex differences in modern, patriarchal societies and inappropriately concluded that humans evolved sex-typed psychological dispositions in ancestral times that correspond to these differences.

CONCLUSION

In summary, in our biosocial theory, human mating practices are characterized by behavioral flexibility that is an emergent product of local conditions and prevailing culture, developmental experiences, and evolved attributes. Our approach is in stark contrast to evolutionary psychology theories that treat culture largely as error variance or as a moderating variable that selects for certain pre-existing evolved dispositions (see Buss, Chapter 41, and Thornhill, Chapter 43, this volume).

The principle that sex differences in social roles are emergent from female reproductive activity and male size and strength explains why profound changes occurred in the status of women in the 20th century in most industrialized countries. Weakening both the traditional division of labor and patriarchy are women's increased control over reproduction, the marked decline in birthrates, and the decrease in the proportion of productive activities that favor male size and strength. Accordingly, women have increased their participation in the paid labor force, and young women's rates of education now equal or exceed men's in many nations. It is also not surprising that research tracking sex differences across recent time periods in the United States suggests that many psychological attributes and related behaviors of women have changed with women's entry into formerly male-dominated roles (see Wood & Eagly, 2002). The demise of many sex differences with increasing gender equality is a prediction of our theory that will be more adequately tested to the extent that societies equalize opportunities for women and men.

REFERENCES

Buss, D. M. (1989). Sex differences in human mate preferences: Evolutionary hypotheses tested in 37 cultures. *Behavioral and Brain Sciences, 12,* 1–49.

Eagly, A. H., & Wood, W. (1999). The origins of sex differences in human behavior: Evolved dispositions versus social roles. *American Psychologist, 54,* 408–423.

Eastwick, P. W., Eagly, A. H., Glick, P., Johannesen-Schmidt, M., Fiske, S. T., et al. (in press). Is traditional gender ideology associated with sex-typed mate preferences?: A test in nine nations. *Sex Roles.*

Gaulin, S. J. C., & Schlegel, A. (1980). Paternal confidence and paternal investment: A cross-cultural test of a sociobiological hypothesis. *Ethology and Sociobiology, 1,* 301–309.

Harris, C. R. (2005). Male and female jealousy, still more similar than different: Reply to Sagarin (2005). *Personality and Social Psychology Review, 9,* 76–86.

Hupka, T. B., & Ryan, J. M. (1990). The cultural contribution to jealousy: Cross-cultural aggression in sexual jealousy situations. *Behavior Science Research, 24,* 51–71.

Plavcan, J. M., & van Schaik, C. P. (1997). Interpreting hominid behavior on the basis of sexual dimorphism. *Journal of Human Evolution, 32,* 345–374.

Reiss, I. L. (1986). *Journey into sexuality: An exploratory voyage.* Englewood Cliffs, NJ: Prentice-Hall.

Richerson, P. J., & Boyd, R. (2005). *Not by genes alone: How culture transformed human evolution.* Chicago: University of Chicago Press.

Sweeney, M. (2002). Two decades of family change: The shifting economic foundations of marriage. *American Sociological Review, 67,* 132–147.

Tomasello, M., Carpenter, M., Call, J., Behne, Y., & Moll, H. (2005). Understanding and sharing intentions: The origins of cultural cognition. *Behavioral and Brain Sciences, 28,* 675–735.

Whyte, M. K. (1978). *The status of women in preindustrial societies.* Princeton, NJ: Princeton University Press.

Wood, W., & Eagly, A. H. (2002). A cross-cultural analysis of the behavior of women and men: Implications for the origins of sex differences. *Psychological Bulletin, 128,* 699–727.

Wrangham, R. W., Jones, J. H., Laden, G., Pilbeam, D., & Conklin-Brittain, N. (1999). The raw and the stolen: Cooking and the ecology of human origins. *Current Anthropology, 40,* 567–577.

43

The Evolution of Women's Estrus, Extended Sexuality, and Concealed Ovulation, and Their Implications for Human Sexuality Research

RANDY THORNHILL

By 1930, research showed that women's ovulation occurs near the midpoint of the menstrual cycle (not during or just after menses, as previously thought), that it is facilitated by the same hormones as ovulation in other mammals, and that estrogen plays a central role (etymologically, the "gen" or creator of estrus). These discoveries led to the hypothesis that women have estrus or "heat" that functions to motivate female eroticism at ovulation because sperm are needed for conception. Multiple reviews of the large body of literature produced in the 1970s, 1980s, and 1990s to test this hypothesis concluded that no overall, clear-cut patterns indicate estrus in women. Women's sexual motivation and mating does not show a definite periovulatory peak that corresponds with the high proceptivity (initiation of mating) and receptivity (allowing mating) that characterizes estrus in other mammals; nor was the attractivity component of mammalian estrus evident at midcycle, which would be observed in pair-bonded humans as a distinct periovulatory sexual attraction of males to their partners. Scholars' conclusion, therefore, that women had lost estrus led to numerous hypotheses to try to explain the loss.

Recent research, however, has questioned the earlier conclusion that estrus is nonexistent in women. Research published by my colleagues and myself was inspired by a fundamentally different theoretical framework than the earlier thinking. We propose that estrus does not function to get sperm per se. The focus of past selection on estrous females, instead, has been on getting a mate(s) with traits that, through inheritance, enhanced the reproductive value (health, survival, and/or mating success) of offspring. Sperm are, of course, obtained by estrus, but this is incidental to its function of good-genes sire choice. The view that the sexual motivation of estrous females functions for the indiscriminate pursuit of any old sperm is still widely held in mammalian reproductive biology (see Nelson, 2000) despite taxanomically widespread evidence that estrous females prefer males with traits that connote potential or actual superior genetic quality.

New research also reasons that the genetically superior sire for offspring may not be the main pair-bond partner of a female. This is expected to promote adaptive, condition-dependent, extrapair copulation (EPC) behavior by women that functions, during peak fertility in the menstrual cycle, to maximize the genetic quality of offspring when the in-pair partner is of relatively low genetic quality. Relatedly, new research assumes that women will exhibit concealed peak fertility in the menstrual cycle, and that this functions in EPC at peak fertility to disguise their EPC pursuits from primary partners. Thus, the reasoning is that women, like any other female mammals in estrus, will perceive and respond to their peak fertility in the cycle, but women will be cryptic about their motivations to secure the best sire through EPC at peak fertility. Moreover, their full estrous sexual rapture will be manifested only in the context of mating with a good-genes sire. Indeed, the recent research proposes that males always gain from "knowing" (perceiving and responding to) the peak fertility of females, and that a continuous coevolutionary race in humans to hide peak fertility (selection on females) and to detect it (selection on males) should leave each sex adapted, albeit imperfectly so, to the problem presented by the opposite-sex partner.

Finally, the new research assumes that at infertile phases of the menstrual cycle, women will exhibit sexual adaptation that I refer to as "extended sexuality," which is mating motivation outside the fertile phase of the reproductive cycle, and is seen in most Old World primates, pair-bonding birds, and across species in some other taxa. Comparative data indicate that extended sexuality evolves in species in which males provide females with nongenetic, material benefits; it functions to obtain those benefits. The particular benefits gained by females depend on the species. Benefits range from food, social alliances, and protection of self and offspring, including protection of offspring from infanticide and other maltreatment by males in the group.

The research inspired by this new theoretical perspective has provided diverse empirical findings that support the hypothesis that women have estrus that functions to get a good-genes sire. At peak fertility in the menstrual cycle, but not at infertile cycle times, women prefer the following: the body scent, faces, and behaviors of symmetrical men over the same traits of asymmetrical men; the relatively high degrees of facial testosteronization in men, indicating a fertile-phase–specific preference for another marker (in addition to symmetry) of potential male genetic quality; the scents (androstenone) related to high testosteronization; the relatively high degrees of male skin coloration (melanin- and hemoglobin-based) that may correspond to elevated testosterone; and the relatively high degrees of mental functioning in men (creative intelligence); women also show relatively high levels of disgust about incestous and other maladaptive matings. These effects are reviewed by Gangestad, Thornhill, and Garver-Apgar (2002), Thornhill and Gangestad (2003), Fessler and Navarrete (2003), and Haselton and Gangestad (2006). A number of these effects are seen primarily or solely in women's preferences for short- rather than long-term mates, as would be expected if the preferences function in pursuing sires, not longterm partners. Moreover, multiple studies indicate that only high-fertility-phase women seem to modify their behavior to reduce the risk of rape and, hence, insemination by men who may be unsuitable sires (see Bröder & Hohmann, 2003). It also appears that the effects mentioned are not seen in women using hormonal contraception (e.g., the pill), which means that the changed periovulatory sexuality of women depends on ovulatory cycle hormonal factors.

Another supportive line of recent work has examined normally ovulating women's sexual attractions and fantasies across the menstrual cycle. In general, nonpartner men, rather than the main pair-bond partner, are the focus of women's sexual interests at peak fertility, according to two separate studies (Thornhill & Gangestad, 2003). (One additional study, however, did not find this pattern; instead, it found that high-fertility women focus more sexual interest toward the main partner than toward nonpartner men.) Another study indicated that fertile-phase women paired with relatively symmetrical males showed more sexual interest in their partners than in nonpartner men, but fertile-phase women paired with asymmetrical men showed the reverse (Gangestad, Thornhill, & Garver-Apgar, 2005).

Collectively, this new research indicates that women perceive and respond to their peak fertility in the cycle in relation to changes in menstrual
cycle hormones. Additionally, it suggests that the peak fertility sexuality of
women is functionally organized to obtain a sire of high genetic quality.
Thus, in terms of self-knowledge of and adaptive design of estrus, women
at midcycle may be no different than other female mammals in estrus.

Moreover, women's estrus appears to have the attractivity component
seen in mammalian estrus in general. Three separate studies of normally
ovulating women have indicated that men rate the body scent of fertile-
phase women as more attractive than that of infertile-phase women. One of
these studies showed also that there is no menstrual cycle variation in the
body scent attractiveness to men of women using hormonal contraception
(see Kuukasjärvi et al., 2004; Thornhill & Gangestad, 2003). In addition,
two studies have found that men respond by increasing their mate guarding
during their partners' peak fertility in the cycle (Gangestad, Thornhill, &
Garver, 2002; Haselton & Gangestad, 2003).

Although men have far more knowledge of women's peak fertility in
the cycle than earlier scholars thought, men are not as astute as other male
mammals at detecting fertility. Men's incomplete knowledge is demonstrated by their great interest in copulation across the menstrual cycle, not
just at peak fertility. Men's limited knowledge implies selection on females
for crypsis of peak fertility in the menstrual cycle. However, given that men
have some knowledge, it also implies selection on males to circumvent the
crypsis and identify peak menstrual cycle fertility.

I refer to the sexuality of woman at peak fertility in the menstrual cycle
as "estrus" because of both its homology and function. Estrus apparently
had its phylogenetic debut in the species that was ancestral to all the vertebrate groups (fishes, amphibians, reptiles [including birds], and mammals).
This phylogenetic inference is supported by the apparent presence of estrus
in all of these groups, as seen in the similarity across vertebrates of the endocrinology and neurobiology of female sexual motivation at peak fertility
during the reproductive cycle (e.g., Nelson, 2000). Research also indicates
that estrus has the same general function throughout vertebrates, including
fishes, birds, and mammals. The function of estrus as sire choice seems to
be the reason for its evolutionary maintenance by selection after its phylogenetic origin. This persistence involved taxon-specific selection that molded
estrus for adaptive sire choice in each vertebrate taxon.

Previous discussion of women's sexuality in the literature has been
confused by the popular view that the loss of estrus is the same as the absence of female sexual swellings. This view claims, erroneously, that

women have no estrus, because their sexual swelling was lost in evolutionary history. Estrus and sexual swellings, however, are not equivalent. The
females of most species of nonhuman mammals lack swellings, but all
mammals have estrus. Also, contrary to conventional wisdom, swellings do
not likely function as signals of fertility in the ovarian cycle. Sexual selection acting on males guarantees that peak-fertility females conceive (Pagel,
1994). Instead, swellings are a form of female ornamentation that, like
sexual ornamentation in both sexes, probably functions honestly to signal
individual quality. In the hominin lineage, sexual swellings that function to
signal ovulation probably never existed, and ornamentation specific to
women—fat displays of breasts, hips, and thighs, as well as certain features
of face and skin—arose. Women's ornaments are not permanent, deceptive
signals of cycle-related fertility, as some have proposed. Instead, they probably function to obtain material benefits from males by honestly signaling
residual reproductive value.

Another popular view that confused prior thinking about women's
sexuality is the notion that loss of estrus is equal to concealed ovulation.
Estrous sexuality in women apparently is not lost, but is concealed, partially and conditionally, probably by design to mask it in the service of female EPC for superior genes. Equating the loss of estrus with concealed
ovulation is based on the very unlikely, but widely accepted, notion that
estrus functions to reveal ovulation.

Women's extended sexuality is also the subject of exciting recent research. It appears to be a distinct adaptation that functions to secure material benefits. For example, normally ovulating women at infertile phases of
their menstrual cycle, in contrast to fertile-phase women, prefer men with
less facial testosteronization; such men appear to be more willing to provide benefits to mates than men with greater degrees of testosteronization.
Also, the preferences of fertile-phase females for symmetry (mentioned earlier) seem to be contrary to material benefit by women. Symmetrical men,
like highly testosteronized men, invest less in their romantic relationships
(Thornhill & Gangestad, 2003). Women are designed by past selection to
exercise choice across the cycle, but the functional significance of their
choices seems to differ importantly between infertile and fertile phases. Extended sexuality allows women to achieve material benefit from mating
with men with low risk of conception by a sire of inferior genetic quality,
and estrus can facilitate production of offspring of high genetic quality.

The recent findings about human sexuality call for a program of research that addresses the design of each of women's two functionally distinct sexualities, the evolved products of arm races between men and

women in relation to estrus, and the relationship between honest signal theory and the sexual ornaments of both sexes. I hope that future research will appreciate more fully the value of understanding phylogenetic origin. Complete knowledge of the evolutionary history of human sexuality requires equal attention to both phylogenetic origin and persistence (typically with elaboration) of the features of human sexuality (see my essay in Chapter 1, this volume, on these two, distinct categories of ultimate causation).

ACKNOWLEDGMENT

Rosalind Arden, Steve Gangestad, Jeff Simpson, and Paul Watson provided useful comments on the manuscript.

REFERENCES

Bröder, A., & Hohmann, N. (2003). Variations in risk taking behavior over the menstrual cycle: An improved replication. *Evolution and Human Behavior, 24,* 391–398.

Fessler, D. M. T., & Navarrete, C. D. (2003). Domain-specific variation in disgust sensitivity across the menstrual cycle. *Evolution and Human Behavior, 24,* 406–417.

Gangestad, S. W., Thornhill, R., & Garver, C. E. (2002). Changes in women's sexual interests and their partners' mate retention tactics across the menstrual cycle: Evidence for shifting conflicts of interest. *Proceedings of the Royal Society of London B, 269,* 975–982.

Gangestad, S. W., Thornhill, R., & Garver-Apgar, C. E. (2005). Women's sexual interests across the ovulatory cycle depend on primary partner developmental instability. *Proceedings of the Royal Society of London B, 272,* 2023–2027.

Haselton, M. G., & Gangestad, S. W. (2006). Conditional expression of women's desires and men's mate guarding across the ovulatory cycle. *Hormones and Behavior, 49,* 509–518.

Kuukasjärvi, S., Eriksson, C. J. P., Koskela, E., Mappes, T., Nissinen, K., & Rantala, M. J. (2004). Attractiveness of women's body odors over the menstrual cycle: The role of oral contraception and received sex. *Behavioral Ecology, 15,* 579–584.

Nelson, R. J. (2000). *An introduction to behavioral endocrinology* (2nd ed.). Sunderland, MA: Sinauer.

Pagel, M. (1994). Evolution of conspicuous estrous advertisement in Old-World monkeys. *Animal Behaviour, 47,* 1333–1341.

Thornhill, R., & Gangestad, S. W. (2003). Do women have evolved adaptation for extra-pair copulation? In E. Voland & K. Grammer (Eds.), *Evolutionary aesthetics* (pp. 341–368). Heidelberg, Germany: Springer-Verlag.

Whither Science of the Evolution of Mind?

Steven W. Gangestad
Jeffry A. Simpson

We begin with two statements of gratitude. The first is directed to our contributors. We began this project, confident that authors, all respected scholars in their respective fields, would bring readers interesting, engaging, and clearly stated ideas about the state of human evolutionary behavioral science, ingredients that together would comprise a tantalizing intellectual dish. They most certainly did. We are pleased to offer this dish to readers and are very thankful to the authors for their thoughtful contributions.

Our second statement of gratitude is a more generalized one that is metaphorically directed to "the heavens," but more specifically to our intellectual forebears (dating back to Darwin), current scholars in the field, and the winds of fate that swept all of us into this fascinating field. We are thankful to be part of a scientific enterprise that is as intellectually vigorous, challenging, and stimulating as the present state of human evolutionary behavioral science. As our contributors make clear, these are exciting times. The goals are lofty—to understand human nature, its flexibility, and its cultural expression—and the intellectual challenges to reach them are daunting. Fortunately, the power of the theoretical tools available—the corpus of evolutionary biology—is now proven. Important progress is possible, and that prospect is exhilarating.

Nonetheless, as detailed in our introduction and reflected in this collection of essays, thoughtful minds disagree about how the available tools should be best used to make progress and, indeed, what progress has been made thus far. In this final chapter, we attempt both to distill some of the major points of consensus (or near-consensus) and to discern major issues that remain controversial and/or unresolved. In some cases, there may be clear ways to resolve certain outstanding issues empirically. In other cases, differences of opinion about the plausibility of assumptions deeply embedded in approaches probably mean that different researchers will choose different theoretical roads to travel. Time will tell which roads go farther.

We hope not to "overcook" the ingredients here or add many new ingredients of our own. Rather, our goal in this concluding chapter is to point out how some of the various flavors mix, stirring in a dash of spice here and there to bring out the zest and rich flavor of the various perspectives.

THE MAJOR APPROACHES TO HUMAN EVOLUTIONARY BEHAVIORAL SCIENCE

As we outlined in our Introduction, four major approaches characterize the study of the evolution of human behavior: sociobiology and three perspectives arising out of the sociobiology debates (human behavioral ecology, evolutionary psychology, and gene–culture coevolutionary approaches). Given that sociobiology has largely channeled into these three perspectives, we focus on each of them. In so doing, however, we also address the possible emergence of a distinctive brand of evolutionary psychology rooted in developmental systems theory (see Sterelny, Chapter 18, this volume) and discuss roles for historic and comparative data. We then briefly describe the main assumptions of each major approach. Following this, we identify several major metatheoretical and methodological issues of contention and discuss possible means by which they can be resolved.

Before proceeding, some general remarks are in order. As we noted in the introduction, debates have led to rather polarized positions. Some polarization has perhaps been due to advocates of certain positions carving out their own unique stands. But perhaps more of it has arisen because each side has caricaturized alternative views—presenting them in an imagined way that advocates of those positions do not truly endorse. Hence, debates have sometimes been between straw men, not actually believed by anyone.

These straw men debates have frustrated proponents whose views have been caricatured (even though these same proponents may have frustrated advocates of alternative positions in a similar fashion). Ultimately, of course, the field's long-term interests are served if we move beyond debates between straw men and center on issues of real, substantive disagreement.

At the same time, some—probably most—oversimplified presentations of positions been neither mischievous nor completely devoid of benefit. Critical examination of a perspective often requires making fully explicit the assumptions of that perspective. Individuals most motivated to examine a position critically—those who advocate an alternative perspective—may sometimes be most motivated to make clear any implicit assumptions of that perspective as well. Even when attempts to "fill in" these implicit assumptions are misguided or inaccurate, they may move debate ahead by forcing advocates of the criticized position to clarify their implicit assumptions. (For instance, as we discuss below, developmental systems theorists have made claims about foundations of evolutionary psychology that evolutionary psychologists reject. Evolutionary psychologists have countered by trying to clarify the true assumptions of their perspective, thereby sharpening their perspective.) In an effort to sharpen extant debates, we ourselves may at times be guilty of presenting some positions in overly simplistic or caricatured terms, even if unintentionally.

As a matter of convention, we reference essays by listing the last name (or names) of the author(s) followed by the number of the issue their essay addressed in brackets. We begin with the evolutionary psychology approach.

Evolutionary Psychology

Evolutionary psychology is an *adaptationist* approach. As Thornhill [1] and Andrews [1] note, adaptationism does *not* commit one to the idea that most or all organismic features are adaptive (or were ancestrally adaptive). Indeed, by-products of selection (incidental effects carried along with selected traits but having no adaptive advantages themselves, such as the belly button, the foveal blind spot) greatly outnumber adaptations (features selected because they promoted gene propagation better than alternatives, typically because they enhanced individual reproductive success). Rather, adaptationism is a *method* for discerning *which* organismic features are adaptations and which are likely by-products of selection.

Selection that had implications for *current* human behavior occurred *ancestrally*; that is, adaptations arose sometime in the past. This definition of "adaptation" is a historic one. Adaptations need not be adaptive in the modern world. As discussed in the Introduction, a classic illustration is taste preferences for calorically rich foods that were adaptive in ancestral environments, when nutritional stress was common, but not in modern environments in which the health risks of obesity are a major cause of death. An "adaptation" is a feature that arose in ancestral environments and may or may not be adaptive now. Selection may operate now (e.g., against these same taste preferences), but this new selection cannot itself explain *current* behavior (Borgerhoff Mulder [2]). According to an adaptationist perspective—hence, according to evolutionary psychology—if an understanding of natural selection tells us anything about contemporary human behavior (whether in modern or traditional societies), then it tells us that selection operated *historically*.

Evolutionary psychology is not the only adaptationist perspective in the human behavioral evolutionary sciences, however. In the 1980s and early 1990s, Symons (1987, 1990) argued that human behavioral ecologists were not adaptationists but rather were *adaptivists*—interested merely in whether certain features are adaptive now, not in the ancestral past. In this volume, Reeve and Sherman [2] argue differently. They claim that two, nonopposing methods can be used to study selection. One, the forward method, focuses directly on attempts to understand *historic* selection. Evolutionary psychologists typically adopt this method. The other, the backward method, can also be applied to understand *historic* selection, but it does so indirectly by studying *current* selection. Behavioral ecologists typically adopt this latter method (e.g., Smith [1]; Borgerhoff Mulder [2]). *No one among our contributors argues for an adaptivist approach over an adaptationist one;* that is, no one argues that an evolutionary perspective is centrally about what is adaptive today; instead, everyone appears to agree that *ancestral selection* is key to understanding the implications of selection for current behavior. This issue is resolved. However, as discussed below, differences of opinion persist about the utility of examining current fitness for purposes of revealing past selection.

Here, then, are key components of a standard evolutionary psychology approach.

A Forward Method for Understanding Selection

Using this method, researchers try to understand and test the implications of past selection by (1) creating a model of past selection, (2) making hypotheses about current adaptations based on it, then (3) testing those hypotheses (Reeve & Sherman [2]). To create a model of past selection, a researcher must either know of or hypothesize a specific selection pressure in the ancestral past. This selection pressure is typically expressed as *an adaptive problem* (i.e., a need) whose solution should have been selected over alternatives, all else being equal (e.g., a need to recognize kin, to identify and select fertile mates, and to avoid predation). One then specifies the requirements of design features that would have succeeded in solving that problem (or satisfying the need) ancestrally and should therefore have been favored by selection. Successful design features purportedly satisfy a general requirement, which is the basis for the second component of evolutionary psychology.

Functional Specialization

The human body reveals intricate functional specialization throughout. Livers, hearts, spleens, stomachs, blood vessels, immune systems are all functionally specialized. When we examine subtypes and subcomponents of these organs and systems (e.g., capillaries, valves, leukocytes, individual cytokines), we see even further functional specialization. Hagen and Symons [1], Ermer, Cosmides, and Tooby [5], and Barrett [5] lay out reasons we should not be surprised to see functional specialization everywhere. General purpose (or even multipurpose) devices do not effectively and efficiently solve particular problems well, but problems that require information processing abound (e.g., kin recognition, identification of fertile mates, avoidance of predators). Based first on principles, then, evolutionary psychologists typically expect psychological design features to be *functionally specialized* in a manner analogous to that of the human body.

As Ermer and colleagues [5] and Hagen and Symons [1] further note, functionally specialized information processing can take advantage of the recurrent structure of specific information embodied in the world relevant to particular adaptive problems then to efficiently and effectively solve those problems. For instance, because most ancestral individuals who saw their female caretakers breast-feed an infant were biological siblings of that infant, kin recognition could be validly inferred from this cue. An effective and cheap kin recognition device, then, might partly compute kin relatedness as a function of this cue (e.g., Lieberman [6]). Successful psychological design features are not just functionally specialized; many also process information of specific *content*; that is, they are also *domain-specific*.

The standard evolutionary psychology approach, then, encourages the following research strategy: (1) A researcher first identifies an *adaptive problem* that recurred in ancestral human groups; (2) the researcher performs a *task analysis*, which asks what kind of computations (information acquisition and processing) would have effectively and efficiently solved the problem in an ancestral world, typically in a domain-specific manner; (3) the researcher tests the hypothesis that modern humans possess these computational procedures. (See Tooby & Cosmides, 1992, for a more elaborate description of this research strategy and other strategies adopted by evolutionary psychologists.)

Human Behavioral Ecology

As noted in our Introduction, the human behavioral ecology approach grew as an extension of animal behavioral ecology. Animal behavioral ecologists ask how ecological selective pressures have shaped the way members of species behave. They often use optimality models of how selection pressures operate to affect optimal behavioral strategies (under the constraints of limited time and energy budgets). Models have both generality and specificity with respect to individual species. They often are presumed to apply generally to many species. Because different species differ with respect to important ecological variations specified in the models (e.g., resource patchiness, mortality hazards), however, the models also make different predictions for different species. Human behavioral ecology applies similar logic and theoretical tools to understand why individuals in the same and in different cultural groups (who often encounter different ecological and socioecological variants) behave differently.

As Reeve and Sherman [2] argue, the behavioral ecology approach, like evolutionary psychology, is adaptationist in nature but it differs from evolutionary psychology in its focus and methodology. As typically practiced, the behavioral ecology approach is characterized by three major components.

A Backward Method for Understanding Selection

Reeve and Sherman [2] describe the backward method for understanding selection, the one typically employed by both human and nonhuman animal behavioral ecologists. One observes outcomes favored by selection in current environments in which organisms reside to infer which outcomes may have been selected in ancestral environments.

An Optimality Modeling Approach

To predict and explain observations of what is favored, behavioral ecologists use models of what selection *should* favor. They prefer rigorous, quantitative models that incorporate trade-offs between allocations of effort to various tasks (e.g., growing vs. reproducing, parenting vs. finding mates). These models of selection are the primary theoretical tools that behavioral ecologists employ.

Agnosticism with Regard to Psychological or Cognitive Mediators

Behavioral ecologists have traditionally been interested in using models of selection to predict and explain how organisms behave in their environments. They are not typically concerned with building theories about the psychological or cognitive mechanisms that might have been selected to generate adaptive behavior (Smith [1]). Instead, they are satisfied with their explanations, if their selection models correctly predict observed behavior. It is not so much that behavioral ecologists deny that selection has shaped psychological processes. Rather, they tend to think that models of psychological process are fallible (because they involve unobservables) and add little to understanding behavior (see Smith, Chapter 4).

We sketched out a typical research strategy within behavioral ecology in our Introduction. Behavioral ecologists often develop quantitative models to identify which kinds of behavior should be optimal in promoting reproductive fitness within a given ecology (e.g., the allocation of time to hunting that would maximize net calorie gain). To derive optima when testing these models, researchers estimate parameters within the model with actual data (the rate of return per unit time as a function of hunting, gathering roots, picking fruits, etc.). In some instances, they might estimate the rate of actual reproduction as a function of a particular behavior. They then measure actual performance (e.g., the actual amount of time spent hunting) and compare it to the estimated optimum. If a discrepancy exists, they usually refine the model by taking into account benefits or costs not specified in the initial optimality model (e.g., the benefits of obtaining mates through hunting success) or entertain the possibility that behavior does not optimize fitness in the environment, because it contains evolutionarily novel elements.

Gene–Environment Coevolutionary Theory

In many respects, coevolutionary approaches endorse components of the adaptationism underlying evolutionary psychology and behavioral ecology. Proponents of this approach, however, also emphasize ways these approaches are limited and simplified. As we noted in the Introduction, they argue that selection operates on a system of "inherited" information based on the replication of ideas (cultural evolution), as well as a system based on the replication of genes (genetic evolution). Cultural evolution has implications for understanding human behavior. Increasingly, proponents of this approach have been interested in specifying the ways the two systems of inheritance do not evolve independently. Specifically, humans purportedly have adaptations for culture and cultural transmission. As Boyd and Richerson [11] argued, cultural transmission permits remarkable ability to adapt rapidly and to invade new niches (see also Kurzban [11]). However, it also leads humans to act in highly maladaptive ways, and not merely because of "misfits" between adaptations and novel environments. The potential for maladaptation may be inherent in the nature of adaptations for culture.

MAJOR METATHEORETICAL
AND METHODOLOGICAL ISSUES

We now turn to major issues of contention that remain unresolved and are matters of debate. We identified 10 such issues pertaining to metatheory and methodology. Many of the debates surround specific assumptions of particular approaches that critics maintain are implausible or untested. In most instances, proponents of the criticized position have responded, often vigorously, sometimes in ways that defend the standard approach, other times in ways that modify it in particular ways. Although this list is not exhaustive, many of the key controversies in the human evolutionary behavioral sciences center on these criticisms and counterresponses.

Issue 1: How Much Do and Can We Know about
Environments in Which Past Selection Occurred?

As discussed by Reeve and Sherman [2], the forward approach to understanding past selection of evolutionary psychology requires assumptions about the nature of past selective environments; that is, based on assumptions of an ancestral selective environment, a researcher using this method hypothesizes what kinds of traits would have been favored. Some critics of this approach make the obvious observation that selection in the past can no longer be observed and measured. We cannot know through direct observation what was selected ancestrally; hence, we cannot possibly perform a critical test of any hypothesis about past selection (e.g., Reeve & Sherman [2], Borgerhoff Mulder [2]). The implication is that although we can tell stories, we cannot scientifically test them. Other critics claim that we simply do not know enough about the ancestral world even to make good guesses about what was selected. The historic archival data on *Homo ergaster*, for instance, are very thin, particularly when it comes to understanding social structure and relations (e.g., Mithen [1]).

The standard adaptationist response to these criticisms is articulated by Thornhill [1]: Past selection can be inferred from *special design*. Adaptations have been selected to perform functions, which, in specialized evolutionary terminology, refers to the means by which the feature propagated gene transmission relative to alternatives. A trait exhibits special design for a particular function when it performs that function very effectively within a particular environment, and it is difficult to imagine an alternative evolutionary process generating it. The classic illustration is vertebrate eyes: They are very good for seeing, and it is difficult to imagine an evolutionary process that would have led to eyes other than selection for their optical properties. Because special design evidence can be very powerful evidence for ancestral selection, one can validly infer past selection even without direct observation of the selection process. No biologist doubts that passerine bird wings were, at some point in their history, selected for flight. And biologists do not fret about not being able to witness that selection process directly to test that hypothesis "scientifically."

As Buller (2005) recently argued, however, a methodological problem may remain. Again, because we cannot observe ancestral environments, we do not know what psychological features were selected. Evolutionary psychologists respond that psychological design itself is a footprint of ancestral selection pressures, containing telltale clues of past selection. But how can one use ideas about historical environments to *discover* psychological design, as evolutionary psychologists claim we should, as well as *simultaneously* to infer historical selective environments *from* design? Doesn't this strategy suffer from a catch-22?

Strange as it may seem to some, it *can* work this way; indeed, science often works this way. Scientists regularly bootstrap understanding of unobserved events by using imperfect understandings of those events (scientific conjectures) to guide empirical inquiry, which then feeds back to refine theories. This process is perhaps a more extended, iterative, and deductive–inductive one than implied by many simple descriptions of the evolutionary psychology approach. However, it is consistent with the basic principles of the evolutionary psychology approach and the forward method of investigating selection. More generally, it is consistent with the notions of construct validation in psychology: *Systematic programs* of research, which simultaneously *are guided by and guide* theory, refine theory and at the same time test it (see Cronbach & Meehl, 1955).

How adequate is this response? Judged against standards within philosophy of science, probably pretty good. Many phenomena claimed to be well documented in physics, for instance, have not been directly observed; only the effects of electrons, protons, and many other subatomic particles are used to test rigorously high-energy physical theory. Moreover, hypotheses and assumptions are conjectural, which is a part of normal science. Iteratively applied, conjecture → test → theory refinement processes can build detailed accounts that powerfully explain wide nets of observations. They account for how theoretical physics arrived where it is today—as well as historical scientific enterprises such as astronomy, geology, and other aspects of evolutionary biology (e.g., all of phylogenetics), in which meaningful scientific investigation began with imperfect understandings of unobserved pasts. This philosophy of science lies at the core of construct validation (Cronbach & Meehl, 1955).

Even if this iterative, forward method of investigating selection is perfectly consistent with accepted scientific principles and procedures, one can still wonder how well it works *in practice,* specifically *within evolutionary psychology.* How many examples in human evolutionary behavioral science approach the kind of strong inference we can make about selection relative to bird wings or vertebrate eyes? Investigating and testing ideas about the "structure" of the mind might be much more difficult than investigating the structure of morphological characters. Andrews [1], who is sympathetic to the general special design approach, recognizes the difficulties; a related article (Andrews, Gangestad, & Matthews, 2002) expands upon them and discusses procedures that might help the cause. Evolutionary psychologist Crawford [2] and behavioral ecologists Smith [1] and Borgerhoff Mulder [2] make similar points, namely, that a deep understanding of adaptation will require data from multiple kinds of studies (e.g., lab experiments, field studies in traditional societies, correlational studies in modern societies; see also Mithen [1], who argues for attention to the historic record as well). Nevertheless, differences in opinion about which precise "recipes," combining different empirical ingredients, will lead to success are likely to persist.

We think that there are some good, paradigmatic examples of systematic research programs that have made progress. One is the inference that female estrus sexuality most likely evolved for the function of obtaining good genes from mates for offspring (Thornhill [12]). Others include work on adaptations involved in maternal–fetal conflict (e.g., Haig, 1993) and kin recognition (Lieberman [6]).

How many examples, however, meet the rigorous standards of Williams's (1966) "onerous" concept of adaptation, those exemplified by the case made for the vertebrate eye? There may be many, though some critics may disagree. Borgerhoff Mulder [2], Smith [1], and Reeve and Sherman [2] remain skeptical of the plausibility of reconstructions of past environments used in special design arguments. (See also Stanford [3], who implies that evolutionary hypotheses not backed by data on reproductive outcomes remain "just-so" stories, a claim that many evolutionary psychologists would deny; see Thornhill [1].) Hagen and Symons [1] make the interesting point that rather than being *too* speculative in thinking about past environments, evolutionary psychologists perhaps should do *more* in the way of specifying the kinds of environments in which specialized adaptations purportedly function adaptively. The general idea is that rigorous demonstrations of functional hypotheses through special design, which show lock-and-key kinds of fit between adaptation and environment, *require* specification of environments. Accordingly, special design tests may suffer from *lack* of aggressive speculation about environmental features rather than overspeculation. No doubt, important discussion about appropriate adaptationist methodology will continue. We remain optimistic that debate will only sharpen methodologies and, eventually, provide more convincing empirical evidence for certain adaptationist claims.

Issue 2: What Can and Need We Know about the Time Span of Past Selective Environments?

Many evolutionary psychologists at least imply that we should be thinking about what would have been the adaptive environments in which ancestral humans evolved, a Pleistocene existence. What adaptations would have been favored by such an "environment of evolutionary adaptedness" (EEA)? This concept of "an EEA" has been extensively criticized by behavioral ecologists. When Symons (1990) and Tooby and Cosmides (1990) first used the term (borrowed from Bowlby, 1969), many took what they said to imply that the Pleistocene was our EEA and that, accordingly, we should expect psychological adaptations to be adaptive in a hunter-gatherer existence. Many of our adaptations, of course, predate the Pleistocene and hunting-gathering ways (including many psychological traits); some adaptations may have arisen post-Pleistocene (even within the past 10,000 years). The Pleistocene is not a monolithic time period (e.g., much evolutionary change in hominins occurred between 2 million and 100,000 years ago), and many adaptations may be just as adaptive now as they were in traditional hunter-gathering societies (Reeve & Sherman [2]). The EEAs of any two specific traits, then, may be quite different. Indeed, Tooby and Cosmides agree with all these points and actually proposed a concept of the EEA that was more diverse than the one that has been criticized. Smith [1] argues that the concept of the EEA is not so much wrong as it is oversimplified. For these reasons, Irons (1998) proposed that a better way to talk about fit between traits and environments is to speak of "adaptively relevant environments" with respect to particular traits. Hence, despite the fact that the vertebrate eye first emerged in the distant past, it may nonetheless be functional in modern human environments, which are "adaptively relevant environments" with respect to vertebrate eyes. The same may be true of many psychological adaptations. The strategy of simply thinking about what would have been adaptive for humans living in hunter-gatherer bands (even if we knew precisely how those bands lived, which we do not), according to critics, does not derive from first principles.

Phylogenetic comparisons may reveal which human adaptive traits evolved in ancestors shared with other extant species. Humans, of course, did not "evolve from" close relatives (e.g., chimpanzees); we evolved from common ancestors (Stanford [3]; Silk [3]; Thornhill [1]). According to Stanford [3], evolutionary psychologists too often assume that important human cognitive traits first appeared in hominids, when in fact some important ones may have evolved in more distant relatives. More generally, phylogenetic data can support or cast doubt on hypotheses about human traits. Silk [3] provides an intriguing example. The social brain hypothesis for human intelligence would appear to have much going for it. Yet apes, she argues, are an embarrassment to it. Some have little social complexity, such as many Old World monkeys, yet they have large brains. Apes innovate, however, and perhaps that is why they have large brains. Human brain evolution may have launched from these origins. (See Dunbar [9], however, for one possible explanation for the ape–monkey grade-shift in brain size, independent of group size, but consistent with the social brain hypothesis.) Similarly, Lancaster and Kaplan [3] argue that differences between humans and close relatives may clarify the nature of human adaptive complexes. As these authors make clear, phylogenetic comparisons have received far too little attention from many human evolutionary behavioral scientists, particularly those stuck on thinking about important human traits arising in a Pleistocene EEA (see also Thornhill [1]).

Issue 3: What Is the Implication of the Fact That Adaptation Involves Tinkering, Not a Priori Design?

A simple description of the task analysis of evolutionary psychology is that it answers the question, "What kinds of design features (e.g., information-processing capabilities) would have solved adaptive problem X (where X could be any purported adaptive problem) in ancestral environments, and therefore possibly evolved?" Related to Issue 2, but separate, is Issue 3. Humans were not constructed anew in "the EEA." They were the outcome of eons of evolutionary process, appearing approximately 400 million years since the appearance of the first vertebrates and perhaps 200 million years since the origin of mammals. Never across these vast timescales were ancestral species formed anew as a set of solutions for their environments. Rather, in each generation, selection had to operate on variations on a preexisting design. "Reverse engineering" is an approach for trying to understand the function of something designed for a particular purpose, and attempts to understand the function of biological features are sometimes compared to attempts to understand the function of objects designed by humans. Unlike human artifacts, however, biological "design features" were not constructed from scratch. The evolution of adaptations probably involves "tinkering" more than "engineering" (e.g., Jacob, 1977). Hence, evolutionary psychologists should perhaps be trying to "reverse tinker" rather than "reverse engineer." The problem with this task is that we do not necessarily know what preexisting design there was to be tinkered with at any point in evolution. How do we separate what has been tinkered with from the outcomes of tinkering itself? (See also Andrews et al., 2002.)

Finlay [9] tells a related cautionary tale. Primates possess trichromatic color vision. Other mammals do not. Does this mean that color vision was more strongly selected in primates than in other mammals? Possibly not. Primates are the only mammalian species with high-definition focal vision, presumably selected for reasons other than those that favored trichromatic color. Yet trichromatic color vision is particularly useful in species with high-definition focal vision. Hence, primates may stand alone as mammals that possess trichromatic color vision, because they alone have high-definition focal vision, not because their environments selected color discrimination particularly strongly. Outcomes that could be favored if preconditions were met may nonetheless not evolve because these preconditions never evolved.

Adaptationist logic perhaps rarely takes into account conditions of evolvability (though see Barrett et al. [8] and Hill [11] for examples in this volume).

A response to these criticisms is that one need not always know the full history of a biological feature to reverse engineer it effectively. Mammary glands originally were "tinkered" sweat glands. But they too contain telltale signs of selection for a particular function, feeding young (Thornhill [6]). Features of mind may also possess telltale signs of selection, despite being outcomes of "tinkering" with prior features.

Still, some features surely do possess "mixed designs"—mixtures of features reflecting design for a phylogenetically older function, as well as design for a more recent function. This point was one of Gould and Vrba's (1982) key arguments for the importance of the concept of exaptation (see also Andrews et al., 2002). But if a trait possesses mixed design, with no special design for any single specific function, it may not appear to have been designed for either. In these cases, phylogenetic methods may be useful. By examining the distribution of individual features across phylogenetically related species, researchers may be able to identify an older design separately, including how it was altered by recent function (see Silk [3], Stanford [3]). Thornhill's [6] call for greater attention by evolutionary psychologists to questions of phylogeny is relevant here. A more complete evolutionary psychology should take questions of origins much more seriously.

Issue 4: What Is the Relevance of Current Selection and Fitness Differentials to an Understanding of Evolved Outcomes?

As evolutionary psychologists have long argued (e.g., Symons, 1987), current selection is neither a necessary nor sufficient criterion to establish adaptation. In this volume, Crawford [2] repeats this argument, while also noting some valid uses for measures of reproductive success in modern environments (e.g., when patterns of reproductive success in modern environments differ from those found in traditional societies). As discussed earlier, evolutionary psychologists prefer to infer ancestral selection using criteria of functional design.

Related to this criticism is the argument that current (or even past) fitness differentials do not reveal design per se. Suppose one finds that individuals who exhibit submissive displays have lower reproductive success than those who are dominant. Even if one assume that this pattern existed ancestrally, does it imply that selection disfavors submissive displays? Not necessarily. Submissive display may be a best strategy for individuals who have low power and, may therefore have been selected as a conditional tactic. More generally, patterns of correlation do not directly imply anything about the nature of the underlying design that was selected.

In response to these criticisms, Borgerhoff Mulder [2] acknowledges the premise of this argument: Current selection for a trait is neither a necessary nor a sufficient criterion of adaptation. She argues, however, that the conclusion that a trait's association with current reproductive success *cannot provide useful information* does not follow. As she notes, studies of current fitness are useful for addressing a range of important questions relevant to understanding human adaptation (e.g., what environments favor particular traits, whether hypotheses about selection fit relevant data [particularly when evaluated in environments presumed similar to ancestral ones], questions about conflicting selection pressures). As she also explains, the key is to appreciate results of these studies within a sophisticated adaptationist framework, not simplistically (see also Smith [1]; Reeve and Sherman [2]). Her commentary moves discussion of these matters well beyond the polarized evolutionary psychology versus evolutionary anthropology controversy of the early 1990s.

Reeve and Sherman [2] similarly argue for the utility of examining current selection on a trait for understanding ancestral selection, even when maladaptation is observed, given that patterns of adaptation and maladaptation can constrain hypotheses about what kinds of ancestral environments would have favored observed traits (see also Crawford [2]). But they go on to make stronger claims. They argue that because past selection would have favored organisms that could project their own fitness outcomes based on available information, individuals should be expected often to behave adaptively in current environments. Some evolutionary psychologists will no doubt disagree with these arguments on grounds that any strategy must rely on computations performed on relevant information. And, it is not clear what kinds of workable computational procedures are robustly adaptive in all possible environments (see Issue 5 below). Again, a preference for sweet foods, contributing to a modern epidemic of obesity, is often offered as an illustration of how a computational procedure that worked fine in past environments (choosing calorie-rich foods—ones that taste sweet or fatty) can be maladaptive in current ones. Some fundamental disagreements between some behavioral ecologists and perhaps most evolutionary psychologists on these issues are likely to persist.

Issue 5: What Should the Role of Optimality Modeling Be for Understanding Adaptation?

Behavioral ecologists often use precise, rigorous optimality models to predict what adaptive behaviors should be observed. Smith [1] reiterates his preference for these sorts of theoretical tools (see also Smith, Borgerhoff Mulder, & Hill, 2001). Hill [11] argues that the optimality approach, and the trade-offs recognized by it, have deep metatheoretical consequences. Organisms are selected to maximize fitness under the constraints of finite time and energy budgets. Just as finite household financial budgets entail trade-offs between different expenditures (e.g., the more that is consumed, the less can be saved), organisms face trade-offs between different forms of resource expenditure. This fact has two major implications. First, organisms will not be selected to perform any particular function, solve any adaptive problem, or satisfy any "need" perfectly; trade-offs always entail compromises (Kaplan & Gangestad [4]). Second, under different circumstances, organisms may optimize fitness through different forms of energy expenditure. Hence, selection should lead to systems that adaptively modulate resource allocation to various functions, depending on the circumstances. According to some critics, standard evolutionary psychology does not sufficiently appreciate these implications. For instance, Hill [11] argues that the strong modular thesis of evolutionary psychology is not plausible, because modulation of different systems requires some central processes not specific to particular domains.

Kaplan and Gangestad [4] discuss ways that individuals may modulate expenditure of effort consistent with adaptive trade-offs. Endocrine hormonal systems (e.g., those involving testosterone, estrogen, or cortisol) illustrate adaptations that function to modulate effort by simultaneously affecting the operation of multiple modular systems. Though evolutionary psychologists may have largely neglected trade-offs to date, an evolutionary psychology that attends to trade-offs seems possible.

Some evolutionary psychologists do use optimality modeling in their work, though they typically use it to understand how *past* selection operated, not to predict which outcomes should be observed in modern settings (see DiScioli & Kurzban [4]; Kaplan & Gangestad [4]). Reeve and Sherman [2] might argue that there is a place for using these models to also predict *current outcomes* within the context of a backward method for understanding past selection (see also Smith [1]). As Kenrick and Sundie [4] note, many psychologists (evolutionary and otherwise) do not feel that they need quantitative models in their work; these authors illustrate how models may sometimes, and sometimes not, be useful. We hope that evolutionary psychologists will become more acquainted with quantitative models (both formal techniques and simulations) applied to evolutionary processes and increasingly use them in their work.

Issue 6: How Much Specification of Computational Design Is Needed in a Compelling Account of Adaptation?

Whereas behavioral ecologists argue that evolutionary psychologists are not sufficiently rigorous in the way they theorize about selection pressures, evolutionary psychologists complain that many behavioral ecologists are not sufficiently rigorous in the way they theorize about resulting adaptations. Organisms are selected to respond adaptively to their environments. To do so, they must attend to information available in the environment and alter their behavior accordingly in fitness-promoting ways. An adequate model of how they do so must state what information is processed, how the information would have recurrently appeared in environments in which the adaptation evolved, how organisms are designed to respond to this information, and why that pattern of responses would have promoted fitness. On the basis of the idea that no very general procedure with respect to content ("domain-general" procedures) could solve all adaptive problems, evolutionary psychologists argue that functional psychological traits tend to be specialized for specific purposes (e.g., "domain-specific" procedures)—in other terms, that psychological traits are modular (Ermer et al. [5]; though see Barrett [5] on the need to explicate further a workable notion of modularity). The most fundamental premise here is not that psychological adaptations are modular, but that any complete account of psychological adaptations must rigorously specify the procedures involved.

Some behavioral ecologists argue that domain-general kinds of reasoning or learning have evolved to solve many human adaptive tasks. Even evolutionary psychologists accept that some psychological adaptations are not highly domain-specific (see our discussion of general intelligence below). Reeve and Sherman [2] argue that organisms have evolved a suite of psychological adaptations that compute flexibly and continually compute the alternative strategies' expected fitness outcomes (i.e., Darwinian algorithms), then selects the strategy (behavior or behavioral suite) that will maximize fitness. Furthermore, they argue that because ancestral humans often occupied novel environments, these psychological adaptations would have been selected to operate adaptively even in novel modern circumstances.

Some evolutionary psychologists might respond by asking that behavioral ecologists specify the procedures that have evolved in precise terms. What information, for instance, is acted upon? If organisms can track fitness consequences in novel environments (where new behaviors in novel circumstances promote fitness), and what information that tracks fitness consequences, specifically, do they pick up (see also Tooby & Cosmides, 1990)? Most evolutionary psychologists would not argue against the claim that psychological adaptations have evolved to respond "flexibly" to environmental changes (thus, they would disagree with Reeve and Sherman's [2] characterization of their views). But they might argue that much adaptive flexibility requires specificity with respect to adaptive domains. Indeed, Barrett [5] argues that "plasticity" is a property of modules, not an alternative to them. Similarly, Ermer and colleagues. [5] discuss an issue illustrated by the "Stoppit" problem: Can the goal of maximizing fitness contingently in all domains, when the domains may have little in common with one another, be served by a single adaptation? Hence, evolutionary psychologists might argue that Reeve and Sherman's "active fitness projector" requires a psychological architecture that is highly specialized, which would be evident if one tried to specify with precision the kinds of procedures that are truly workable. They might also argue that such a specialized system could not actually project fitness accurately in all novel environments. How much disagreement remains between proponents of views such as those expressed by Reeve and Sherman and those of evolutionary psychologists (e.g., Ermer et al. [5]; Barrett [5]) may depend on precise specification of the nature of the psychological adaptations claimed to be involved.

Issue 7: What Are the Consequences of the Fact That Organisms Themselves Create Environments and Do Not Merely to Adapt Preexisting Environments?

The concept of adaptation may imply that organisms "adapt" to something, namely, an environment, and in so doing "solve" a problem that the environment "poses." Indeed, the task analysis of evolutionary psychology assumes a preexisting environment that poses problems for organisms to solve. As Sterelny [6] emphasizes, this view of the relation between organisms and their environments is overly simplistic (see also Lewontin, 1983). Organisms both create and respond to their environments. Perhaps more profoundly, however, neither organisms nor their environments can be fully defined without reference to the other. They are part of a coevolved system in which neither element can be separated from the other (see Sterelny [6]).

The coevolved nature of organisms and their environments is illustrated by work on niche construction. Organisms are adapted to their environments partly because they find niches for which they possess adaptive features. Did humans *adapt to* the hunter-gatherer lifestyle? Or did they develop a hunter-gatherer lifestyle because they *already possessed features* (evolved for other reasons, either for other functions or as by-products) that rendered hunting and gathering successful? In all likelihood, the answer to both questions is "yes." Sterelny [6] argues that the methods of evolutionary psychology (task analysis, reverse engineering) ignore the latter possibility.

Of course, task analysis and reverse engineering *have* proven useful. Many organismic features evolved in response to features of the environment (e.g., immune systems to pathogen stress; means of kin detection to the problem discriminating kin; mate choice criteria to the problem of identifying suitable mates), and standard adaptationist methods have successfully identified evolved function in many such cases. For some questions, however, a broader approach is perhaps needed. Boyd and Richerson [11], for instance, argued that a key human "trick" allowing people to spread rapidly across the globe was the invention of culture, which permitted much useful information to be stored in and transmitted through the minds of people. Is it useful to think of the invention of culture as a solution to a particular problem the environment posed? Perhaps. (See Flinn and Coe [11] on aspects of culture that evolved in response to social selection.) But another possibility is simply that human intellectual capacities and social predilections that evolved for other reasons permitted humans to transmit information horizontally and create a component of culture. If so, much adaptive behavior in humans—that which solves problems through information embodied in culture—is due to features *not* evolved as solutions to particular problems now solved by those features.

Are organism–environment coevolutionary phenomena of this sort readily incorporated into the standard framework of evolutionary psychology, one that gives priority to evolutionary task analysis and reverse engineering? Or is a new metatheory for evolutionary psychology needed (e.g., Sterelny [6])? This issue will no doubt continue to be debated.

Issue 8: How Should Development Be Incorporated into the Concept of Adaptation?

Selection is not a creative force. Selection on phenotypic variants can change the frequencies of genotypes or other components of developmental systems, but it cannot create elements that do not already exist. As Thornhill [6] notes, every phenotypic variant that selection operates to increase in frequency or to eliminate from a population begins as a variation in a developmental process (e.g., through introduction of a new genetic mutation or a new environmental element). To understand processes involved in the origin of adaptations, one must understand development. Furthermore, every adaptation of every organism must be constructed anew during the lifetime of the organism. Once it appears in the population, the trait does not automatically appear; rather, it must emerge through development. This notion, Honeycutt and Lickliter [6] argue, should be fundamental to the concept of adaptation, but it is missing in the thinking of many evolutionary psychologists. They outline some deeper implications of evolutionary psychology's neglect of development. Standard adaptationist approaches separate out different kinds of causes. Questions of what causes a trait or behavior to occur in the current situation are questions of proximate causation. These causes include the brain systems or mechanisms responsible for behavior, the situations that affect those brain systems and, hence, behavior, and the developmental processes that lead to those brain systems. Questions of how traits evolved are questions of ultimate causation. Ultimate causes include causes of the origins of traits and causes for the spread and maintenance of traits (e.g., random drift, selection). Evolutionary psychologists purportedly use theory about ultimate causation (selection) to guide inquiry into the nature of proximate causes. Honeycutt and Lickliter and some other developmental systems theorists argue that because this distinction is not legitimate, this adaptationist program is not sound. Specifically, development, a *proximate* process, is key to the appearance of every adaptation whose causes are purportedly *ultimate* in nature.

Thornhill [6], a self-proclaimed adaptationist, agrees that evolutionary psychologists have ignored development, for they have generally ignored questions of evolutionary origin. Barrett [6] agrees with developmental systems theorists' point that every adaptation requires a developmental process to be created anew within the lifetime of the organism. At the same time, he argues that the developmental process leading to adaptations is itself often selected for its robustness. Important outcomes are not typically the result of highly fickle developmental processes. This point is also implicit in Crawford's [3] distinction between an innate adaptation (DNA) and an operational adaptation (the adaptation as it develops). Developmental systems theorists would probably take exception to delimiting the evolved basis of adaptation to DNA (e.g., Honeycutt & Lickliter [6]).

An important question for evolutionary developmental biologists (evo-devos) is how developmental processes can evolve to become robust (see West-Eberhard, 2003). Barrett [6] and Thornhill [6] claim that developmental systems theorists often ignore or downplay the fact that selection shapes developmental systems. Developmental systems theorists might counter by noting that robust developmental systems should be empirically demonstrated rather than assumed a priori. Lieberman [6] describes how selection has purportedly shaped systems underlying the development of kin discrimination and illustrates how an adaptationist approach can tackle some key questions of developmental process in a principled, generative way. She leaves open the possibility that developmental systems theory can offer incremental insight, but asks for the same kind of principled, predictive approach from this theory.

The claim that there is no fundamental distinction between proximate and ultimate causation, Thornhill [6] argues, is confused. Development is actually both kinds of cause. Which it is in any specific context depends on what outcome one is trying to explain. Development is an ultimate cause of any novel variation that is subsequently maintained in a population (and hence evolves). It is a proximate cause of any feature, including adaptations. That development is both sorts of causes should not obscure the fact that ultimate causation is separate from proximate causation.

The evo-devo approach in biology has produced considerable integration of developmental phenomena into an adaptationist framework (e.g., West-Eberhart, 2003). We hope to see similar attempts at integration within evolutionary psychology. Exactly how evolutionary psychology should integrate developmental perspectives will be a major topic for future discussion.

Issue 9: How Should Cultural Variation Be Understood?

Evolutionary psychology emphasizes human universals. Kin discrimination, cheater detection, and mate choice are all adaptive problems assumed to be solved through the same adaptations by all people (or at least all same-sex people). Yet human behavior varies considerably. Given its emphasis of human universals, evolutionary psychology largely neglects this variation (Smith [1]; Borgerhoff Mulder [2]; Hill [11]; Schaller [11]).

In principle, evolutionary psychology addresses cultural variation through the concept of "evoked culture," grounded in behavioral ecologists' notion of environmentally contingent responses, which in turn is grounded in adaptive trade-offs (e.g., Gangestad, Haselton, & Buss, 2006a; Tooby &

Cosmides, 1992). As Boyd and Richerson [11] argue, however, much cultural variation does not appear to be due simply to ecologically contingent responses. Commentaries on a recent article by Gangestad and colleagues (2006a) point out a variety of cultural phenomena that appear to require theories that extend beyond the concept of evoked culture (e.g., Flinn, 2006; Norenzayan, 2006). Schaller's [11] call for evolutionary psychologists to put serious effort into accounting for cultural variation is timely. Though some evolutionary psychologists and gene–culture coevolutionary theorists have proposed that humans have specialized adaptations for processing cultural information, Smith [1] calls this idea "quixotic" and instead suggests that more domain-general information processing handles cultural input.

Issue 10: What Is the Role of Group Selection in Evolution?

Debate over whether selection can effectively operate on differential reproduction of group-level features, or effectively operate on features defined at the individual level has a longstanding and contentious history in evolutionary biology. For decades, resistance to the idea of selection at the group level was strong (see Wilson & Sober, 1994), based largely on the arguments advanced by Williams (1966) in his classic treatment of Wynne-Edwards's (1962) claims for group-level selection. Proponents argued that Williams's arguments do not pertain to particular forms of group-level selection (see Boyd & Richerson [7]). Persistence on their part has paid off. Acceptance of "multilevel selection theory"—the idea that selection can operate on properties affecting gene propagation defined at a number of different levels (species [clade selection], within-species groups, individuals, genes) is now widespread. Indeed, all of our commentators on this issue (Boyd & Richerson [7]; Kurzban & Aktipis [7]; Wilson [7]) endorse it.

This shift in thinking represents a major theoretical advance. Disagreements that remain center on whether group-level selection has been an important selective force on human traits and, if so, which ones and what evidence supports such claims. Kurzban and Aktipis [7] propose that one should look for evidence of group-level selection in the design of the adaptations it might have forged; that is, one might expect that social adaptations that have been favored by group-level selection have signatures of that history of selection, features that cannot be explained by individual-level selection accounts.

We now turn to more specific substantive issues addressed by the chapters in the latter part of the book. These chapters addressed one of four general sets of questions dealing with specific evolved outcomes in humans: the evolutionary history of our large brains, our superior general intelligence and abstractive abilities, the emergence and purpose of culture, and patterns of human mating.

SPECIFIC SUBSTANTIVE ISSUES

In addition to posing questions about metatheoretical and methodological issues, we asked some authors to respond to questions about specific evolved outcomes in humans: our large brains, our general abstractive intelligence, culture, and human mating patterns. We also posed an open-ended question to a few authors about which key evolutionary changes during hominid evolution have been the most central in understanding human psychology. Several important themes recur in the responses to these various questions.

Large Brains, Abstract Reasoning Ability, and Key Evolved Outcomes in Human Psychology

Two major themes arose in responses to questions about why large brains evolved, the nature and function of abstract reasoning ability, and key evolved outcomes in human psychology: (1) entry of hominids into the cognitive niche, and (2) the importance of coevolutionary social selection processes for understanding humans.

Hominid Entry into the Cognitive Niche

Selection on humans resulted in massive encephalization, resulting in our very large brains. Moreover, our brains do things that no other species' brains can do. We speak complex language, we reason with arbitrary symbols, we think in highly abstract ways, and we create forms of culture not observed in other species. Many authors believe that our ability to reason abstractly is intimately tied to massive encephalization. What specific selection pressures led to these abilities and the brain mass to support them? Few questions are more central to understanding changes that occurred during hominid evolution. Despite much speculation, answers to this question remain open to debate.

One set of answers focuses on human entry into the *cognitive niche*. As discussed by Barrett and colleagues [8], humans have an extensive array of adaptations dedicated to the acquisition, manipulation, and application of information. These adaptations include those resulting in subsistence economics of use of information and knowledge that involves (for example) greater use of lower quality information and novel interrelationships among information, and breakthroughs in lowering the cost to acquire and maintain large bodies of information. Variations on these ideas emerge in essays by Mithen [8] and Kaplan, Gurven, and Lancaster [9].

What are the key components of this array of adaptations? According to Barrett et al. [8], one core component is *improvisational intelligence*. Dedicated intelligences solve targeted problems, typically through specialized manipulation of information that capitalizes on the recurrent structures of encountered environments (e.g., the invariant mechanics of objects in three-dimensional space). Improvisational intelligence, by contrast, improvises solutions to novel problems in real ontogenetic time. One advantage of this capacity is that a species armed with it does not have to ratchet up adaptations slowly that permit entry into new niches over long evolutionary timescales. Rather, it can create adaptive solutions to new niches within single generations. Modern humans are the only species that has developed this ability to extraordinary levels; hence, humans have rapidly expanded into new habitats, have developed amazing diversity relative to subsistence and to resource extraction methods, have caused the extinctions of innumerable prey species in the environments they penetrated, and have generated an immensely greater array of social systems, artifacts, and representational systems than those found in any other single species (Barrett et al. [8]).

Kaplan and colleagues [9] place evolution of this capacity into a larger ensemble of important human traits, which they term the "human adaptive complex." These traits include a particular life history in which juveniles mount large deficits in caloric production relative to consumption and are "subsidized" by adults. This life history is possible only when a period of excess productivity during adulthood is long—that is, when mortality is low, when senescence is slow, and productive activity yields caloric surpluses. Large human brains and, in Barrett and colleagues' [8] terms, "improvisational intelligence" are key to human food production, which involves extensive extractive foraging (e.g., hunting).

Kaplan and colleagues [9] provide one answer to an issue raised by Barrett and colleagues [8]. Improvisational intelligence would benefit any species, but it has evolved in extreme forms in only humans. It must therefore have large costs, or there must be preconditions to its evolution that are uncommon (see Finlay's [9] "cautionary tale"). How could it have evolved in humans despite heavy costs? Other components of the human adaptive complex is the answer that Kaplan and colleagues provide. Human children and young adults spend a prolonged period of time acquiring the "embodied capital" represented by large brains and the knowledge they store and apply. While doing so, they are subsidized by adults, which is possible because of the very high levels of productivity afforded by human embodied capital, in combination with low mortality rates, slow senescence, and a system enabling intergenerational flow of resources from adults to juveniles (including heavy paternal investment).

Other authors characterize improvisational intelligence or related capacities in somewhat different ways. Silk [3] posits the importance of innovation for the evolution of human (and possibly ape) intelligence. Smith refers to "deliberative" processes as forms of general problem solving. Mithen [8, 10] refers to cognitive fluidity—the ability to integrate information manipulated by domain-specific modules. Relatedly, Barrett and colleagues [8] note that improvisational intelligence is built on an array of dedicated intelligences. Without these, improvisational intelligence would not have leverage to solve novel problems. In addition, to be adaptive, application of outputs of improvisational intelligence must be restricted to the particular novel problems they solve and not bleed into domains in which they do not work. Framing the application of solutions to novel problems requires supporting adaptations (e.g., "scope-syntax"; Barrett et al. [8]). Identifying and characterizing what computational procedures are required for human "general intelligence" is no small task. Interfaces between evolutionary science and cognitive and neuroscience approaches will be important to progress on this front (but see Boyer [11]).

Miller [9] questions whether solutions that solve ecological problems might account for human brain evolution. Other species, for instance, with much smaller brains appear to solve very complex problems of foraging. The computational capacity of the human brain, then, may be overkill for solving most ecological problems. On this basis, Miller favors explanations that posit coevolutionary, positive-feedback selection processes, notably, social selection (see below). In a related vein, Dunbar [9] discusses comparative evidence favoring the social brain hypothesis of brain size evolution in primates and argues that current data do not favor an extractive foraging view. Some of our authors might respond that dismissal of models positing selection on capacities to solve ecological problems based on comparative data is premature. Barrett and colleagues [8] and Kaplan and colleagues [9] claim that humans evolved to solve ecological problems through computational capacities that are simply unparalleled in any other evolutionary line (enabled by the cost-absorbing features outlined in the embodied capital framework); that is, humans represent a major evolutionary transition (see Kaplan et al. [9]; see also Wilson [7]). Given that we currently do not know the extensiveness of the computational procedures required for these capacities, it is difficult to infer whether human brains represent computational overkill. Comparisons with other species that solve ecological problems in dramatically different ways are not unambiguously informative.

Coevolution through Social Selection

Another set of authors argues that social selection processes have been the major force behind human brain expansion. Social selection is a leading candidate for two primary reasons. First, social selection is a positive feedback (or "Red Queen") process that can lead to runaway evolution (e.g., Flinn & Alexander [8]; Miller [9]; see also Rice & Holland, 1997). Solutions to problems of social living are often not stable. A tactic that permits deception of a conspecific rival, for instance, may become nonadaptive at a later time, when conspecifics have evolved a counteradaptation permitting detection of the deception, leading to selection favoring new tactics of deception, new counteradaptations, and so forth. Because social success is based on relative superiority, the bar is constantly raised and the selection process can be autocatalytic, leading to extravagance (Flinn & Alexander [8]). The claim with respect to social selection is that humans have evolved an extensive arsenal of adaptations applied to problems of social competition, which include, but are not limited to, competition for mates (Miller [9]). Second, solutions applied to social living are computationally demanding, because the social world is a virtual one (Dunbar [9]). One must consider information about not only entities immediately present but also many individuals (and their relationships with others) not immediately present.

What is the nature of the cognitive processes resulting from social selection? Presumably, they are highly variable. They are likely to include an extensive and well-developed theory of mind (e.g., Mithen [8]) and processes that support theory of mind (e.g., Dunbar [9]). According to Geary [10], they also include the hallmarks of abstract reasoning. In his view, abstract reasoning—the ability to represent the world symbolically—evolved as an elaboration of folk psychological systems, elaborations that permitted self-centered scenario building to evolve through social selection. Hence, the social selection view argues that even highly unique human cognitive abilities ultimately have their functional roots in social competition.

Of course, the social selection theory of human brain evolution is incomplete without an explanation of why *humans* in particular were under strong social selection pressures. Dunbar [9] makes the valuable observation that the social brain hypothesis *is* a kind of ecological hypothesis. Individuals do not adapt to group living simply for the sake of group living. Group living affords individuals in some species occupying particular kinds of ecological niches advantages over individuals that lack group living. Adaptations for group living, then, are likely to evolve in particular kinds of ecologies. The social selection theory of human brain evolution, therefore, must ultimately be grounded in an *ecological* theory of human living.

Flinn and Alexander [8] and Geary [10] argue that humans experienced strong social selection because they attained ecological dominance— a relative lack of selection as a result of extrinsic causes compared to the relative importance of selection as a result of interactions with conspecifics (Flinn & Alexander [8]). Their idea is that humans became so successful in obtaining food, freedom from predators, and so on, that selection pressures on their abilities to succeed in these domains became weak relative to their abilities to compete with conspecifics. Here, then, is a major contrast between authors' viewpoints. Those who defend ecological theory believe that humans' ability to achieve tremendous success in obtaining food occurred through *strong* selection imposed by ecological factors within the human niche on brain size, which Flinn and Alexander [8] believe became weak, *after* which extensive pressures on elaborate human cognitive skills resulted. Because authors such as Barrett and colleagues [8] and Kaplan and colleagues [9] might not agree with Flinn and Alexander's view of ecological dominance, more discussion of this concept might be useful.

Kaplan and colleagues [9] extend their embodied capital view to incorporate a role for social selection. They argue, however, that the kinds of social selection pressures on humans are unusual, if not unique, and are situated within a broader array of adaptive human features. In particular, they propose that extensive cooperative behavior (and corresponding incentives to cheat cooperators) is part of the human adaptive complex as well (a view consistent with that of Flinn and Coe [11]). Human foraging requires it. In addition, surpluses in food production mean that much food is distributed through social networks. In line with Dunbar's [9] claims, navigating the social world is cognitively demanding. However, whereas Dunbar understands the human case as a quantitative extrapolation of primate social complexity, Kaplan and colleagues [9] emphasize ways in which humans represent a qualitatively different form of social intelligence, one based on the unique nature of evolved human cooperative relations. Again, as

Dunbar [9] argues, sociality did not evolve for the sake of sociality per se; it evolved in specific ecological niches because of the fitness benefits it afforded in those niches. Kaplan and colleagues [9] sketch out one way that features of human sociality distinct from those of other species could be adapted to a human niche, as outlined within their embodied capital view.

A similar sentiment is echoed by Barrett and colleagues [8]. Improvisational intelligence, they argue, vastly expands the potential for mutually beneficial trade, because information garnered through both improvisational intelligence and applications of information (e.g., new technologies) can be exchanged. Gains in trade from improvised solutions can only be achieved, however, when potential cooperators can infer what others want, believe, and plan to do. Moreover, cognitive adaptations supporting cultural transmission coevolved with improvisational intelligence. Hence, according to Barrett and colleagues, entry into the cognitive niche led to new social selection pressures, not because humans were "released" from ecological selection pressures (cf. Flinn & Alexander [8]) but because social living allowed individuals to solve ecological problems within the cognitive niche more effectively. Once again, the juxtaposition of different positions reveals some key points of disagreement in need of further discussion and resolution.

One who takes the view of Miller [9], who has argued for the importance of sexual selection in human brain evolution, might suggest that ecology is itself not central to understanding human brain expansion. The human brain, according to this view, is partly a kind of "peacock tail," a wasteful extravagant display that evolved to signal genetic quality (Miller, 2000). Costly, sexually selected signals may be arbitrary with respect to ecology. Just as the peacock presumably did not evolve a costly tail as a signal in response to some unique ecological selection pressure on tails, this view might propose that humans did not evolve large brains because of any unique ecological selection pressure on brains. Alternatively, displays of cognitive ability in particular may have evolved as signals (e.g., of genetic fitness), because those cognitive abilities did in fact have functional importance for other reasons, a view favored by Kaplan and colleagues [9].

Toward an Integrative View

As indicated earlier, integration of ecological and social selection views of human brain evolution is not only possible but perhaps also required. One issue we raised earlier is what forms of ecological and social factors have been selective forces, and how might they fit together in a coherent picture of the human niche (if in fact they do fit)? A second issue concerns sequencing (e.g., Kaplan et al. [9]). Were the initial benefits that launched the evolution of massive brains social in nature? Were they ecological in nature? And how did specific capacities permit the evolution of additional capacities (see Geary [10])?

Finlay [9] accepts the view that a variety of different forms of ecological and social benefits probably contributed to brain evolution. She is not optimistic, however, about the prospect of accurately sequencing the evolution of particular abilities. One reason is that the primary area in which brain expansion has occurred in humans, the neocortex, is not specialized for one particular kind of ability. As a result, we have no telltale sign that human brain expansion was driven by one particular form of benefit. As Kaplan and colleagues [9] argue, some cognitive capacities (e.g., scenario building) can have both social and ecological benefits. Finlay notes, however, that the challenge of sequencing is particularly difficult, because brain evolution may have involved not only enlargement but also introduction of new functions into the enlarged space. She proposes that the issue of sequencing is not a major evolutionary question that needs to be answered, and that we should stop arguing about it. Instead, we might direct our efforts to understanding the human brain in the context of the evolution of brains in general, including abilities dynamically to reallocate brain structure to function.

An even broader issue centers on the nature of capacities that are uniquely well-developed in humans, such as improvisational intelligence. Dedicated intelligences (forms of intuitive physics, many mating adaptations, kin recognition, etc.) take advantage of recurrent structure of information in the world. As Hagen and Symons [1] argue, effective reverse engineering can rely on an understanding of the recurrent structure of information in the world. Based on a lock-and-key analysis of information and its processing, it will be clearly evident that some dedicated information-processing procedures (e.g., processing of cues of kin detection) are designed to solve particular problems. Because improvisational intelligence is not geared to particular domains of information, reverse engineering its function may be considerably more challenging.

Consider, for instance, Kanazawa's [10] provocative proposal that general intelligence is a domain-specific adaptation that evolved to solve novel problems in ancestral environments, particularly new or irregular problems that could not be solved by other domain-specific psychological mechanisms. Contrary to other theorists (e.g., Barrett et al. [8]), Kanazawa [10] argues that general intelligence evolved to solve narrow sets of novel problems and predicaments that hindered survival and/or reproduction, particularly those that demanded the ability to reason inductively and deductively, to think abstractly, to synthesize information rapidly, and to apply these new insights in future situations. But this set of problems, he claims, was not tremendously important in many ancestral environments. In Kanazawa's view, general intelligence predicts greater success in modern life, because we now live in chronically novel environments that differ in innumerable ways from our ancestral past. Indeed, he suggests that the high level of general intelligence exhibited by humans may be an "accident" of human evolutionary history. Can we test between competing theories about the function of general intelligence on the basis of design features per se? Perhaps, but the task appears more difficult than reverse engineering many other kinds of dedicated psychological adaptations.

Miller [9] reminds us, however, that perhaps we can glean empirical findings about brains that allow us to narrow the range of plausible scenarios leading to massive human brain size. He draws attention to several features of human brains. One feature, for instance, is its cost. If brain tissue supporting general intelligence per se is highly expensive, one might think that it had payoffs in ancestral environments more frequently than Kanazawa's view implies. As we discussed earlier, proponents of views that Miller suggests are not likely to explain the benefits of large brains, may disagree with his particular conclusions. Nonetheless, Miller's fundamental conceptual and methodological point—that we should continue to look to human cognitive capacities for telltale footprints of its evolutionary heritage—is an excellent one. In line with our earlier remarks about methodology, other sources of information (e.g., phylogenetic reconstructions, the historic record, observations of hunter-gatherers) may also yield important insights. The challenge of reconstructing the evolution of uniquely human forms of intelligence may be daunting, but resourceful researchers will, we believe, continue to make progress.

It is worthwhile to echo a theme that Barrett and colleagues [8] begin with—that it is a mistake to think that human evolution will be understood in terms of a few underlying, powerful laws, as in physics. The evolution of big brains, general intelligence, culture, or any other unique human trait does not define human evolution. Documenting the important outcomes that affect human functioning will be an enterprise of cataloguing. Many key features affecting human well-being and distress that are to be understood through evolutionary functional analysis made their debut well before the appearance of our first hominid ancestors. The luminance of unique human features should not blind us to understanding the functional design and nature of human traits with more ancient roots as well (e.g., Stanford [3]; Silk [3]; Thornhill [1]).

The Evolution of Culture

No one doubts that humans create culture. Neither do our contributors doubt that culture reflects important outcomes of human evolution. How are we to understand these outcomes, however? Differences of opinion abound, even on just how this question should be framed. What constitutes cultural phenomena? What are the important, underlying human psychological features that give rise to them? Are cultural phenomena unselected-for by-products—incidental effects—of these features? Indeed, are the psychological features that give rise to culture themselves adaptations or by-products? Or are the cultural effects of these features fundamental to their functional explanation? Have we evolved adaptations *to* cultural phenomena? If so, what were the selection pressures involved? Have some features been selected through group-level selection?

It is almost certainly wrong to think that "culture" is one, unitary phenomenon. Hill [11] explicitly speaks to this point. He identifies three major components of what behavioral scientists refer to as culture: (1) Culture is a means of social transmission of information, one involving representation of knowledge, language, and persuasion; (2) culture is a set of normative stipulations of which acts are permitted and which acts are to be sanctioned through direct punishment or social isolation; and (3) culture consists of ritual behaviors, which are nonverbal signals that function to reinforce norms. And even this list may be incomplete. Different forms of each could be discriminated, at least on functional bases (e.g., norms aimed at aggressive behavior could function differently than norms aimed at incestuous behavior). Thus, different components of culture should probably be framed in terms of different selection pressures and underpinning adaptations.

As emphasized by Boyd and Richerson [11], a vast body of knowledge is embodied in culture. "Tricks" that enabled individuals in our great-grandparental generation to solve particular problems through trial and error or innovative processes become our solutions for these problems by word of mouth or mere demonstration years later. In some cases, these solutions transmit through single lineages (e.g., a grandmother's recipes).

In others, they transmit horizontally through vast segments of the population (e.g., the solution afforded by Edison's light bulb). Boyd and Richerson [11] further argue that transmission of information occurs through adaptations designed specifically for transmission of knowledge. Although these adaptations are not "domain-specific" (designed for particular forms of knowledge), they are, according to Boyd and Richerson, "special purpose." According to this view, humans have adaptations that function to generate core aspects of what we refer to as "culture."

What selection pressures led to these adaptations in humans? As Boyd and Richerson [11] make clear, these adaptations partly explain why humans are so smart. But why did they specifically evolve in humans? Barrett and colleagues [8] offer one possibility. Improvisational intelligence—the ability to solve novel problems in real ontogenetic time—must have considerable costs. Social transmission processes reduce its costs considerably, in that they permit the costs to be distributed across a large number of individuals. Indeed, many improvised solutions can be learned at low cost through social transmission. According to this view, then, adaptations underlying social transmission—and more generally, population-wide economies of knowledge acquisition and sharing—coevolved with improvisational knowledge. Language and underlying adaptations play a critical role in knowledge representation and communication, of course, and presumably were either a precondition for the evolution of improvised solutions (see Finlay [9]) and their transmission or coevolved with these features.

We throw into the mix another avenue through which improvisational intelligence and social transmission may have coevolved. Once social transmission exists, innovation may gain fitness value. Without social transmission (or even observational learning), innovators solely reap not only the benefits of an innovation but must also pay all of its costs. With social transmission, innovators can accrue fitness benefits through social exchange of valued information. These fitness benefits can, potentially, help pay for the cost of innovation and bolster selection for improvisational intelligence. They may also account for the fact that human social hierarchies are organized along lines of not only dominance but also prestige based on specialized and valued skills.

Just as there are two broadly competing classes of explanation for the evolution of large human brains, there are also two parallel classes of explanation for human cultural transmission. While Barrett and colleagues [8] point to the coevolution of social transmission with improvisational intelligence, Flinn and Coe [11] raise the alternative possibility that social transmission adaptations coevolved with forms of social intelligence, fueled by runaway social selection processes. Strategies of competition in social arms races selected for intense cooperation as well. Cooperation between coalitions of individuals with like interests became a dominant, overarching strategy of competing to win in the hominin social game. Keeping up with competing coalitions required imitation of dominant tactics. Getting ahead required innovation, but because random changes are unlikely to be effective, innovation should have been tightly constrained. Thus, Flinn and Coe emphasize that much cultural transmission, far from facilitating rapid change and adoption of novelties, is a highly conservative process. They focus on cultural transmission of traditions within groups of individuals with shared genetic interests, namely, kin.

A major issue, then, concerns what kind of intelligence fueled the evolution of social transmission processes: ecological or social intelligence? Given that ecological hypotheses of brain evolution and social brain theories are not incompatible, both may speak to the evolution of social transmission. But what coherent picture paints a reasonable role for each?

How Specialized Are the Psychological Adaptations Underlying Transmission of Knowledge?

Boyd and Richerson [11] claim that humans have special-purpose adaptations for social transmission. These adaptations, they argue, make people very smart. Because a culturally shared pool of "knowledge" can also accumulate much silly content, however, they also render us dumb. Boyd and Richerson suggest that the "silly" must come along with the "smart." Humans have been selected to be gullible in taking advantage of good innovations, but one cost of gullibility is susceptibility to silly beliefs.

Kurzban [11] explores the question of whether people can, in fact, discriminate between circumstances in which they should be either gullible or skeptical when presented with new information. Noting that the transmission and processing of new information is complex, Kurzban points out that social learning is an active process, and that certain social situations or contexts are likely to be associated with greater gullibility (i.e., readiness to accept and use new information), whereas others should be associated with greater skepticism (i.e., disinclination to accept or use new information). Arguing for models that are more context-dependent, he suggests that people should be more gullible when the costs of making errors or mistakes that could harm reproductive fitness are low and when the evolutionary interests of teachers, learners, and others generally coincide. Examples include the learning of language and the technological development and dissemination of tools (see also Flinn & Coe [11] on intergenerational transmission of traditions across kin). Conversely, people should be more skeptical of new "strategic social information" that might be used for deceptive purposes, especially when the potential costs of believing and using the new information are high. Examples include social influence attempts from unknown individuals, communications of personal intentions or power, and communications involving local norms, obligations, mores, or the distribution of resources. Kurzban's [11] ideas suggest that investigators might profitably explore adaptations that frame acceptance of or resistance to new information (see also Gangestad, Haselton, & Buss, 2006b). This focus on when individuals tend to be receptive or antagonistic to novel information nicely illustrates how specific contextual factors in different cultures may explain why certain practices and innovations (e.g., the development of sophisticated weapons) proliferate, whereas others (e.g., trust of outgroups) rarely materialize.

Similar themes are found in comments by Boyer [11], who laments the current state of understanding of how evolved cognitive dispositions affect cultural content—a scarcely explored frontier of human knowledge (see also Hill [11]). To say that cultural content merely reflects "cultural creations" is no explanation at all. Boyer [11] stresses the need to use evolutionary biology to guide an understanding of the cognitive dispositions that underlie acquisition and generation of cultural information. Fundamental misunderstandings must be overcome, notably, the confusion that results from the belief that evolved dispositions are "closed programs" resulting in specific behaviors or beliefs. Psychological adaptations do not result in specific, universal outcomes; rather, they lead to adaptive, contingent variability. Variation in moral systems across different cultures, for instance, does not imply a lack of any dispositions specific to moral feelings. Instead, it contains clues of just what moral concepts, in concert with local conditions (e.g., affecting how trust between individuals is established), frame the development of moral systems (see also Schaller [11]). Only by adopting an evolutionary framework, Boyer suggests, can scientists hope to make progress toward understanding underlying cognitive dispositions.

How Did Norm Regulation Evolve?

Culture consists of not only content that is socially transmitted but also sets of prescriptions about what is acceptable behavior within a group and sanctions, if those prescriptions are violated. The rightness and wrongness of behavior entailed in these prescriptions are rooted in values, defined by a social community, rather than nonsocial contingencies. Hill [11] observes that language may be necessary for enforcement of norms, a reason that humans may be the only species in which norm regulation has evolved (as least in any extensive form). But we can still wonder what benefit led to its appearance in humans. As Hill also notes, norm regulation may have evolved because it permitted groups or subgroups to outcompete others by reducing the costs of intergroup conflict (see also Boyd & Richerson [7]). Still, precisely what processes led to widely observed practices that underpin norm enforcement, such as punishment of noncooperators, remain topics of debate.

Another topic in need of further exploration concerns what kinds of processes regulate the explicit or implicit bargaining process that results in specific norms (Hill [11]). Individuals have unequal power to exert social influence (e.g., differing amounts of prestige, dominance, and status, which lead them to have differing abilities to attract coalition partners). Some individuals share interests with more group members than do others. In theory, weighted effects of individuals exerting influence over rules and customs affect their outcomes. Despots who acquire enormous amounts of power, for example, can establish rules unilaterally. Establishment of rules itself, then, may be a dynamical outcome of individuals strategically acting in self-interest, a theme consistent with the perspective laid out by Flinn and Alexander [8] and Flinn and Coe [11]. At the same time, some sets of norms could allow groups to outcompete other groups by reducing overall costs to group members, leading them to be favored by cultural group selection (Boyd & Richerson [7]; Hill [11]). Since these sets of norms need not, in theory, result from competition within a larger group between coalitions to maximize self-interest, this form of group selection might conflict with selection on individuals within groups imposing their own interests on other group members.

More generally, Schaller [11] argues that a theoretical leading edge in evolutionary behavioral science should be application of evolutionary psychology to an understanding of cultural processes, including those that give rise to cultural variation. We concur with his call for evolutionary psychologists to attend more intently to cultural processes, including cultural variation.

The Evolution of Human Mating Systems

Given the central role of mating in reproduction, a considerable amount of theory and research has focused on how evolutionary forces could have sculpted human mating preferences, tactics, and strategies. Largely due to Trivers's (1972) theory of parental investment and sexual selection, much of this work has tried to explain the noteworthy sex differences that tend to exist relative to many sociosexual attitudes and behaviors. Collectively, this work has spawned some of the most heated and contentious debates in human evolutionary science. Some of the theoretical diversity that characterizes this area is captured in the positions advocated by Buss [12], Wood and Eagly [12], and Thornhill [12].

A key topic of debate is the extent to which differential sexual selection on the sexes has contributed to sex differences. Trivers (1972) argued that the sex that exerts greater parental effort—effort exerted to increase the quality of offspring—is a limited reproductive resource for the sex that invests less parental effort. The latter sex is therefore under relatively stronger sexual selection to exhibit features that increase access to the former sex, which is selected to wisely choose between competitors. In most mammalian species, females typically exert greater parental investment than do males; hence, males are typically under stronger sexual selection than females. As reflected in Buss's [12] contribution, many evolutionary psychologists have attributed a variety of human sex differences to sexual selection processes (e.g., physical attributes, such as muscularity; psychological attributes, such as interest in uncommitted sex).

Wood and Eagly [12] question the role of sexual selection in creating sex differences. They note that sexual dimorphism in physical size and canine tooth size is actually relatively small in humans compared to that in other primates. In addition, selection pressures other than differential intrasexual competition (e.g., selection for specialized roles in parenting) may cause sexual dimorphism. There is no clear disagreement between many evolutionary psychologists' claims and these arguments. As Buss [12] emphasizes, human reproduction does differ from that of our closest relative, chimpanzees, in some dramatic ways. Men and women often do form lasting pair-bonds and have multiple offspring together. Men, Buss argues, often invest heavily in offspring. (Some theorists argue that men have not been selected to invest parentally. What appears to be paternal effort may, in fact, be effort that functions to obtain mates; thus, it could be sexually selected [e.g., Hawkes, 2004]. Hence, some theorists argue for greater differences in sexual selection than what many evolutionary psychologists have suggested.) Accordingly, men and women should differ in size less than the sexes of many other primates. Indeed, Trivers (1972) himself argued that humans probably represent a case of modest differences in sexual selection. Relatively small differences in sexual selection pressures, however, do not imply the complete absence of differences. And Wood and Eagly [12] do not present evidence that differences in sexual selection on men and women have been absent. Some sizable sex differences (e.g., differences in interest in sex without commitment) may reflect differential sexual selection. More data are needed on this issue.

Another issue of contention concerns male interest in sexual control of females. Buss [12] cites evidence that men are more concerned with the sexual infidelity of their partners than are women. This sex difference purportedly reflects differential ancestral selection due to the fact that, ancestrally, men could have been cuckolded, whereas women could not. Wood and Eagly [12] argue that men's interest in controlling women's sexuality emerged after the development of more complex socioeconomic societies in which heritable wealth became a concern; hence, control of female sexuality gained economic utility. Double standards of sexuality are indeed more prevalent in societies that have patrilineal inheritance and patrilocal arrangements.

These data, however, do not imply complete absence of male interest in controlling female sexuality. As Hill [11] notes, established norms do not reflect the interests of all individual members of a society. Lack of a double standard within a society, then, does not imply that men and women's interests in controlling each others' sexuality are identical. Though Wood and Eagly [12] imply that levels of male and female sexual jealousy do not differ in "simpler," more traditional societies (e.g., those lacking heritable wealth), our reading of the literature is not consistent with this conclusion. For instance, Wood and Eagly (2002) cite the Canela (a group in Brazil that, traditionally, engages in ritual extramarital sex) as lacking sexual dimorphism in jealousy. Yet a careful reading of the writings of the ethnographer they cite reveals a different picture. Whenever sexual jealousy is mentioned (and it was common in the Canela), the reference is almost always *only* to male sexual jealousy (see Crocker, 1984, 1990). Exclusive reference to female sexual jealousy never occurs, references to both sex's jealousy are quite rare, and one reference to both sexes explicitly refers to "primarily" males. Similarly, Hill and Hurtado (1996; also cited by Wood & Eagly, 2002) discuss male sexual jealousy but not female sexual jealousy in the Aché of Paraguay. Undoubtedly, debate on sex differences in sexual jealousy will continue.

Wood and Eagly [12] dedicate much of their contribution to discussion of cultural variation in mating arrangements and roles the sexes play in reproduction and parenting. The cross-cultural variation in mating and parenting practices, relations between the sexes, and differences in mate preferences are indeed fascinating and worthy of greater attention from evolutionary psychologists (see also Schaller [11]). As Wood and Eagly also note, cultural variation does not imply a blank slate with respect to the underpinnings of variations. And as Boyer [11] observed, to claim that cultural variation reflects "cultural creation" is no explanation. A key task will be to understand what adaptations or other psychological features underlie the emergence of cultural variations. With regard to human mating, Wood and Eagly [12] focus on social roles. Social roles and role prescriptions partly reflect processes of norm establishment and enforcement. As noted by Hill [11], norms frequently address issues related to reproduction, so it is not surprising that norms also apply to men's and women's roles in mating. Just as norms surrounding incest may reflect dispositions to acquire, through epigenetic processes, aversion to incest (Lieberman, Tooby, & Cosmides, 2003), so too may norm regulation of the behavior of the sexes reflect similar dispositions. But what are the underlying adaptations (see Boyer [11])? Buss [12] would argue that some have been sexually selected. He proposes that both men and women have a menu of both long- and short-term mating strategies on which to draw. In two different cultural settings, the subsets drawn may differ.

Thornhill [12] adopts a strong adaptationist perspective to human mating, focusing on the evolution of estrus, extended sexual receptivity, and concealed ovulation in human females. Borrowing principles from "good genes" theorizing, he reviews evidence suggesting that human females evolved to prefer men who display certain traits likely to signal better genetic quality, particularly in short-term mating contexts. Collectively, these findings point to the possibility that women have evolved cognitive adaptations motivating them to be more attracted to men who have markers of genetic quality, primarily when women are ovulating and evaluating such men as possible short-term mates. The highly specific pattern of these effects was anticipated by "good genes" sexual selection models and cannot be easily explained by most competing models. This body of work is important, because it indicates that women may not have "lost" estrus, and that the mating patterns of human females may be more similar to females of other species than some nonsexual selection theories imply.

The conflicts of interest between the sexes implied by Thornhill [12] are discussed in a broader theoretical framework by Buss [12], who notes, however, that relations between the sexes involve both highly cooperative and conflictual elements. An evolutionary perspective should strive to understand the specific contexts in which each operates. Love remains a fascinating and not fully understood phenomenon from an evolutionary perspective. What benefits led to adaptations underlying the various phenomena we refer to as "romantic love"? Buss sketches out one possibility and calls for great attention to these phenomena, a call we echo.

CONCLUSION

As evidenced by the excellent chapters in this book, the evolutionary sciences are rapidly expanding and have a very bright future. Answers to certain foundational questions are still being formed, and debates are bound to continue. Nevertheless, a great deal has been discovered about human evolution since the theoretical "reawakening" of the evolutionary sciences in the 1960s and early 1970s. In the future, we hope that scientific discovery and debate will be structured more around the fundamental questions, issues, and tentative solutions outlined in this book than around traditional disciplinary or theoretical camps. The three major perspectives that now define the evolutionary sciences—human behavioral ecology, evolutionary psychology, and gene–culture coevolution—each have much to contribute to our understanding of human social behavior. Each perspective brings special strengths and advantages to this cause. Evolutionary scientists of all stripes need to identify, appreciate, and apply the strengths that different approaches can offer their *own* programs of research. A complete evolutionary understanding of human nature demands it.

REFERENCES

Andrews, P. A., Gangestad, S. W., & Matthews, D. (2002). Adaptationism—how to carry out an exaptationist program. *Behavioral and Brain Sciences, 25,* 489–504.

Bowlby, J. (1969). *Attachment: Vol. 1. Attachment and loss.* London: Hogarth.

Buller, D. J. (2005). *Adapting minds: Evolutionary psychology and the persistent quest for human nature.* Cambridge, MA: MIT Press.

Crocker, W. H. (1984). Canela marriage: Factors in change. In K. M. Kensinger (Ed.), *Marriage practices in lowland South America* (pp. 63–98). Urbana and Chicago: University of Illinois Press. Available online at *www.mnh.si.edu/anthro/canela/ literature/marrriage.pdf*

Crocker, W. H. (1990). *The Canela (Eastern Timbira), I: An ethnographic introduction* (Smithsonian Contributions to Anthropology, No. 33). Washington, DC: Smithsonian Instiution Press. Available online at *www.mnh.si.edu/anthro/canela/literature/monograph/toc.htm.*

Cronbach, L. J., & Meehl, P. E. (1955). Construct validity in psychological tests. *Psychological Bulletin, 52,* 281–302.

Flinn, M. V. (2006). Cross-cultural universals and variations: The evolutionary paradox of informational novelty. *Psychological Inquiry, 17,* 118–123.

Gangestad, S. W., Haselton, M. G., & Buss, D. M. (2006a). Evolutionary foundations of cultural variation: Evoked culture and mate preferences. *Psychological Inquiry, 17,* 75–95.

Gangestad, S. W., Haselton, M. G., & Buss, D. M. (2006b). Toward an integrative understanding of evoked and transmitted culture: The importance of specialized psychological design. *Psychological Inquiry, 17,* 138–151.

Gould, S. J., & Vrba, E. S. (1982). Exaptation: A missing term in the science of form. *Paleobiology, 8,* 4–15.

Haig, D. (1993). Genetic conflicts in human pregnancy. *Quarterly Review of Biology, 68,* 495–532.

Hawkes, K. (2004). Mating, parenting, and the evolution of human pair bonds. In B. Chapais & C. M. Berman (Eds.), *Kinship and behavior in primates* (pp. 443–473). Oxford, UK: Oxford University Press.

Hill, K., & Hurtado, A. M. (1996). *Aché life history: The ecology and demography of a foraging people.* New York: Aldine de Gruyter.

Irons, W. (1998). Adaptively relevant environments versus the environment of evolutionary adaptedness. *Evolutionary Anthropology, 6,* 194–204.

Jacob, F. (1977). Evolution and tinkering. *Science, 196,* 1161–1166.

Lewontin, R. C. (1983). Gene, organism and environment. In D. S. Bendall (Ed.), *Evolution from molecules to men* (pp. 273–285). Cambridge, UK: Cambridge University Press.

Lieberman, D., Tooby, J., & Cosmides, L. (2003). Does morality have a biological basis? *Proceedings of the Royal Society of London B, 270,* 819–826.

Miller, G. F. (2000). *The mating mind: How sexual choice shaped the evolution of human nature.* New York: Doubleday.

Norenzayan, A. (2006). Evolution and transmitted culture. *Psychological Inquiry, 17,* 123–128.

Rice, W. R., & Holland, B. (1997). The enemies within: Intragenomic conflict, interlocus contest evolution (ICE), and the intraspecific Red Queen. *Behavioral Ecology and Sociobiology, 41,* 1–10.

Smith, E. A., Borgerhoff Mulder, M., & Hill. K. (2001). Controversies in the evolutionary social sciences: A guide to the perplexed. *Trends in Ecology and Evolution, 16,* 128–135.

Symons, D. (1987). If we're all Darwinians, what's the fuss about? In C. Crawford, M. Smith, & D. Krebs (Eds.), *Sociobiology and psychology: Ideas, issues, and applications* (pp. 121–146). Hillsdale, NJ: Erlbaum.

Symons, D. (1990). Adaptiveness and adaptation. *Ethology and Sociobiology, 11,* 427–444.

Tooby, J., & Cosmides, L. (1990). The past explains the present: Emotional adaptations and the structure of ancestral environments. *Ethology and Sociobiology, 11*, 375–424.

Tooby, J., & Cosmides, L. (1992). Psychological foundations of culture. In J. H. Barkow, L. Cosmides, & J. Tooby (Eds.), *The adapted mind: Evolutionary psychology and the generation of culture* (pp. 19–136). New York: Oxford University Press.

Trivers, R. (1972). Parental investment and sexual selection. In B. Campbell (Ed.), *Sexual selection and the descent of man: 1871–1971* (pp. 136–179). Chicago: Aldine.

West-Eberhard, M.-J. (2003). *Developmental plasticity and evolution.* New York: Oxford University Press.

Williams, G. C. (1966). *Adaptation and natural selection.* Princeton, NJ: Princeton University Press.

Wilson, D. S., & Sober, E. (1994). Re-introducing group selection to human behavioral sciences. *Behavioral and Brain Sciences, 17*, 585–654.

Wood, W., & Eagly, A. H. (2002). A cross-cultural analysis of the behavior of men and women: Implications of the origins of sex differences. *Psychological Bulletin, 128*, 699–727.

Wynne-Edwards, V. C. (1962). *Animal dispersion in relation to social behavior.* Edinburgh, UK: Oliver & Boyd.

Index

Page numbers followed by *f* indicate figure; *t* indicate table